SELECTED READINGS

UNDERSTANDING VICTIMOLOGY

Peggy M. Tobolowsky
University of North Texas

anderson publishing co.
2035 Reading Road
Cincinnati, OH 45202
800-582-7295

Understanding Victimology: Selected Readings

Copyright © 2000
Anderson Publishing Co.
2035 Reading Rd.
Cincinnati, OH 45202

Phone 800.582.7295 or 513.421.4142
Web Site www.andersonpublishing.com

Library of Congress Cataloging-in-Publication Data

Understanding victimology : selected readings / [edited by] Peggy M. Tobolowsky.
        p.   cm.
    Includes bibliographical references and index.
    ISBN 1-58360-501-0 (pbk.)
    1. Victims of crimes--United States.   I. Tobolowsky, Peggy M., 1952-   .
    HV6250 .3. U5U5   1999
    362.88 ' 0973--dc21   99-30348
                                                            CIP

Cover digital composition and design by Tin Box Studio, Inc.

EDITOR Ellen S. Boyne
ASSISTANT EDITOR Sharon L. Boyles
ACQUISITIONS EDITOR Michael C. Braswell

In memory of my father,

an incomparable role model in life, love, and the law

Preface

Although individuals have been victimized by crime since the beginning of recorded human life, the study of crime victims, or *victimology*, is of relatively recent origin. Victimology emerged from the seminal works of Hans von Hentig and Beniamin Mendelsohn in the 1940s and 1950s. Interest in crime victims was further fostered by the evolution of a *victims' movement* in this country in the 1970s, which was devoted to increasing victim services and assistance and expanding victim rights and remedies in the criminal justice process.

In the last two decades, thousands of federal and state laws providing crime victim rights and remedies have been enacted; victim services programs have been established; and research and policy analyses addressing victim issues have been published. The study of victimology has increasingly been incorporated as an important component of the criminal justice and criminology curricula at colleges and universities across the country. Students with academic backgrounds in victimology are in demand to assist in the continuing research work in this area and to staff positions in the expanding victim services field.

The idea for this anthology evolved through my work with the Center for Victim Studies, administered by the Department of Criminal Justice at the University of North Texas. By participating in the Center's efforts to foster research and academic training regarding victims of crime and violence, as well as by conducting victim-related research of my own, I have become acquainted with much of the excellent victimological research and policy analysis that has been performed since the emergence of victimology and the victims' movement. I am also familiar with the victimology courses offered by criminal justice programs across the country and the existing texts available for these courses.

It is my hope that this text will be a meaningful addition to available course materials by providing in-depth selections by some of the foremost victimological researchers and policy analysts on the primary areas addressed in most victimology courses. Accompanying each section of the text are introductory overview materials, related learning experiences for students, and bibliographical materials for further research. Thus, the text provides an overview of each general subject area as well as detailed research or policy analyses of specific issues in each area. It strives to demonstrate the relationships between research and policy. The text can be used either as a supplementary reader to an overview text or as a primary text.

The selections chosen for this anthology have satisfied several criteria. They have been written by well-respected researchers and policy analysts. They address important research and policy issues in each area of the text. The selections, individually or collectively as a group, represent a balance of the sometimes conflicting viewpoints regarding victimology and the victims' movement. Finally, they are "readable" and understandable by college students and are written in a manner to stimulate discussion on the topics covered. The selections, in combination with the accompanying learning experiences, are designed to bring the world of victimological research and policy "to life."

These selections have been included without deletions from their original sources. Every attempt has been made to ensure their accuracy.

Finally, I would like to acknowledge the support and encouragement of Robert W. Taylor, Eric J. Fritsch, Donna Dickert, Veronica Kronvall, and Dominque Gray, at the University of North Texas, and of Mickey Braswell, Ellen Boyne, and Kelly Grondin at Anderson Publishing Co. They each deserve my thanks and appreciation.

Peggy M. Tobolowsky

Table of Contents

Each section has suggested learning experiences and an extensive bibliography.

Section 1
VICTIMOLOGY AND THE VICTIMS' MOVEMENT

Individuals have been victimized by the criminal acts of others since the beginning of recorded history. Early victim-centered private proceedings that focused on retribution and restitution for the victim from the offender evolved long ago into the prevailing model of government-centered prosecutions that seek societal redress from and punishment for the offender. Victims had only a limited role in—and received little attention from—these government-sponsored prosecutions of offenders. As a result of the confluence of a variety of factors in the middle of the twentieth century, however, crime victims have begun to receive much greater attention from the individuals and institutions responsible for the administration of the American criminal justice and social service delivery systems, as well as the research community.

The catalyst for this renewed interest in the victim of crime was the emergence of a theoretical approach that became known as *victimology*. Most scholars trace the modern study of victimology to the seminal works of Hans von Hentig and Beniamin Mendelsohn in the 1940s and 1950s. Both explored the relationships between victims and offenders. They developed victim typologies that identified victim characteristics that might increase a person's risk of victimization (e.g., factors that might make a person more physically or mentally vulnerable to crime, such as age or mental impairments) or even contribute to or precipitate the victimization (e.g., provocative behavior by the victim). Social scientists, such as Marvin Wolfgang in his study of homicide victimization, also began to examine the role that victim precipitation might play in the commission of crime.

Some accused these early theorists and researchers of "blaming the victim" due to their identification of ways in which a victim might influence or contribute to a crime. Rather than focusing solely on the victim's role or the offender's role in the commission of crime, they argued for a more integrative approach in examining the relationship between the offender and the victim. New theories to explain victim-

1

ization were developed, such as those focusing on the lifestyles, proximity, and even the "routine activities" of victims and offenders. Still other theorists proposed to expand victimology into new areas, such as the ways society defines individuals as victims and criminals. Others suggested expanding victimology beyond the study of victims of crime to the study of victims of forms of discrimination, technology, and the environment. These expanded areas of study have been identified by such designations as "critical," "radical," "progressive," and "general" victimology. Many of these themes of victimology and their implications are discussed in Chapter 1, the selection by Viano.

The primary focus of victimology, however, remains the study of victims of crime. In this country, the study of crime victims has led to changes in the way crime is measured; a broader understanding of the theories, risk, and impact of victimization; and an expansion of the victim's role in the criminal justice system. The selections in this book (and those in the accompanying bibliographical materials) explore these topics.

The evolution from victimological theory and research to implementing action began in this country in the 1960s as a result of a renewed interest in and concern about crime and its victims. Following the models of early grassroots movements, individual victims and victim service providers and advocates began to "network" at the local level during this period. By the 1970s, a "victims' movement" had emerged that was committed to making the crime victim an integral part of the administration of criminal justice once again. During the 1970s, significant victim-centered achievements were accomplished, including the enactment of legislation in a majority of states to provide compensation for victims of violent crimes, the creation of victim service and assistance programs in many locations throughout the country, and the establishment of several national organizations addressing crime victim issues. The efforts of the victims' movement were aided by the initiation, in 1973, of the Department of Justice National Crime Victimization Survey (formerly named the National Crime Survey), which used survey methodology to generate annual national estimates of the extent of victimization in several personal and property crime categories. This survey provided much more detailed information about crime victims and the victimization experience than that available through the FBI's Uniform Crime Reports, and reflected higher levels of crime and fear of crime than were generally reported in the UCR.

As significant as these victim-centered developments were, crime victim issues were truly raised to national prominence when President Ronald Reagan established the President's Task Force on Victims of Crime in 1982. After several months of study, the Task Force issued a Final Report that included more than 60 action recommendations addressed to federal and state executive and legislative branches, criminal justice system agencies, and other professionals involved in crime victim service delivery. These recommendations were designed to "restore balance" to the criminal justice system by better integrating the concerns and needs of crime victims into the system.

In the years since the President's Task Force Final Report, significant federal legislation supporting crime victim needs and rights has been enacted. Every state has constitutional and/or legislative victim rights, compensation, and services provisions. Almost 10,000 victim services programs are currently in existence. Although some critics have raised concerns about the goals and objectives of the victims' movement, as illustrated in Chapter 2, by Fattah, such concerns have not prevented the dramatic changes in the criminal justice system that have been effected since its emergence. The selections in this book reflect the evolution of victim-related theory and action following the development of victimology and the victims' movement.

LEARNING EXPERIENCES

1. In Chapter 1 on victimization, Viano examines the concept of harm and its causes. Obtain the most recent National Crime Victimization Survey report and identify the demographic characteristics of the persons most frequently victimized by the violent crimes reported in the survey. Discuss the causal factors that contribute to the more frequent victimization of persons with these characteristics.

2. Have you (or has someone you know) been the victim of a crime or other harm described by Viano? Describe your progression (or that of the other person) through the four stages in the definition of victimization outlined by Viano. If you (or the other person) did not progress through all four stages, discuss the obstacles that prevented such a progression and how they might be overcome.

3. In Chapter 2, Fattah identifies some potential dangers of the "victim movement." Locate a victim rights or advocacy organization in your community. Interview a representative of the organization to determine whether any of the concerns that Fattah identifies exist in the organization.

4. One of the concerns with the victims' movement that Fattah identifies is that of increased fear of victimization. Discuss class members' fears about being victims of property and violent crimes and the actions they take on a regular basis to prevent such victimization (e.g., security devices, locking car doors, avoiding certain places).

5. One of the concerns Fattah identifies with the victims' movement is that the "professionalization" of victim services will replace previously existing social networks that can assist in the process of recovery from victimization. What types of such social networks are available in your community to assist crime victims? What kinds of assistance do they provide?

BIBLIOGRAPHY

Amir, M. (1971). *Patterns in forcible rape*. Chicago: University of Chicago Press.

Bard, M., & Sangrey, D. (1986). *The crime victim's book* (2nd ed.). New York: Brunner/Mazel.

Carrington, F., & Nicholson, G. (1984). The victims' movement: An idea whose time has come. *Pepperdine Law Review, 11*, 1-13.

Baumer, T.L. (1985). Testing a general model of fear of crime: Data from a national sample. *Journal of Research in Crime and Delinquency, 22*, 239-255.

Clarke, R.V., & Felson, M. (Eds.). (1993). *Routine activity and rational choice*. New Brunswick, NJ: Transaction.

Cohen, L.E., & Felson, M. (1979). Social change and crime rate trends: A routine activity approach. *American Sociological Review, 44*, 588-608.

Conaway, M.R., & Lohr, S.L. (1994). A longitudinal analysis of factors associated with reporting violent crimes to the police. *Journal of Quantitative Criminology, 10*, 23-39.

Davis, R.C., Taylor, B.G., & Titus, R.M. (1997). Victims as agents: Implications for victim services and crime prevention. In R.C. Davis, A.J. Lurigio, & W.G. Skogan (Eds.), *Victims of crime* (2nd ed., pp. 167-179). Thousand Oaks, CA: Sage.

Doerner, W.G., & Lab, S.P. (1998). *Victimology* (2nd ed.). Cincinnati, OH: Anderson.

Drapkin, I., & Viano, E. (Eds.). (1974). *Victimology*. Lexington, MA: Lexington.

Dubow, F., McCabe, E., & Kaplan, G. (1979). *Reactions to crime: A critical review of the literature*. Washington, DC: U.S. Government Printing Office.

Elias, R. (1985). Transcending our social reality of victimization: Toward a new victimology of human rights. *Victimology, 10*, 6-25.

Elias, R. (1986). *The politics of victimization: Victims, victimology, and human rights*. New York: Oxford University Press.

Elias, R. (1993). *Victims still: The political manipulation of crime victims*. Newbury Park, CA: Sage.

Fattah, E.A. (1979). Some recent theoretical developments in victimology. *Victimology, 4*, 198-213.

Fattah, E.A. (1986). Prologue: On some visible and hidden dangers of victim movements. In E.A. Fattah (Ed.), *From crime policy to victim policy: Reorienting the justice system* (pp. 1-14). New York: St. Martin's.

Fattah, E.A. (Ed.). (1992). *Towards a critical victimology*. New York: St. Martin's.

Ferraro, K.F., & LaGrange, R. (1987). The measurement of fear of crime. *Sociological Inquiry, 57*, 70-101.

Franklin, C.W., II, & Franklin, A.P. (1976). Victimology revisited: A critique and suggestions for future direction. *Criminology, 14*, 125-136.

Freedy, J.R., Resnick, H.S., Kilpatrick, D.G., Dansky, B.S., & Tidwell, R.P. (1994). The psychological adjustment of recent crime victims in the criminal justice system. *Journal of Interpersonal Violence, 9*, 450-468.

Friedman, L.N. (1985). The crime victim movement at its first decade. *Public Administration Review, 45,* 790-794.

Friedrichs, D.O. (1983). Victimology: A consideration of the radical critique. *Crime & Delinquency, 29,* 283-294.

Garofalo, J. (1981). The fear of crime: Causes and consequences. *Journal of Criminal Law & Criminology, 72,* 839-857.

Gobert, J.J. (1977). Victim precipitation. *Columbia Law Review, 77,* 511-553.

Gottfredson, M.R. (1981). On the etiology of criminal victimization. *Journal of Criminal Law & Criminology, 72,* 714-726.

Hale, C. (1996). Fear of crime: A review of the literature. *International Review of Victimology, 4,* 79-150.

Hindelang, M.J., Gottfredson, M.R., & Garofalo, J. (1978). *Victims of personal crime: An empirical foundation for a theory of personal victimization.* Cambridge, MA: Ballinger.

Jensen, G.F., & Brownfield, D. (1986). Gender, lifestyles, and victimization: Beyond routine activity theory. *Violence and Victims, 1,* 85-99.

Kidd, R.F., & Chayet, E.F. (1984). Why do victims fail to report? The psychology of criminal victimization. *Journal of Social Issues, 40,* 39-50.

Kilpatrick, D.G., Best, C.L., Veronen, L.J., Amick, A.E., Villeponteaux, L.A., & Ruff, G.A. (1985). Mental health correlates of criminal victimization: A random community survey. *Journal of Consulting and Clinical Psychology, 53,* 866-873.

Kilpatrick, D.G., Saunders, B.E., Veronen, L.J., Best, C.L., & Von, J.M. (1987). Criminal victimization: Lifetime prevalence, reporting to police, and psychological impact. *Crime & Delinquency, 33,* 479-489.

Levine, J.P. (1976). The potential for crime overreporting in criminal victimization surveys. *Criminology, 14,* 307-330.

Mawby, R.I., & Walklate, S. (1994). *Critical victimology: International perspectives.* Thousand Oaks, CA: Sage.

Maxfield, M.G. (1987). Household composition, routine activity, and victimization: A comparative analysis. *Journal of Quantitative Criminology, 3,* 301-320.

McShane, M.D., & Williams, F.P., III. (1992). Radical victimology: A critique of the concept of victim in traditional victimology. *Crime & Delinquency, 38,* 258-271.

Meier, R.F., & Miethe, T.D. (1993). Understanding theories of criminal victimization. *Crime and Justice, 17,* 459-499.

Mendelsohn, B. (1956). The victimology. *Etudes Internationales de Psycho-Sociologie Criminelle, July,* 23-26.

Mendelsohn, B. (1976). Victimology and contemporary society's trends. *Victimology, 1,* 8-28.

Miethe, T.D. (1985). Myth or reality of victim involvement in crime: A review and comment on victim-precipitation research. *Sociological Focus, 18,* 209-220.

Miethe, T.D. (1987). Stereotypical conceptions and criminal processing: The case of the victim-offender relationship. *Justice Quarterly, 4,* 571-593.

Miethe, T.D., & McDowall, D. (1993). Contextual effects in models of criminal victimization. *Social Forces, 71,* 741-759.

Miller, T.R., Cohen, M.A., & Wiersema, B. (1996). *Victim costs and consequences: A new look.* Washington, DC: U.S. Department of Justice.

Nicholson, G. (1992).Victims' rights, remedies, and resources: A maturing presence in American jurisprudence. *Pacific Law Journal, 23,* 815-841.

Norris, F.H., & Kaniasty, K. (1994). Psychological distress following criminal victimization in the general population: Cross-sectional, longitudinal, and prospective analyses. *Journal of Consulting and Clinical Psychology, 62,* 111-123.

President's Task Force on Victims of Crime. (1982). *Final report.* Washington, DC: U.S. Government Printing Office.

Quinney, R. (1972). Who is the victim? *Criminology, 10,* 314-323.

Rand, M. (1998). *National crime victimization survey: Criminal victimization 1997.* Washington, DC: U.S. Department of Justice.

Reiss, A.J., Jr. (1986). Policy implications of crime victim surveys. In E.A. Fattah (Ed.), *From crime policy to victim policy: Reorienting the justice system* (pp. 246-260). New York: St. Martin's.

Sampson, R.J., & Lauritsen, J.L. (1990). Deviant lifestyles, proximity to crime, and the offender-victim link in personal violence. *Journal of Research in Crime and Delinquency, 27,* 110-139.

Sampson, R.J., & Wooldredge, J.D. (1987). Linking the micro- and macro-level dimensions of lifestyle-routine activity and opportunity models of predatory victimization. *Journal of Quantitative Criminology, 3,* 371-393.

Schafer, S. (1977). *Victimology: The victim and his criminal.* Reston, VA: Reston.

Singer, S. (1981). Homogeneous victim-offender populations: A review and some research implications. *Journal of Criminal Law & Criminology, 72,* 779-788.

Skogan, W.G. (1976). Victimization surveys and criminal justice planning. *University of Cincinnati Law Review, 45,* 167-206.

Skogan, W.G. (1981). *Issues in the measurement of victimization.* Washington, DC: U.S. Government Printing Office.

Skogan, W.G. (1987). The impact of victimization on fear. *Crime & Delinquency, 33,* 135-154.

Smith, B.L., & Huff, C.R. (1992). From victim to political activist: An empirical examination of a statewide victims' rights movement. *Journal of Criminal Justice, 20,* 201-215.

Sparks, R.F. (1981). Multiple victimization: Evidence, theory, and future research. *Journal of Criminal Law & Criminology, 72,* 762-778.

Symposium on Victimization and Victimology. (1981). *Journal of Criminal Law & Criminology, 72,* 704-857.

U.S. Department of Justice. Office for Victims of Crime. (1998). *New directions from the field: Victims' rights and services for the 21st century.* Washington, DC: Author.

U.S. Department of Justice. Office of Justice Programs. (1986). *Four years later: A report on the President's Task Force on Victims of Crime.* Washington, DC: Author.

Viano, E. (1983). Victimology: The development of a new perspective. *Victimology, 8(1-2),* 30.

Viano, E.C. (1989). Victimology today: Major issues in research and public policy. In E.C. Viano (Ed.), *Crime and its victims: International research and public policy issues* (pp. 3-14). New York: Hemisphere.

Viano, E. (Ed.). (1990). *The victimology handbook: Research findings, treatment, and public policy.* New York: Garland.

Von Hentig, H. (1941). Remarks on the interaction of perpetrator and victim. *Journal of Criminal Law, Criminology, & Police Science, 31,* 303-309.

Von Hentig, H. (1948). *The criminal and his victim: Studies in the sociobiology of crime.* New Haven, CT: Yale University Press.

Walklate, S. (1989). *Victimology: The victim and the criminal justice process.* London: Unwin Hyman.

Walklate, S. (1994). Can there be a progressive victimology? *International Review of Victimology, 3,* 1-15.

Warr, M. (1987). Fear of victimization and sensitivity to risk. *Journal of Quantitative Criminology, 3,* 29-46.

Warr, M., & Stafford, M. (1983). Fear of victimization: A look at the proximate causes. *Social Forces, 61,* 1033-1043.

Weed, F.J. (1995). *Certainty of justice: Reform in the crime victim movement.* New York: Aldine de Gruyter.

Wolfgang, M.E. (1958). *Patterns in criminal homicide.* Philadelphia: University of Pennsylvania Press.

Wolfgang, M.E., & Singer, S.I. (1978). Victim categories of crime. *Journal of Criminal Law & Criminology, 69,* 379-394.

Young, M.A. (1997). Victim rights and services: A modern saga. In R.C. Davis, A.J. Lurigio, & W.G. Skogan (Eds.), *Victims of crime* (2nd ed., pp. 194-210). Thousand Oaks, CA: Sage.

Chapter 1

Victimology Today: Major Issues in Research and Public Policy

Emilio C. Viano
School of Public Affairs, The American University, Washington, D.C.

INTRODUCTION

This chapter examines four major areas of inquiry that can be identified in contemporary victimology. They correspond to four different and complementary stages in the definition of victimization. These stages also constitute a process which confers official victim status on someone if it is carried out to its conclusion. The chapter examines the nature, development, and dynamics of each stage, utilizing a *process approach*. This approach is important because it helps focus research on the question of who will be in each stage, who will move from one stage to the next, and when, how, and why. At the end of the chapter, major questions for research and public policy are raised.

Persons at one stage will have a different perception of their status as "victim" than those at other stages. This will affect their behavior and will influence (or even determine) who will make the transition from one

Emilio Viano is a professor at the Department of Justice, Law and Society, The American University, Washington, D.C. He is also the editor of *Victimology: An International Journal*. He has been active in the field of victimology and victim-witness services since the early 1970s. He has conducted research and has organized and chaired several national and international congresses and meetings in the field. He has also directed several programs, including the National Victim and Witness Resource Center, and has served as a national and international expert on various projects. He has published various books and articles in victimology and in other fields of justice. Professor Viano can be reached at 2333 North Vernon Street, Arlington, VA 22207.

Source: Viano, E.C. (1989). Victimology today: Major issues in research and public policy. In E.C. Viano (Ed.), *Crime and its victims: International research and public policy issues* (pp. 3-14). New York: Hemisphere. Reprinted by permission of Taylor & Francis.

9

stage to the next and who will not. The process approach also stresses the dynamics of the situation and the impact that social and cultural values and forces have on the determination of who is a "real" victim. Different research and policy questions belong to each stage.

The four stages are as follows:

1. In the first stage, individuals experience harm, injury, or suffering caused by another person or institution.

2. In the second stage, some of these individuals perceive such harm as undeserved, unfair, and unjust, and they therefore perceive themselves as victims.

3. In the third stage, some of these individuals, perceiving themselves as harmed or victimized, attempt to get someone else (e.g., family, friends, helping professionals, or authority figures) to recognize the harm and validate the claim that they have been victimized.

4. Finally, some of these individuals receive validation of their claim to victim status, become "official" victims, and possibly benefit from various types of support, depending on various variables.

For the purposes of our discussion, a *victim* is any individual harmed or damaged by another or by others who perceives him- or herself as harmed, who shares the experience and seeks assistance and redress, and who is recognized as harmed and possibly assisted by public, private, or community agencies.

While the emphasis here is on the individual, note that institutions, corporations, commercial establishments, and groups of people can also be victimized and claim victim status—basically following the same stages.

STAGE 1: HARM AND ITS CAUSES

According to the traditional view, the essential element for victim status is the presence of harm, suffering, or injury caused by a crime. However, some argue that there is no compelling reason to limit the cause of the harm to a criminal act committed by an individual against another. Institutional victimization, abuse of power, collective victimization, and illegal or illegitimate governmental actions should be considered causes of victimization as well. Similarly, not only acts of commission but also acts of omission should be taken into account. Whether victims of natural disasters, war, environmental pollution, the closing of a factory, etc., should be included in this definition is debatable. One could argue that why or how one is harmed is irrelevant, that what counts is being in crisis, injured, harmed, and needing to recover and regain mastery over one's life and surroundings.

One can experience harm without defining oneself as a victim. Many experience considerable harm or suffering, often harm clearly caused by other individuals, without defining themselves as victims. On the contrary, cultural, traditional, or religious beliefs may supply rationalizations leading them to consider themselves responsible for or the cause of what they suffer and to blame themselves and not the actual perpetrators. Domestic violence, sexual assault, and sexual harassment offer classic examples of these rationalizations. The concepts of susceptibility, vulnerability, and life-style are also important tools in approaching this dimension.

Questions

There has been considerable research about the epidemiology of certain crimes, including research on who is killed, or killed the most, in homicides and who gets robbed, burglarized, and sexually assaulted. Groups or categories of people have also been studied to identify what type of harm they may suffer disproportionately. The vulnerability of women, children, and the elderly to certain types of abuse and neglect and the vulnerability of young males to violence have been stressed by this approach.

Moving beyond mere statistics and frequencies, one might next consider why certain segments of the population are harmed in relatively specific ways. One might also ask why patterns of harm can change. For example, the large number of women entering the work force may create new situations with harmful potential for them (e.g., an increase in cases of sexual harassment on the job or of robbery or assault while at work or traveling on business). The fact that a group is found to suffer disproportionately in a certain way can lead to new discoveries or perspectives and reveal deeper causes for such victimization.

For example, the victimization of children, women, elderly people, and minorities is better and more realistically understood if we shift away from analyzing what they did, where they were, or how they behaved and instead look at the cultural, social, and economic values supporting a certain view of them which leads to attitudes condoning or actively generating their victimization. Sexism, racism, and ageism were not always acknowledged to exist. Some still deny the existence of these powerful forces and prefer to "blame the victim." Thus, as one can see, changing the focus of the inquiry leads to a very different understanding of what causes certain individuals or groups in society to be subject to harm.

This, in turn, enlightens us about the appropriate strategy for change. In this sense, the Stage 1 analysis provides a strong foundation for preventive efforts. The policy question here is, How do we reduce the amount of harm people encounter, whether or not they consider themselves victims? The analysis also leads us to ask other fundamental questions like, What does an increasing victimization rate mean for a culture? How do our data bear on the meaning of society as a positive and beneficent entity? What fundamental restructuring is needed to stop the victimization? Or are our efforts to be limited to treating the victims without questioning and attacking the processes that generate them? Moreover, it reminds us of the need to look at and understand the "before" of victimization and its gestation, when it still lurks about as an unthematized, unspoken possibility, an undefined fear, a mere turbulence in the sky appearing against the still predominant horizon of safety.

On the other hand, this approach can have its downside too. For example, the possible pitfalls and the potential for trivialization and for "blaming the victim" that are inherent in the "life-style" approach are pretty clear.

Some do not agree that victimology should include these processes, claiming that victimological inquiry should begin only at the level of the victims' awareness and realization of their victimization and, even better, of their willingness to publicly acknowledge and report it.

Others disagree and feel instead that the questions raised during this stage and during the transition to the next stage can generate important research questions and support vigorous and useful research efforts.

STAGE 2: SEEING ONESELF AS A VICTIM

The transition from suffering harm to seeing oneself as a victim is crucial, and it has been neglected, possibly because of the recent emphasis on sociologically oriented macroresearch (e.g., national victimization surveys) versus the more psychologically oriented microapproaches.

One of the major obstacles to recognizing victimization, even on the part of the victim, is often silent public tolerance of it. Such tolerance can result from a system of values, beliefs, mores, and laws that actively support, justify, and legitimize victimization. At times this silent tolerance is enshrined into a formal code of honor and behavior, as in the case of the *omertá* enforced by organized crime. Danilo Dolci, a social reformer who cast his lot in recent years with the exploited and the dispossessed of Sicily, attracted international attention exactly because he defied the silence and openly spoke about organized crime's evil empire. The fact that high prelates and some parish priests in Sicily recently also openly acknowledged the existence and the activities of organized crime caused a sensation—not so much because they revealed something new but because they defied the accepted code of silence and the pretense that nothing was wrong.

The tacit acceptance of victimization can be the result of a "nonconscious ideology," a system of beliefs and attitudes that are implicitly accepted but remain outside conscious awareness because of prevailing stereotypes. It can also be due to the fact that sometimes alternatives are not available, possible, or even imaginable. In order to avoid the surfacing of troubling "cognitive dissonance," the awareness of injustices and prevarications is blotted out and normalcy is restored by legitimizing and incorporating the victimization into the accepted values, mores, and ways of life of a particular society.

Victims themselves are raised to accept and internalize such patterns as "the way things are," at times even supporting them and opposing reform because of intricate social and psychological dynamics. The few who become aware of the abnormal situation and speak up are ignored, ridiculed, silenced, crushed, cast away, declared insane, or driven to insanity.

It often takes drastic social changes like industrialization, urbanization, the growth of educational and career opportunities, and the opening up of life-style alternatives to shake the status quo and bring relevant issues into the open. This in turn educates the victims about their victimization, heightens their awareness, encourages their quest for change and, most of all, leads them to see themselves as victims of an unjust system. The realization that "this should not have happened to me: I did not deserve it or cause it" constitutes the key psychological dynamic in this complex process. The difficulty of accomplishing this stems from the fact that well-ingrained beliefs, values, and social systems must be challenged and changed and that trusted authority and guidance figures must be rejected with no immediate guarantee of ultimate success. This perceived riskiness of the choice is coupled with the awareness that defeat would bring a crushing backlash.

A major reason why people have difficulty in seeing themselves as victims is the novel, threatening, and shattering nature of the experience of being victimized. Normally, an atmosphere of safety and social harmony supports our activities. Being victimized is not a reality normally facing us. If there is any thought of victimization at all, the tendency is to think "I might be—anyone could be" or, more likely, "I know it happens, but it will not happen to me." Prior to its occurrence, victimization is at most an empty possibility which we are not concerned about in normal, routine daily life.

Being victimized is the dawning of a *new configuration of meaning*, and it occurs in lived experience through a developmental process. In the beginning of this process, it presents itself as strange, unfitting, unfamiliar, perhaps problematic and confusing. Even when victimization becomes a lived reality, the disbelief expressed in victims' reports indicates that it is still a relatively empty sort of quasi-reality. It has not been fully articulated, realized, and understood. This is because the person's previous world of meaning was built on the foundations of safety and social harmony. Now that these foundations are shattered, the victim is delivered to a strange, unfamiliar, shocking, hardly believable new realm outside the usual norms and experiences of life.

Victimization (or at least the first instance of it) is originally surprising, alien, and unpredictable as it tears away the familiar world. Thus, even when it becomes clear to the person that his or her preferred situation is being destroyed by another, what results is a kind of a void which only gradually begins to be understood. The victim has been torn from his or her life and swept into another which is contrary to it, thus emptying the victim's world of its usual meaning.

There are three major components of victimization that make it particularly threatening and difficult to absorb:

1. The victim's ability to control his or her life is lost, and the victim stands helplessly vulnerable, isolated, and immobilized.

2. All helpful and cooperative social support systems have receded and are out of the victim's reach.

3. A predator has invaded the victim's life and destroyed in various degrees the victim's well-being.

Victimization strikes the victim's sphere of ownness. It is not indifferent or trivial matters which are involved here but the victim's personal world or ownmost world, the *eigenwelt*, whose center is the victim and others intimately related to the victim. Thus, the seriousness and profundity of victimization can be measured by questions like these: How close to home did the crime strike? How essentially was the victim's life affected? There are of course variations in seriousness and significance which reflect individual values and idiosyncrasies. For some, their cars or pets may indeed be more important than their spouses or children!

Seeing oneself as a victim and accepting one's victimization is important for another crucial reason: It can be the beginning of the recovery process. Understanding overcomes shock and confusion and opens the way for the struggle to overcome.

Questions

As a general comment, research questions for Stage 2 could be borrowed from the labeling school of criminology, which has developed questions mostly with deviants and criminals in mind. Acknowledging that one is a victim is indeed a process of *self-labeling*.

What are the circumstances in which people react to harm as unfair and requiring redress? What role do significant others and the larger culture play in this process of self-labeling? Is there a critical mass of ideological communication and consensus that makes it possible for victims to "come out," cast aside previous rationalizations, and acknowledge their victimization? What are the major factors that create a climate favorable to the success of this process? What other givens must be in place for such factors to be successful? For example, the factors often cited to explain our awareness of sexual and domestic violence against women do not seem to cause the same changes in non-Western societies, although on the surface these factors exist there as well (e.g., increased education, affluence, communications, travel, work outside the home and related income, etc.). The current resurgence of fundamentalism in most major religions, which directly impacts the level and awareness of victimization of women and children, also poses interesting questions about the dialectics of this process.

Cultural values also influence which forms of harm are readily and clearly accepted as being injurious so that people easily see themselves as having been victimized. For example, interestingly enough, crimes against property are more easily considered clearly injurious to the victims than crimes of violence or physical harm. Psychological harm is even more difficult to identify, attribute, label, and place a valuation on. How do we take into account individual variations in the perception and evaluation of seriousness and harm? Should we strive for a consensus on a general continuum of victimization that would ultimately govern society's recognition and intervention in a standardized and agreed manner? (At one end of this continuum would be trivial losses and at the other would be the extreme form of destruction of someone's world—homicide.)

Harms affecting a large number of people and harms caused by impersonal entities are similarly difficult. When government, business, or trade decisions adversely affect someone's life, does the victim go through the same process of feeling victimized as someone hurt by an attacker? Can we learn anything from studying the similarities and differences in how people react to personally versus impersonally caused harm? And what are the long-term consequences of this apparent indifference to impersonal harm in our society, in which high levels of technology and computer-driven functions will dramatically increase the sense of impersonality and loss of community in the future?

Another related question is, How do we go about perceiving ourselves as victimized by entire societal systems, like racism, sexism, ageism? What factors and dynamics make it possible for our perceptions to coalesce so that we can see patterns of harm that go beyond individual decisions and actions and are instead part of a larger and entrenched system of beliefs and practices?

Stage 2 alerts us to the importance of *public education and consciousness raising* so that people can transcend particular explanations and justifications of victimization and grasp the systemic and widespread nature of the harm affecting them. This should then lead to the development of a sense of outrage and to a decision that something must be done to change the situation—and not just in a particular case but for an entire class of actual or potential victims, which would thus attack the problem at its roots and solve it in a definitive manner.

The importance of public education and consciousness raising is far-reaching. In most Western systems of justice, it is the jury that determines guilt or innocence. If the public has not been reached and educated, the likelihood is small that the jury will be able to understand the dynamics of victimization and to agree with the victim's vision of him- or herself and of the events. While considerable efforts have been recently undertaken to educate people in the criminal justice system about the plight of victims, if the public from which juries are selected is ignored, all these efforts can easily come to naught.

The implications for social policy are clear. Approaching victimization as an individual, discrete situation leads to interventions that are meant to alleviate the discomfort and suffering of victims but do not challenge or attempt to change (1) the system that is producing and will continue to produce more victims and that will even revictimize again and again those who are healed, and (2) the underlying values that support such a system.

There might even be collusion between the healer and the victimizer in perpetuating the cycle of victimization. The healer might, without challenging the inequity of the system, (1) mold the victim so he or she accepts the unjust situation and (2) change the victim's behavior accordingly so the victim can escape harm at the individual level. This process of acceptance and accommodation ultimately recognizes, legitimizes, and increases the victimizer's power and grip.

Serious questions have been raised by some in recent times about the role of psychology, psychiatry, social work, and counseling vis-à-vis the victim. Should these professions help a person with psychological problems accept the existing social order as a given that should not be challenged? In other words, should they try to improve the "fit" by changing the individual? Or should they be willing and trained to support the individual whose problems stem from an unjust social order and try to reform it to fit the individual?

Even more troubling is the role of other healing professionals (e.g., medical doctors), who may utilize their knowledge and skills to keep a victim alive for further torturing or to determine how far torture can go before jeopardizing the life of the victim (e.g., when the torturer wants to keep the victim alive for further interrogation or abuse). The role of psychiatry has also been criticized when it supports the status quo in certain countries by declaring social reformers and opponents of the power structure to be mentally ill and confining them to psychiatric institutions.

From a policy perspective, we should also ask ourselves whether or not it is always desirable to make people aware of their status as victims if they are not aware of it and have adapted to the injustice and the oppression. Are there circumstances when this may cause more harm than good? How should this process be conducted to minimize additional trauma? What if there are no available remedies, so that the awareness of victimization is useless and actually inflicts additional pain? What if it leads to isolated and fruitless attempts at changing the situation, attempts that will only result in more repression? Is it right to cause dissatisfaction and raise false hopes when one cannot effectively introduce change or guarantee some success?

Some experts believe that people who have been harmed should at least be willing to consider themselves victimized before victimology considers them victimized. Others argue that no stage by itself constitutes the proper focus of victimology. Rather, in their opinion, victimology must focus on the entire process of victimization. The major questions here are, What are the proper and correct borders of victimology? When does someone become the legitimate object of victimological inquiry?

STAGE 3: CLAIMING THE STATUS
AND ROLE OF VICTIM

After an individual has recognized an experience as victimization, he or she must still decide what to do about it. Several formal and informal avenues are open to the victim. There is evidence that victims validate their experience and their conclusions with someone they trust—a family member, friend, spouse, neighbor, doctor, or priest—more often than one would think. Such validation strongly influences whether or not they will ultimately notify official agencies of society (e.g., police, consumer protection agencies, professional societies or boards, ombudsmen, etc.).

Many variables affect the victim's decision to publicly report the victimization: the perceived probability of the police finding the culprit; the amount of damage or harm suffered; the relationship with the victimizer and the impact of reporting on it; the obstacles, expense, and time involved in reporting; the perceived complexity of bureaucratic proceedings; the fear of being ridiculed or of retaliation and revenge; the lack of privacy at the initial stages of reporting; and the place of residence (rural dwellers find it even more difficult to report than urban residents).

Social, cultural and psychological factors may stop a victim from publicly claiming the status of victim. This can at times lead to continued victimization, with the victimizer taking advantage of the lack of action on the part of the victim. A basic and pervasive factor giving victims pause is the value placed on winning and on being successful in society. In the eyes of many, a victim is a loser, even though an innocent one. As a result, the victim can pay a high price when acknowledging victimization. This is why, for example, it may be more difficult for males to admit and report their victimization and seek appropriate help.

In societies where setting the limits of sexual activity is strictly the woman's responsibility, fornication a serious crime, and rape no excuse, one can readily understand a victim's reluctance to report a victimizing event. Reporting it could be the equivalent of passing a death sentence on herself, or at least it could seriously jeopardize her own social status, respectability, and desirability in the community and the social status of her family.

In other words, where victim blaming is prevalent and, worst of all, internalized by the victims themselves, the psychological and social price to be paid in reporting may simply be too high. Similarly, the victims' perception or realization that they will not be believed could effectively close all avenues for reporting and seeking redress for an indeterminate period of time and could possibly lead to prolonged victimization. Moreover, the social devaluation consequent to reporting may make the victim an easy target for harassment and further victimization at the hands of the original victimizer or at the hands of others. Examples of this situation include incest, sexual harassment or assault, domestic violence, and elder abuse.

The reluctance to claim the status and role of victim is not confined to individuals. Corporations, businesses, even governments may not report being victimized in order to maintain a certain image or for other practical reasons. For example, a company may not report a virus invasion or a breach of security in its computer system. Instead, it will absorb the losses to avoid bad publicity, which might shake its customers' confidence and adversely affect its ability to function. The acquiescence of small and even large businesses to the extortionist demands of organized crime or of corrupt customs, government, or police officials also reflects many of the same dynamics affecting the willingness of individual victims to acknowledge and claim their role as victim and seek redress.

Questions

What influences the decision to claim the status and role of victim? What influences the choice of whom to report the victimization to (family, friends, acquaintances, police, private or public agencies, rape crisis center, etc.)? Some victims initially limit the disclosure to closer people and then later extend it to outsiders. When reporting to outsiders, some choose to avoid official or law enforcement agencies in favor of community-based, grass roots, or victim-staffed organizations. There is also evidence that many victims prefer to share their victimization and seek the assistance of informal, rather than formal, networks of social support.

What are the reasons why some people do not claim the status and role of victim? What are the psychological and social consequences of such a decision? How can society increase the likelihood of victim reporting? What do victims anticipate or expect, positively or negatively, when they report?

What is the victims' level of satisfaction with those they interact with when they report? Does the existence of reputable treatment and rehabilitation programs for some types of offenders increase the probability of reporting by victims? How do the different operational philosophies of helping organizations affect whether someone claims the role of victim?

How does reporting unfold (in terms of frequency, nature, and degree of willingness to pursue the matter further) once social and cultural changes make it respectable or safe to report a particular type of victimization? Is there a feedback loop which rewards reporting by changing cultural values in favor of the victim, thus making it progressively easier for later victims to report because of the reporting of previous ones? Is reporting truly to the benefit of the victim or is it officially encouraged because it is mostly advantageous to the system?

Claiming the role of victim can be seen as an important step toward recovery. It represents the victim's struggle with victimization. It is an attempt by the victim to reclaim some active control over his or her own life by coming to terms with reality and by moving toward a resolution of the crisis. It is also an attempt to reestablish and strengthen the helpful, peaceful, and cooperative social supports that may have failed the victim at the time of victimization. Finally, it means taking positive action against the predator.

On the other hand, the inability to claim victim status can lead to very negative consequences. Some repeated victims, seeing no way out, commit suicide—a desperate way to finally take "control" of one's own life.

STAGE 4: RECEIVING SOCIETY'S RECOGNITION AND POSSIBLE SUPPORT

Overcoming victimization is an exact reversal of its meaning and cannot be taken for granted. If the social world causing or supporting victimization does not change or continues to be detrimental, if the victim does nothing about his or her misfortune, or if others remain indifferent and unavailable, victimization deepens. Society and others play a crucial role in the victim's overcoming victimization and forming a newly constituted world. The active help of others restores a sense of trust and harmony in the victim's destroyed sociality and helps the victim make the difficult transition into the new world "after" victimization.

It is vital for the well-being of the victim as an individual and as a member of society that the damage of victimization be overcome and that the crisis generated by it be successfully resolved. Every victim's task and need is to reestablish the world as he or she prefers it and knows it. This involves rising out of immobility and seizing the initiative, ending isolation and establishing contacts and networks, escaping danger and entering into a safe harbor.

This process requires three interrelated elements: active effort, the world's assertion of predictable safety, and active help from others. It is through this process that victimization will appear as avoidable, preventable, and possible to overcome. Society's understanding and recognition of victimization is crucial to the unfolding of this recovery process.

A substantial amount of victimological research has been conducted on (1) the factors affecting the transition from Stage 3 to Stage 4 (i.e., the factors that determine whether a claim to the status of victim is recognized and acted on by society's agents) and (2) the actions of agents offering support, retribution, restitution, and compensation. Research and writing on the victim and the criminal justice system, victim-witness assistance programs, compensation and restitution, treatment for the victim, legal and criminal justice system reform, etc., clearly dominate the field.

Society's reaction and involvement are greatly affected by Stage 3. The increasing number of victims "coming out" reinforces and intensifies public awareness of victimization and contributes to further establishing it as part of the constellation of issues that cannot be ignored and about which something should be done. It also provides firsthand information on the victims, their numbers, the dynamics of victimization, the needs of the victims, and on how to reach them.

Once victims come out and public and professional interest is heightened, the logical next step will be to formulate appropriate public policy and provide related services. Such planning is required to ensure that society will be able to respond adequately and promptly when victims acknowledge and claim their status and seek the recognition and support of the community. It is not unusual for politicians and others in positions of power to give lip service to a legitimate cause in response to pressure but then fail to provide the adequate infrastructure and the means to responsibly address the problem once the intended target population takes them seriously and requests the services. Overpromising and underdelivering would be a serious setback to the resolution of victimization and would ultimately revictimize the victims.

Questions

How society will react to a victim's claim will inevitably depend on various variables linked to status, visibility, and power. What impact do the status of the victim, the type of victimization, its circumstances, the victim's belonging to a specific group (which may be receiving more or less recognition from official agencies depending on its numbers, visibility, and organized strength) have on the probability that the victim's claim will be honored?

The impact of these variables can be quite dramatic. For example, runaways for a long time were considered delinquents. It was only recently that a different view of runaways—the view that many are victims of abuse, neglect, and incest ("throwaways")—has finally begun to be accepted because of the vigorous efforts of skilled advocates and organizers of shelters.

A crucial concept that affects society's recognition is *victim precipitation*. What exactly is victim precipitation? In what ways does it affect the legitimation of the status of victim?

How can we increase the likelihood that public and private agencies, family, friends, and others will respond positively and show support when the victim asks for assistance?

Another important dimension here is what occurs once an agency, particularly an official one, recognizes a victim's claim to being a "real" victim. Does this recognition keep the victim in that role? If not, how exactly is the victim helped to move out of that role and back to "normal"? And what is normal particularly after a serious victimization? Which treatment is appropriate for which type of victim? Also, whose interests are being served when treatment is offered? Should this treatment include reeducating the victim to see the world differently or should those providing assistance accept victims for what they are, even though they may be returning to a world where they will be revictimized?

What can we learn from research in other fields of victimization (natural disasters, accidents, torture, abuse of power, etc.)? How do other types of victims cope with crisis, deal with the forced recognition of their vulnerability, and begin the recovery process?

What are the consequences of being denied victim status? How do people cope and make sense of the rejection of their claim? What impact does such denial have?

At a time of surging and competing claims within the framework of limited resources, how does one ensure that society will respond affirmatively and adequately to the needs of victims? How should society prepare to meet their claims? As for the most appropriate locus for victim services, should they be established in the private or public sector? Should they be in existing agencies or new ones? Should the programs be self-help or professionally controlled?

CONCLUSION

The framework provided here represents a comprehensive and dynamic approach to the understanding of victimization. It is our responsibility to review and evaluate past work in this field and to develop a future agenda that will spur, guide, and support future research and policy intervention.

Struggling with these issues will allow us to approach the attainment of a fuller understanding of the patterns and dynamics of victimization, It will also allow us to create an equitable society with less suffering, violence, and oppression while we respect the individuality and uniqueness of each victim.

BIBLIOGRAPHY

Birkbeck, C. (1983). "Victimology is what victimologists do" but what should they do? *Victimology: An International Journal, 8* (3-4), 270-275.

Burt, M. (1983). A conceptual framework for victimological research. *Victimology: An International Journal, 8* (3-4), 261-269.

Giorgi, A. (1985). *Phenomenology and psychological research*. Pittsburgh, PA: Duquesne University Press.

Viano, E. (1983). Violence, victimization and social change: A sociocultural and public policy analysis. *Victimology: An International Journal, 8* (3-4), 54-79.

Chapter 2

Prologue: On Some Visible and Hidden Dangers of Victim Movements

Ezzat A. Fattah

Recent years have witnessed a revival of interest in the victims of crime. Today there seems to be a genuine concern in our society for this disenfranchised and neglected group of citizens who suffer the direct consequences of criminality. Ever since the State monopolized the right to criminal prosecution and converted the "Wergeld," i.e. the indemnity payable to the victim or his family, to a fine destined for the king's coffers, the victim has been the forgotten man in the criminal process, the party in the shadow, used to buttress the State's case and abused if he refused to co-operate or testify. And despite some progress in the last decade society's reaction to crime victims has not changed much. When a crime is committed, society's energies and resources are mobilized to find, catch and punish the culprit. Very little is done to help the victim recuperate from the traumatic effects of victimization or recover the material losses incurred as a result of the crime. The millions and millions of dollars society willingly spends on punishment and incarceration are in sharp contrast to the token amount devoted to compensate the victims. Society has failed the victims of crime, has ignored, neglected and often mistreated those who are criminally victimized.

The current renewed interest in the victim manifests itself in both research and action. At present, every aspect of criminal victimization is being studied and analyzed. Every facet of the plight of the victim is being debated and scrutinized. Criminologists are trying to assess the

Source: Fattah, E.A. (1986). Prologue: On some visible and hidden dangers of victim movements. In E.A. Fattah (Ed.), *From crime policy to victim policy: Reorienting the justice system* (pp. 1-14). New York: St. Martin's. Copyright © E.A. Fattah (ed). Reprinted by permission of Dr. E.A. Fattah; St. Martin's Press, Incorporated; and Macmillan, Ltd.

needs of crime victims and to find ways and means of alleviating their suffering and distress. On the applied side, groups have been formed in many
countries, not only to offer help and assistance to crime victims but also to
lobby on their behalf. Although in many cases the action of these groups is
neither orchestrated nor coordinated, the term "victim movements" is
appearing with amazing consistency in the popular and scientific literature.
It should be futile to challenge the need for victim advocacy or to deny that
the time has come for the victims of crime to have their voice heard in matters of criminal policy. There are, however, certain dangers associated with
the present trend. And although "victim movements" as organized action-
and-pressure groups are still in the early stages of development, some of
these dangers are becoming more and more apparent. Identifying and
debating these dangers is necessary to prevent the exploitation of these
movements for political purposes and to ensure that their action is geared
toward the achievement of their primary and foremost goal, namely justice
for the victims of crime. The ultimate success of the movements in reaching
this worthwhile goal will naturally depend on the future orientation they
will take. The aim of this chapter is to outline and discuss some of the visible and hidden dangers that loom on the horizon of victim movements in
Canada, the United States, and many other countries.

THE DANGER THAT VICTIM MOVEMENTS MIGHT TURN INTO OFFENDER-BASHING CAMPAIGNS

As Elias points out (Chapter 15),* the now long-term cry for addressing
victim needs and for orienting the criminal process away from the
offender and toward the victim, has been closely associated with a "law
and order" approach to law enforcement. Get-tough criminal policies
have combined nicely with an apparent concern for the victim.

  Most victim advocates do not restrict their demands to a charter of
victim rights or to a better lot for those who are victimized. These
demands are usually coupled with, and in fact overshadowed by, calls for
harsher penalties, stricter measures and more oppressive treatment of
offenders. Getting-tough with offenders is often advanced as the central or,
at least, as an essential component, of society's obligation to the victims of
crime and as a *sine qua non* for redressing the wrong done unto the victim. In this way, the noble cause of the victims of crime is used as a pre-
text to unleash suppressed vindictive impulses or as an excuse to act out
the inhibited aggression against the offender. The danger is that a healthy
victim movement might thus be transformed into a backlash against criminals and that the progress that has been realized over the years in human-
izing the criminal policy and the criminal justice system will be reversed.

---

*Chapter references in this material refer to chapters in the book edited by Dr. Fattah (*From Crime
Policy to Victim Policy: Reorienting the Justice System*), the source of this Fattah reading.

THE DANGER OF WIDENING THE NET OF SOCIAL CONTROL

Recent experience with well-intentioned criminal justice programs, such as diversion and community service orders, reveals the inherent tendency of these programs to widen the net of formal social control and to intensify the mechanisms of such control. Many of the new services for crime victims carry with them a similar danger. As Elias (Chapter 15) points out, victim services are associated with building police forces and are more concerned with controlling social discontent than crime. His evaluation of victim services in the USA inevitably leads to the conclusion that most seem oriented more to either narrowly controlling victims or broadly controlling discontent than to controlling crime or meeting victim needs. According to Elias, most government-sponsored victim services seem devoted to more than merely restoring the victim in some way. They also seek some kind of control. In particular, victim-witness programs seek to control victims in the criminal justice process. Victims seem to be channeled into the process for official needs and perspectives, instead of providing a co-operative spirit, greater citizen participation, and effective crime control.

Other evidence shows that victims of crime are being used for political purposes and as a vehicle that serves only the interests of opportunistic politicians and criminal justice practitioners. Rock (Chapter 2) notes that very few of the organizations supposedly set up for helping victims were in fact established in a world figured by a politics of victims. They were founded to accomplish distinct sets of purposes which touched only obliquely on victims. This is echoed by Joanna Shapland (Chapter 10) who points out that the major projects aimed at fulfilling victims' needs have been set up without regard to, or even investigation into, victims expressed needs. Elias (Chapter 15) provides at least a partial explanation to this obvious paradox. He notes that victim compensation programs were set up in many American states because they were regarded as very valuable for building public opinion and electoral support. They did not imply a strong commitment to victims or to the notion of compensation. He also refers to the reputation victim-witness programs have for "using" victims to pursue certain criminal cases deemed important by the prosecution and for preferring official over victim needs.

THE DANGER OF APPLYING BAND-AIDS TO THE SYMPTOM OF CRIME WITHOUT ADDRESSING OR COUNTERACTING ITS SOURCES

One of the dangers of the present orientation of the victim movement is to divert attention and to direct funds and resources away from effective crime control policies and promising crime prevention strategies. Existing victim services are geared to the alleviation of the effects of victimization. As such, they are more concerned with what happens after the crime than they are with reducing victimization or preventing people from becoming victims in the first place. Actually crime prevention does not appear on the program of most victim advocates. And by advocating a retributive criminal justice policy they are apt to increase the cost of the punitive segments of the system to the detriment, or at the expense, of the system's preventive components. In the current climate created by the victim movement the root causes of crime are bound to be overshadowed and the conditions that breed crime are bound to be neglected.

Elias (Chapter 15) points out that victim services and schemes do not seek to fundamentally root out the problem they are addressing. They do not genuinely seek to eliminate crime. In fact they seem to ignore the value of serious crime control for preventing victims in the first place. He notes that while official rhetoric consistently emphasizes an apparent concern for reducing crime, the effectiveness of the policies actually promoted is very questionable. And there is little evidence to indicate that the programs have any concrete effect on reducing crime. One might argue, he writes, that government-inspired victim services, as currently constituted, actually increase crime by promoting discredited policies that only encourage crime, and do not effectively combat it. Furthermore, the victim orientation of these programs may serve to abdicate responsibility for addressing the sources of crime since they emphasize a false contest of rights (not needs) and promote a kind of complacency towards crime, now that some post-victimization relief appears available.

THE DANGER OF PLACING TOO MUCH EMPHASIS ON CONVENTIONAL CRIMES TO THE NEGLECT OF OTHER ACTIONS CAUSING GRIEVOUS SOCIAL HARMS

As Anttila (Chapter 12) points out, a victim-centered approach would put the emphasis on the traditional offenses more than is already done today. This would especially be true of those offenses that cause immediately perceptible damage. Offenses of endangerment, and offenses which only cause indirect or slowly accumulating damage (such as labor and environmental offenses) would be left without sufficient attention. The emergence of the victim movement seems to have refocused the notion of criminality on the traditional crimes which have a direct, immediate and tangible victim. White collar crimes, corporate actions causing grievous social harms, whether they are legally defined as crimes or not, have been once again relegated to the background. Victim movements have focused their attention on, and directed their action to, the so-called conventional crimes. This is understandable. Homicide, rape, robbery, assault, burglary have visible, identifiable victims. This is not always the case with corporate and business crimes which may victimize millions and millions of people and still go largely unreported and unprosecuted. Despite the scope of white collar crime and despite the fact that its depredations far exceed those of conventional crime it is totally left out from victim campaigns. And so are other socially harmful actions such as the pollution of the environment, the production of hazardous substances, the manufacture and sale of unsafe products, and so on, although they cause more death, injury and harm than all violent crimes combined. And what about victims of violations of health and safety codes, victims of social injustice and of racial discrimination, victims of state terrorism, victims of abuse of political and/or economic power? The lot of these latter victims is even a sadder one than that of victims of conventional crime. The reason is that they lack any means of redress and usually have no recourse against the perpetrators of the abuse.

THE DANGER OF INCREASING ANXIETY OVER CRIME AND HEIGHTENING THE FEAR OF VICTIMIZATION

To awaken the social conscience and to gain sympathy and support for the noble cause of crime victims, victim movements try as much as possible to emphasize the dangers and consequences of victimization and to highlight the plight and misfortunes of those who are victimized. The danger of this strategy is that it could inadvertently raise anxiety over crime and heighten the fear of victimization. Placing too much stress on the weakness and vulnerability of certain groups can produce similar effects. It may well be that the exaggerated fear women and the elderly have of crime is due in all or in part to the great attention being given to their potential status as victims. As Christie (Chapter 1) notes, singling out certain groups such as the old or women and paying excessive attention to their proneness to victimization is likely to produce fear and anxiety in their minds and the more attention they are given as victims, the more they fear. And although empirical evidence is still lacking the hypothesis of a positive link between attention and fear seems, at least, plausible. The record high level of fear of crime reported in Canada and the USA in recent years (Skogan, Chapter 8) may not be totally unrelated to the growing attention and publicity being given to the victims of crime. The publicity given to the risks and effects of victimization, the graphical portrayal of the sufferings and anguish victims go through, can only arouse feelings of anxiety about crime and amplify the fear of becoming victim. This can indirectly hurt the cause of the victims by discouraging samaritan interventions. There is an inverse relationship between the degree of fear of crime and the willingness to intervene, the higher the fear, the less willing are people to come to the rescue of fellow citizens being victimized for fear of personal injury or harm (van Dijk, Chapter 7).

THE DANGER OF INTENSIFYING THE CONFLICT RATHER THAN SOLVING IT

No one would dispute the fact that there is an urgent, pressing need to care for and to protect the victims of crime. Any initiative and every move aimed at achieving this goal should therefore be welcomed and encouraged. But as with other noble, worthy social causes, there is always the danger of too much paternalism, of too much interference in victims' personal lives, of overreaction and of overdoing what we set out to do. One of the dangers of the present orientation of the victim movement is that rather than bringing the feuding parties together it will widen the gap that separates them, that it will intensify the conflict instead of solving it. Some victim programs have a well-deserved reputation for discouraging reconciliation and for urging victims not to accept any settlement that does not involve the punishment of the offender. An example from the area of family violence would help illustrate this policy. Many shelter homes for battered wives set as a formal or informal requirement for admission that the wife does not return to her husband under any circumstances. Residents may even be threatened with dismissal from the shelter in case they agreed to mediation that might lead to the resumption of marital cohabitation. While some of these requirements may be essential in certain cases to protect the woman against further abuse, they are usually dictated not by the best interests of the victims but by the ideological orientation of those running the service.

Some of the actions advocated by the victim movement might also be in conflict with other goals of the criminal justice policy. Giving victims a say in parole decisions may result in unnecessarily lengthy incarceration and in delaying the social reintegration of the offender. Victim impact statements are likely to bring about more prison sentences and might discourage the use of prison alternatives. Victims' involvement in plea bargaining negotiations is apt to make the justice process slower and render the system more inefficient than it is at present.

THE DANGER OF STIGMATIZING THE VICTIMS AND OF CREATING VICTIM STEREOTYPES

The labelling approach has amply shown the nefarious effects of stigmatizing offenders and deviants and of branding them as social enemies, misfits or outcasts. This should sensitize us to the dangers of formal, intensive intervention with at least certain categories of crime victims. The labelling of certain crime victims as a weak, vulnerable group in dire need of assistance, care and compassion carries with it the danger of attaching to those who are victimized a social stigma similar to the one attached to welfare recipients, beneficiaries of unemployment insurance and other unprivileged groups. Rock (Chapter 2) refers to such stigma when he quotes the arguments often made by feminists urging raped and battered women to resist the ignoble title of "crime victim."

The dangers of stigmatization are greater still when popular stereotypes of certain victims are created. Even more general programs such as state compensation schemes do not escape the pitfalls of stereotyping. Shapland (Chapter 10) draws attention to the prevailing view in terms of society's attitudes to victims and victim assistance according to which it is the deserving, innocent victim who should be compensated or helped and that help should be given as a form of charity. A stereotype is thus created and only those who fit this stereotype (and this is decided by the schemes themselves) become entitled to compensation!

The dangers of stigmatization and stereotyping could be reduced if laws and programs designed to help, assist or compensate crime victims were to emphasize their right not their plight, their strength not their weakness and if they were based on the notion of risk not of vulnerability.

Stressing the weakness, the vulnerability, the helplessness and the plight of crime victims carries with it yet another danger, the danger of ostracizing the offender. By casting offenders and victims into socially predefined antagonistic roles as predators and prey, as outsiders and insiders, by amplifying their differences rather than their similarities (similarities so well described by Hough—Chapter 5—and by Garofalo—Chapter 6) and by magnifying the guilt of the doer and the innocence of the sufferer, the wickedness of the former and the virtue of the latter, we risk to reach what Rock (Chapter 2) calls "the most extreme form of the divide" encountered in totalitarian societies which banish criminals and deviants to a metaphysical exile outside the true community. By so doing, and by dismissing criminals as strangers, totalitarian societies intentionally propagate the view that these criminals are less than human thus rationalizing and justifying the cruel, inhuman or extremely repressive measures that are usually taken against them.

THE DANGER OF WEAKENING SOCIAL TIES AND INCREASING DEPENDENCY ON SOCIAL SERVICES

The welfare state has often been criticized for generating insatiable demands for social services and for breeding an army of citizens totally or partially dependent on these services. The critics maintain that social services in the welfare state, whether run by professionals or volunteers, whether they cater to the needs of the young or the old, the poor, the unemployed or the handicapped, have a tendency to develop dependency among their clients and even to extract these clients from their natural social networks. The truth of such allegations is, of course, open to challenge. There can be no doubt, however, that many social services do in the long run weaken social ties by freeing the members of the traditional social network (relatives, friends, neighbors, peers and so on) from some of their social obligations. Social services provide an alibi for our conscience. They allow us to turn our backs on the needs of those fellow citizens closest to us and to lay these needs at the doorstep of state agencies.

Victims of crime are now being defined as "society's orphans," as the new herd of society's weaklings who are in dire need of the care of the welfare state. Setting up social services for the victims allows us to escape our own social responsibilities. And when victims are not helped, when their needs are not met, when they are ultimately left to suffer alone and in silence we need not feel guilty about our inaction, we need not blame ourselves for not having lived up to our social and civic obligations, we can always blame the authorities for their inefficiency.

The professionalization of victim services presents yet other dangers. The personalized care of the victim's social network is replaced by the depersonalized care of the state. The victim who within his family, his neighborhood or his small community is treated as a person and who in such setting feels and acts as an individual is converted into "a client," or a "recipient of services." He/she has to suffer the dehumanization of being transformed from a person to a number. In addition, the psychological support and regeneration the victim feels when cared for by family or friends is replaced by the agony and humiliation of having been placed within the hands of strangers who have to deal daily with dozens of other victims.

THE DANGER OF DELAYING
THE NATURAL HEALING PROCESS

The psychology of the victim remains an unexplored field. To understand the physical and emotional effects of victimization it is necessary to turn to research done in other older disciplines such as psychiatry and child psychology.

Child care is an area where psychologists have made important contributions. They advise parents to protect their children but warn them not to be overprotective. Too much attention, too much concern, too much care tend to develop weak, dependent, fearful, passive and withdrawn individuals. In providing the care, help and support victims need, caution should be exercised to avoid causing greater harm to the victim. Intensive and/or excessive intervention can delay the natural healing process. It can prolong the agony and the trauma resulting from the offense, create undue anxieties about the crime situation and the risks of victimization, and nurture attitudes of distrust or mistrust among actual and potential victims. There is already some empirical evidence that should sensitize us to such danger. Psychiatrists have always been amazed at the remarkable healing capacity of the human psyche. Studies of victims of violent victimization revealed that though the immediate and short-term effects might in some cases be both dramatic and traumatic, the victim is likely, in the long run, to make a healthy recovery and to come away from the experience with little or no damage to his or her psyche. Catamnestic studies of sexually molested children showed that the victims whose cases were handled properly without too much fuss, too much fanfare, did not suffer lingering ill effects. On the other hand, in cases where the parents overreacted, the victims were likely to suffer, years after the experience, from emotional side effects. Follow-up studies of Austrian women gang-raped by Russian soldiers in the final days of World War II reported that even such grave, humiliating, and highly traumatic experience did not leave permanent scars on the psyche of most victims.

The difficulty many victimization survey respondents have in recalling the incidents of which they were victims (Skogan, chapter 4) indicates that such experiences do not occur often enough to make a major impact on their lives or to affect their way of life to any considerable extent. Furthermore, even those offenses which do occur sufficiently often do not seem to be important enough in people's lives to be remembered vividly for any length of time (McIntyre, 1967). McIntyre concluded that ". . . most incidents of victimization do not appear to constitute very important events in a person's life experience" and hence are not readily recalled in an interview.

Conklin (1975) found that personal victimization does not seriously affect victims' attitudes and behaviour except perhaps in the short run. He attributes this to the fact that most of the crimes people suffer are trivial in nature such as the theft of a small sum of money. He writes

> Reaction to such crimes is minimal, even in the short run. Also, reaction to even the more serious crimes of robbery and rape is apt to diminish over time; a sense of invulnerability returns after a period during which no additional crimes occur.

Findings of recent studies, however, paint a drastically different picture. To cite just one example, a study by Rich and Salasin in the USA, reported in 1983, found that 90% of rape victims suffer long-term emotional problems and the percentage was even higher for burglary victims, 94%. These victims were found to be suffering from what the authors called the "post-traumatic stress syndrome." How can these findings, in sharp contrast with previous ones cited above, be explained? They can be interpreted as indicating that researchers in the social sciences tend to see what they want to see and to find what they set out to find. The second and more plausible explanation is that the traumatic effects suffered by crime victims are, at present, more widespread, more profound, more intense than they used to be, and last longer than they used to last. If that is true, could there be a relationship between the change in our attitudes to crime victims, between our new interventionist techniques with victims and the growing pains of victimization? Could the heightened fear of victimization reported in recent years be related in any way to the increasing attention, the outpour of sympathy and the wide publicity being given to the victims of crime? Do policies of intervention prolong rather than shorten the traumatic effects of victimization?

THE DANGER OF CREATING EXPECTATIONS AMONG CRIME VICTIMS THAT ARE NOT OR COULD NOT BE MET

The publicity currently being given to victim services is apt to create or heighten expectations among crime victims. Such expectations, if not met, can only lead to various levels of insatisfaction and frustration with the criminal justice system and with the greater society. The history of victim services, as brief as it is, is one of unfulfiled [sic] promises and unmet expectations. This does not imply that victim needs are so diverse or that their expectations are so high that they cannot be met. It is simply a realistic assessment based on various evaluations of existing victim services. The chapters by Shapland and Elias (Chapters 10, 11 and 15) provide evidence of the inadequacy of the services and the frustrations that ensue. In her studies of crime victims in England, Shapland detected a mismatch between victims expectations of the system and the system's assumptions about victim needs. Consequently she warns that public statements about the worth of victims, which are later shown to be hollow, may rebound on any who set up such ineffective schemes. This is confirmed by her finding that by the end of police and court processes, there was a significant decline in victim's satisfaction with the police handling of the case and also a decline in attribution of positive qualities to the police generally.

Elias's assessment of the state of victim services in the USA paints a more negative and gloomier picture. Referring to victim compensation, he notes that there is overwhelming evidence that the most apparent goal of compensation schemes, namely to help restore victims by providing financial payments, is not being met. For a variety of reasons, only a very small percentage of victims receives any assistance, and when it does come, it is with much delay and considerable inconvenience. Elias notes further that for the most part offender restitution is unused and ineffective. Regarding social service referrals, he observed that most social services do not address victim needs and do not accept victim cases.

The inadequacy of existing victim services may be traced to many factors not the least of which is the insufficient funding and the shortage of personnel. In the present climate of austerity and financial restraint it seems totally unrealistic to expect major commitments of funds and resources to victim services even when such commitments entail the prospect of political gain. If that is the case then it may not be too pessimistic to expect most justice for victims initiatives to remain, at least in the near future, in the realm of political rhetoric rather than becoming a social reality.

CONCLUSION

The claim that victims' desire for justice can only be satisfied through the infliction of harsher penalties is neither logical nor rational and is belied by empirical research on what victims really want. Inhumane treatment of the offender is not and need not be an outcome or a corollary of humanitarian consideration for the victim. And it is not necessary to sacrifice the basic or the constitutional rights of the offender in order to affirm and safeguard the rights of the victim. Unfortunately, most of the so-called victim bills passed or are being considered by legislatures of some American states contain dispositions that amount to the abrogation of some of the legal safeguards which for centuries have been the pride of criminal justice in the USA. How regressive and retrograde it would be to sacrifice, under the guise of protecting the victim, any of the fundamental principles of democratic justice, be it the presumption of innocence, the requirement of corroboration in certain crimes, or the exclusionary rule. Such action can only backfire! How easy it is to forget that "we are all potential aggressors—differently placed and variously motivated to harm our fellows." Yes, it is always easier to see or to perceive ourselves as potential victims than as potential aggressors.

The suffering of the victim is not diminished by increasing the suffering of the offender. Inflicting undue pain on the perpetrator of the crime does not alleviate the victim's distress. And the humiliation suffered by the victim is not erased by the degradation of the offender. Humaneness is indivisible. We cannot be humane to one party and inhumane to the other, be kind to the victim and cruel to the offender. We cannot preach justice for the aggressed and at the same time tolerate injustice toward the aggressor.

Furthermore, our concern for the victim's plight should not blind us to the fact those we label as criminals are more often than not victims themselves. Without subscribing to a purely deterministic view of criminal behavior, without negating individual responsibility, we cannot but recognize that criminal behavior has causes. And whether one believes in nature or nurture, in the bad seed or the bad environment, in theories of innate criminal tendencies or theories of learning, we cannot escape the conclusion that everytime [sic] a crime is committed against one of our fellow citizens, we as parents, brothers, neighbors, educators, friends or peers, have failed in someway [sic]. We have to accept a share in the blame and a part of the responsibility. The crime, therefore, does not create a one-sided obligation, but a dual responsibility on our part, to the one who transgressed and the one who suffered. Both need help and support, both need sympathy and compassion. It would be against the teachings of Christ and the spirit of Christianity to care for the aggressed but not for the aggressor or inversely to care for those who have sinned but not for those sinned against. And in the long run, the interests of victims and of society at large are best served by humanity and compassion, by tolerance and forgiveness, by the development of conciliatory and forgiving communities rather than hostile and vengeful ones.

Whether for political, ideological or practical reasons, victim movements have been largely selective (I would even say discriminating) in their focus, emphasis and action, in the victim groups they adopt as well as in the types of crimes they chose to fight against. As a result, the vast majority of victims have been left unprotected, unassisted and unheard. If victim movements are claiming justice for victims, then let it be justice for all victims. Can we stress the distress and anguish of victims of conventional crimes and still remain oblivious or indifferent to the pain and suffering done to the victims of crimes committed by businessmen, politicians, and government officials? And why single out the victims of intentional violent crimes when acts of negligence, imprudence, and recklessness claim many more lives and hurt many more victims? If we are to emphasize and publicize the plight of victims of traditional criminality then let us not forget or neglect the victims of social injustice, racial discrimination, gross inequities in wealth and power, nor the victims of abuse of power.

As social scientists, as criminologists, as policy-makers, as criminal justice practitioners, and as concerned citizens we should advocate a justice system based on restitution not retribution. We should urge society to abandon punishment and retaliation in favour of compensation, mediation and reconciliation. We have to try to break the vicious cycle of vengeance which does nothing but eternalize the conflict and perpetuate the dispute. Let us prevent a return to the summary justice of Lex Talionis or the arbitrary justice of the classical and neoclassical schools. Let our reaction to crime be marked by sympathy, pity and compassion *vis-à-vis* those unfortunate members of our society whether they are victims or offenders, aggressed or aggressors. Let us build our society on love not hate, on forgiveness not vindictiveness, on commiseration not retaliation. Only then can we hope to create for our children and grandchildren a better society and a safer environment to live in.

Section 2
HOMICIDE

In this country, as well as in societies since the beginning of recorded history, prosecuting authorities have given high priority to the investigation and prosecution of homicide. This priority has certainly not changed with the emergence of victimology and the victims' movement. If anything, these developments have simply increased an already keen desire to understand the factors that contribute to or influence homicide victimization and to address the needs of homicide survivors.

Fortunately, compared to other crimes, criminal homicide is a relatively infrequent event in this country. According to the 1997 Uniform Crime Reports compiled by the FBI, the rate of reported criminal homicides was just under seven per 100,000 persons. Although this is the lowest such reported homicide rate since 1967, homicide rates have not exceeded approximately 10 per 100,000 at any time during this period. In the 1997 reporting year, the majority of homicide victims and offenders were male and 18 years or older. There was approximately the same percentage of white homicide victims and black homicide victims and a slightly higher percentage of black offenders than white offenders. Approximately one-half of the murder victims knew their assailants. Firearms were used in approximately 70 percent of the reported murders, but more homicides resulted from arguments than from felonious activities such as robbery or burglary. Even these aggregate data dispel some common stereotypes by demonstrating that most murders are intraracial (with disproportionately minority victims) and are as likely to be committed by intimates or acquaintances as by strangers and for personal reasons as for felonious ones.

Yet, as Chapter 3, by Zahn and Sagi, and Chapter 4, by Finkelhor, indicate, it is important to separate these aggregate data by age, gender, racial and ethnic background, and more detailed circumstances of the occurrence to understand more clearly the varying nature of murder victimizations. In this vein, diverse theories of homicide victimization have been explored. Some of the earliest empirical research conducted following the initial victimological focus on victim precipitation factors was Wolfgang's research regarding the role of victim precipitation in criminal homicide. Other researchers have focused less on victim initiation of events and more on the escalating circumstances of an encounter that may result in homicide. Still others have examined the contributing role of lifestyle factors, media-portrayed violence, and medical resources in homicide victimization.

Researchers have also attempted to better understand the impact that homicide victimization has on survivors. Survivors of homicide victims generally have no time to prepare for the sudden and traumatic death of a parent, spouse, child, or sibling due to murder. Research and clinical observation indicate that grief and recovery patterns may be different for homicide survivors than for others who suffer more "normal" losses. These findings have important implications for treatment and social service providers, as well as for police and prosecutors who interact with such survivors.

There have been some changes in criminal justice policies and procedures that relate specifically to homicide victimization. Some changes have been as basic as the establishment of death notification procedures by police departments to inform survivors of the victim's death in a manner more appropriate to the circumstances. At the other end of the process, a jurisdiction may authorize the witnessing of a murder offender's execution by a victim's family members. In between these events, the general innovations in the criminal justice process that have been advocated by the victims' movement—such as greater victim input regarding disposition and sentencing (see Section 6 of this text)—apply in homicide cases.

In our society, which is increasingly permeated by violent images and events, homicide victimization will certainly continue to be among the highest priorities. Research, such as that illustrated by the Zahn and Sagi and Finkelhor selections, that seeks to disaggregate the homicide data in an attempt to understand the diverse causal factors that contribute to its occurrence is critical to the development of causal theories and, more importantly, prevention strategies regarding homicide victimization. Treatment, social service, and criminal justice efforts to address the needs of homicide survivors more effectively and appropriately must also continue to be priorities.

LEARNING EXPERIENCES

1. The homicide analysis provided in Chapter 3, the Zahn and Sagi article, was based on 1978 homicide data from urban areas. Using the most recent Uniform Crime Reports homicide data, or another available data source, determine whether the general analysis provided by Zahn and Sagi has remained consistent. If you are able to obtain these data for your own community, determine whether the homicide patterns identified by Zahn and Sagi are reflected in your community. If they are not, what factors might account for any differences?

2. Zahn and Sagi suggest that, with regard to the various categories of homicide studied, further research is necessary regarding the role of the public as witnesses to homicide, additional variables (e.g., alcohol or drug use by victims and offenders), and causal theories of homicide. Explore what types of research have been conducted in these areas since the Zahn and Sagi article was written.

3. In Chapter 4, Finkelhor discusses the incidence of child abuse fatalities. Interview a child protective service worker in your community. What procedures are used to investigate child abuse reports and to remove a child from a home, temporarily or permanently?

4. Some researchers have explored the role of medical care in the incidence of homicides. Find out what hospitals in your community provide the most trauma care to homicide victims. What protocols do they use in treatment? What are their fatality rates and survival rates regarding similarly situated patients?

5. The responsibility of notifying family members of a homicide often rests with police officers. Does the police department in your community have a standard protocol it uses to make these notifications? If so, how was it developed? If not, how are these notifications made?

BIBLIOGRAPHY

Allen, N.H. (1980). *Homicide: Perspectives on prevention.* New York: Human Sciences.

Allen, R.B. (1986). Measuring the severity of physical injury among assault and homicide victims. *Journal of Quantitative Criminology, 2,* 139-156.

Amick-McMullan, A., Kilpatrick, D.G., Veronen, L.J., & Smith, S. (1989). Family survivors of homicide victims: Theoretical perspectives and an exploratory study. *Journal of Traumatic Stress, 2,* 21-35.

Barnett, A., Essenfeld, E., & Kleitman, D.J. (1980). Urban homicide: Some recent developments. *Journal of Criminal Justice, 8,* 379-385.

Block, C.R., & Christakos, A. (1995). Intimate partner homicide in Chicago over 29 years. *Crime & Delinquency, 41,* 496-526.

Cheatwood, D. (1993). Notes on the theoretical, empirical and policy significance of multiple-offender homicides. In A.V. Wilson (Ed.), *Homicide: The victim/offender connection* (pp. 443-460). Cincinnati, OH: Anderson.

Chilton, R. (1987). Twenty years of homicide and robbery in Chicago: The impact of the city's changing racial and age composition. *Journal of Quantitative Criminology, 3,* 195-214.

Cook, P.J. (1985). Is robbery becoming more violent? An analysis of robbery murder trends since 1968. *Journal of Criminal Law & Criminology, 76,* 480-489.

Crittenden, P.M., & Craig, S.E. (1990). Developmental trends in the nature of child homicide. *Journal of Interpersonal Violence, 5,* 202-216.

Deane, G.D. (1987). Cross-national comparison of homicide: Age/sex-adjusted rates using the 1980 U.S. homicide experience as a standard. *Journal of Quantitative Criminology, 3,* 215-227.

Decker, S.H. (1993). Exploring victim-offender relationships in homicide: The role of individual and event characteristics. *Justice Quarterly, 10,* 585-612.

Doerner, W.G. (1988). The impact of medical resources on criminally induced lethality: A further examination. *Criminology, 26,* 171-179.

Edwards, S.S.M. (1985). A socio-legal evaluation of gender ideologies in domestic violence assault and spousal homicides. *Victimology, 10,* 186-205.

Ewing, C.P. (1997). *Fatal families: The dynamics of intrafamilial homicide.* Thousand Oaks, CA: Sage.

Farrell, R.A., & Swigert, V. L. (1986). Adjudication in homicide: An interpretive analysis of the effects of defendant and victim social characteristics. *Journal of Research in Crime and Delinquency, 23,* 349-369.

Felson, R.B., & Steadman, H.J. (1983). Situational factors in disputes leading to criminal violence. *Criminology, 21,* 59-74.

Finkelhor, D. (1997). The homicides of children and youth: A developmental perspective. In G. Kaufman Kantor & J.L. Jasinski (Eds.), *Out of the darkness: Contemporary perspectives on family violence* (pp. 17-34). Thousand Oaks, CA: Sage.

Gartner, R., Baker, K., & Pampel, F.C. (1990). Gender stratification and the gender gap in homicide victimization. *Social Problems, 37,* 593-612.

Gartner, R. (1990). The victims of homicide: A temporal and cross-national comparison. *American Sociological Review, 55*, 92-106.

Goetting, A. (1990). Child victims of homicide: A portrait of their killers and the circumstances of their deaths. *Violence and Victims, 5*, 287-296.

Goetting, A. (1991). Female victims of homicide: A portrait of their killers and the circumstances of their deaths. *Violence and Victims, 6*, 159-168.

Harries, K. (1993). A victim ecology of drug-related homicide. In A.V. Wilson (Ed.), *Homicide: The victim/offender connection* (pp. 397-414). Cincinnati, OH: Anderson.

Harries, K.D. (1997). *Serious violence: Patterns of homicide and assault in America* (2nd ed.). Springfield, IL: Charles C Thomas.

Heide, K.M. (1993). Parents who get killed and the children who kill them. *Journal of Interpersonal Violence, 8*, 531-544.

Herjanic, M., & Meyer, D.A. (1976). Psychiatric illness in homicide victims. *American Journal of Psychiatry, 133*, 691-693.

Hickey, E.W. (1991). *Serial murderers and their victims*. Pacific Grove, CA: Brooks/Cole.

Holmes, R.M., & Holmes, S.T. (1994). *Murder in America*. Thousand Oaks, CA: Sage.

Holmes, R.M., & Holmes, S.T. (1998). *Serial murder* (2nd ed.). Thousand Oaks, CA: Sage.

Kennedy, L.W., & Silverman, R.A. (1990). The elderly victim of homicide: An application of the routine activities approach. *Sociological Quarterly, 31*, 307-319.

Kposowa, A.J., Singh, G.K., & Breault, K.D. (1994). The effects of marital status and social isolation on adult male homicides in the United States: Evidence from the national longitudinal mortality study. *Journal of Quantitative Criminology, 10*, 277-289.

Lehman, D.R., Ellard, J.H., & Wortman, C.B. (1986). Social support for the bereaved: recipients' and providers' perspectives on what is helpful. *Journal of Consulting and Clinical Psychology, 54*, 438-446.

Long-Onnen, J., & Cheatwood, D. (1992). Hospitals and homicide: An expansion of current theoretical paradigms. *American Journal of Criminal Justice, 16(2)*, 57-74.

Lord, J.H. (1990). *No time for goodbyes: Coping with sorrow, anger and injustice after a tragic death*. Ventura, CA: Pathfinder.

Luckinbill, D.F. (1977). Criminal homicide as a situated transaction. *Social Problems, 25*, 176-186.

Lyon, E., Moore, N., & Lexius, C. (1992). Group work with families of homicide victims. *Social Work with Groups, 15*, 19-33.

Macdonald, J.M. (1986). *The murderer and his victim* (2nd ed.). Springfield, IL: Charles C Thomas.

MacKellar, F.L., & Yanagishita, M. (1995). Homicide in the United States: Who's at risk? *Population Trends and Public Policy, No. 21*. Washington, DC: Population Reference Bureau.

Mann, C.R. (1988). Getting even? Women who kill in domestic encounters. *Justice Quarterly, 5*, 33-51.

Massey, C.R., & McKean, J. (1985). The social ecology of homicide: A modified lifestyle/routine activities perspective. *Journal of Criminal Justice, 13*, 417-428.

Messner, S.F., & Golden, R.M. (1992). Racial inequality and racially disaggregated homicide rates: An assessment of alternative theoretical explanations. *Criminology, 30*, 421-447.

Messner, S.F., & Tardiff, K. (1985). The social ecology of urban homicide: An application of the "routine activities" approach. *Criminology, 23*, 241-267.

Phillips, D.P. (1982). The impact of fictional television stories on U.S. adult fatalities: New evidence on the effect of mass media on violence. *American Journal of Sociology, 87*, 1340-1359.

Phillips, D.P. (1983). The impact of mass media violence on U.S. homicides. *American Sociological Review, 48*, 560-568.

Poussaint, A.F. (1983). Black-on-black homicide: A psychological-political perspective. *Victimology, 8(3-4)*, 161-169.

Rasko, G. (1976). The victim of the female killer. *Victimology, 1*, 396-402.

Riedel, M., & Przybylski, R.K. (1993). Stranger murders and assault: A study of a neglected form of stranger violence. In A.V. Wilson (Ed.), *Homicide: The victim/offender connection* (pp. 359-382). Cincinnati, OH: Anderson.

Riedel, M., Zahn, M.A., & Mock, L.F. (1985). *The nature and patterns of American homicide*. Washington, DC: U.S. Government Printing Office.

Segall, W.E., & Wilson, A.V. (1993). Who is at greatest risk in homicides?: A comparison of victimization rates by geographic region. In A.V. Wilson (Ed.), *Homicide: The victim/offender connection* (pp. 343-356). Cincinnati, OH: Anderson.

Silverman, R.A., & Kennedy, L.W. (1988). Women who kill their children. *Violence and Victims, 3*, 113-127.

Smithey, M. (1997). Infant homicide at the hands of mothers: Toward a sociological perspective. *Deviant Behavior, 18*, 255-272.

Stout, K. (1992). Intimate femicide: An ecological analysis. *Journal of Sociology and Social Welfare, 19(3)*, 29-50.

Stout, K.D. (1991). Intimate femicide: A national demographic overview. *Journal of Interpersonal Violence, 6*, 476-485.

Straus, M.A. (1987). State and regional differences in U.S. infant homicide rates in relation to sociocultural characteristics of the states. *Behavioral Sciences & the Law, 5*, 61-75.

Trocme, N., & Lindsey, D. (1996). What can child homicide rates tell us about the effectiveness of child welfare services? *Child Abuse & Neglect, 20*, 171-184.

Unnithan, N.P. (1994). Children as victims of homicide: Making claims, formulating categories, and constructing social problems. *Deviant Behavior, 15*, 63-83.

Unnithan, N.P. (1994). The processing of homicide cases with child victims: Systemic and situational contingencies. *Journal of Criminal Justice, 22*, 41-50.

Unnithan, N.P. (1997). Child homicide in developed countries. *International Review of Victimology, 4,* 313-326.

U.S. Advisory Board on Child Abuse and Neglect. (1995). *A nation's shame: Fatal child abuse and neglect in the United States.* Washington, DC: U.S. Government Printing Office.

U.S. Department of Justice. Federal Bureau of Investigation. (1998). *UCR press release—Crime in the United States, 1997.* Washington, DC: Author.

Williams, K.R., & Flewelling, R.L. (1987). Family, acquaintance, and stranger homicide: Alternative procedures for rate calculations. *Criminology, 25,* 543-560.

Wilson, A.V. (Ed.). (1993). *Homicide: The victim/offender connection.* Cincinnati, OH: Anderson.

Wolfgang, M.E. (1958). *Patterns in criminal homicide.* Philadelphia: University of Pennsylvania Press.

Wortman, C.B., Battle, E.S., & Lemkau, J.P. (1997). Coming to terms with the sudden, traumatic death of a spouse or child. In R.C. Davis, A.J. Lurigio, & W.G. Skogan (Eds.), *Victims of crime* (2nd ed., pp. 108-133). Thousand Oaks, CA: Sage.

Zahn, M.A. (1975). The female homicide victim. *Criminology, 13,* 400-415.

Zahn, M.A., & Sagi, P.C. (1987). Stranger homicides in nine American cities. *Journal of Criminal Law & Criminology, 78,* 377-397.

Chapter 3

Stranger Homicides in Nine American Cities*

Margaret A. Zahn[**]
Philip C. Sagi[***]

I. INTRODUCTION

Past studies of homicide have focused either on the general demographic characteristics of homicide or on causal factors or processes descriptive of selected types, such as homicides within the family or those associated with felonies.[1] Few studies have examined homicide comparatively by describing ways in which various types of homicide differ from each other.[2] Even fewer studies describe the interactions between demographic variables such as age, sex, and race between and

* The collection of data reported here was supported by a grant from the National Institute of Justice (LEAA-USDJ-00920). The views expressed in this Article are those of the authors and do not necessarily represent the views of the National Institute of Justice.

** Associate Professor of Sociology, Temple University. Ph.D., M.A., B.A., Ohio State University, 1969, 1964, 1963.
*** Professor Emeritus, University of Pennsylvania. Ph.D., University of Minnesota, 1956; M.S., Ph.B., University of Wisconsin, 1951, 1949.

[1] E.g., Farley, *Homicide Trends in the United States*, 17 DEMOGRAPHY 177 (1980); Klebba, *Homicide Trends in the United States*, 90 PUB. HEALTH REP. 195 (1975); Loftin, *Homicide Related to Crimes Other Than Drug Traffic*, 62 BULL. N.Y. ACAD. MED. 517 (1986); Zimring, *Determinants of the Death Rate From Robbery: A Detroit Time Study*, 6 J. LEG. STUD. 317 (1977).
[2] For one complete study that analyzes types of homicide, see M. RIEDEL & M. ZAHN, THE NATURE AND PATTERNS OF AMERICAN HOMICIDE (1985).

Source: Zahn, M.A., & Sagi, P.C. (1987). Stranger homicides in nine American cities. *Journal of Criminal Law & Criminology*, 78, 377-397. Reprinted by special permission of Northwestern University School of Law, *Journal of Criminal Law and Criminology*, vol. 78, issue 2, 1987.

within types of homicide.[3] For example, while numerous studies have established a greater volume of homicide victimization for young black males,[4] these studies seldom determine whether such victimization exists in all contexts, such as within the family, between friends, and in robbery situations.[5] This Article will first describe different types of homicide in terms of characteristics of victims, offenders, location, method of attack, and presence of witnesses.

This Article will next explore the types of homicide in terms of interactions among the variables of age, sex, and race.

II. TYPES OF HOMICIDE

While numerous typologies of homicide have been suggested,[6] a typology used in homicide research is generally based on differences in victim-offender relationships.[7] Classification schemes for such studies are diverse and inconsistent across studies. Wolfgang has classified victim-offender relationships into thirteen categories;[8] Boudouris has used twelve categories;[9] and Curtis has used four primary categories.[10] In Curtis' study of seventeen American cities in 1967, 24.7% of homicides were found to be within the family; 9% were within other primary relationships, which include lovers and close friends; 45.4% were within nonprimary relationships, which include prostitutes, acquaintances, neighbors, and strangers (15.6% of the combined group were strangers); and 20.9% were unknown.[11] Studies using such classifications often provided frequencies of the type of killing.[12] No study has compared the characteristics of homicide types in order to elucidate structure and process.

---

[3] For a study that attempted to analyze race in relation to homicide type, see Zimring, Mukherjee & Van Winkle, *Intimate Violence: A Study of Intersexual Homicide in Chicago*, 50 U. CHI. L. REV. 910 (1983).

[4] *E.g.*, M. WOLFGANG, PATTERNS IN CRIMINAL HOMICIDE 31-33 (1975); Farley, *supra* note 1, at 179; Klebba, *supra* note 1, at 199.

[5] For one study that has explored victimization in various contexts, see M. RIEDEL & M. ZAHN, *supra* note 2.

[6] For a review of typologies, see M. RIEDEL, A REVIEW OF HOMICIDE TYPOLOGIES (1980).

[7] Numerous studies have used the victim-offender relationship as the basis for homicide typologies. *E.g.*, L. CURTIS, CRIMINAL VIOLENCE 45-64 (1974); M. WOLFGANG, *supra* note 4, at 254-57; Boudouris, *A Classification of Homicide*, 11 CRIMINOLOGY 525 (1974).

[8] M. WOLFGANG, *supra* note 4, at 254-57.

[9] Boudouris, *supra* note 7.

[10] L. CURTIS, *supra* note 7.

[11] *Id.* at 52.

[12] *See, e.g.,* Boudouris, *supra* note 7 at 536.

More recent studies, such as Straus, Gelles, and Steinmetz in 1980,[13] Loftin in 1986,[14] and Cook in 1985,[15] have focused on violence or homicide within specific relationships, such as family homicide versus robbery homicide. These studies have added immensely to our understanding of family and robbery murders. Gelles, for example, found that the families which have the most violence within them are those families which are isolated and lack social supports.[16] Unlike family homicides, robbery-motivated homicides are relatively more likely to occur in urban environments.[17] High rates of robbery-murder are likely to be found in urban areas which have concentrated poor populations and which have young males who possess guns and are ready to use them to secure material goods.[18] Types of homicide and whether there is variation between and within these types have seldom been examined systematically.[19] Smith and Parker in 1980[20] and Parker in 1984,[21] however, studied felony types of homicide and discovered important differences in causal factors for intimate versus felony-related homicides. In their work, Smith and Parker examined predictors of four types of homicide: robbery murders; other felony murders; homicides occurring between friends and acquaintances; and homicides occurring among family intimates.[22] Some predictors were type-specific. For example, racial composition is a factor in the robbery and the friends and acquaintances homicide types, but not in the other types.[23] In his 1984 study, Parker concluded that the composition of homicide types needed greater elaboration.[24] Such elaboration is important both theoretically and practically.

Theoretically, as Parker has shown, the search for the causes of homicide can only be effectively completed with a refined set of appropriate categories of types of killings.[25] Pragmatically, strategies for intervention should be quite different if there are clearly different types of homicide with different populations involved. For example, if stranger murders involve young male felons and family homicides involve mid-

---

[13] M. STRAUSS, R. GELLES & S. STEINMETZ, BEHIND CLOSED DOORS: VIOLENCE IN THE AMERICAN FAMILY (1980). *See also* R. GELLES, THE VIOLENT HOME: A STUDY OF PHYSICAL AGGRESSION BETWEEN HUSBANDS AND WIVES (1972).

[14] Loftin, *supra* note 1.

[15] Cook, *Is Robbery Becoming More Violent? An Analysis of Robbery Murder Trends Since 1968* 76 J. CRIM. L. & CRIMINOLOGY 480 (1985).

[16] R. GELLES, *supra* note 13, at 132.

[17] Parker & Smith, *Deterrence, Poverty and Type of Homicide*, 85 AM. J. SOC. 614 (1979).

[18] Loftin, *supra* note 1, at 528.

[19] M. RIEDEL & M. ZAHN, *supra* note 2; Parker & Smith, *supra* note 17.

[20] Smith & Parker, *Type of Homicide and Variation in Regional Rates*, 59 SOC. FORCES 136 (1980).

[21] R. Parker, Poverty, Subculture of Violence and Type of Poverty on Urban Homicide (1984) (unpublished manuscript) (paper presented at American Society of Criminology meetings, Atlanta).

[22] Smith & Parker, *supra* note 20.

[23] R. Parker, *supra* note 21, at 18.

[24] *Id.* at 19.

[25] *Id.*

dle-aged adult females, the causes and strategies of intervention and prevention will most likely differ.

Four types of homicide will be examined in this Article. The first two categories are homicide within the family and homicide among friends and acquaintances.[26] The third and fourth categories emerge as a result of the distinction between two types of stranger murders: those associated with felonies and those not associated with felonies. To date, the research literature has for the most part associated robbery or felony-related murders with stranger killings as though the two were synonymous.[27] Statistical evidence from a national study suggests, however, that stranger felony and stranger non-felony homicides may be distinct.[28] These data show that stranger homicides are associated with felonies in 57.3% of the cases and are not so associated in 42.7% of the cases, although the ratio between felony-related and non-felony-related stranger murders is as low as 1:1 in some cities.[29] Table 1 reveals these patterns. Given these data and the importance of this issue, this Article stresses the importance of the investigation of factors affecting the two types of stranger murder and how such murders differ from murders in more intimate circles.

TABLE 1
PERCENT OF STRANGER HOMICIDES ASSOCIATED
WITH A FELONY IN EIGHT CITIES, 1978

| | STRANGER HOMICIDES | |
	FELONY ASSOCIATED	NOT FELONY ASSOCIATED
Philadelphia	52.5% (53)	47.5% (48)
Newark	66.7% (18)	33.3% (9)
Chicago	60.0% (54)	40.0% (36)
St. Louis	62.2% (23)	37.8% (14)
Memphis	65.2% (15)	34.8% (8)
Dallas	55.6% (35)	44.4% (28)
Oakland	50.0% (7)	50.0% (7)
"Ashton"	50.0% (10)	50.0% (10)
Total 8 Cities	57.3% (215)	42.7% (160)

Source: Marc Riedel and Margaret A. Zahn. *The Nature and Patterns of American Homicide,* U.S. Government Printing Office, May, 1985, p. 59.

---

[26] These categories are congruent with previous homicide research. *E.g.,* L. Curtis, *supra* note 7; M. Riedel & M. Zahn, *supra* note 2; M. Wolfgang, *supra* note 4.

[27] L. Curtis, *supra* note 7, at 46-47; M. Wolfgang, *supra* note 4, at 203-21.

[28] M. Riedel & M. Zahn, *supra* note 2.

[29] *Id.* at 59.

III. METHODS

Data for this report were drawn from a nation-wide study of the nature and patterns of homicide in the United States.[30] The nine cities selected for study were: Philadelphia and Newark, New Jersey in the Northeast; Chicago and St. Louis in the Midwest; Memphis and Dallas in the South; and Oakland, San Jose,[31] and "Ashton"[32] in the West. In these cities, with the exception of Chicago, data on all cases of homicide occurring in 1978 were collected. In Chicago, because of the large number of homicide cases (over 800), a 50% sample was used.

In each of the nine cities, police and medical examiner departments were asked to supply records for all homicide cases which had occurred in their jurisdictions in 1978. This particular year was selected because the departments have closed active investigations on most of the cases occurring in 1978, yet the data were sufficiently recent to have relevance for current policy and understanding of current homicide patterns. Once permission was secured, coders, persons familiar with the extensive data form used, went to each site and coded information on various aspects of each case, including: characteristics of the offender, such as age, sex, race, and past criminal history; characteristics of the victim; the relationship between the victim and the offender; and a variety of elements surrounding the homicide event, such as the number of witnesses present and the type of weapon used.

Data on a total of 1,748 homicide cases in the nine cities were collected. The original data collection included seventy killings by police in which a police officer was the "offender" and a number of cases in which data were either missing from the files or in which the relationship between the victim and the offender remained unknown (N=260). For the most part, police killings and those homicides in which offender-victim relationship remained unknown have been eliminated from this analysis. After eliminating police killings and those killings in which the relationship was unknown, 1,373 homicide cases with known victim-offender relationships remained.

Victim-offender relationships were classified into four types. The first type, homicides within the family, includes immediate family members, unmarried couples living together, and separated or divorced couples. The within family type does not include heterosexual partners who have had some sexual relationship but have not lived together or had

---

[30] *Id.*

[31] Data from San Jose were not included in the national study, *see* M. RIEDEL & M. ZAHN, *supra* note 2, because the focus of that study was on cities with 100 or more cases of homicide in 1978. San Jose did have that many cases. Adding data from San Jose helps provide a more complete picture of homicide and so are included in this survey.

[32] "Ashton" is a code name for a city in the Far West. The police chief of "Ashton" required the use of a code name in exchange for release of information of the city's homicides.

some other more extended relationship. These types of cases were classified as the friends and acquaintances homicide type. This second type, friends and acquaintances, includes people who have known each other in some way, ranging from neighbors and business associates to close personal friends. Stranger killings are those in which there is no evidence of prior acquaintance between the victim and the offender. The stranger type is further subdivided into those situations in which a felony is involved and those in which a felony is not involved. Most stranger felonies are robbery-connected, while stranger non-felonies represent a variety of situations. The following four situations, based on actual police records, are examples of stranger non-felony homicide. First, a thirty-one year old black female parked her car in a driveway for a short time in a heavy snow. The car got stuck. When she returned, the offender's father yelled at her and hit her child. The offender, a twenty year old black male, came out of the house, shot and killed the victim, and wounded her two children. Second, the victim and three companions were riding down the street when they became involved in an argument with the occupants of another car. When the car pulled over, the victim, a twenty-two year old white male, got out as did the person in the other car. The latter killed the victim with a shotgun. Third, the offender picked up a hitchhiker and drove down to a deserted creek bottom, where both got out and started drinking some beer. According to the offender, the victim made homosexual advances to him. The offender pushed him away, got a steel pipe from his car and beat the victim to death by hitting him over the head with the pipe. Fourth, the victim, a sixty year old white female, was the owner of a gift store. The offender, a seventeen year old white male, walked into the store and stabbed the victim twice in the chest. He stated that his sister and he had been in the store earlier to buy some "stuff." When they left, he said, "something came into my head to hurt the lady." He went home, got a butcher knife, went back to the store and stabbed the victim after talking to her for about five minutes. The offender's father informed the police that the offender had deep mental problems and had killed a six year old boy in Texas in 1975. As is apparent from these examples, stranger non-felony homicides differ in both weapon and victim characteristics.

General descriptive data for the four types of homicide will be presented. The types of homicide will be described by the age, race, and sex of both the victims and offenders, as well as by method of assault, the location of the killing, and whether or not witnesses were present. Following the discussion of general characteristics, the types of homicides will be examined, with race, age, and sex held constant in the statistical analysis. White, black and hispanic groups will be examined. Homicides among "other" races were too sparsely represented in the data set to justify inclusion in the analysis and, therefore, were eliminated.

IV. RESULTS

A. TYPES OF HOMICIDE IN NINE CITIES

As shown in Table 2, of the 1,373 cases with known victim-offender relationships, 18% occurred within the family, 54% occurred between friends and acquaintances, 16% were stranger felonies and 12% were stranger non-felonies. Clearly, the largest percentage of murders were those in which the killer and victim were acquainted. Twenty-eight percent of those with known relationships, however, were stranger killings, and stranger killings surpassed the percentage of people killed by family members. These data indicate that, among murder victims in the nine cities, the most likely offender was a friend or an acquaintance, and the second most likely offender was a stranger.

TABLE 2
FREQUENCY, PERCENTAGE AND RATE OF
VICTIMIZATION OF FOUR TYPES OF HOMICIDE
IN NINE CITIES, U.SA., 1978

	f.	%	RATE PER 100,000
Family Homicide	247	18	3.41
Acquaintance Homicide	736	54	10.47
Stranger Felony Homicide	219	16	2.95
Stranger Non-felony Homicide	171	12	2.28
Relationship Unknown	*	*	4.86
Total	1,373	100%	

* The above percentage table includes only those cases in which data on the victim-offender relationship is known. There are 260 cases where the relationship is not known (14.8% of total); 36 cases where all data are missing from files (2%); 9 cases of stranger murders which could not be classified into felony or non-felony types (.5%) and 70 police killings (4.0%). Total number of homicides = 1,748.

B. CHARACTERISTICS OF TYPES OF HOMICIDE

1. Gender and Type of Homicide

The differential involvement of males and females as victims and as offenders in homicide is shown in Tables 3 and 4. The majority of victims and offenders in all four types of homicide were males. In terms of victimization, both a percentage and a rate analysis show males to be at a greater risk than females. In situations which the victim-offender relationship is known, 82% of the victims were male and 18% were female. Both male and female victims were more likely to be killed by someone that they knew (70% for males and 81% for females). The victims of stranger killings were predominately male; 85% of the victims involved in stranger felony killings and 92% of the victims involved in stranger non-felony killings were male. Although males were killed in many relationships, females were primarily killed within the friends and acquaintance,[33] and family categories.

TABLE 3
FREQUENCY AND PERCENT OF VICTIMIZATION BY SEX OF VICTIM

| TYPE OF HOMICIDE | SEX OF VICTIM | | | |
| | MALE | | FEMALE | |
	f	%	f	%
Family	167	14.8	80	32.9
Acquaintance	619	54.7	117	48.1
Stranger Felony	187	16.5	32	13.2
Stranger Non-Felony	157	13.9	14	5.8
Total	1,130	99.9	243	100.0

* Rates of male and female victimization were also computed using 1980 census data for each of the nine cities as a base. The race and sex specific rates are provided in Table 5. All rates in the paper are calculated similarly.

Furthermore, males were more frequently the offenders in each of the four homicide types, with this dominance increasing as the relationship between the victim and the offender became more distant. Males were almost exclusively the offenders in stranger murders, with 96% of stranger felonies having male offenders and 93% of stranger non-felonies having male offenders.

TABLE 4
FREQUENCY DISTRIBUTION OF FOUR TYPES OF HOMICIDE BY SEX OF OFFENDER*

| TYPE OF HOMICIDE | SEX OF OFFENDER | | | | | |
| | MALE | | FEMALE | | TOTAL | |
	f	%	f	%		
Family	145	60.0	97	40.0	242	100%
Acquaintance	623	88.0	86	12.0	709	100%
Stranger Felony	167	96.0	7	4.0	174	100%
Stranger Non-Felony	140	93.0	11	7.0	151	100%
Total	1,075		201		1,276	

* Cases where sex of the offender is unknown are not included in the table.

[33] Within the friends and acquaintance category it is likely that women were killed by their boyfriends. See M. Zahn & N. Cazenave, Women, Murder, and Male Domination: A Research Note on Domestic Homicide in Chicago and Philadelphia (1986) (paper presented at American Society of Criminology meetings in Atlanta). That research note suggested that women were frequently killed by husbands or boyfriends when women attempt to end a relationship. Furthermore, women seldom kill other women. See L. CURTIS, supra note 7, at 32. Thus, women were usually killed by men with whom there was prior involvement.

2. Race and Type of Homicide

This Article makes contrasts only among the race categories of White, Black and Hispanic.[34] As Table 5 shows, the victimization rates are dramatically higher for black males than for any other group, with 84.4 per 100,000 black males killed as compared to 46.8 per 100,000 for hispanic males and 16.2 per 100,000 for white males. In addition, black females have higher victimization rates than white or hispanic females, although these rates are not as high as the rates for any male victims. As Table 6 shows, the highest rates of victimization for black males were in the friends and acquaintances, and family types of homicide. The highest rates for white males were in the friends and acquaintances, and stranger felony types. The highest rates for hispanic males were in the friends and acquaintances, and stranger non-felony contexts. Women in all three racial groups were more frequently killed within intimate circles and had very low rates of victimization in stranger contexts.

TABLE 5
RATES OF VICTIMIZATION AND OF OFFENDING BY RACE AND SEX
(PER 100,000 POPULATION)

	VICTIMIZATION	OFFENDING
White Male	16.2	10.5
Black Male	84.4	72.7
Hispanic Male	46.8	42.8
White Female	3.6	1.2
black Female	14.4	13.2
Hispanic Female	5.3	1.7

TABLE 6
RATES OF VICTIMIZATION IN FOUR TYPES OF HOMICIDE
BY RACE AND SEX OF OFFENDER.

	WHITE MALE	BLACK MALE	HISPANIC MALE	WHITE FEMALE	BLACK FEMALE	HISPANIC FEMALE
Family	1.6	10.9	3.7	.8	4.3	1.7
Acquaintance	4.7	41.5	21.5	1.0	6.5	1.9
Stranger Felony	3.7	8.7	3.5	.7	.7	1.5
Stranger Non-Felony	2.5	7.0	5.7	.2	.8	0
Unknown & Other	3.7	16.3	12.4	1.0	2.1	.2
Total	16.2	84.4	46.8	3.7	14.4	5.3

---

[34] Homicides among "other" races were too sparsely represented in the data set to justify inclusion in the analysis.

Rates for offenders follow the same pattern, with black males having much higher rates than any other population group. Rates of offenders by race and sex, from highest to lowest, are: black males, hispanic males, black females, white males, hispanic females, and white females. Seventy-one percent of the offenders were black, 16% were white, and 12% were hispanic. Black males were more likely to be, in both rate and percentage, offenders in all type of killings. As shown in Table 7, differences in rates between black and white offenders vary, although black male rates always exceed white male rates across types of homicide.

In terms of offending, the general pattern is the same for black and white males. While black males killed more frequently in all contexts, these contexts were the same for Blacks and Whites. The major difference by race seems to be the decreased relative frequency of killing within the family by hispanic males and hispanic females and the higher relative frequency of hispanic male offending and victimization in stranger non-felony killing within the family by hispanic males and hispanic females and the higher relative frequency of hispanic male offending and victimization in stranger non-felony killings. Rates for each type are given in Table 7.

TABLE 7
RATES OF OFFENDING IN FOUR TYPES OF HOMICIDE BY RACE
& SEX OF OFFENDER (PER 100,000 POPULATION)

	WHITE MALE	BLACK MALE	HISPANIC MALE	WHITE FEMALE	BLACK FEMALE	HISPANIC FEMALE
Family	1.4	8.7	4.3	.85	6.0	.43
Acquaintance	4.4	41.2	22.1	.27	5.7	1.06
Stranger Felony	1.4	11.4	4.5	.00	.49	.00
Stranger Non-Felony	1.1	7.1	8.4	.04	.73	.21
Unknown & Other	2.2	4.2	3.5	.04	.2	.00
Total	10.5	72.7	42.8	1.2	13.12	1.7

3. Racial Homogeneity and Type of Homicide

Among all types of homicide in which the victim-offender relationship is known, 14% of the victims were Whites killed by Whites, 68% were Blacks killed by Blacks, and 3.7% were Hispanics killed by Hispanics. Thus, approximately 86% of these types of homicides were intraracial, and 14% of the homicides occurred between racial groups. These percentages, however, change dramatically within types.

As would be expected, 95% of the homicides in the family category and 92% of the homicides in the friends and acquaintances category were interracial [sic]. The highest percentage of interracial killing occurred in the stranger felony category. As Table 8 shows, 40% of the stranger felonies were interracial. In stranger felony killings with a white offender, 34.4% were interracial homicides. In stranger felony killings with a black offender, 38.8% were interracial homicides. While the numbers are small for stranger felonies involving a hispanic offender (n = 17), 41% of the homicides involving a hispanic offender were interracial.

Although 89% of the black victims were victimized by Blacks, 74% of the white victims in stranger felony homicides were victims of interracial homicides. Among hispanic victims, 41% were inter-ethnically assaulted.

Stranger non-felonies displayed a lower percentage of interracial killings than did stranger felonies. Twenty-one percent of the stranger non-felonies were interracial homicides. White offenders seldom crossed racial lines in a non-felony stranger homicide. Thus, race appears to determine the rate of homicide and, to a limited extent, the type of homicide.

TABLE 8
INTRARACIAL AND INTERRACIAL CHARACTERISTICS
OF STRANGER FELONY HOMICIDES*

OFFENDER/VICTIM	WHITE OFFENDER	BLACK OFFENDER	HISPANIC OFFENDER	TOTAL
White Victim	19 (26%) 65.5%	43 (60%) 35.5%	10 (14%) 58.8%	72 100.0%
Black Victim	9 (11%) 31.0%	74 (89%) 61.2%	0 (0%)	83 100.0%
Hispanic Victim	1 (8.3%) 3.4%	4 (33.3%) 3.3%	7 (58.3%) 41.2%	12 99.9%
Total	29 99.9%	121 100.0%	17 100.0%	167

* (Figures percentaged across rows are in Parentheses; Column percentages are not in parentheses.)

4. Age and Type of Homicide

The mean ages of victims and offenders in the four types of homicide are given in Table 9. Victims were older than offenders in all four types of homicide. The difference in mean age between victim and offender is small in all types except stranger felonies. In stranger felonies, the mean age of the victim was forty years, while the mean age of the offender was twenty-six years. Clearly, the stranger felony murder is distinct from the other three types by virtue of the greater age difference between victim and offender. The offenders in family killings were also somewhat older than the offenders in the other three homicide types.

TABLE 9
Mean Age of Victims and Offenders in Four Types of Homicide

Type of Homicide	Mean Age of Victims/Mean Age of Offenders
Family	31/33
Acquaintance	31/30
Stranger Felony	40/26
Stranger Non-Felony	30/29

5. Location, Witnesses, and Type of Homicide

The homicides occurred in a variety of locations. Locations were divided into public space, such as a street, subway, bar or other commercial establishment, and private space, such as the victim's residence or other residence. As Table 9 shows, the largest single group of victims (641 out of 1323, or 46%) were murdered on the street. The second largest group of homicides occurred in the victim's residence (521 out of 1373, or 38%). Fifty-five percent of the homicides took place in public spaces, as compared to 42% in private spaces.

TABLE 10
Percent of Victims Killed in Public versus Private Space in
Four Types of Homicide

	Public Space	Private Space	Total	
Family	53 (22%)	193 (78%)	246	100.0%
Acquaintance	368 (50%)	366 (49.9%)	734	99.9%
Stranger Felony	145 (66%)	74 (34%)	219	100.0%
Stranger Non-Felony	145 (85%)	26 (15%)	171	100.0%
			1,370	

Not unexpectedly, the percentage of family killings occurring at home was higher (78%) than with other types of killings. The percentage of killings occurring in public settings increased as the relationship between the victim and the offender became more distant. The stranger non-felony homicide is clearly the most public homicide type, with 85% of these killings occurring in a public space. The public nature of the stranger non-felony homicide is also revealed by analyzing the number of witnesses to the event.

As Table 11 shows, most killings outside of the family were witnessed. While family killings were the most private (53.7%), stranger non-felony homicides were the most public. Eighty-nine percent of stranger non-felony homicides were witnessed by at least one other person. It appears, therefore, that there is an absence of caution in stranger non-felony homicides.

6. *Method of Assault and Type of Homicide*

Methods of assault included guns, knives, beatings and strangulation, and other methods.[35] As Table 12 shows, guns predominated as the means of killing in all types of homicide; 65% of all homicides involved firearms. This percentage was somewhat lower for family killings and was somewhat higher for the other three types. Stabbing accounts for 21% of the homicides, with a higher percentage in the family homicides and a lower percentage in stranger felonies. Beatings and strangulation occurred in only 11% of the cases, with a higher percentage in family killing only.

TABLE 11
NUMBER OF EYEWITNESSES BY TYPE OF HOMICIDE

TYPE OF HOMICIDE	NUMBER OF EYEWITNESSES				TOTAL	
	0	1	2	3+		
Family	132 (53.7%)	46 (18.7%)	39 (15.9%)	29 (11.8%)	246	100.1
Acquaintance	212 (29.2%)	210 (28.9%)	121 (16.6%)	184 (25.3%)	727	100.0
Stranger Felony	69 (31.9%)	79 (36.6%)	19 (8.8%)	49 (22.7%)	216	100.0
Stranger Non-Felony	19 (11.4%)	52 (31.1%)	24 (14.4%)	72 (43.1%)	167	100.0
Total	432 31.9%	387 28.5%	203 15.0%	334 24.6%	1,356	100.0

TABLE 12
METHOD OF ASSAULT IN FOUR TYPES OF HOMICIDE

TYPE OF HOMICIDE	METHOD OF ASSAULT								TOTAL	
	GUN		KNIFE		BEATINGS		OTHER			
	f	%	f	%	f	%	f	%		
Family	125	51.0	65	26.5	42	17.1	13	5.3	245	99.9
Acquaintance	499	67.8	174	23.6	53	7.2	10	1.4	736	100.0
Stranger Felony	146	66.7	35	16.0	19	8.7	19	8.7	219	100.1
Stranger Non-Felony	116	67.8	36	21.1	14	8.2	5	2.9	171	100.0

Important differences emerge in a comparison of the mean age differences between offender and victim by method of assault. As Table 13 shows, in family homicides and in both types of stranger killings, offender mean age was older when a gun was used and younger when stabbing or beating and strangulation was the method of assault. The average age of an offender who used a gun was older (mean age = 32) than the offender who used a knife (mean age = 27). The youngest offenders used their hands, feet, or other means of beating (mean age = 25).

---

[35] Other methods may include arson, poisoning, and pushing from high places.

TABLE 13
MEAN AGE OF OFFENDERS IN FOUR TYPES OF HOMICIDE
BY METHOD OF ASSAULT*

TYPE OF HOMICIDE	METHOD OF ASSAULT							
	GUN		KNIFE		BEATINGS		OTHER	
	Mean Age	f	Mean Age	f	Mean Age	f	Mean Age	f
Family	37	125	29	64	26	39	27	12
Acquaintance	30	471	30	167	29	50	28	10
Stranger Felony	27	113	24	29	22	13	21	8
Stranger Non-Felony	31	99	26	31	22	10	22	4
Total		808		291		112		34

* Since fewer offenders' ages are known than victims' ages, the totals in this table are smaller than in Table 14.

Comparatively, as Table 14 shows, victim mean age also varies by weapon type, especially in family and stranger killings. In family type homicide, the mean age of those killed by a gun or a knife was decidedly older (35 and 33 years respectively) than in those situations in which the victim was killed by beating and strangulation. In homicides in which the offender beat and strangled the victim, the mean age of the victim was eighteen years old. Stranger felony killings, when divided by method, show pronounced mean age differences between victims, according to method. A victim of a stranger felony killed with a gun averaged thirty-six years of age; a victim killed by a knife averaged forty-six years of age; and a victim killed by beating and strangulation averaged fifty-nine years of age. The mean ages for victims in friend and acquaintances homicides and in stranger non-felony killings do not show dramatic differences, although, in stranger non-felony homicides, victims of beating and strangulation were older (mean age = 38) than victims of other methods.

TABLE 14
MEAN AGE OF VICTIMS IN FOUR TYPES OF HOMICIDE BY METHOD OF ASSAULT*

TYPE OF HOMICIDE	METHOD OF ASSAULT							
	GUN		KNIFE		BEATINGS		OTHER	
	Mean Age	f	Mean Age	f	Mean Age	f	Mean Age	f
Family	35	125	33	65	18	41	17	13
Acquaintance	31	498	32	174	31	53	41	9
Stranger Felony	36	145	46	35	59	19	42	19
Stranger Non-Felony	30	115	27	36	38	14	30	5
Total		883		310		127		46

This analysis suggests that it is the age of the victim, not the relationship between victim and offender, which determines the method of assault used. Specifically, those victims who are young and those victims who are old were more likely to be killed by beatings and strangulation than by any other method. As Table 14 shows, such victims were also killed by more youthful offenders. It could be argued that youthful offenders choose victims who they perceive as being defenseless because these offenders are less likely to posess [sic] a weapon.[36]

V. OVERVIEW OF HOMICIDE TYPES

This Article has discussed the interactions of methods of assault, victims' and offenders' ages, and types of homicide. An examination of Tables 15 through 18 show that there is considerable variation in the mean age of victims and offenders by type of homicide, race, and sex. This pattern of variation is an indication of main and interaction effects among the variables of race, sex, and homicide type in the determination of the mean ages of offenders and victims. Each variable affects the mean age of the victim and the offender, and particular combinations of variables also affect mean age.

TABLE 15
MEANS ($\overline{X}$) AND STANDARD DEVIATIONS (SD) OF AGES OF OFFENDERS IN FOUR TYPES OF HOMICIDE BY RACE AND SEX OF OFFENDER

| | | OFFENDER'S RACE AND SEX | | | | | |
| | | MALE OFFENDERS | | | FEMALE OFFENDERS | | |
		WHITE	BLACK	HISPANIC	WHITE	BLACK	HISPANIC
Family	$\overline{X}$	38	33	30	35	30	21
	SD	18	13	11	15	11	6
	N	31	96	18	20	72	2
Acquaintance	$\overline{X}$	30	30	28	31	30	33
	SD	12	13	12	15	12	13
	N	90	445	75	6	70	5
Stranger	$\overline{X}$	31	25	22	0	21	0
Felony	SD	13	10	6	0	3	0
	N	29	110	17	0	7	0
Stranger	$\overline{X}$	31	31	24	19	29	25
Non-Felony	SD	14	13	8	0	13	0
	N	22	79	29	1	9	1

[36] In looking at a specific racial groups, there were few differences in method of assault. For all three racial groups of offenders, approximately 65% used a gun in the killing, 18-25% used knives, and 10-16% used their hands or feet as a method of beating or strangulation or used some other means. While a somewhat higher percentage of Whites used their hands or feet, the difference between racial groups were small. The only clear differences in terms of race was that hispanic offenders in stranger felonies and stranger non-felonies used knives more frequently than did their black and white counterparts.

TABLE 16

MEANS ($\overline{X}$) AND STANDARD DEVIATIONS (SD) OF AGES OF VICTIMS IN FOUR
TYPES OF HOMICIDE BY RACE AND SEX OF VICTIM

		MALE VICTIMS			FEMALE VICTIMS		
		WHITE	BLACK	HISPANIC	WHITE	BLACK	HISPANIC
Family	$\overline{X}$	34	31	29	37	26	31
	SD	22	17	21	18	18	18
	N	34	115	16	19	55	5
Acquaintance	$\overline{X}$	36	31	28	29	31	38
	SD	16	14	10	17	16	12
	N	95	449	71	24	83	8
Stranger	$\overline{X}$	46	35	34	59	32	21
Felony	SD	18	15	15	18	19	12
	N	72	94	14	16	10	6
Stranger	$\overline{X}$	31	30	24	36	31	0
Non-Felony	SD	15	12	9	19	17	0
	N	46	86	23	4	10	0

TABLE 17

MEANS ($\overline{X}$) AND STANDARD DEVIATIONS (SD) OF AGES OF VICTIMS IN FOUR
TYPES OF HOMICIDE BY RACE AND SEX OF OFFENDER

		MEAN AGE OF VICTIM					
		MALE OFFENDERS			FEMALE OFFENDERS		
		WHITE	BLACK	HISPANIC	WHITE	BLACK	HISPANIC
Family	$\overline{X}$	38	28	27	32	31	22
	SD	20	18	22	21	17	21
	N	31	96	17	20	72	2
Acquaintance	$\overline{X}$	30	32	29	33	33	30
	SD	13	15	12	18	14	9
	N	89	450	75	6	70	5
Stranger	$\overline{X}$	33	39	41	0	40	0
Felony	SD	14	18	18	0	17	0
	N	29	120	16	0	7	0
Stranger	$\overline{X}$	32	29	26	40	37	36
Non-Felony	SD	13	12	12	0	9	0
	N	22	81	30	1	9	1

TABLE 18
MEANS ($\overline{X}$) AND STANDARD DEVIATIONS (SD) OF AGES OF OFFENDERS IN FOUR
TYPES OF HOMICIDE BY RACE AND SEX OF VICTIM

		MALE VICTIMS			FEMALE VICTIMS		
		WHITE	BLACK	HISPANIC	WHITE	BLACK	HISPANIC
Family	$\overline{X}$	34	31	28	42	32	34
	SD	15	13	10	17	12	14
	N	34	113	16	19	52	6
Acquaintance	$\overline{X}$	29	30	28	29	33	29
	SD	12	12	10	15	16	8
	N	89	422	71	22	82	8
Stranger	$\overline{X}$	23	28	28	21	27	33
Felony	SD	9	12	13	5	10	0
	N	56	70	11	12	7	1
Stranger	$\overline{X}$	28	31	26	30	22	0
Non-Felony	SD	12	13	9	8	8	0
	N	38	72	21	2	9	0

The Tables, especially Tables 15 through 18, in conjunction with the earlier analyses, support the following general picture of homicide types. The features that distinguish family homicides from other homicide types are the lack of witnesses and the proportion of homicides involving a female offender. While males were the predominant offenders in this homicide type, a much higher proportion of family homicides involved a female offender than any other type. Males were almost equally likely to offend against males and females in the family. Women offenders, conversely, had victims who were almost exclusively male. The one exception to this general pattern of female offenders was hispanic women, who seldom offended within the family group at all. The interaction between race, age, and sex categories, therefore, is quite important within the family homicide type.

The friends and acquaintances homicides are distinguishable from other homicide types by their relative frequency of occurrence. Fifty-four percent of homicides with known victim-offender relationships occurred between friends and acquaintances. The friend and acquaintance killing involved predominately a male with an average age of thirty years killing a somewhat older male in the same racial group. Black males had much higher offender and victimization rates than other racial groups of this type of homicide.

The striking features that distinguish stranger felony homicides from other homicide types are the proportion of intraracial homicides and the difference in mean ages between victims and offenders. The age disparities and the victim-offender age ratios become accentuated for white victims, both male and female. The average age of white male victims is twice that of their offenders (ages 46 and 23, respectively). The average age for white females victims is nearly three times that of their offenders (ages 59 and 21, respectively). With black and hispanic victims, mean age differences persist, but the differences are smaller, thus making the victim-offender ratio smaller. The average age of black male victims is 1.4 times that of their offenders (ages 35 and 25, respectively). The average ages for hispanic male victims is about 1.6 times that of their offenders (ages 35 and 22, respectively).[37] Although most victims of homicide were victims of offenders of the same race, stranger felony homicide is characterized by the highest interracial rate. Young black and hispanic male offenders appear more likely to victimize older whites. Finally, there were very few women offenders in stranger felony homicides (n = 7). All of the women were black and had an average age of twenty-one.

The stranger non-felony homicides category had the lowest rate of occurrence of the four homicide types. Both victims and offenders were overwhelmingly males and were of similar ages. The average age of the victim was thirty, and the average age of the offender was twenty-nine. The victim and offender mean ages did not vary dramatically by race or sex, although hispanic male victims and offenders were younger than their black and white counterparts. The stranger non-felony homicides were similar to the friends and acquaintances homicides in characteristics of victims and offenders. Stranger non-felony homicides are distinguished from other types, however, by their public character. A high percentage of stranger non-felonies occurred in public, and a high percentage were witnessed.

VI. CONCLUSION

The preceding analysis shows that there are clear differences between types of homicide. The importance of age, sex, and race specific studies on both victims and offenders of types of homicide also has been established. The finding that white victims and offenders were older in most types of homicide and that hispanic victims and offenders were younger deserves closer scrutiny. This phenomenon, as in the disparity between the victim-offender ages in stranger felony homicides, may reflect differences among age-race structures in American cities.[38] In the data base of the nine cities, it is quite possible that Whites in central areas of the cities were older than the Blacks and Hispanics in the area,[39] because in the

---

[37] *See supra* Tables 15 through 18.

[38] For an examination of the age-race structure in the United States, see Morrison, *Urban Growth and Decline in the United States: A Study of Migration's Effects in Two Cities,* in INTERNAL MIGRATION: A COMPARATIVE PERSPECTIVE 235 (A. Brown & E. Neuberger eds. 1977).

[39] *Id.* at 248-50.

past, white families with young children have tended to leave central cities for the suburbs, while older Whites remained.[40] Blacks and Hispanics have migrated to cities,[41] have higher birth rates than Whites,[42] and, therefore, constitute younger populations. The age-race findings in homicide victimization and offending, especially in family and stranger murders, may reflect these demographic-ecological city realities.

This Article has also demonstrated that the general category of stranger homicide, frequently used in homicide research,[43] is too heterogeneous and needs to be subdivided. The stranger felony type is one subdivision which seems distinct and useful for analysis. The stranger non-felony category, however, needs additional exploration. The stranger non-felony homicide type is similar to the friends and acquaintances homicide type along most dimensions examined. The major exceptions are the locations and the percentage of cases with witnesses. The stranger non-felony homicide was often a very public act; this quality suggests that subsequent research should focus on the role of the public as witnesses to murder. Witnesses may facilitate such killings either by becoming actively involved in the disputes or by providing a climate which facilitates a lethal conclusion. In other types of homicide, such as killings within the family, witnesses may inhibit aggressive responses. This inhibition by the presence of witnesses does not appear to be the case in the stranger non-felony type. Perhaps society's notions of social control should be re-examined to better understand how and when audiences inhibit rather than facilitate homicide. Subsequent research should also examine the perpetrator's view of witnesses and the public.

Additional variables which might subdivide the stranger non-felony type into homogeneous categories include: the use of drugs and alcohol by offenders and victims, past history of violent behavior or mental illness, and the nature of the disputes. The presence of psychotic disturbance may be more highly associated with stranger non-felony homicides than with other types.[44] This hypothesis, as well as the interplay of these factors with situational variables, clearly deserve further attention.

---

[40] This effect is known as "white flight." For an study of "white flight" from the city of St. Louis, see *id.* at 246.

[41] BUREAU OF THE CENSUS, U.S. DEP'T. OF COMM., THE STATISTICAL ABSTRACT OF THE UNITED STATES 14 (102 ed. 1981).

[42] *Id.* at 59; Morrison, *supra* note 38, at 250.

[43] *E.g.*, F. LOYA & J. MERCY, THE EPIDEMIOLOGY OF HOMICIDE IN THE CITY OF LOS ANGLES [sic], 1970-79: A COLLABORATIVE STUDY BY THE UNIVERSITY OF CALIFORNIA AT LOS ANGELES AND THE CENTERS FOR DISEASE CONTROL 104 (1985); A. TIMROTS & M. RAND, VIOLENT CRIME BY STRANGERS AND NONSTRANGERS 1-7 (1987); M. WOLFGANG, *supra* note 7, at 203-21.

[44] Articles in the popular press have suggested the possible connection of psychotic disturbances and stranger non-felony homicides. *See, e.g.,* Gest, *On the Trail of America's Serial Killers*, U.S. NEWS & WORLD REP., April 30, 1984, at 53; Starr, *The Random Killers*, NEWSWEEK, Nov. 26, 1984, at 100.

Theories addressing causes of homicide also need further development. Such theories must pay attention to the observed differences within and between types of homicide. Types of homicide may not only have different causes, but also may bear different relations to public order. Subsequent research needs to focus on these and related issues.

Chapter 4

The Homicides of Children and Youth: A Developmental Perspective

David Finkelhor

Murders of children, the ultimate form of child victimization, have received a great deal of deserved public notoriety in recent years, whether in the form of homicides by strangers, as in the death of Polly Klaas, kidnapped from her home in Petaluma, California, or homicides by relatives, such as Susan Smith, the South Carolina mother who drowned two sons, or Joel Steinberg, the New York lawyer who battered his daughter to death. Indeed, the statistics on child murder in the United States are grim and alarming. In 1994, according to Federal Bureau of Investigation data, 2,521 persons under 18 were victims of homicides.[1] That rate of 3.8 per 100,000 (over six children per day) makes the United States first among developed countries in juvenile homicide. In fact, the U.S. rate is dramatically out of line with other places in the world, really double even the next most murderous country for all ages of children except infants. (Table [1] illustrates this, albeit somewhat piecemeal because World Health Organization data do not have a consolidated category for ages 0-17.) Of course, the U.S. "gold medal" in child homicide is not unrelated to the generalized American prowess in lethal violence: The homicide rate for all persons in the United States is 10.1 per 100,000, 3 times higher than any other developed country.

AUTHOR'S NOTE: I would like to thank Kathy Christoffel, Lauren Duncan, Michael Durfee, Sherry Hamby, Anne Keith, Milling Kinard, Murray Straus, and Carolyn West for helpful comments. Nancy Asdigian and Janis Wolak provided assistance with data analysis, and Kelly Foster helped with manuscript preparation. This research was supported by a grant from the Boy Scouts of America.

TABLE [1]

Child and Youth Homicide Rates for 22 Developed Nations With Populations Greater Than 1 Million (by age, per 100,000)

Country	<1 Year Old	Country	1-4 Years Old	Country	5-14 Years Old	Country	15-24 Years Old
United States	8.0	United States	2.5	United States	1.5	United States	19.3
Denmark	7.3	Switzerland	1.2	Sweden	0.8	UK N. Ireland	7.9
UK Scotland	6.0	Canada	1.1	Canada	0.7	UK Scotland	5.8
Austria	5.1	Japan	1.1	Japan	0.5	Finland	4.2
New Zealand	5.1	Netherlands	0.9	Switzerland	0.5	Canada	3.1
Switzerland	4.6	New Zealand	0.9	New Zealand	0.4	Italy	2.7
Portugal	4.4	Norway	0.9	Australia	0.3	New Zealand	2.3
Japan	3.9	Sweden	0.9	Austria	0.3	Australia	2.1
Germany	3.5	Finland	0.8	Belgium	0.3	Israel	2.1
Norway	3.2	Germany	0.8	Finland	0.3	Portugal	1.7
Canada	2.9	UK Scotland	0.8	France	0.3	Austria	1.6
France	2.3	Australia	0.7	Germany	0.3	Belgium	1.5
Belgium	1.7	Belgium	0.7	Italy	0.3	Switzerland	1.5
Sweden	1.7	France	0.5	Netherlands	0.3	Netherlands	1.3
UK Wales, England	1.7	Portugal	0.5	Portugal	0.3	Sweden	1.3
Finland	1.5	UK Wales, Eng.	0.5	Denmark	0.2	Denmark	1.2
Italy	0.9	Denmark	0.4	Norway	0.2	Germany	1.2
Netherlands	0.5	Italy	0.3	UK Wales, Eng.	0.1	France	0.7
Australia	0.4	Austria	–	UK Scotland	0.1	UK Wales, Eng.	0.7
Ireland	-	Ireland	–	Ireland	-	Norway	0.6
Israel	-	Israel	–	UK N. Ireland	-	Ireland	0.5
UK N. Ireland	-	UK N. Ireland	–	Israel	-	Japan	0.4

SOURCE: Figures are from World Health Organization (1995).

Murder is actually one of the few crimes in which children are *not* more victimized than adults. But the homicides of children have been increasing quite dramatically in recent years. They rose 53% from 1976 to 1992 according to FBI data, most of the jump coming since 1987 (Figure [1]). Importantly, homicide is the only major cause of childhood death to have increased in incidence in the past 30 years. While deaths due to accidents, congenital defects, and infectious diseases were falling, growing numbers of children were being murdered. Homicide is now among the five leading causes of childhood mortality, accounting for 1 out of 20 deaths for those under age 18. More children now die from homicides than from cancer or infectious disease (Table [2]).

Overall, juvenile homicides are among the most unequally distributed form of child victimization, with certain groups and certain localities experiencing the brunt of the problem. Minority children are particularly affected, making up 69% of all child homicide victims. Overall rates for Black children (8.4 per 100,000) and Hispanic children (4.7 per 100,000) dwarf the rate for Whites (1.7 per 100,000). The maldistribution is geographic, too. The difference between the states with the highest rates (California and Illinois) and those with the lowest rates (Maine,

Montana, South Dakota, and Iowa) is a factor of about 25 (Table [3]). Large cities have exposures that greatly exceed that of rural areas. Washington, D.C., which is entirely urban and heavily African American, has 10 times more child murders than the national average. On a regional basis, the West has the most child homicide. And boys are substantially more likely to be victims than girls.

However, a global summary like this of statistics on juvenile homicide is misleading and masks the multifaceted nature of the problem. There are really several different forms of the child homicide problem that are only revealed by taking a developmental perspective. Not all of them are increasing. They have different sources, and ultimately different strategies for preventing them. This chapter tries to look at them individually.

Figure [1]
Child Homicide Rates, 1976-1992 (rate per 100,000 U.S. children, ages 0-17)

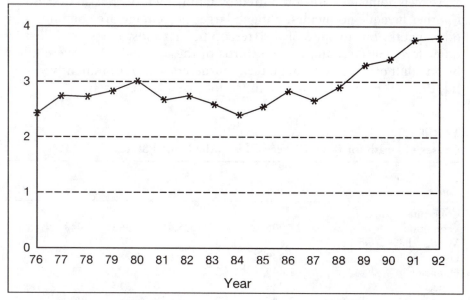

SOURCE: Uniform Crime Report

From a developmental perspective, juvenile homicides should be broken down into at least three distinct segments, each of which has its own reality: young children, including infanticide and child abuse homicide; school-aged children; and teenagers. This chapter will discuss each in order of decreasing frequency, starting with teens, then young children, and finally, school-aged children. It will conclude with some general principles about development and violent victimization.

Teen Homicides

The murder of teenagers has received substantial publicity in recent years in part because it has been the most rapidly increasing form of homicide. Whereas the overall homicide rate was growing 44% from the early 1980s to the early 1990s, teen homicides were increasing 80%. Teens (ages 13-17) now are killed at a rate that is 50% higher than the average rate for all persons. Age 13 is clearly the line of demarcation for this phenomenon: That is the age at which rates begin to rise dramatically (Figure [2]) and the age above which the recent historical increase has occurred (Figure [3]).

The murder of teenagers is the type of juvenile homicide that most resembles and appears to be an extension of the adult homicide problem. Like adult homicides, teen homicides overwhelmingly involve male victims (83%), killed by other males (96%), using firearms (86%) and knives (10%). In contrast to other juvenile homicides, relatively few of these teen homicides are committed by family members. Also in contrast to other juvenile homicides, a much larger percentage are committed by other youth. But in spite of the stereotype that most teens are killed by other teens, in fact, almost two thirds of these teens (62%) were killed by an adult offender. Although teen murderers are predominantly youthful, they are primarily young adults, not juveniles themselves.

TABLE [2]
Causes of Death for 0- to 17-Year-Olds in the United States

Cause	Total	Rate Per 100,000	<1	1-4	5-14	15-17
Congenital/perinatal condition	27,005	41.9	25,452	963	448	142
Motor vehicle accidents	6,679	10.3	190	783	1,975	3,731
Other accidents	5,339	8.3	740	1,783	1,675	1,141
Homicide	2,449	5.3	332	377	512	1,228
Cancer	2,243	3.5	90	513	1,094	546
Heart/circulatory disease	2,145	3.3	1,019	342	409	378
Suicide	1,725	2.7	–	–	264	1,461
Infectious diseases	1,329	2.1	734	294	188	113

NOTE: Figures are for 1990 and are from World Health Organization (1995). Figures for 15- to 17-year-olds were calculated by taking 30% of the number of deaths for 15- to 24-year-olds.

The big jump in teenage homicides in recent years has been popularly attributed to the rise of gangs, the spread of drugs, and increasing availability of handguns. The statistics clearly bear this out. In assigning a circumstance to the homicide, over half (56%) the teen killings for which a circumstance was listed were labeled by police as gang related.

Drug-related homicides made up another 15%. There has been an enormous proliferation of handguns in the youth population, instigated by youth in the drug trade who needed to protect valuable drugs and money, but accelerated as other youth acquired guns to protect themselves from other armed youth (Sheley & Wright, 1995; Simonetti Rosen, 1995).

TABLE [3]
Child Homicide Rates by State, 1991-1992, per 100,000

State	1991-1992 Rate Per 100,000 U.S. Children	State	1991-1992 Rate Per 100,000 U.S. Children
Washington, D.C.	36.71	Ohio	2.72
California	6.60	Connecticut	2.67
Illinois	5.83	Tennessee	2.64
Missouri	5.25	Mississippi	2.55
New York	5.16	Hawaii	2.50
Texas	5.12	Delaware	2.45
Maryland	5.08	Indiana	2.33
Arkansas	4.35	Utah	2.23
Nevada	4.04	Vermont	2.10
Louisiana	4.00	New Mexico	2.01
Michigan	3.94	Kentucky	1.99
Virginia	3.92	Massachusetts	1.85
North Carolina	3.74	Rhode Island	1.77
Arizona	3.66	Florida	1.71
Colorado	3.61	Alabama	1.70
Oregon	3.59	Minnesota	1.63
Georgia	3.47	Nebraska	1.63
Oklahoma	3.35	South Carolina	1.41
Kansas	3.17	West Virginia	1.35
Wisconsin	3.10	Idaho	1.30
Wyoming	2.95	New Hampshire	1.08
New Jersey	2.94	North Dakota	.85
Alaska	2.90	Iowa	.28
Pennsylvania	2.79	South Dakota	.25
Washington	2.78	Montana	.23
		Maine	0

But sinister as this arms race is, this ecology of teenage homicide suggests also that it is somewhat limited in scope demographically and geographically, primarily to communities with gang and drug problems. Available data do bear out that in spite of the widespread publicity about the jump in teen homicides, the increase has not affected all segments of the population equally. Most dramatic has been disproportionate rise in

risk for minority group teens. Teen homicide rates for Whites have been
almost flat (up only 9% since the early 1980s), whereas they have skyrocketed for minorities, doubling in the same period. The rate for Blacks
is up 132% and Hispanics up 93%. Most disturbing is the astronomic
rise of rates for Asian teens, up 343%. Rural areas seem also to have
been relatively unaffected. Rates barely rose between the early 1980s
and 1990s in towns with populations under 25,000 while teen homicides
were more than doubling in cities over 250,000.

Figure [2]
Race of Child Homicide Victims by Victim Age
(rate per 100,000 U.S. children)

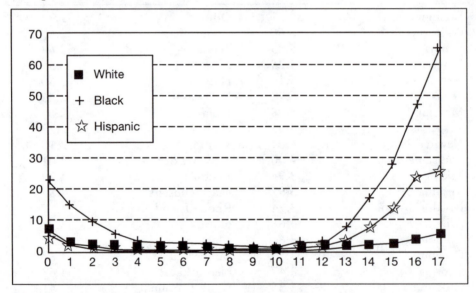

SOURCE: Uniform Crime Report, 1991-1992.

The particular risk of homicide victimization among minority teens
has led criminologists to look there for possible underlying explanations.
For example, Sampson (1987) analyzed the social correlates of specifically Black teen homicide using 1980 data (that is prior to the big recent
uptick in rates). Whereas communities with high levels of Black teen
homicide had more economic adversity (higher unemployment, lower
income, and lower welfare payments), the even more highly associated
factor was the percentage of Black households headed by a woman.
Sampson speculated that Black family disruption meant among other
things less effective social control over children, less involvement in community activities, and less general neighborhood surveillance, all of
which permitted more delinquent activity and more vulnerability to
homicidal violence.

Figure [3]
Percentage Change in Homicide Rate for U.S. Youth, 1981-1982 to 1991-1992

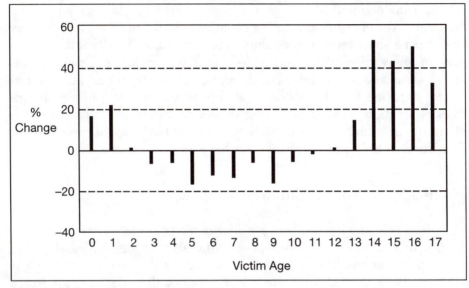

SOURCE: Uniform Crime Report, 1991-1992.

Beyond the question of why homicide victimization rates may be high for minority teens is the question of why they are high for teens in general. Certainly, a major part of the explanation has to do with the marginal and transitional status of youth. As a group with relatively weak ties to and a lower stake in many conventional roles (family and job), they are available for risky and dangerous activities. The powerlessness of the status (less access to money, prestigious work, or influential individuals) gives them a motivation for quick but potentially high-risk avenues to money, power, and respect. But even the many teens who are not prone to risk taking themselves may be made vulnerable because they have relatively frequent and involuntary contact with others who are.

Although the increase in the teen homicide rate is serious in its own right, Fox (1995) has added to the alarm, arguing that it is just a harbinger of a future escalation in adult homicides as today's violent teens age and carry forward their violent habits. Moreover, the current demographic trends project a 28% increase in Black teens and a 50% increase in Hispanic teens by the year 2005, potentially more fuel for homicide rates, if the sources of alienation for these minority groups remain unchanged. Although Fox describes one plausible development, other scenarios are possible, too. It may be that the age for involvement in lethally risky activities has declined in recent years but primarily for those who would have become violent as adults anyway, meaning that there will not necessarily be an increase in the number of such individuals overall compared to historical rates. It may also be that such individuals kill one another off, perhaps earlier than later now, so some homeostasis is maintained. Moreover, some of the etiologic factors behind the increase in youth homicides such as competition for the drug market may have been a short-term phenomenon and may abate. In 1995, to the surprise of many, there was a decline in overall homicide rates, demographics notwithstanding. In any case, the prediction of future crime rates has been a notoriously risky endeavor. Although the problem of teen homicides is a tragic problem requiring urgent remedies, it is not clear that alarm about future violent explosions will create more policy willpower than concern about the explosion we have already experienced.

Homicides of Young Children

Often eclipsed by the concern about teen murders is the fact that very young children are also quite vulnerable to homicide, although under different conditions. The official rate for children under age 5 is 3.6 per 100,000, and for many years was equal to the rate for teens, before the latter's recent rise. In fact, the rate of homicide for White children under age 5 is still nearly as high as the rate for White teens.

Moreover, there are strong hints that the actual homicide rate for young children is substantially higher than official statistics suggest. The homicides of young children are among the most difficult to document, because their presentation so often resembles deaths due to accidents and other causes. Thus, it is difficult to distinguish children who are suffocated from those who die from sudden infant death syndrome (SIDS). It is difficult to distinguish young children who are dropped, pushed, or thrown from those who die from falls. Even in many so-called accidental deaths, such as falls or auto fatalities, there may be a major component of willful parental negligence that is difficult to establish.

Thus, knowledgeable physicians have in recent years urged more careful examinations of child fatalities (Christoffel, Zieserl, & Chiaramonte, 1985), and most states have established child death review teams to ferret out child abuse fatalities that may have been previously overlooked (Durfee, Gellert, & Tilton Durfee, 1992; U.S. Advisory Board, 1995). When a team of such experts in Missouri carefully examined all the fatalities for children age 0-4 over a 4-year period, they found a great underestimation of the true extent of child maltreatment deaths using any individual record source, such as coroners' death certificates or police reports. In particular, only 39% of definite maltreatment fatalities and 18% of the combined definite/possible maltreatment fatalities got reported as homicides for purposes of the FBI Uniform Crime Report (UCR) (Ewigman, Kivlahan, & Land, 1993). This highlights how many actual homicides the official homicide data may miss.

This underestimation of young children's inflicted deaths has several distinguishable sources. One part is the definition of homicide that does not include many deaths that may have a large component of child maltreatment. So, for example, deaths due to gross negligence (a child left unsupervised on a window ledge falls to his death) may not meet a criminal standard of homicide or even manslaughter, so they are not counted. A second problem is the ambiguity of evidence in many child deaths and the lack of well-trained and systematic investigators. Finally, many states do not list a child fatality as a homicide unless charges are actually filed. Charges may not be filed for a variety of reasons.

All this means that some analysts have estimated the actual rate of homicides for young children to be double the official rate (see also Christoffel, 1990; McClain, Sacks, Froehlke, & Ewigman, 1993). The Centers for Disease Control and Prevention (CDC) believes the true rate of deaths due to child abuse and neglect is between 5.4 and 11.6 per 100,000 (U.S. Advisory Board, 1995). If child abuse deaths can all be equated with homicide, the upper bound of the CDC estimate would mean that young children have homicide rates higher than the rest of the population.

Moreover, the homicide rates for young children have been on the rise over the past 10 years. This is true whether one looks at the UCR data or at national child abuse fatality statistics, which, for example, show a rise between 1985 to 1992 from 1.30 to 1.94 per 100,000 (McCurdy & Daro, 1993; Weise & Daro, 1995). However, most of that increase has been among the youngest children, those age 0-1, and there are reasons to think that it could be artifactual. Because of the potentially large quantity of undiagnosed or unlabeled child homicide, particularly among these very young children, better efforts to screen for it in ambiguous cases of child death could easily pump the numbers. As we indicated, many states have established child death review teams in recent years and it is very possible that this greater scrutiny has pushed up rates without any true underlying increase. Others, though, noting the growth of births to unmarried young mothers in very disorganized, drug- and crime-ridden environments, have believed that the rise was real.

Infanticides

Most of the homicides of very young children are committed by parents and caretakers and thus fall into what would be defined as child abuse. But within this group there appears to be justification for distinguishing a special category called "infanticide," although the boundaries of this distinction are sometimes unclear. A definition of infanticide suggested by the legal tradition in Britain and Canada is the killing of a recently born child by a relative in situations where the relative does not want the child, is ill-equipped to care for him or her, or is suffering from a childbirth-related psychiatric disturbance such as postpartum depression or psychosis. A prototypical situation is a mother who smothers, strangles, or drowns an unwanted child shortly after the birth. It is characterized by an actual intent to destroy the child, unlike much other child abuse, which tends to be an expression of frustration, anger, or extremely reckless or negligent behavior that goes too far. Unfortunately, instead of following some such definition, many studies of infanticide simply define it as murders by parents of children under the age of 6 or 12 months (Christoffel, Anzinger, & Amari, 1983; Jason, Carpenter, & Tyler, 1983). This is probably overly broad. In Canada, which has a special crime of infanticide similar to our proposed definition, more than 40% of the homicides by mothers of children under age 6 months did not qualify for this crime category (Silverman & Kennedy, 1988). Moreover, 13% of the homicides of children between ages 6 and 12 months did qualify. Thus, generalizations about infanticide from statistical profiles based on age, as most are, are possibly misleading.

If infanticides are defined by motive, and not age, it would appear that mothers are the predominant perpetrators. Studies suggest that these women tend to be teenage, single mothers, who receive very little or no prenatal care, some of whose births occur outside the hospital and involve low-birth-weight children (Emerick, Foster, & Campbell, 1986). This suggests a clearly defined group of young women, who do not wish to be pregnant, are very ambivalent about it or are psychiatrically disturbed, and who kill their children because they do not want them, are overburdened, or see them as a threat to themselves.

But men can be the perpetrators of infanticide, too. Fathers and boyfriends may assist mothers in killing unwanted children. Grandfathers and other relatives may participate in killing children whose out-of-wedlock birth brings shame on the family. Fathers may kill new babies when they disagree over the decision to have the child or feel resentful over the competition for the mother's attention. And boyfriends may kill children of girlfriends when they know or suspect that the child is not their own. It is significant to note that according to FBI homicide statistics, men predominate overall as the murderers of children under age 1.

One curious sociological fact about infant homicides, however, is that they show much less international variation than other homicide. Thus, although the United States has twice as much child homicide as even the next highest developed country, there is only a marginal difference for infant homicide (Table [1]).

One possibility is that infant homicide is more related than other homicides to biological factors that have less variation across populations and socioeconomic strata. So, for example, if postpartum depression and colicky, difficult babies are significant contributors to the infant homicide and such conditions occur at similar rates across most groups of women and children, regardless of environment or nation, then we might expect that this form of child murder to be less related to social indicators or to vary less from country to country.

Child Abuse Homicides

Child abuse homicides are homicides of children by persons who are charged with their care, which would include parents, family members, baby-sitters, and friends who were taking responsibility for the children. The vast majority of child abuse deaths (92%) are to children age 5 and under (McClain et al., 1993), and a majority of what get recorded as homicides for children under age 5 are due to child abuse. Most statistics or studies on child abuse homicide do not segregate out the special group of "infanticides" that we have described above, so that generalizations from those statistics include the infanticide group. Moreover, statistics on child abuse *fatalities,* as opposed to *homicides,* which is how many studies are organized (Ewigman et al., 1993; U.S. Advisory Board, 1995), often encompass more than what gets recorded as homicide per se, counting also deaths due to neglect or negligence. Neglect deaths generally include situations in which a child dies because parents fail to feed the child or get obviously needed medical attention, and deaths due to negligence involve parents who fail to provide such basic supervision or precaution that the child dies in some obviously preventable accident, for example, a child left unattended on an open windowsill. About 42% of what are counted by child protection authorities as child abuse fatalities are classified as due to neglect, 54% to abuse, and 5% to both abuse and neglect (Weise & Daro, 1995).

Fatal outcomes in child abuse result most often among the youngest children, with 40% occurring to children under age 1, 18% to children between ages 1 and 2, and 13% to children ages 2 to 3 (McClain et al., 1993; see also Weise & Daro, 1995). The figures for children under 1, however, certainly include a large number of the homicides that we have termed infanticide (i.e., a recently born child killed because the parent does not want the child, is incapable of caring for him or her, or is suffering a childbirth-related psychiatric disturbance). But even excluding an estimated one third of the caretaker-inflicted deaths to children under 1 that might be classified as infanticides, child abuse homicides are still heavily concentrated among very young children.

Three factors account for the unusual vulnerability of this particular group of young children. First, of course, is the large burden and responsibility that such children impose on caretakers. The complete dependence and constant attention required by young children who are needy, impulsive, and not amenable to verbal control can readily overwhelm vulnerable parents. Not surprisingly, two of the most common triggers for fatal child abuse are crying that will not cease and toileting accidents (Krugman, 1985). Second, and perhaps most important, children of this age are small and physically vulnerable. This has several implications. They can still be picked up and shaken or thrown. Moreover, a limited amount of physical force is able to cause serious damage, and the immaturity of certain anatomical features (such as the relatively large size of the head and weakness of the neck) means that they are more likely to suffer fatal traumas than older children. As an indication of this, fatal child abuse is more concentrated among very young children than nonfatal child abuse. The major cause of death is cerebral trauma (Copeland, 1985), especially for the youngest victims. Third, there is often a delay in help-seeking that accompanies violence against young children. When such children are injured, but not fatally, they may not be able to communicate the seriousness of their injuries, and they are isolated in the care of those who may have hurt them, who also are reluctant to seek help. Thus, nonfatal injuries may turn fatal in the absence of care.

Child abuse homicides are more common in conditions of poverty, in families marked by paternal absence or divorce, and perhaps as a result, also among African Americans (2 to 3 times that of other racial groups). Drug use is implicated in 29%. Several studies show that boys and girls are at roughly equal risk for fatal abuse, but boys are at slightly higher risk for fatal neglect (Levine, Freeman, & Compaan, 1994). A possible explanation may be that young boys, more active and aggressive on average, may be more difficult to supervise, or treated as needing less care and supervision (Margolin, 1990). Interestingly, male caretakers account for a disproportionate share of the child abuse homicides, whereas females, who spend more time caring for young children, are responsible for a greater portion of the child neglect fatalities (Levine et al., 1994). The inadequate preparation men receive for assuming the caretaking role with young children may result in lower levels of tolerance for crying, soiling, and disobedience.

A tragic fact about child abuse fatalities is that a large minority, ranging from 24% to 45% (Alfaro, 1988; Levine et al., 1994; Weise & Daro, 1995), occur in families that are already known to child protective authorities because of some family or child care problem they had been having. In as many as one in eight, the case was currently active (Levine et al., 1994). This clearly raises the hope that many deaths could, with proper intervention, somehow be prevented. Unfortunately, the 2,000 child abuse fatalities need to be placed in the context of over 1 million cases of child abuse and neglect that are substantiated by child welfare authorities every year. Some observers have doubted that the homicidal subgroup could ever be reliably detected from that larger pool, in part because the fatalities are so comparatively rare, and in part because so many of the factors that contribute to an actual death may be unpredictable (U.S. Advisory Board, 1995). Others, however, have noted that an important subgroup of child abuse homicides occurs in families with a long and serious history of child maltreatment and parental incompetence and that better research and more aggressive child welfare intervention might save a substantial number of lives (Kaufman Kantor, Williams, & Jasinski, 1995).

Interestingly, there is quite a bit of evidence that the homicides of young children are a very distinct social phenomenon. Unlike homicides for other age groups, the rate for young children does not appear to vary in close correlation with the overall murder rate. This has been found in state-to-state analyses (Straus, 1987) and in international comparisons (Christoffel & Liu, 1983; Fiala & LaFree, 1988). Some countries like Japan that have very low overall homicide rates have relatively high levels of young child homicide. The United States, which has an overall homicide rate 3 times higher than any other developed countries is only modestly higher when it comes to infants (Table [1]). Straus has found that the sociodemographic variables that predict overall homicide levels in states have no predictive power when it comes to infant homicides, and reduced power for children ages 1 to 4.

If general violence levels do not predict young child homicide, what does? Fiala and LaFree (1988), analyzing the international data, find that levels of child homicide for young children are most closely related to conditions that affect the lives of women and mothers. When women have high labor force participation in the absence of access to education and generous social welfare spending, child homicide rates tend to be higher. Thus, in countries where females were less likely to work like Ireland and Italy (the data were for the 1960s and 1970s), the young children appeared to be more protected from homicide. When women worked but had substantial social welfare supports and education like in Sweden and Denmark, young children had low murder rates. By contrast, the United States has high female labor force participation but comparatively low social welfare spending, and this tended to account for the higher rates.

Baron (1993), analyzing U.S. state data, found gender inequality also a factor that predicted young children's homicide rates, possibly because it increases stress on women and undercuts their ability to protect children. Interestingly, Baron also found the percentage of households headed by females and the level of alcoholism (as measured by deaths due to cirrhosis) to be correlated with young child murders.

Thus, the implication from several comparative studies is that the homicides of young children are a quite distinct social problem from homicide in general and may be most closely related to the conditions of life for women and mothers.

Homicides of Middle Childhood

Middle childhood, the period from age 5 to age 12, marks a time of relative immunity from the risks of homicide. Although children of this age face substantial violence, in the form of both parental assaults at home and peer aggression at school, relatively little of it is lethal. The overall rate of 1.5 per 1,000 is far smaller than that for any other age, and the rate is even low among some of the population subgroups in which there are high overall child murder rates, such as Blacks. It is a rate lower than any other segment of the population including elderly persons.

This is a period of transition, which probably accounts for the low rate (Holinger, Holinger, & Sandlow, 1985). Children in middle childhood have outgrown some of the characteristics that create vulnerability for the very young, but have not begun to engage in the activities that make the rate so high for adolescents. Thus, they are less dependent, require less continual care, and have a certain self-sufficiency and socialization and verbal skills. This makes them less of a burden and less potentially frustrating for their parents and other adult caregivers, who are the primary perpetrators of early childhood homicide. They are also bigger and better able to hide, dodge blows, and get away from angry parents. It also takes more force and more energy to inflict a lethal injury on them. By the same token, children of middle childhood still are protected from some of the dangers that affect adolescents. They are under adult supervision and protection most of the time. They have yet to get access to weapons, drugs, and cars. Gang activity, although starting for some of them, is yet to become highly dangerous. Other criminally minded older children and adults are less likely to consider these children as threats or as candidates for involvement in criminal enterprises.

Yet children still do get murdered in this period, and the murders appear to be from a mixture of causes, some related to the homicides of early childhood and some to those of adolescence. Related to their still dependent status, children of middle childhood, like younger children, tend primarily to get murdered by family members (52% of the perpetrators). But unlike the case of younger children, these are not murders committed by hand. Over half are actually committed with firearms. Moreover, reflecting their greater independence, children in middle childhood begin to be prey for stranger homicides. One out of seven children killed in this period is killed by a stranger, more than 3 times the percentage for younger children. Children in this age group, especially the older ones, begin to be touched by the ravages of gang-type violence. About a quarter of these homicides for which police listed a cause were listed as gang related.

The homicides of middle childhood appear to stem from a wide variety of motives. For example, in addition to gang murders, children in this period begin to be vulnerable to sexual homicides. Pedophiles are attracted to children in this age range, and sometimes murder to hide their crimes. There are a significant number of negligent gun homicides for these children. Youth and other family members wield or misuse firearms that they believe to be harmless or unloaded. Some children in this period are killed in the course of other crimes, like robberies or carjackings, in which children happen to be innocent participants. When family members murder children of this age, sometimes it is in the course of whole-family suicide-homicides (Resnick, 1970). The perpetrators of these crimes are typically fathers who shoot their wives and children before turning their weapons on themselves. Family members also play a role in arson murders, when youth or alienated parents start fires to a family household, and other children are caught in the blaze.

One of the most interesting and unrecognized facts about homicides in middle childhood, however, is that they appear to be on the decline, according to FBI data analyzed for this chapter. This decline may have been missed because overall rates for childhood, influenced by big rises for teen homicide, have been on the increase. But when changes in rates are examined by individual ages (Figure [3]), using the FBI's supplementary homicide data file, one notes a marked decline for the ages of middle childhood from the 1980s to the 1990s. The decline has occurred for most nonteenage children down to age 2. In fact, it is quite possible that the decline has even affected the infants and 1-year-olds and that the appearance of a statistical increase is due, as suggested earlier, to the recent effect of child death review committees and the more intensive scrutiny being given to the deaths of very young children in ambiguous situations such as accidents and SIDS. But if we exclude these infants, for whom the increase may have been an artifact, homicide rates for 2- to 12-year-olds have dropped 19% over the decade, a fact all the more impressive in that the rate for teens was rising 80% during the same period.

A look at some of the subcategories of homicide for this age group over this time period shows that the decrease has not been uniform (Figures [4 and 5]). It occurred for Whites and Hispanics, but barely at all for Blacks. It occurred in all regions but the West and all city sizes except for the large ones. It applied to family and acquaintance homicides but not those committed by strangers. And all forms of homicide went down except for those by firearms. It would appear that there has been a decline except for the same kinds of homicides that result in the increase in the rate among teens, that is, African American or Asian victims, involving gangs, drugs, and firearms.

What kinds of factors could be responsible for this apparent decrease in child homicide among nonteenagers? A variety of considerations may be at work. The decade of the 1980s, for example, saw a much intensified effort to identify and report child abuse and neglect and some expansion of treatment programs in this area. This may have protected some children from family homicides who had not previously been pro-

Figure [4]
Percentage Change in Homicide Rate for 2- to 12-Year-Olds, 1981-1982 to 1991-1992, by Race and Region

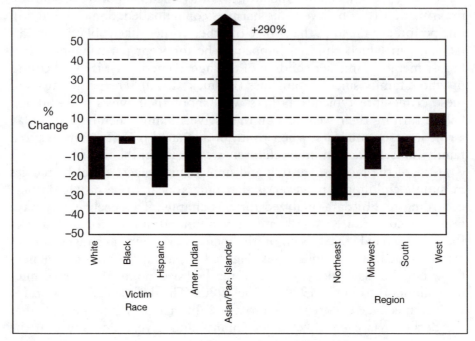

Figure [5]
Percentage Change in Homicide Rate for 2- to 12-Year-Olds, 1981-1982 to 1991-1992, by Relation, Circumstance, and Weapon

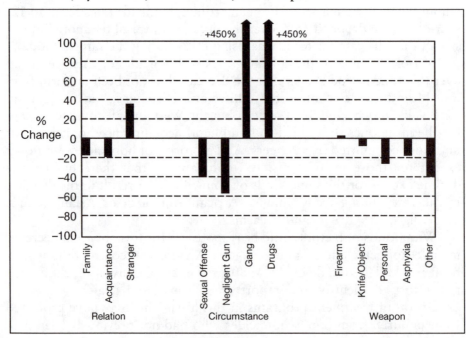

tected. The decade has also seen a dramatic development and dissemination of medical technology and emergency medical care. It may be that many more children are surviving inflicted wounds and injuries than have in the past. The decade has certainly *not* seen a drop in firearm availability, as families from all walks of life have become concerned about crime, but it may be that due to publicity about the problem they are being better safeguarded against misuse. The drop in the 1981-1991 rate for negligent gun homicide was particularly marked. There was also a marked drop in the number of children killed as a result of arson: The 1980s saw a great expansion in the use of smoke detectors. A host of other factors may be at work in explaining the decline. This drop is not entirely isolated in that it corresponds to a drop that has also occurred for middle-age Americans (MacKellar & Yanagishita, 1995), and may share common roots. But because apparent successes in the fight against crime seem so infrequent, this is a phenomenon that warrants further study.

Child Homicide: The Developmental Perspective

The preceding sections, breaking down juvenile homicide into three different subcategories, was organized in a largely developmental framework. The analysis could have, alternatively, organized the discussion in other ways, for example, emphasizing the perpetrator-victim relationship or the weapon choice, regardless of the children's age. However, the developmental framework has been particularly compelling in the analysis of child homicide (see also Christoffel et al., 1983; Crittenden & Craig, 1990) because it helps make sense of much of the other information about the crime. Elsewhere we have coined the term *developmental victimology* to describe this approach, one that asserts that the nature of crime victimization (and its effects) vary in certain patterned ways as children pass through the life cycle (Finkelhor, 1995; Finkelhor & Dziuba-Leatherman, 1994).

Juvenile homicide is particularly amenable to this kind of developmental analysis for a number of reasons. First, the definition of homicide is relatively clear and uniform across most of childhood. This is not true for other kinds of victimization. For example, in dealing with assault victimization, one is faced with the problem of how to categorize corporal punishment by parents, or in dealing with sexual assault, one is faced with the fact that the crime definition may differ for adolescents compared to prepubertal children. Second, because it is so serious, better and more complete data are available for homicide than for other kinds of crime and victimization. Most homicides are reported to authorities, even if they do not all get counted as homicides, which minimizes the problems of reporting biases. Third, homicide data are available across the whole age spectrum. Much other crime victimization data, like the

National Crime Survey, only covers youth ages 12-17 or like the UCR, is not broken down by age at all.

A goal of developmental victimology is to demarcate developmental patterns that can be formulated as general principles regarding crime victimization. Three such principles are relatively easy to observe in the case of homicide and are worth articulating in the possibility that they might in fact be applicable to other kinds of crimes.

Principle 1: As children get older, family perpetrators make up a smaller portion of all perpetrators. With increasing age, children interact with a larger and larger circle of other individuals. They also spend less time with family members. So family-perpetrated homicides should decline as a proportion of the total. The data on homicide clearly bear this out (Figure [6]), as the percentage of homicides declines with age, with three particular drops, after infancy, after age 7 and then again after age 12.

Figure [6]
Relationship of Child Homicide Victims to Perpetrators

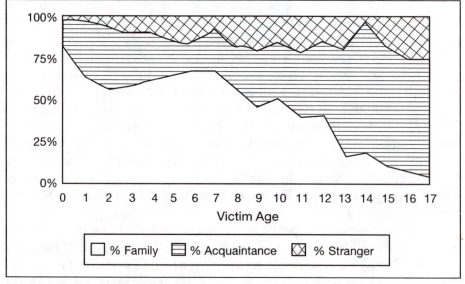

SOURCE: Based on 1991-1992 homicide data.

Principle 2: As children get older, their victimizations come to resemble those of adults. Thus, as children engage in more and more adult activities and take on adult responsibilities and characteristics, their crime victimization patterns should become more like adults. Indeed, the data on homicide show that in addition to more acquaintance homicides, as children age, more of the homicides involve firearms (Figure [7]), one of the hallmark distinctions between child homicide and adult homicide.

Figure [7]
Homicide Weapon by Victim Age

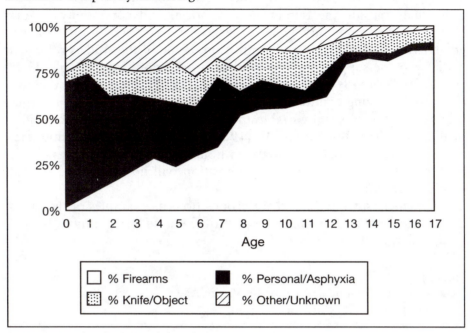

SOURCE: Based on 1991-1992 homicide data.

Principle 3: As children get older, gender patterns become more specific. Among younger children, there is less differentiation between the sexes, so presumably gender would be less of a factor in differentiating the patterns or rates of victimization. As children age and activities and physical characteristics are more differentiated by gender, patterns of victimization should become more gender specific. In the case of homicide, we do see that there is a marked divergence of rates for boys and girls as they age (Figure [8]). Prior to age 12, the male and female rates are extremely similar. After age 12, rates for males rise much more rapidly, so that they are nearly 7 times that of girls by age 17. Interestingly, unlike the previously indicated patterns, this is not a change that occurs gradually or in several steps over childhood, but undergoes a single, marked shift with the onset of adolescence.

One additional principle seems plausible from the prior principles, but we do not have data to explore it so clearly.

Principle 4: As children get older, their risk for victimization is decreasingly determined by family-related factors and increasingly related to more general social factors. Because families and parents govern the lives of younger children much more directly, factors such as maternal well-being, family composition, and quality of parenting should have a correspondingly greater effect on their risk of victimization. As children age and begin to interact with community institutions like schools and other individuals outside the family, general social and community factors such as race, community violence levels, and so forth should play a greater role in their risk for victimization. Some of the studies reviewed earlier provide support for this kind of proposition, for example, Fiala and LaFree's (1988) findings that maternal conditions affect the homicide rate for young children internationally and Straus's (1987) findings that general sociological variables do better at predicting the homicides of older children. But Sampson's (1987) research finds that family factors are important in predicting teen homicide rates as well. It may be that in spite of its logic, such a proposition will not withstand careful empirical scrutiny.

Nonetheless, we present these propositions as examples of the kinds of empirical issues that might be part of the domain of a more formal field of developmental victimology.

Figure [8]
Gender of Child Homicide Victims by Victim Age
(rate per 100,000 U.S. children)

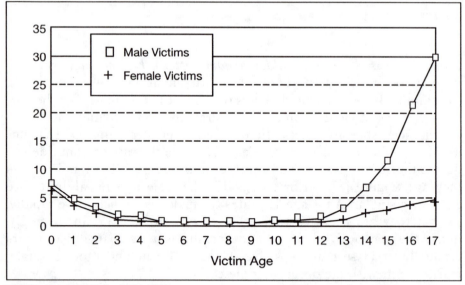

NOTE: Average rate for 1991-1992.

Child Homicide Statistics

As illustrated by these examples, homicide statistics have a utility and credibility that other crime and abuse statistics often do not. Because of the seriousness of the crime, and other factors such as the common performance of a criminal investigation or an autopsy, there is often a substantial amount of information about the crime on which the statistics are based. Assault and abuse statistics may be based on a single self-report, as in the case of the National Crime Survey, or on a professional decision that is not subject to much review, as in the UCR or child abuse reports. Moreover, national homicide statistics are available for the whole universe of homicides over an extended period of time, rather than being based on a sample or on the aggregation of possibly incompatible state data.

Because homicide statistics exist when other data do not exist or are seen as inferior, analysts often want to use them to answer more general questions, such as trends in nonlethal violence against youth or level of child abuse. So, for example, people have been eager to read success (Besharov, 1990; Pritchard, 1992) or failure (Weise & Daro, 1995) in the fight against child abuse in general from decreases (in the United Kingdom) or increases (in the United States) in the child homicide rate.

But there are good arguments against trying to use homicide statistics and particularly child homicide statistics as indicators for other, more general kinds of crime, violence and maltreatment of children (Trocme & Lindsey, 1995). For one thing, homicides generally constitute only an extremely tiny fraction of the universe of violence and abuse suffered by children. Compared to estimates of child abuse homicides (1,200 to 2,000 per year) estimates of nonfatal child abuse run from 500,000 to 4 million per year, making the homicides far less than even 1% of the total. The ratio of homicides to assaults is equally lopsided. It is risky to make generalizations from such a tiny portion of the problem to something so much bigger and potentially more diverse.

One of the risks of making such generalizations is that small factors can affect the small problem but have little relevance for the larger problem. Thus, if improvements in emergency medicine result in saving the lives of a few dozen more severely assaulted children every year, it could make a dramatic change in the child homicide rate, but have no bearing on the overall issue of child assault or child abuse in general.

In addition, there is good evidence that homicide is a problem very distinct from the general problems of child abuse or violence against children in general. Studies of homicide suggest that it is not distributed in the same way or predicted by the same characteristics as the more general problems (Gelles, 1991; Trocme & Lindsey, 1995). For example, older teens are much more likely to be murdered than younger teens, but the two groups have generally equivalent risks for being assaulted. Teen homicides seem to be much more disproportionately distributed geographically than assault. Similarly, child abuse homicides are much more heavily concentrated among very young children than child abuse in general.

Thus, much as we would like to be able to use child homicide data to interpret general trends in youth victimization, it is risky to do so. Child homicide needs to be considered a distinct phenomenon from other child victimization, and child homicide statistics primarily tell us about child homicide.

Another more general problem in using homicide statistics is that, even if better than other crime data, they have themselves many serious imperfections, particularly in regard to children. This was illustrated by a study in Missouri that scrutinized all deaths of children ages 0-4 in Missouri between 1983 and 1986 (Ewigman et al., 1993) and found many cases of homicide and child abuse deaths, even some of the obvious ones, being missed by the data-gathering systems. The three major sources of information—the FBI's UCR, child protective services agencies (CPS), and the death certificates that get reported as vital statistics—all had large areas where they failed to overlap. Of all the cases identified as definite child maltreatment deaths by one of the systems, the UCR failed to record 61%, vital statistics failed to identify 52%, and the CPS system failed to identify 21%. Part of the issue for the UCR data is that not all child maltreatment deaths can be classified as "homicides." But, remarkably, the UCR data failed to identify fully one third of the cases in which there was a *criminal* conviction as a result of the death. The death certificates missed many cases of child homicide for a number of additional reasons including a restrictive definition of homicide and the practice of filling out the certificates before criminal and child welfare investigations are complete. The CPS system misses homicide cases especially when the perpetrator is not a caretaker or when the case goes directly to the police and there are no additional children in the household who need to be protected.

In addition to these obvious missed cases, the systems almost certainly miss a great deal of homicide and child abuse that is more subtle and hidden. It is frequently hard to distinguish between intentional injuries and those due to accidents or natural causes or SIDS. Crimes against children are also relatively easy to conceal. Thus, the careful review of child deaths in Missouri determined that in addition to the definite maltreatment cases, there were an equal number of possible or probable maltreatment cases, most of which had been classified on death certificates as accidents. It would seem that a great deal of child homicide is being overlooked. Taking into account the lack of overlap among known cases and the hidden portion of the problem, some analysts have estimated that the actual rate of child homicide or child maltreatment fatality may be about double the numbers officially reported (U.S. Advisory Board, 1995).

Statistics on the homicides of older children have not been subject to the same scrutiny as those on younger children. But because accidents and intentional killings for this group may be more easily distinguished, the data may be more accurate for this group.

The existence of a large number of potentially uncounted homicides of young children has a number of important implications. One is simply that the problem may be much more serious than previously thought, rivaling in size the problem of teenage homicide. Another implication is that trends in homicide statistics for young children risk being affected by social change artifacts. If police get more training in child abuse issues, if autopsies and coroners' reviews become more systematic, if child death review teams bring more professional points of view to bear on child deaths, the number of child homicides may rise without any true underlying increase. In Los Angeles, for example, the local child death review team took credit for increasing from 50% to 87% the percentage of child abuse and neglect deaths that were sent to the district attorney for prosecution from 1989 to 1992 (U.S. Advisory Board, 1995). It is not certain that this sending of cases to the DA increased the number of cases that were classified in the UCR system as child homicides, but it seems quite probable that this would be one effect. In short, homicide statistics for young children in particular have a substantial imprecision and need to be well understood by those who compile them as well as those who use them.

Note

[1] This chapter is concerned about persons ages 17 and younger because that is the statutory age of dependency in most states for most purposes. As the time when secondary education ends for most young people in the United States, it is also the point of an important life stage transition.

References

Alfaro, J.D. (1988). What can we learn from child abuse fatalities? A synthesis of nine studies. In D. J. Besharov (Ed.), *Protecting children from abuse and neglect. Policy and practice* (pp. 219-264). Springfield, IL: Charles C Thomas.

Baron, L. (1993). Gender inequality and child homicide: A state-level analysis. In A.V. Wilson (Ed.), *Homicide: The victim/offender connection* (pp. 207-225). Cincinnati, OH: Anderson.

Besharov, D. (1990). Gaining control over child abuse reports. *Public Welfare, 48(2),* 34-40.

Christoffel, K.K. (1990). Violent death and injury in U.S. children and adolescents. *American Journal of Diseases of Children, 144,* 697-706.

Christoffel, K.K., Anzinger, N.K., & Amari, M. (1983). Homicide in childhood: Distinguishable pattern of risk related to developmental levels of victims. *American Journal of Forensic Medicine and Pathology, 4(2),* 129-137.

Christoffel, K.K., & Liu, K. (1983). Homicide death rates in childhood in 23 developed countries: U.S. rates atypically high. *Child Abuse & Neglect, 7,* 339-345.

Christoffel, K.K., Zieserl, E.J., & Chiaramonte, J. (1985). Should child abuse and neglect be considered when a child dies unexpectedly? *American Journal of Diseases of Children, 139,* 876-880.

Copeland, A.R. (1985). Homicide in childhood: The Metro Dade County experience from 1956-1982. *American Journal of Forensic Medicine and Pathology, 6*(1), 21-24.

Crittenden, P.A., & Craig, S.E. (1990). Developmental trends in the nature of child homicide. *Journal of Interpersonal Violence 5,* 202-216.

Durfee, M., Gellert, G., & Tilton Durfee, D. (1992). Origins and clinical relevance of child death review teams. *Journal of the American Medical Association, 237,* 3172-3175.

Emerick, S.J., Foster, L.R., & Campbell, D.T. (1986). Risk factors for traumatic infant death in Oregon, 1973 to 1982. *Pediatrics, 77*(4), 518-522.

Ewigman, B., Kivlahan, C., & Land, G. (1993). The Missouri child fatality study: Under-reporting of maltreatment fatalities among children younger than five years of age, 1983 through 1986. *Pediatrics, 91(2),* 330-337.

Fiala, R., & LaFree, G. (1988). Cross-national determinants of child homicide. *American Sociological Review, 53,* 432-445.

Finkelhor, D. (1995). The victimization of children in a developmental perspective. *American Journal of Orthopsychiatry, 65*(2), 177-193.

Finkelhor, D., & Dziuba-Leatherman, J. (1994). Victimization of children. *American Psychologist, 49*(3), 173-183.

Fox, J.A. (1995, March). *Homicide offending patterns: A grim look ahead.* Paper presented at the annual meeting of the American Academy for the Advancement of Science, Atlanta, GA.

Gelles, R.J. (1991). Physical violence, child abuse, and child homicide: A continuum of violence, or distinct behaviors. *Human Nature, 2*(1), 59-72.

Holinger, P.C., Holinger, D.P., & Sandlow, J. (1985). Violent deaths among children in the United States, 1900-1980: An epidemiologic study of suicide, homicide and accidental deaths among 5- to 14-year olds. *Pediatrician, 12,* 11-19.

Jason, J., Carpenter, M.M., & Tyler, C.W. (1983). Underrecording of infant homicide in the United States. *American Journal of Public Health 73*(2), 195-197.

Kaufman Kantor, G., Williams, L., & Jasinski, J. (1995, November). *Detection and prevention of fatal child abuse: Is prevention possible?* Paper presented at the annual meeting of the American Society of Criminology, Boston.

Krugman, R.D. (1985). Fatal child abuse: Analysis of 24 cases. *Pediatrician, 12,* 68-72.

Levine, M., Freeman, J., & Compaan, C. (1994). Maltreatment-related fatalities: Issues of policy and prevention. *Law & Policy, 16*(4), 449-471.

MacKellar, F.L., & Yanagishita, M. (1995). *Homicide in the United States: Who's at risk?* Washington, DC: Population Reference Bureau.

Margolin, L. (1990). Fatal child neglect. *Child Welfare, 69*(4), 309-319.

McClain, P.W., Sacks, J.J., Froehlke, R.G., & Ewigman, B.G. (1993). Estimates of fatal child abuse and neglect, United States, 1979 through 1988. *Pediatrics, 91,* 338-343.

McCurdy, K., & Daro, D. (1993). *Current trends in child abuse reporting and fatalities: The results of the 1992 annual fifty state survey* (Working Paper No. 808). Chicago: National Committee for Prevention of Child Abuse.

Pritchard, C. (1992). Children's homicide as an indicator of effective child protection: A comparative study of Western European statistics. *British Journal of Social Work, 22*(6), 663-684.

Resnick, P.J. (1970). Murder of the newborn: A psychiatric review of neonaticide. *American Journal of Psychiatry, 126*(10), 1414-1420.

Sampson, R.J. (1987). Urban Black violence: The effect of male joblessness and family disruption. *American Journal of Sociology, 93*(2), 348-382.

Sheley, J.F., & Wright, J.D. (1995). *In the line of fire: Youth, guns, and violence in urban America*. New York: Aldine de Gruyter.

Silverman, R.A., & Kennedy, L.W. (1988). Women who kill their children. *Violence and Victims, 3*(2), 113-127.

Simonetti Rosen, M. (1995, April 30). A *Law Enforcement News* interview with Prof. Alfred Blumstein of Carnegie Mellon University. *Law Enforcement News*, pp. 10-13.

Straus, M.A. (1987). State and regional differences in U.S. infant homicide rates in relation to sociocultural characteristics of the states. *Behavioral Sciences and the Law, 5*(1), 61-75.

Trocme, N., & Lindsey, D. (1995). What can homicide rates tell us about the effectiveness of child welfare services? *Child Abuse & Neglect, 20*(3), 171-184.

U.S. Advisory Board. (1995). *A nation's shame: Fatal child abuse and neglect in the United States* (Report of the U.S. Advisory Board on Child Abuse and Neglect). Washington, DC: U.S. Department of Health and Human Services.

Weise, D., & Daro, D. (1995). *Current trends in child abuse reporting and fatalities: The results of the 1994 annual fifty state survey* (Working Paper No. 808). Chicago: National Committee to Prevent Child Abuse.

World Health Organization. (1995). *World health statistics annual*. Switzerland: Author.

Section 3
SEXUAL ASSAULT

One of the most visible products of the combined efforts of the women's and victims' movements has been this country's evolution from traditional concepts of the crime of rape to more expansive notions of the crime of sexual assault. Prior to the efforts of those associated with these movements, most American jurisdictions utilized common law principles in their definitions of rape as forcible sexual intercourse by a male with a female. Husbands were traditionally exempt from prosecution for the rape of their wives. Over the last 20 years, however, most jurisdictions have abandoned this narrow definition of rape in favor of sexual assault prohibitions that are gender-neutral regarding the perpetrator and victim and that expand the range of prohibited sexual conduct as well as the concept of lack of consent. Most jurisdictions have also narrowed or eliminated the spousal exemption from prosecution for sexual assault.

Despite these expanded definitions of the crime, sexual assault remains one of the least frequently reported violent crimes in this country. Consequently, there is considerable variation in the estimates of the extent of this crime. A conservative national estimate, based on traditional rapes reported to the police compiled by the FBI in its Uniform Crime Reports, reflects that 70 out of every 100,000 females were victims of reported forcible rape in 1997. The National Crime Victimization Survey, using a gender-neutral and more expansive definition of sexual assault, estimated that there were 140 attempted and completed rape/sexual assault victimizations per 100,000 persons age 12 or older in 1997. In a national survey, sponsored by the National Institute of Justice and the Centers for Disease Control and Prevention, 18 percent of surveyed women and 3 percent of surveyed men said that they had experienced an attempted or completed sexual assault at some point in their lives. Thus, although the annual frequency rate of sexual assault may appear relatively small, the lifetime prevalence rate is quite significant.

The increased attention given to sexual assault in recent years has not been limited to changes in the definition of the crime. Increased attention has also been given to research regarding theories explaining the occurrence of the offense and its impact on victims. Traditionally, rape had been viewed as a "sex crime" only, perpetrated due to impairments or inadequacies of the individual offenders. Subsequent theorists have expanded the list of causal motivations to include anger, power, and control, as well as sexuality. Some theorists view sexual assault as symptomatic of gender inequality existing in the larger society. As with most crimes, it is doubtful that there is a single theory that explains the occurrence of sexual assault. Instead, it has been recognized as the complex and multifaceted offense that it is.

Just as sexual assault perpetrators and their motivations are multifaceted, so is the impact that the crime has on its victims. In the past, most attention has focused on the victim's physical recovery from the crime. It has been recognized, however, that the psychological impact of the crime is often far more extensive and long-lasting than its physical effects. As discussed in Chapter 5, the Resick selection, sexual assault victims frequently suffer from such symptoms as fear, anxiety, depression, loss of self-esteem, and impaired social adjustment and sexual functioning. Researchers have noted increased levels of alcohol and drug abuse and suicide-related behavior among sexual assault victims. Some researchers have identified the characteristics of post-traumatic stress disorder in sexual assault victims. Although some of the most acute reactive symptoms of many sexual assault victims are reduced or resolved within the first few months after the crime, victims often experience some continuing symptoms for extended or indefinite time periods. As the Resick selection indicates, research is also focusing on the pre-assault, assault, and post-assault variables that contribute to these victim reactions and influence victims' recovery from them.

Both the increased understanding of the factors motivating sexual assault offenders and the range of harmful reactions experienced by their victims have provided support for advocates seeking reforms in the treatment of sexual assault by the criminal justice system. As indicated previously, most American jurisdictions have adopted significant changes in their definitions of the crime of sexual assault, including making the crime gender-neutral, expanding the range of prohibited sexual conduct, eliminating the absolute requirements of force and resistance by expanding the concepts of lack of consent, narrowing or eliminating the spousal exemption from prosecution for sexual assault, and eliminating corroboration requirements. To alter the tendency of traditional rape trials to "try the victim" by exploring the victim's prior sexual history, most jurisdictions have adopted rape "shield laws" that restrict testimony regarding the victim's sexual conduct prior to the crime. Greater attention has also been given to sexual assaults that occur among acquaintances and intimates, which represented well over half of the rape and sexual assault victimizations estimated in the 1997

National Crime Victimization Survey. Many police departments and prosecutor's offices have also revised their procedures for handling sexual assault victims. Despite these substantial changes, however, as described in Chapter 6, the Bachman and Paternoster selection, researchers have yet to document any *significant* changes in the levels of rape reporting, arrests, convictions, and imprisonment of offenders, although some increases have been detected in some of these areas.

Although empirical research has not yet been able to document a significant impact of rape law reforms on criminal justice system outcomes, the change from a perceived "victim blaming" system to a more "victim friendly" system has certainly had effects in individual cases. Moreover, as more is learned about the underlying nature of this complex crime and its impact on victims, the criminal justice system will be better equipped to prosecute and punish its perpetrators and aid its victims.

LEARNING EXPERIENCES

1. Research cited in Chapter 5, the Resick selection, suggests that initial reactions to sexual assault victims might play a meaningful role in victim recovery. Does your local police department have a specific protocol it follows when dealing with sexual assault victims and complaints? Do police officers receive any special training regarding dealing with sexual assault victims? What procedures do local hospitals use in conducting the forensic examination of the victim? Does the local prosecutor's office have any special procedures to handle sexual assault victims and cases?

2. Does your community have a rape crisis center? If so, what services does it provide? What additional services are needed? If your community does not have such a center, does any agency or organization provide any of the services usually provided by a rape crisis center?

3. Is "acquaintance rape" a problem on your campus? Discuss its prevalence and the circumstances that contribute to or impede its incidence. What is your school doing and what more could it be doing to discourage this behavior?

4. Review your state laws regarding sexual assault to determine which of the rape law reforms identified in Chapter 6, the Bachman and Paternoster selection, have been enacted. Regarding those that have been enacted, interview a local prosecutor to determine whether such reforms have made a difference in the prosecution of sexual assault cases. Regarding those reforms that have not been enacted in your state, interview a state legislator to determine why such reforms have not been enacted.

BIBLIOGRAPHY

Alicke, M.D., & Yurak, T.J. (1995). Perpetrator personality and judgments of acquaintance rape. *Journal of Applied Social Psychology, 25,* 1900-1921.

Allison, J.A., & Wrightsman, L.S. (1993). *Rape: The misunderstood crime.* Newbury Park, CA: Sage.

Amir, M. (1971). *Patterns in forcible rape.* Chicago: University of Chicago Press.

Bachman, R., & Paternoster, R. (1993). A contemporary look at the effects of rape law reform: How far have we really come? *Journal of Criminal Law & Criminology, 84,* 554-574.

Benson, D., Charlton, C., & Goodhart, F. (1992). Acquaintance rape on campus: A literature review. *Journal of American College Health, 40,* 157-165.

Berger, R.J., Searles, P., & Neuman, W.L. (1988). The dimensions of rape reform legislation. *Law and Society Review, 22,* 329-357.

Berger, V. (1977). Man's trial, woman's tribulation: Rape cases in the courtroom. *Columbia Law Review, 77,* 1-103.

Bohmer, C., & Parrot, A. (1993). *Sexual assault on campus: The problem and the solution.* New York: Lexington.

Brems, C., & Wagner, P. (1994). Blame of victim and perpetrator in rape versus theft. *Journal of Social Psychology, 134,* 363-374.

Brownmiller, S. (1975). *Against our will: Men, women, and rape.* New York: Bantam.

Bryden, D.P., & Lengnick, S. (1997). Rape in the criminal justice system. *Journal of Criminal Law & Criminology, 87,* 1194-1384.

Burgess, A.W. (Ed.). (1985). *Rape and sexual assault: A research handbook.* New York: Garland.

Burgess, A.W. (Ed.). (1988). *Rape and sexual assault II.* New York: Garland.

Burgess, A.W., & Holmstrom, L.L. (1979). *Rape, crisis and recovery.* Bowie, MD: Brady.

Call, J.E., Nice, D., & Talarico, S.M. (1991). An analysis of state rape shield laws. *Social Science Quarterly, 72,* 774-788.

Campbell, R., & Johnson, C.R. (1997). Police officers' perceptions of rape: Is there consistency between state law and individual beliefs? *Journal of Interpersonal Violence, 12,* 255-274.

Chappell, D., Geis, R., & Geis, G. (Eds.). (1977). *Forcible rape: The crime, the victim, and the offender.* New York: Columbia University Press.

Cohen, L.J., & Roth, S. (1987). The psychological aftermath of rape: Long-term effects and individual differences in recovery. *Journal of Social and Clinical Psychology, 5,* 525-534.

Davis, R.C., & Brickman, E. (1996). Supportive and unsupportive aspects of the behavior of others toward victims of sexual and nonsexual assault. *Journal of Interpersonal Violence, 11,* 250-262.

Dripps, D.A. (1992). Beyond rape: An essay on the difference between the presence of force and the absence of consent. *Columbia Law Review, 92,* 1780-1809.

Drugge, J.E. (1992). Perceptions of child sexual assault: The effects of victim and offender characteristics and behaviour. *Journal of Offender Rehabilitation, 18(3-4),* 141-165.

Ellis, L. (1989). *Theories of rape: Inquiries into the causes of sexual aggression.* New York: Hemisphere.

Felson, R.B., & Krohn, M. (1990). Motives for rape. *Journal of Research in Crime and Delinquency, 27,* 222-242.

Foa, E.B., Rothbaum, B.O., Riggs, D.S., & Murdock, T.B. (1991). Treatment of post-traumatic stress disorder in rape victims: A comparison between cognitive-behavioral procedures and counseling. *Journal of Consulting and Clinical Psychology, 59,* 715-723.

Frazier, P.A., & Borgida, E. (1992). Rape trauma syndrome: A review of case law and psychological research. *Law and Human Behavior, 16,* 293-311.

Frazier, P.A., & Haney, B. (1996). Sexual assault cases in the legal system: Police, prosecutor, and victim perspectives. *Law and Human Behavior, 20,* 607-628.

Frohmann, L. (1991). Discrediting victims' allegations of sexual assault: Prosecutorial accounts of case rejections. *Social Problems, 38,* 213-226.

Galvin, J., & Polk, K. (1983). Attrition in case processing: Is rape unique? *Journal of Research in Crime and Delinquency, 20,* 126-154.

George, L.K., Winfield, I., & Blazer, D.G. (1992). Sociocultural factors in sexual assault: Comparison of two representative samples of women. *Journal of Social Issues, 48(1),* 105-125.

Giannelli, P. (1997). Rape trauma syndrome. *Criminal Law Bulletin, 33,* 270-279.

Gidycz, C.A., & Koss, M.P. (1991). Predictors of long-term sexual assault trauma among a national sample of victimized college women. *Violence and Victims, 6,* 175-190.

Gilbert, N. (1993). Examining the facts: Advocacy research overstates the incidence of date and acquaintance rape. In R.J. Gelles & D.R Loseke (Eds.), *Current controversies on family violence* (pp. 120-132). Newbury Park, CA: Sage.

Gordon, M.T., & Riger, S. (1991). *The female fear: The social cost of rape.* Urbana, IL: University of Illinois Press.

Grauerholz, E., & Koralewski, M.A. (Eds.). (1991). *Sexual coercion: A sourcebook on its nature, causes, and prevention.* Lexington, MA: Lexington.

Gray, E. (1993). *Unequal justice: The prosecution of child sexual abuse.* New York: Free Press.

Hazelwood, R.R., & Burgess, A.W. (Eds.). (1995). *Practical aspects of rape investigation: A multidisciplinary approach* (2nd ed.). Boca Raton, FL: CRC Press.

Holmstrom, L.L., & Burgess, A.W. (1978). *The victim of rape: Institutional reactions.* New York: Wiley.

Horney, J., & Spohn, C. (1991). Rape law reform and instrumental change in six urban jurisdictions. *Law and Society Review, 25,* 117-153.

Horney, J., & Spohn, C. (1996). The influence of blame and believability factors on the processing of simple versus aggravated rape cases. *Criminology, 34*, 135-162.

Jensen, G.F., & Karpos, M. (1993). Managing rape: Exploratory research on the behavior of rape statistics. *Criminology, 31*, 363-385.

Kerstetter, W.A., & Van Winkle, B. (1990). Who decides? A study of the complainant's decision to prosecute in rape cases. *Criminal Justice and Behavior, 17*, 268-283.

Kilpatrick, D.G., Edmunds, C.N., & Seymour, A.K. (1992). *Rape in America: A report to the nation*. Arlington, VA: National Victim Center.

Koss, M.P. (1992). The underdetection of rape: Methodological choices influence incidence estimates. *Journal of Social Issues, 48*, 61-75.

Koss, M.P. (1993). Detecting the scope of rape: A review of prevalence research methods. *Journal of Interpersonal Violence, 8*, 198-222.

Koss, M.P., & Burkhart, B.R. (1989). A conceptual analysis of rape victimization: Long-term effects and implications for treatment. *Psychology of Women Quarterly, 13*, 27-40.

Koss, M.P., Dinero, T.E., Seibel, C.A., & Cox, S.L. (1988). Stranger and acquaintance rape: Are there differences in the victim's experience? *Psychology of Women Quarterly, 12*, 1-24.

Koss, M.P., & Harvey, M.R. (1991). *The rape victim: Clinical and community interventions* (2nd ed.). Newbury Park, CA: Sage.

Kramer, E.J. (1998). When men are victims: Applying rape shield laws to male same-sex rape. *New York University Law Review, 73*, 293-331.

Larson, J.E. (1997). "Even a worm will turn at last": Rape reform in late nineteenth-century America. *Yale Journal of Law & the Humanities, 9*, 1-71.

LeBeau, J.L. (1987). Patterns of stranger and serial rape offending: Factors distinguishing apprehended and at large offenders. *Journal of Criminal Law & Criminology, 78*, 309-326.

Marhoefer-Dvorak, S., Resick, P.A., Hutter, C.K., & Girelli, S.A. (1988). Single- versus multiple-incident rape victims: A comparison of psychological reactions to rape. *Journal of Interpersonal Violence, 3*, 145-160.

Mio, J. S., & Foster, J.D. (1991). The effects of rape upon victims and families: Implications for a comprehensive family therapy. *American Journal of Family Therapy, 19*, 147-159.

Muehlenhard, C.L., Powch, I.G., Phelps, J.L., & Giusti, L.M. (1992). Definitions of rape: scientific and political implications. *Journal of Social Issues, 48(1)*, 23-44.

Muram, D., Miller, K., & Cutler, A. (1992). Sexual assault of the elderly victim. *Journal of Interpersonal Violence, 7*, 70-76.

Murphy, S.M., Kilpatrick, D.G., Amick-McMullan, A., Veronen, L.J., Paduhovich, J., Best, C.L., Villeponteaux, L.A., & Saunders, B.E. (1988). Current psychological functioning of child sexual assault survivors: A community study. *Journal of Interpersonal Violence, 3*, 55-79.

Pirog-Good, M.A., & Stets, J.E. (Eds.) (1989). *Violence in dating relationships: Emerging social issues*. New York: Praeger.

Rand, M. (1998). *National Crime Victimization Survey: Criminal Victimization 1997*. Washington, DC: U.S. Department of Justice.

Resick, P.A. (1993). The psychological impact of rape. *Journal of Interpersonal Violence, 8,* 223-255.

Resick, P.A., & Nishith, P. (1997). Sexual assault. In R.C. Davis, A.J. Lurigio, & W.G. Skogan (Eds.), *Victims of crime* (2nd ed., pp. 27-52). Thousand Oaks, CA: Sage.

Resick, P.A., & Schnicke, M.K. (1990). Treating symptoms in adult victims of sexual assault. *Journal of Interpersonal Violence, 5,* 488-506.

Rothbaum, B.O., Foa, E.B., Riggs, D.S., Murdock, T., & Walsh, W. (1992). A prospective examination of post-traumatic stress disorder in rape victims. *Journal of Traumatic Stress, 5,* 455-475.

Scully, D. (1990). *Understanding sexual violence: A study of convicted rapists.* Boston: Unwin Hyman.

Siegel, J.M., Golding, J.M., Stein, J.A., Burnam, M.A., & Sorenson, S.B. (1990). Reactions to sexual assault: A community study. *Journal of Interpersonal Violence, 5,* 229-246.

Spears, J.W., & Spohn, C.C. (1996). The genuine victim and prosecutors' charging decisions in sexual assault cases. *American Journal of Criminal Justice, 20,* 183-205.

Spears, J.W., & Spohn, C.C. (1997). The effect of evidence factors and victim characteristics on prosecutors' charging decisions in sexual assault cases. *Justice Quarterly, 14,* 501-524.

Spohn, C., & Horney, J. (1992). *Rape law reform: A grassroots revolution and its impact.* New York: Plenum.

Spohn, C., & Spears, J. (1996). The effect of offender and victim characteristics on sexual assault case processing decisions. *Justice Quarterly, 13,* 649-679.

Stitt, B.G., & Lentz, S.A. (1996). Consent and its meaning to the sexual victimization of women. *American Journal of Criminal Justice, 20,* 237-257.

Tjaden, P., & Thoennes, N. (1998). *Prevalence, incidence, and consequences of violence against women: Findings from the National Violence Against Women Survey.* Washington, DC: U.S. Department of Justice.

Ullman, S.E., & Siegel, J.M. (1993). Victim-offender relationship and sexual assault. *Violence and Victims, 8,* 121-134.

U.S. Department of Justice. Federal Bureau of Investigation. (1998). *UCR press release—Crime in the United States, 1997.* Washington, DC: Author.

Waldner-Haugrud, L.K., & Magruder, B. (1995). Male and female sexual victimization in dating relationships: Gender differences in coercion techniques and outcomes. *Violence and Victims, 10,* 203-215.

Walsh, A. (1986). Placebo justice: Victim recommendations and offender sentences in sexual assault cases. *Journal of Criminal Law & Criminology, 77,* 1126-1141.

Warr, M. (1985). Fear of rape among urban women. *Social Problems, 32,* 238-250.

Wiehe, V.R., & Richards, A.L. (1995). *Intimate betrayal: Understanding and responding to the trauma of acquaintance rape.* Thousand Oaks, CA: Sage.

Chapter 5

The Psychological Impact of Rape

Patricia A. Resick
University of Missouri—St. Louis

The purpose of the present article is to review the literature on the psychological impact of rape on adult female victims. Typical patterns of recovery, types of symptoms, and variables affecting recovery are all reviewed. Among the problems discussed are fear and anxiety, posttraumatic stress disorder, depression, poor self-esteem, social adjustment issues, and sexual dysfunctions. The moderating variables that are reviewed are preassault variables such as prior psychological functioning and life stressors; within-assault variables such as acquaintanceship status, level of violence, and within-crime victim reactions; and postassault variables such as social support and participation in the criminal justice system.

It was my charge to review the impact of rape on psychological functioning. Research on the impact of rape has been important in several respects. Until the impact of the crime was more fully understood and appreciated, rape was a misinterpreted crime that was too often not taken seriously enough by professionals and the significant others in the victims' lives. This misinterpretation of rape as merely unwanted sex, rather than as a life-threatening and traumatic event, affected reporting rates, prosecution, and the development and availability of appropriate forms of treatment for victims. This problem of misinterpretation is still evidenced with acquaintance rape victims.

A thorough understanding of the impact of rape is also important for theory development, for early identification of those victims who are likely to experience particularly difficult reactions or slow recovery, and

Source: Resick, P.A. (1993). The psychological impact of rape. *Journal of Interpersonal Violence*, 8, 223-255. Copyright © 1993 by Sage Publications, Inc. Reprinted by permission of Sage Publications, Inc.

for the development and assessment of appropriate therapy techniques. Extant research on the psychological effects of rape has already contributed substantial information toward these goals. It is the purpose of this article to describe the most typical pattern of reactions and recovery that has been observed, to delineate the most frequently occurring symptoms found among rape victims, and to review variables that may influence recovery. Finally, recommendations for future research will be made.

PATTERNS OF REACTION AND RECOVERY

As part of the first assessment in a longitudinal study of rape victims' reactions, Veronen, Kilpatrick, and Resick (1979) asked participants to describe their emotional and physical reactions during the crime and a few hours later. Ninety-six percent of the victims said they were scared, worried, and were shaking or trembling. Ninety-two percent were terrified and confused. These reactions abated only slightly in the two to three hours following the rape and depression (84%), exhaustion (96%), and restlessness (88%) increased. Burgess and Holmstrom (1974, 1979a) found similar reactions immediately after the assaults in their landmark study of rape conducted at the emergency room of a hospital.

Rothbaum, Foa, Murdock, Riggs, and Walsh (1992) have studied early patterns of reaction by assessing 95 victims of rape or attempted rape weekly for 12 weeks following the crime. They found a consistent pattern with most of the assessment measures they used. At 1 week postcrime, 94% of the subjects met the symptom criteria for posttraumatic stress disorder (PTSD) and were clinically depressed. By 3 months postcrime, 47% still met full criteria for PTSD. The bulk of the improvement occurred within the first month postcrime. Those women who eventually developed chronic PTSD showed little further improvement after the first month on any of the symptom scales. Those women who eventually recovered continued to show gradual improvement through the 3 months of assessment.

Other studies that have assessed women within 2 weeks postassault (Atkeson, Calhoun, Resick, & Ellis, 1982; Calhoun, Atkeson, & Resick, 1982; Feldman-Summers, Gordon, & Meagher, 1979; Kilpatrick, Veronen, & Resick, 1979a; Resick, 1986) have found that the majority of rape victims experience clinically significant fear, depression, other mood states, sexual dysfunctions, and problems with self-esteem and social adjustment.

The longitudinal studies by Calhoun and her associates (Atkeson et al., 1982; Calhoun et al., 1982; Resick, Calhoun, Atkeson, & Ellis, 1981) and more recently by Resick (1988) have found that these reactions tend to continue to be quite strong at 1 month postrape, but begin to improve by 2 to 3 months postrape. Although scores on many symptom scales have returned to normal, many of the scales measuring fear, anxiety, self-esteem, and sexual dysfunctions remain somewhat elevated in rape victims compared to nonvictim comparison groups. One year after the crime, rape victims were still likely to be exhibiting these problems.

In the initial report from their longitudinal study, Kilpatrick et al. (1979a) reported the same pattern of reactions and recovery. However, after increasing their sample size from 35 to 149 rape victims, they found that their sample did not improve to normal levels at 3 months (Kilpatrick & Veronen, 1984). Although there was substantial improvement by the 3-month assessment and no change thereafter on the repeated measures analyses, these women scored as significantly more distressed than nonvictims on 26 out of 28 measures at 3, 6, and 12 months. A dramatic improvement was reported at the 18-month assessment. The 46 rape victims who remained in the study reported significantly greater distress than 69 nonvictims on only one of the 28 measures, phobic anxiety. Apparently, some of the improvement was transitory. At 2 and 3 years postrape, there were differences on several of the fear and anxiety measures between raped and nonraped women.

Studies that have continued to assess rape victims over time (Resick, 1988, for 18 months; Kilpatrick & Veronen, 1983, for 3 years) or have assessed women after an extended period (Burgess & Holmstrom, 1978, after 6 years; Ellis, Atkeson, & Calhoun, 1981, from 1-16 years) have found continued problems with fear or depression. It should be noted at this point, however, that samples in these studies may be biased because of attrition in the longitudinal studies, and initial sample selection bias (e.g., Ellis et al., 1981).

The only studies that have succeeded in obtaining a representative sample of the population to assess the long-term effects of rape are the prevalence study and follow-up assessment study by Kilpatrick and his associates (Kilpatrick, Best, et al., 1985; Kilpatrick et al., 1987). They, too, found significant long-term problems in fear, social adjustment, depression, and sexual disorders in women who had been raped an average of 6 years previously.

An overall pattern has emerged with reasonable consistency in all of these studies. Most rape victims experience a strong acute reaction that lasts for several months. By 3 months postcrime, much of the initial turmoil has decreased and stabilized. Some victims continue to experience chronic problems for an indefinite period of time. These problems fall under the categories of fear/PTSD, depression, loss of self-esteem, social adjustment problems, sexual disorders, and other anxiety disorders (social phobia or obsessive-compulsive disorder). The next section will explore these reactions in more depth.

SYMPTOMS FOLLOWING RAPE

Fear and Anxiety

The most frequently observed symptoms following rape are fear and anxiety. Using the Modified Fear Survey (MFS; Veronen & Kilpatrick, 1980), an instrument specifically designed to assess fear in rape victims, or the Derogatis Symptom Check List-90-Revised (SCL, 90-R; Derogatis, 1977), which has a phobic anxiety subscale, several studies have found differences in fear levels between victims and nonvictims. In their longitudinal study, Kilpatrick and Veronen (1984) found that rape victims had significantly higher scores than nonvictims on seven of the eight MFS subscales and the SCL-90-R phobic anxiety subscale at the 6-to-21-day, 1-month, 3-month, 6-month, and 1-year assessments. As mentioned earlier, fear, as measured by the MFS, decreased at 18 months but reemerged at 2 and 3 years postcrime. Calhoun et al. (1982) reported similar results. Their sample of rape victims exhibited improvement between 2 weeks and 2 months postcrime but continued to score significantly higher than nonvictimized women through 1 year postcrime.

In a longitudinal study comparing rape and robbery victims, Resick (1988) found no differences on the total MFS scores between the two groups for 18 months of assessment, and differences on only one of the subscales, sexual fears, for 6 months following the crime. Rape victims reported significantly more sexual fears than robbery victims. On the Brief Symptom Index (BSI), a shorter version of the SCL-90-R, rape victims reported greater phobic anxiety for 6 months. However, on the Impact of Event Scale (IES; Horowitz, Wilner, & Alverez, 1979), and the Lifestyle Questionnaire, which was developed for Resick's study to assess behavioral changes and fear/intrusion symptoms following crime, rape victims reported more avoidance and intrusion of thoughts of the event, and more symptoms for 18 months and behavioral changes for 6 months than robbery victims.

It should be noted at this point that Kilpatrick and Veronen (1984) also examined the Impact of Event Scale, but could not compare the scores of rape victims with their nonvictim sample because the scale refers to an event and the nonvictims had no referent trauma for comparison. However, they did find that victims' scores were elevated for 6 months and then declined and stabilized. On their follow-up of the random survey of lifetime victimization, Kilpatrick et al. (1987) had victims of a variety of crimes complete the IES. They found that victims of completed rape exhibited higher levels of intrusion and avoidance than victims of aggravated assault, although both crimes produce significantly higher levels of these two symptoms than do other crimes.

Bulman et al. (1988) conducted a probability survey with 3,132 households and found that 13.2% of the sample had been victims of sexual assault. In comparison with those who did not report sexual assault, the victims reported significantly greater onset of phobias and panic disorder after the assault. These disorders were diagnosed by means of the National Institute of Mental Health Diagnostic Interview Schedule. This sample included men (9.4%) as well as women (16.7%) and childhood as well as adult victimization.

Several studies have examined the development of general anxiety reactions in response to rape. The SCL-90-R (or BSI) Anxiety subscale and the State-Trait Anxiety Scale (Spielberger, Gorsuch, & Luchene, 1970) have both been used to assess these reactions. Kilpatrick and Veronen (1984) found trait anxiety scores to be higher than state anxiety scores at all sessions. They also found rape victims to score higher than nonvictims at all sessions through 1 year postcrime. On the anxiety scale of the SCL-90-R, victims scored higher than nonvictims through the 2-year assessment but not at 3 years postcrime.

In comparing the reactions of rape and robbery victims, Resick (1988) found that rape victims reported more anxiety on the BSI at all sessions through 18 months postcrime. Kilpatrick et al. (1987) also found that anxiety was a more significant long-term problem in rape victims than other crime victims, although both of these studies found anxiety to be a continuing problem in crime victims.

Posttraumatic Stress Disorder

Because many of the studies on rape were conducted or begun prior to the wide acceptance of the diagnostic category PTSD, or because the studies were more interested in describing symptoms than determining diagnostic categories, PTSD was not studied directly in all but the most recent studies. However, the fear and anxiety reactions that are described in most studies are compatible with a diagnosis of PTSD, although a diagnosis cannot be made without knowing whether a woman exceeds threshold on three criteria: persistent reexperiencing of the trauma, persistently avoiding stimuli or numbing of responsiveness, and increased arousal.

Burgess and Holmstrom (1974) defined such symptoms as traumatophobia in their original study and included all three elements with their description of nightmares, fears and avoidance, feeling of unreality, and physical symptoms. More recently, researchers have conducted structured diagnostic interviews tailored to assess PTSD (Kilpatrick et al., 1987; Rothbaum et al., 1992). As mentioned earlier, Rothbaum et al. (1992) found that at 1 week postcrime 94% of their sample of rape victims met symptom criteria, and at 12 weeks 47% continued to do so. By dividing their sample into two groups, PTSD or non-PTSD, based on their final assessment, Rothbaum et al. (1992) found that those who eventually developed chronic PTSD reported more severe distress initially and showed little improvement after the fourth week, whereas those who eventually recovered continued to improve.

Kilpatrick et al. (1987) found that 3.4% of 204 female victims of crimes, other than rape, sometime during their life, were currently experiencing PTSD. In contrast, 16% of 81 victims of one completed rape currently met the diagnostic criteria, and 20% of victims of two completed rapes (n = 10) had PTSD. Almost 60% of the rape victims met the criteria for having PTSD at sometime in their life.

Most recently "Rape in America: A Report to the Nation" was released by the National Victim Center and the Crime Victim's Research and Treatment Center (Kilpatrick, Edmunds, & Seymour, 1992). This report was released following a longitudinal survey of a large national probability sample of 4,008 adult American women. Of the women surveyed, 507 reported having been raped at least once. Based on this telephone survey, it was found that 31% of all rape victims developed PTSD sometime during their life and 11% still had PTSD at the time of the survey. They estimated that 3.8 million adult American women have had rape-related PTSD and 1.3 million currently have rape-induced PTSD.

Depression

Two groups of researchers have focused primarily on the assessment of depression in rape victims. Frank, Turner, and Duffy (1979) administered the Beck Depression Inventory (BDI; Beck, Ward, Mendelsohn, Mock, & Erbaugh, 1961) to 34 rape victims within 1 month of their assaults. They found that 44% scored in the moderately or severely depressed range. A later study with a larger sample (n = 90) resulted in similar findings (Frank & Stewart, 1984). On the BDI, 56% of those subjects fell into the moderately or severely depressed range and 43% of the women were diagnosed as suffering from a major depression based on a semistructured interview. The depression diminished by 3 months postcrime.

Atkeson et al. (1982) examined depressive reactions in rape victims compared to nonvictims over a 1 year period using the BDI and the Hamilton Psychiatric Rating Scale for Depression (HPRS; Hamilton, 1960). The HPRS is a rating scale developed for use by interviewers following a semistructured interview. They found that rape victims' scores on both the BDI and HPRS were significantly different than nonvictims' scores at 2 weeks, 1 month, and 2 months postassault, but not at later assessment periods. On the BDI, at 2 weeks postcrime, 75% of the victims reported from mild to severe symptoms of depression.

Other studies have found similar levels of depression initially (Kilpatrick & Veronen, 1984; Resick, 1988; Rothbaum et al., 1992) using the BDI, the Depression-Dejection scale from the Profile of Mood States

Scale (POMS; McNair, Lorr, & Droppleman, 1971) or the Depression subscale from SCL-90-R or BSI. However, Kilpatrick and Veronen (1984) continued to find differences between victims and nonvictims for 1 year after the crime on both of the depression scales from the SCL-90-R and POMS. Resick (1988) found significant differences on the BDI and the BSI Depression subscale between robbery and rape victims at the 1-, 3-, 6-, and 18-month sessions, but not the 12-month session, on a larger cross-sectional analysis, but found no differences at any session on a longitudinal analysis with a smaller sample.

Studies of long-term effects of rape have also reported problems with depression among rape victims. Ellis et al. (1981), in assessing women 1 to 16 years postrape, found that rape victims were significantly more depressed than a matched comparison group. Forty-five percent of the rape victim sample were moderately or severely depressed as measured by the BDI. On the Pleasant Events Schedule (MacPhillamy & Lewinsohn, 1976), the rape survivors did not differ from the comparison group in their reports of how often they engaged in activities, but victims did report significantly less enjoyment from the activities.

In their clinical follow-up of the randomly surveyed crime victims, Kilpatrick et al. (1987) found their long-term rape victims (mean length of time postrape was 21.9 years) were more likely to be depressed than nonvictims measured by the SCL-90-R and the Mental Health Problem Interview (Robins, Hetzer, Croughan, & Ratcliff, 1981). In fact, they found that 8.6% of victims of one rape and 20% of victims of two rapes currently met the diagnosis for major depressive disorder, whereas 45.7% of single-incident victims and 80% of two-incident victims met the lifetime diagnosis of major depressive disorder. Burnam et al. (1988) also found that a greater percentage of people who had been sexually assaulted (17.93%) were likely to experience a major depressive disorder than nonvictims (4.68%) in their household probability sample.

The Rape in America Survey by Kilpatrick et al. (1992) found that of the 507 victims of rape they surveyed, 30% had experienced at least one major depression and 21% were currently depressed at the time of the survey. They contrasted these figures to the finding that only 10% of the women who had never been raped had ever experienced major depression and only 6% were currently depressed.

Finally, the level of suicidal ideation and attempts among rape victims is notable. Although the rates of suicidal behavior are not very high in the first month after victimization (2.9% in Frank et al., 1979; 27% in Frank & Stewart, 1984), Ellis et al. (1981) found that 50% of their long-term sample had considered suicide. Resick, Jordan, Girelli, Hutter, and Marhoefer-Dvorak (1988) found that 43% of their sample of 37 women who completed a treatment program had considered suicide after the rape. Seventeen percent made a suicide attempt. Although one might argue that these samples are biased because they were comprised

of treatment-seekers, Kilpatrick, Best, et al. (1985) found in their random survey that 44% of the rape victims had suicidal ideation and that
19% had made a suicide attempt. The Rape in America Survey by Kilpatrick et al. (1992) found that 33% of rape victims versus 8% of nonvictims had ever contemplated suicide, whereas 13% of rape victims versus only 1% of nonvictims had made a suicide attempt.

Self-Esteem

Given that self-blame has been frequently noted in rape victims
(Janoff-Bulman, 1979; Libow & Doty, 1979; Meyer & Taylor, 1985), it
might be expected that self-esteem would be affected. However, there
has been surprisingly little research focusing on self-esteem. Based on
Kilpatrick and Veronen's (1984) longitudinal study, Murphy et al.
(1988) reported on the self-esteem of 204 rape victims and 173 nonvictims over 2 years. The study used the Self-Report Inventory (SRI; Brown,
1961), which includes eight subscales reflecting self-esteem relative to
different arenas such as work, parents, others, and so forth. They found
that victims reported significantly lower self-esteem than nonvictims on
most of the subscales until the 1-year assessment. At that time, self, others, and parents were still sources of lower esteem for the victims. At 18
months postcrime, only the Self subscale was significant and at 2 years
only the Parent subscale was significant.

The longitudinal comparison of rape and robbery victims (Resick,
1988) yielded differences on the Tennessee Self-Concept Scale (TSCS; Fitts,
1965) for 1 year following the crime. Moreover, the TSCS was the only
scale used in the study that resulted in differences between women who
were raped versus those who were both raped and robbed. Analyses were
conducted on three groups: rape victims, robbery victims, and rape-robbery victims. The TSCS consists of an overall self-esteem score and eight
subscales that are different from those assessed by the SRI. The three victim groups differed on overall self-esteem at 1, 3, and 6 months postcrime
and there were trends (p = .07) at the 12- and 18-month assessments.

Post hoc analyses revealed that at 1 and 3 months postassault, rape
and robbery victims continued to have greater self-esteem than rape-robbery victims. At 6 months postcrime, robbery victims continued to have
greater self-esteem than rape-robbery victims. On the multivariate analyses of variance (MANOVAs) for the subscales, there were differences at
all assessment sessions through 1 year. Patterns changed somewhat from
session to session, but overall, rape-robbery victims had lower esteem
regarding physical self, social self, and identity than either rape victims
or robbery victims.

Although there was no comparison group, Resick et al. (1988) found
substantial long-term problems with self-esteem in rape victims seeking

treatment. They found that at the time they entered therapy, the average TSCS scores of rape victims were one-half to one standard deviation below the population norms for the scale. Schnicke and Resick (1990) examined the relationship between self-blame and self-esteem in treatment-seeking rape victims. They found that attributions of self-blame predicted higher self-criticism scores on the TSCS.

Social Adjustment

In some ways the subscales of the Self-Report Inventory may reflect social adjustment as well as self-esteem, because the scales concern work, authorities, parents, children, and others. The other major instrument that has been used to assess social adjustment is the Social Adjustment Scale (SAS) by Weissman and Paykel (1974). In addition to an overall adjustment score, the scale assesses work, social and leisure, extended family, marital, parental, family unit, and economic functioning.

Resick et al. (1981) examined social adjustment in rape victims and nonvictims for 1 year postcrime. They found that the victims had poorer overall economic and social and leisure adjustment for 2 months after the crime than nonvictims. Work adjustment was impaired for 8 months. Marital, parental, and family unit adjustment was not impaired at all, and extended family adjustment was affected for 1 month. To determine the effects of repeated assessment, three other groups of rape victims were tested once at 2, 4, or 8 months postcrime. The single-tested groups at 4 and 8 months were having significantly more social adjustment problems than the longitudinal sample at the same time periods. Perhaps participation in a longitudinal research project lent credibility to the reactions of rape victims such that significant others provided more social support and fostered social adjustment.

Because work adjustment appeared to be a particular problem following crime, Resick (1988) included the work subscale in the battery comparing rape and robbery victims. She found no differences between the groups at the five sessions included in that study. However, another measure of social functioning, the interpersonal sensitivity scale from the SCL-90-R, was found to be more elevated in rape than robbery victims at 3 and 6 months postcrime. Kilpatrick and Veronen (1984) found that victims differed from nonvictims on interpersonal sensitivity until the 18-month assessment and then again at the 2-year assessment.

Social adjustment, measured with the SAS, was also assessed in two studies of long-term reactions. Ellis et al. (1981) found that rape victims differed from controls in only one area, family adjustment. In their randomly surveyed population sample follow-up, Kilpatrick et al. (1987) found that a history of rape was associated with current social adjustment problems. Completed rape was particularly associated with social and leisure, family unit, and marital adjustment problems. They also found that rape victims were 5.8 times more likely than nonvictims of crime and 4.5 times more likely than nonrape victims to be suffering from social phobia as determined by the Mental Health Problem Interview.

Sexual Functioning

Problems in long-term sexual functioning have been observed by a number of researchers (Becker, Abel, & Skinner, 1979; Becker, Skinner, Abel, & Cichon, 1986; Becker, Skinner, Abel, & Treacy, 1982; Burgess & Holmstrom, 1979b; Ellis, Calhoun, & Atkeson, 1980; Feldman-Summers et al., 1979; Miller, Williams, & Bernstein, 1982). Sexual dysfunctions are among the most long-lasting problems experienced by rape victims. The most immediate reaction is probably avoidance of sex. Ellis et al. (1980) found that of the rape victims who had been sexually active prior to the crime, 29% stopped having sex with their partner completely and 32% had sex less often at the 2-week postcrime assessment. At the 4-week assessment 43% of the sample had not been sexually active. However, by 1 year postcrime, the frequency of sexual activity had returned to normal levels for those women who had sex frequently or somewhat frequently before the crime. Women who had sex infrequently before the crime had not returned to prerape levels at the end of a year. Continued avoidance is apparently easier for those women who do not have a regular partner in their lives.

Burgess and Holmstrom (1979b) found very similar patterns. Seventy-eight percent of their sample of 81 sexual assault victims had been sexually active at the time of the crime. Of those women, 38% gave up sex for at least 6 months and 33% decreased their frequency of sexual activity. At the 4- to 6-year follow-up, 30% still considered themselves not recovered.

Studies comparing the sexual satisfaction of rape victims with nonvictims (or robbery victims) are all consistent in their findings that rape survivors experience less sexual satisfaction (Feldman-Summers et al., 1979; Orlando & Koss, 1983; Resick, 1986) and more sexual dysfunctions (Becker et al., 1982; Becker et al., 1986; Kilpatrick et al., 1987; Resick, 1986) even when the rape was unacknowledged by the victim (Orlando & Koss, 1983).

In probably the largest study of sexual functioning in sexual assault survivors, Becker et al. (1986) determined the frequency and types of sexual dysfunctions in 372 survivors of sexual assault including rape, attempted rape, incest and child molestation, compared to 99 nonvictims. They found that 59% of the sexual assault victims had at least one sexual dysfunction compared to 17% of the comparison sample. Of the sexually dysfunctional sexual assault victim sample, 69% reported that the assault was directly responsible for the development of their sexual problems. An analysis of this subsample of 152 sexual assault victims revealed that the vast majority of them (88%) were suffering from early-response-cycle-inhibiting problems, which include fear of sex, arousal dysfunction, and desire dysfunction. Compared to the dysfunctional nonassaulted women, the sexual assault survivors were more likely to experience fear of sex and arousal dysfunction. Unfortunately, this study did not compare the different types of sexual assault so the differential effect of rape, incest, sexual molestation, or attempted rape on sexual functioning is not yet known.

Other Psychological Reactions to Rape

Although less frequently reported, there are some other psychological symptoms and problems that must be noted. As measured by the SCL-90-R or the diagnostic interview, rape victims are more likely to have obsessive-compulsive symptoms than nonvictims (Kilpatrick & Veronen, 1984; Kilpatrick et al., 1987) or robbery victims (Resick, 1988) for an extended period of time. Kilpatrick and Veronen (1984) found differences between victim and nonvictim comparison samples until 18 months, and Kilpatrick et al. (1987) found a history of rape to be associated with current obsessive-compulsive symptoms in their population sample follow-up. Although Resick (1988) found no differences between rape and robbery victims at 1 month postcrime, rape victims reported more obsessive-compulsive symptoms than robbery victims at 3, 6, and 12 months. Burnam et al. (1988) found more frequent obsessive-compulsive disorder in sexual assault victims than nonvictims.

The Profile of Mood States and the SCL-90-R have several other subscales that have differentiated victims from nonvictims. In addition to depression and anxiety, victims report more anger and hostility (Kilpatrick & Veronen, 1984; Kilpatrick et al., 1987), fatigue (Ellis et al., 1981; Kilpatrick & Veronen, 1984), and confusion (Kilpatrick & Veronen, 1984) than nonvictims for extended periods of time.

Burnam et al. (1988) reported that sexual assault victims were more likely to develop alcohol abuse and dependence than nonvictims, but they also reported that male victims were more likely to develop such problems than female victims. Age at the time of the assault was also related to the onset of alcohol abuse. Those victims who were age 15 or younger at the time of the assault were more likely to develop an alcohol problem.

The Rape in America Survey by Kilpatrick et al. (1992) also examined alcohol and drug use. They found that compared to nonvictims, rape victims were 3.4 times more likely to have used marijuana (52% versus 16%); 6 times more likely to have used cocaine (15.5% versus

2.5%); 10 times more likely to have used other hard drugs (12% versus 1%); and 5 times more likely to have used prescription drugs nonmedically (15% versus 3%). Compared to rape victims without PTSD, those with PTSD had much higher rates. For example, those with PTSD were 5 times more likely to have two or more major alcohol-related problems and 4 times more likely to have two or more serious drug-related problems.

Finally, the development of more severe psychopathology subsequent to rape should not be overlooked. Although psychosis has not typically been evaluated in rape victims, they frequently score higher on the psychoticism and paranoid ideation subscales from the SCL-90-R (Kilpatrick & Veronen, 1984; Kilpatrick et al., 1987; Resick, 1988) than either nonvictims or victims of other crimes. Elevations could reflect feelings of fear, alienation, or confusion regarding symptoms such as flashbacks, or could reflect more severe thought disorders.

In the population survey of female crime victims, Kilpatrick, Best, et al. (1985) found rape victims more likely to have suffered a "nervous breakdown" than either nonvictims or other crime victims. Because the term "nervous breakdown" was self-defined by respondents, it is not possible to determine what proportion of the 16% reporting breakdowns were describing acute psychotic reactions versus anxiety attacks, depressive reactions, or severe PTSD. Psychosis, as assessed by the clinical interview, did not appear to be associated with rape in the follow-up study (Kilpatrick et al., 1987). Burnam et al. (1988), in their probability survey, found that sexual assault was not related to a later onset of mania or schizophrenia. Nevertheless, clinicians and researchers should be aware that severe reactions could occur in some victims of rape, particularly in those who are susceptible to such disorders prior to the rape.

Conclusions

Overall, a pattern of reactions has emerged in the research that indicates that rape is a life event that causes considerable upheaval in a victim's psychological functioning for a considerable period of time, perhaps the rest of her life. The research on fear and anxiety has been remarkably consistent; rape victims suffer fear and anxiety reactions, including sexual fears and dysfunctions, that abate somewhat over the first few months postcrime but then continue at an even level for an indefinite period of time.

The findings on depression are not so consistent. Some studies found that depressive symptoms had returned to normal within a few months after the assault. Other studies found that victims continued to experience depressive symptoms for much longer periods of time. And those studies that assessed victims after an extended period of time found very high rates of suicidal ideation among them. It is not clear whether participating in assessment research fairly soon after the crime may have a therapeutic effect or whether there are some differences in the samples of women who report victimization and are willing to participate in research versus those who either do not report their victimization or refuse to participate in research. Nevertheless, it is clear that researchers and clinicians should be aware of this discrepancy in the literature and be sensitive to the importance of depressive symptoms and suicidal ideation and attempts in the aftermath of rape.

Other types of symptoms warrant further research. Self-esteem has been studied all too little, but there is evidence that it may be profoundly affected by sexual assault. Interpersonal functioning is difficult to assess in all its complexities but certainly is affected by rape and needs further investigation. Issues such as loss of trust in others are frequently noted by clinicians but have not been subjected to empirical scrutiny. It is clear that although the research has come a long way in delineating the most typical patterns of reactions and symptoms, there are some areas that need to be examined further.

VARIABLES AFFECTING RECOVERY

Despite the relative consistency of findings in the literature regarding patterns of reaction and recovery, individuals within samples do not all react identically. Some women have relatively mild or short-term reactions whereas others are devastated by rape. A wide range of variables have been examined in an effort to predict those women who will need more assistance in recovering from rape, as well as to obtain more information that may play a role in theory development.

Preassault Variables

Demographic Variables

The role of such demographic variables as age, race, and socioeconomic status (SES) in the extent of reactions and recovery from rape are somewhat equivocal at this time. In both the final analyses from their longitudinal study (Kilpatrick & Veronen, 1984) and their population survey (Kilpatrick, Best, et al., 1985), Kilpatrick and his colleagues found that demographic variables had little effect on victims' responses to crime. Other researchers also found that some demographic variables do not play a role in recovery (Becker et al., 1982; Ruch & Leon, 1983). However, Atkeson et al. (1982) found that greater age and lower SES predicted depression at 12 months postcrime. In a study in Hawaii, Ruch and Chandler (1980) found that Asian victims suffered greater trauma than Caucasian victims and that adult victims expressed greater trauma than child rape (nonincest) victims. Burgess and Holmstrom (1978) also found with their 4- to 6-year follow-up that less economically advantaged rape survivors had more symptoms.

Rather than examining age as a continuous variable, Thornhill and Thornhill (1990a, 1990b) compared three groups: prereproductive, reproductive-aged, and postreproductive women. Using a very limited outcome measure of 13 items they labeled "psychological pain," they found that reproductive-aged women were more traumatized even when the level of force and violence was controlled. These findings need replication because 5 of the 13 variables were concerned with heterosocial and sexual functioning, which by definition, are usually of more concern to reproductive-aged women.

Prior Psychological Functioning and Life Stressors

There is stronger evidence that prior psychological functioning or life stressors play a role in recovery. Although Kilpatrick and Veronen (1984) did not find that psychiatric history predicted distress level at 3 months, several other studies have found such a connection. Ruch and Leon (1983) found preexisting mental health problems one of the most influential variables affecting the level of trauma at intake, which was a maximum of 48 hours after the rapes. Although a history of psychotherapy or hospitalization was not associated with elevations in depression, fear, or anxiety, Frank, Turner, Stewart, Jacob, and West (1981) found that victims with a history of psychotropic medication, alcohol abuse, suicidal ideation or attempts were more distressed in the first month after the rape than victims without such histories.

In another study, Frank and Anderson (1987) found that based on clinical interviews, those victims with a prior diagnosis (using *DSM-III* criteria) were significantly more likely to meet criteria for a psychiatric disorder in the first month after rape than those with no diagnosable disorder in their histories. With regard to longer-term recovery, Atkeson et al. (1982) found that depression, suicidal history, and sexual adjustment prior to the rape significantly predicted depression scores at 4 months postassault. Prior anxiety attacks and obsessive-compulsive behaviors predicted depression at 8 months postcrime. At 12 months postrape, prior anxiety attacks, obsessive-compulsive behaviors, and psychiatric treatment history predicted depression.

Prior victimization and other life stressors have also been examined as possible variables affecting recovery. The research on the effect of prior victimization has been very inconsistent. Ruch and Leon (1983) evaluated rape victims within 48 hours postcrime and then again at 2 weeks postcrime. They found that women with no history of prior victimization showed a decrease in their trauma levels, whereas those with prior victimization exhibited an increase in trauma scores across the 2 weeks. They concluded that women who were multiple-incident victims were especially at risk for delayed responses.

In contrast, Frank, Turner, and Stewart (1980) and Frank and Anderson (1987) found that victims of more than one sexual assault did not differ significantly from single-incident victims on standardized measures of depression, anxiety, or fear from 1 to 4 months postrape. However, the multiple incident victims did report poorer global social adjustment and greater disruption in social functioning in their immediate household. With regard to longer-term reactions, McCahill, Meyer, and Fishman (1979) found that multiple-incident rape victims were not different from single-incident victims at 1 year postrape except that multiple-incident victims reported more intense nightmares and a greater fear of being home alone.

Several studies have examined the effect of prior victimization of any type, not just prior rapes. Participants in Burgess and Holmstrom's (1979a) 4- to 6-year follow-up reported differences in recovery depending on their history of victimization. Eighty-six percent of participants with no prior history of victimization said they felt recovered, but only 53% of victims with such a history felt recovered on follow-up. In assessing treatment-seeking rape victims, Marhoefer-Dvorak, Resick, Hutter, and Girelli (1988) found that single- and multiple-incident rape victims did not differ on any of several standardized measures but those victims with a history of major victimization did differ on assertiveness and somatization. Women who had been victims of a crime that involved the threat or presence of bodily harm prior to the sexual assault reported that they were more assertive but had greater somatic symptoms.

Rather than analyzing prior victimization as a simple presence versus absence categorization, Resick (1988) has studied the extensiveness of prior victimization. Stepwise analyses were conducted to determine how a history of domestic violence, child physical abuse, emotional abuse, incest, observation of violence during childhood, and previous criminal victimization would affect reactions and recovery to a recent rape. Four summary scores were used as the measures of symptomatology: the global severity index (GSI) from the BSI, the total self-esteem score from the Tennessee Self-Concept Scale (TSCSTOT), the total score from the MFS (MFSTOT), and the total from the IES. Subjects' responses were examined at four points in time: 1, 6, 12, and 18 months postcrime.

IES scores were not predicted by these victimization variables at any point in time. History of previous criminal victimization predicted GSI scores at 1 month postcrime, but no other variables were predictive of symptom level at 1 month. At 6 months postcrime, GSI and MFSTOT were predicted by a more extensive history of domestic violence prior to the rape. Self-esteem was influenced by observation of violence in childhood. Fear, as measured by the MFS, was also predicted by a history of child sexual abuse. At 12 months postcrime, physical child abuse, emotional abuse, and prior criminal victimization predicted greater GSI and MFS scores. None of the variables predicted responses at 18 months postcrime. Resick (1988) concluded that although it appeared the victimization factors were related to recovery, there were no obvious and consistent patterns.

With regard to other life stressors, Ruch, Chandler, and Harter (1980) examined the presence of 11 life stressors during the year prior to the rape and found a curvilinear relationship. Women who had experienced major life changes were most traumatized, women with no changes were intermediate and those with minor changes were the least traumatized. Apparently, experience with some life stress may have an inoculating effect but too great a level of stress interferes with the development of coping methods needed to deal with an event as traumatic as rape. Looking at it somewhat differently, Kilpatrick and Veronen (1984) divided rape victims into four groups: low, moderately low, moderately high, and high distress. They found that the two more distressed groups were more likely to have suffered the loss of a spouse in the past year than the low distressed group.

Wirtz and Harrell (1987) examined the relationship of a number of nonvictimization life stress events with MFS scores at 1 and 3 months postcrime. They found that those events that could be construed as life-threatening (death of a friend, major illness) were associated with greater postrape fear, whereas other major, but non-life-threatening events (birth of a child, divorce) were associated with less fear. In fact, the subjects who reported the latter type of stressor in the year prior to the rape reported less fear than subjects who reported no stressors the previous year. The authors concluded that the element of vulnerability to perceived future harm is the link between past life-threatening events and levels of fear subsequent to rape.

Cognitive Appraisals

The effect of preassault cognitive appraisals on postassault functioning has not been studied a great deal at this point but there is some research available that has demonstrated that a perception of unique invulnerability may exacerbate reactions to traumatic events (Perloff, 1983). Apparently, those people who believe they control their lives and environments make the poorest adjustments to events that are out of their control. Further, two studies have found that rape victims who appraised the situation as "safe" prior to the assault had greater fear and depressive reactions than women who perceived themselves to be in a dangerous situation prior to the assault (Frank & Stewart, 1984; Schepple & Bart, 1983). The role of preassault cognitive appraisals and attributions warrants further study.

Although there are probably other relevant prerape variables that may affect reactions and recovery that have not been studied thus far (e.g., pre-existing social network and support or victim's coping style), it can be concluded that prior psychological problems or other major life stressors most probably impinge on the smooth recovery from a current trauma such as a rape. Examining it from a more positive direction, Kilpatrick and Veronen (1984) studied the low-distress group at 3 months postassault to see how they differed from the other rape victims. They concluded that these women were more likely to have higher self-esteem initially and were more likely to have had loving, intimate relationships with men in the year prior to the rape. And as mentioned before, they were also less likely to have experienced major life changes prior to the rape.

Assault Variables

Acquaintanceship Status

There has been a common assumption in the public arena that some rapes are worse than others. Rapes by strangers and those that are more violent (i.e., resulting in injuries) are assumed to be more traumatic for the victim. The available evidence, however, indicates that this may not be the case, particularly regarding the acquaintanceship status of victims and offenders. Hassell (1981) compared victims of stranger and non-stranger rape and found no differences in reactions or recovery except those who were attacked by acquaintances were more likely to have problems with their self-esteem initially. These differences had disappeared by 3 months postrape. McCahill et al. (1979) found that interviewers rated victims raped by casual acquaintances or relative strangers to be more severely maladjusted, than those who were raped by friends, family members, or total strangers.

Although Ellis et al. (1981) and Thornhill and Thornhill (1990c) found that women attacked by strangers had more problems with fear and depression afterward than women attacked by acquaintances, other researchers have not found this to be the case (Girelli, Resick, Marhoefer-Dvorak, & Hutter, 1986; Kilpatrick et al., 1987; Koss, Dinero, & Seibel, 1988; Resick, 1988). Kilpatrick et al. (1987) compared the impact of stranger, marital, and date rapes and found no differences in mental health among the three groups. Koss et al. (1988) found no differences in depression, state anxiety, or sexual satisfaction for victims raped by strangers, nonromantic acquaintances, casual dates, steady dates, or spouses/family members. However, they did find lower ratings of relationship quality among women who were raped by spouses/family members than the other groups of acquaintance rape victims. They also found that acquaintance rape victims were less likely to tell anyone about the incident.

Acquaintanceship with the assailant may affect the victim in other ways. Stewart et al. (1987) compared rape victims who sought out immediate treatment with those who delayed receiving treatment. Women who delayed treatment were more likely to have known their assailants and less likely to have physically defended themselves. Perhaps these women experience more self-blame or perhaps they expect that others will blame them or not believe them. Given that these women are just as likely to experience trauma reactions as those who are raped by strangers, it is unfortunate that they are not seeking help sooner, or not at all.

Level of Violence

Several studies have examined the effect that the brutality of the rape has on the victim's reactions by developing brutality scores or indexes based on several assault variables. Results of these efforts have been mixed. Atkeson et al. (1982) found the amount of rape "trauma" did not predict later reactions. Sales, Baum, and Shore (1984) observed that neither the presence nor extent of violence per se was strongly associated with victim reactions. However, Cluss, Boughton, Frank, Stewart, and West (1983), Ellis et al. (1981), and Norris and Feldman-Summers (1981) all found a combination of assault variables to be predictive of greater distress on some measures.

Cluss et al. (1983) found that their "threat index" was significantly and positively correlated with self-esteem at an initial assessment but not at the 6- or 12-month follow-up. Norris and Feldman-Summers (1981) found assault variables to be predictive of problems with psychosomatic symptoms but not with sexual satisfaction or frequency, or the level of reclusiveness. Examination of individual assault variables has also yielded mixed results. Girelli et al. (1986) found that none of eight assault variables predicted a range of assessed symptoms in rape victims seeking treatment. Sales et al. (1984) found that threats against the victim's life predicted symptomatology within the first 3 months after the assault but not at the follow-up assessment 6 months later. Four assault variables predicted follow-up symptomatology only: the number of assailants, physical threat, injury requiring medical care, and medical complications. Victims who developed PTSD in the Kilpatrick et al. (1987) follow-up study were more likely to have been seriously injured than those who did not develop PTSD but did not differ as to whether a weapon was present. Resick (1988) found that almost none of six assault variables predicted reactions of rape victims over time. The extent of threats predicted global severity of symptoms at 6 months postcrime and restraint predicted PTSD symptoms, also at 6 months postcrime.

Within-Crime Victim Reactions

Sales et al. (1984) have suggested that "it is possible that the *actual* violence of an attack is less crucial to victim reaction than the *felt threat*" (p. 125). A few studies have examined this possibility. Girelli et al. (1986) found that subjective distress was predictive of later fear reactions whereas other assault variables such as threats, weapons, and injuries were not. Kilpatrick et al. (1987) also found cognitive appraisal of life threat to predict later PTSD. Resick (1988) examined the effect of behavior (active, passive, and aggressive resistance), emotions (anger, anxious, calm), and specific cognitions regarding the perception of imminent death or injury, on reactions and recovery. She found that at 1 month postcrime, none of the variables were predictive of symptoms or self-esteem. However, at the other time intervals, greater active resistance was predictive of less distress and greater anger or anxiety during the assault was predictive of greater distress.

In a more recent study, Resick, Churchill, and Falsetti (1990) reported on the within-assault emotions and cognitive states of rape victims. They found that confusion/disorientation during the crime was the best predictor of subsequent chronic PTSD symptoms. The single variable accounted for more than 40% of the variance in their PTSD symptom scores.

Postassault Variables

Postassault factors are the least studied variables that may affect recovery. For example, the effect of participating in the criminal justice system on victim recovery has been studied very little, perhaps because so few cases actually reach trial. The effectiveness of the type of counseling that is usually provided has received very little attention as well. Social support has been mentioned frequently as an important variable but has not been researched extensively thus far. Some other variables such as coping methods by the victim, attributions, or the effect of initial reactions have received a little attention.

Initial Reactions

Kilpatrick, Veronen, and Best (1985) examined how initial reactions affect victims' functioning at 3 months postrape. They found that the level of distress that victims experienced within the first few weeks after rape was highly predictive of subsequent distress. Rothbaum et al. (1992) also found that almost 90% of rape victims who developed chronic PTSD could be correctly classified within the first 2 weeks after the crime.

This finding might appear obvious but it is important to consider that PTSD diagnosis is made when reactions are delayed as well as immediate. Most of the longitudinal studies have found that victim reactions stabilize at 3 months and then continue at the same level from 3 months for as long as the studies continued to assess their samples. Kilpatrick, Veronen, and Best (1985) concluded that delayed reactions are probably not a significant problem for most rape victims and that an assessment of initial reactions will predict which victims are most likely to have difficulty recovering from rape. However, it should be noted that this was not a study of child sexual assault. It is possible that there may be delays in symptomatology among child victims because entering a new developmental level may trigger reactions that were not salient before (e.g., problems in sexual functioning).

Participation in the Criminal Justice System

Few studies thus far have examined the effect of participation in the criminal justice system on victim recovery. Cluss et al. (1983) found that at 12 months postrape there were no differences in the level of depression or social adjustment between those who wished to prosecute the crime and those who did not. However, women who wished to prosecute reported greater self-esteem. Further, women who wished to prosecute and were not able to (no arrest, insufficient evidence, etc.) showed better work adjustment at 6 months postcrime and more rapid improvement in self-esteem than those women who were proceeding with prosecution. Perhaps the desire to prosecute reflects a greater externalization of blame for the event.

Resick (1988), as part of her longitudinal study, found 24 rape and robbery victims who completed the criminal justice system process (through trial or a guilty plea). She compared them with 24 subjects who had not participated at all because no suspect was ever apprehended. The only finding was that the criminal justice participants reported greater self-esteem at 6 months postcrime. Given the number of analyses conducted, Resick advised cautious interpretation.

Sales et al. (1984) reported weak and inconsistent findings with their sample of rape victims. However, it appeared that victims who began the process by reporting the case and whose charges held showed fewer symptoms at the initial interview and the 6-month follow-up. There were also indications that further progress toward trial left victims with more symptoms. The authors suggested that extended court proceedings may inflict additional demands on these women and keep them in a victim role.

Although they were not studying the influence of the criminal justice system on victims directly, two studies (Calhoun et al., 1982; Kilpatrick, Veronen, & Resick, 1979b) have found indications that participating in court may be quite stressful. Using the MFS in both studies, the item "testifying in court" emerged as one of the most fear-provoking stimuli reported by victims when compared to nonvictims.

Social Support

Sales et al. (1984) have discussed the difficulty of measuring and interpreting how social support may affect victim reactions and recovery because postassault support is surely confounded by the quality and quantity of prerape relationships and because studies thus far have varied from very specific questions to global assessments of support. There have been no standardized scales used in studies on rape. Further, support may vary depending on the nature of the assault. It may be that more brutal or "stereotypic" rapes elicit more sustained social support. Sales et al. (1984) found a correlation between the violence of an assault and postassault family closeness. With that in mind, Ruch and Hennessy's (1982) finding that, at intake, 72% of their sample reported that their families were supportive and 87% reported having supportive friends, is encouraging. Unfortunately, the authors did not report whether this perception of support continued over time or whether the support influenced recovery.

Sales et al. (1984) reported that neither the initial reactions of significant others nor the quality of the victim's central relationship to a man at the time of the incident was related to her reaction. They did, however, find that victims reporting greater closeness to family members had fewer symptoms. Ruch and Chandler (1980) also found that victims with supportive families experienced lower levels of trauma fairly soon after the assault. Atkeson et al. (1982) found that social support predicted the level of depression the victims were experiencing at 4 and 8 months postrape. Norris and Feldman-Summers (1981) studied long-term reactions and found that the presence of understanding men and women in the victim's life was related to less reclusiveness.

Popiel and Susskind (1985) studied 25 rape victims 3 months postassault and did not find a relationship overall between social support and adjustment (using the SCL-90-R and the IES). However, they did find a relationship between the perception of supportiveness of physicians and adjustment. Generally physicians were viewed as the least supportive and female friends as the most supportive people following rape. West, Frank, Anderson, and Stewart (1987) asked 52 women to rate the supportive or unsupportive reactions they received from their social network in the first 2 to 4 weeks following being raped. They found that those women who had one or more important, unsupportive network members had more symptoms than the women with only neutral or supportive members. Further, Moss, Frank, and Anderson (1987) reported that poor spousal support was associated with more psychological symptoms postcrime, particularly when the lack of support was unexpected.

Resick (1988) examined perceived social support, the extent to which the rape victims talked about the crime, and the network size in predicting reactions over time. She found that the first two variables were predictive only at 1 month postcrime. Those women who perceived less social support and talked about the crime more were more likely to report greater overall distress. Cluss et al. (1983) examined positive and negative social network responses and found them to be unrelated to whether the women wished to prosecute the assailant.

Cognitive Appraisals and Attributions

Postrape cognitive appraisals and attributions can be viewed as reactions to the assault and as attempts to cope with the event and reactions. There is a growing body of literature that indicates that people have a strong need to search for the meaning of negative events (Silver & Wortman, 1980). Criminal victimization destroys the illusion that we live in a predictable, controllable, meaningful world. In a study of incest victims, Silver, Boon, and Stones (1983) found that those women who were still actively searching for the meaning of the experience were more likely to report recurrent, intrusive, and disruptive ruminations than those who were not. Women who had reported that they were able to make some sense out of their experience reported less psychological distress, better social adjustment, greater self-esteem, and greater resolution of the experience than women who were not able to find any meaning but were still searching.

At this time it is still unclear whether any answer to the question "Why me?" is sufficient to reduce stress, or whether some answers may actually increase the distress that victims experience following rape. Some researchers who have focused on self-blame (Bulman & Wortman, 1977; Lerner, 1980; Wortman, 1976) have proposed that victims are likely to accept responsibility for events in order to maintain a sense of control over their lives and to maintain the belief that the world is just and orderly. But at what cost are such attributions made? Janoff-Bulman (1979) hypothesized that self-blame serves an adaptive function but that behavioral self-blame should be associated with more effective postrape adjustment than characterological self-blame. Meyer and Taylor (1985) and Frazier (1990) did not find this to be the case. Although they, too, found high rates of self-blame in rape victims (50%), they found both characterological and behavioral self-blame were associated with poorer adjustment postrape. Schnicke and Resick (1990) also found that self-blame was associated with greater symptomatology, in particular depression, obsessive-compulsive symptoms, and self-criticism.

McCann, Sakheim, and Abrahamson (1988) have proposed that in response to traumatic events, ones' belief about oneself and the world are disrupted (or prior negative beliefs are confirmed). They proposed examining five areas of beliefs: safety, trust, power/competence, esteem, and intimacy. Resick and Schnicke developed a scale, the Personal Beliefs and Reactions Scale (PBRS), to assess these beliefs as well as self-blame, beliefs about rape, and cognitions that represent efforts to "undo" or not accept the rape (Resick & Schnicke, 1992b; Resick, Schnicke, & Markway, 1991). When the scale was given to 20 rape victims with a range of PTSD symptomatology, they found that intrusive symptoms were associated with more attempts at undoing and more negative beliefs about rape. Avoidance symptoms were significantly predicted by negative trust beliefs. Arousal symptoms were predicted by negative safety beliefs. These cognitions changed significantly following cognitive behavioral therapy.

Conclusions

The study of variables affecting recovery has produced more mixed results than research on symptom patterns. Perhaps this is due to differences in methodology. All but the earliest research on victim reactions has used standardized measures of symptomatology, frequently the same measures, such as the MFS or the SCL-90-R across studies. On the other hand, because there have been no standardized measures of history, assault variables, or postcrime variables for researchers to draw on, every group of researchers developed and used their own idiosyncratic scales. For example, a number of studies were reviewed that attempted to examine the effect of the brutality of the rape on subsequent functioning. Every study developed its own violence index and examined different outcome variables. It is almost impossible to compare these studies and draw conclusions with any confidence. In order to begin to attempt to replicate findings it will be necessary to standardize the methodology that is adopted by researchers in the future.

Nevertheless, some very general conclusions can be attempted. It appears that preassault, assault, and postassault variables may all play a role in victim reactions. Victims' psychological functioning prior to the crime and during the crime are likely to explain some of the variability that is observed in reactions among rape victims. Research on the effect of circumstances of the crime was mixed, but it is possible that the actual amount of violence involved may not be as influential as the victim's appraisal of danger. Initial indications are that social support plays a role in recovery, but more research is needed to investigate this further. It is clear that reactions to sexual assault are multivariate. Not only should researchers continue to search for important variables that influence reactions and recovery, but they should begin to examine the interactions of variables.

DISCUSSION AND RECOMMENDATIONS

As should be apparent by now, reactions to sexual assault are multi-faceted. None of the widely held theories of victim reactions are adequate in explaining the array of symptoms observed and the range of variables that may affect reactions and recovery. Over the past decade there have been three major theories of rape reactions: crisis theory (Burgess & Holmstrom, 1974; Sales et al., 1984), behavioral theory (Holmes & St. Lawrence, 1983; Jones & Barlow, 1990; Kilpatrick, Veronen, & Resick, 1982), and an attribution theory of coping (Janoff-Bulman, 1979, 1992; Meyer & Taylor, 1985). In their approach to the problem, they greatly resemble the parable of the blind men and the elephant. Each interprets the problem from the small part they have access to with their research.

Describing rape reactions as a crisis is axiomatic. However, crisis theory does little to explain why certain symptom patterns are observed and has completely failed to account for the long-term reactions that most typically occur. Research on attributions (e.g., Janoff-Bulman, 1992) demonstrates that cognitive appraisals of blame and postassault attempts at coping may play a role in recovery. However, as a theory, it is too narrow to explain the full range of symptoms or the pattern of improvement in recovery that is most typically observed. These attributions could be considered as intervening variables within a more comprehensive theory of victim reactions. A comprehensive theory of victim reactions is needed that can incorporate all of the disparate findings that have been reviewed in this article without becoming so diluted as to become nonpredictive.

Behavioral theory gives an adequate explanation of the development of fear and anxiety through classical conditioning and operant avoidance, but does little to explain the range of other symptoms observed or to incorporate the variables that affect reactions. Further, if rape reactions were accounted for only by classical and operant conditioning stimulated by the life-threatening nature of the assault, then rape reactions should be no more severe than reactions to robbery or aggravated assault. However, the research indicates that rape victims suffer more severe reactions than victims of other types of crime. These differences must be accounted for by differences in the crimes themselves or in the way that victims or others behave after the crime. Further research is needed to delineate these factors in order to incorporate them into theory.

One behavioral theory that has attempted to account for some of these variables is a theory by Jones and Barlow (1990). They compare PTSD with panic disorder in terms of the development of anxiety through anxious apprehension. This state of anxious apprehension begins with biological vulnerability. On being exposed to a negative life event, the person develops alarm reactions that lead to chronic activation of anxiety and anxious apprehension. Social support and coping skills serve as moderating variables. Although more inclusive, this theory does not explain why rape produces higher rates of PTSD than other life threatening events such as aggravated assault or natural disasters. The model also does not account for the other affective reactions that are observed in rape victims such as depression, humiliation, or guilt.

Over the past few years attention has been directed to information processing theories. A narrow information processing theory of PTSD as an anxiety disorder proposed by both Chemtob, Roitblat, Hamada, Carlson and Twentyman (1988) and Foa, Steketee, and Olasov-Rothbaum (1989) views PTSD as the result of the development of a fear network. The network consists of stimuli, responses, and meaning elements regarding the traumatic event. This network functions as a program to stimulate avoidance behavior. Resick and Schnicke (1990, 1992a) have proposed that reactions represent more than a fear network. Victims report a wide range of affective reactions to traumatic events, not just fear. They proposed that PTSD results from an inability to integrate the event with prior beliefs and experiences. When new, incompatible events occur, the person either assimilates (alters) the new information to fit prior beliefs, or the beliefs are altered (accommodated) to accept the event. Resick and Schnicke (1992a) have also proposed that some victims may overaccommodate to the event (i.e., "No one can be trusted" or "I am never safe."). PTSD symptoms of intrusion and avoidance represent unsuccessful attempts to accommodate or assimilate the event.

McCann et al. (1988) have proposed a similar theory of trauma reactions that is much broader in scope than the other information processing theories and is developed from Horowitz's theory (1976) on the adaptation of people to stressful events, and the work of Piaget and Beck. They propose that people develop core schemas about themselves, others, and the world in five areas that are likely to be affected by victimization: safety, trust, power/competence, esteem, and intimacy. These schemas affect adaptation to and are affected by life experiences. A traumatic experience such as rape disrupts prior positive beliefs and appears to confirm preexisting negative beliefs. Clearly, with theorists converging on information processing theory from several directions, it will be important to begin conducting research to test these theories.

Thus far, no extant theories on rape-related PTSD have incorporated the emerging findings on the biological changes that are associated with PTSD. Although it is beyond the scope of this article to review the biological correlates of PTSD, there have been a number of notable findings with regard to sympathetic nervous system hyperarousal, and dysfunctions of the hypothalamic-pituitary-adrenocortical axis and the endogenous opoid system (Friedman, 1991; Mason, Griller, Kosten, & Yehuda, 1990; Orr, 1990; Pitman et al., 1990; Yehuda, Southwick, Perry, Mason, & Griller, 1990). Most of the research on these biological changes has been conducted with combat veterans. Research on rape victims is almost nonexistent and needs to be conducted. Comprehensive theories of victim reactions, and PTSD in particular, will need to account for the role of these biological dysfunctions in the development and maintenance of symptoms.

Research on victim reactions must also attend to methodological differences among studies that could account for the differences in findings. For example, when variables are categorized and subjected to analyses of variance (ANOVAs), more information may be lost than when they are treated as continuous variables and analyzed by means of regression analyses. However, with regression analyses, the magnitude of the relationship must be examined so that weak findings are not given more importance than they deserve. Multiple dependent measures have been treated differently from study to study. Some studies have analyzed data by means of multiple ANOVAs or correlations, which may lead to problems with experimentwise error. Few studies have taken this into account. Multivariate analysis procedures have been used in some studies but unfortunately they require a large sample size that is sometimes difficult to obtain with as sensitive a problem as rape. In some cases the lack of findings may reflect small sample sizes rather than no differences between groups or variables.

Despite the possible discrepancies in findings due to methodological differences, it is possible to make some public policy recommendations. First of all, it is quite probable that although professionals and the public have become aware that rape is traumatic, the extent to which it disrupts victims' lives and the length of time that it takes to recover have been underestimated. More public education and professional training are needed.

Increased public education could also help in several other respects. Women still frequently blame themselves for rape and reporting rates remain low. Public education could help remove the stigma from reporting the crime. Women who tell others about what has happened are more likely to receive support and have greater access to counseling and therapy should they need it. Public education could also help remove the stigma about receiving counseling. Many people still believe that one has to be "crazy" to need therapy and that talking about one's problems is not likely to be helpful. A greater understanding of the impact of rape and of the benefits of therapy could prevent victims from feeling isolated or despairing of the future.

Finally, there is a need for more long-term care for victims of rape. Most rape crisis centers and victim assistance agencies have been established to counsel victims in the immediate aftermath of the crime or to help them through criminal prosecution. Victims who continue to experience symptoms beyond these time periods may feel that they are on their own or that they are having a uniquely bad reaction. It is important that agencies who work with victims provide access to long-term care and conduct outreach efforts directly with victims or through the media. Women who do not report the crime to the police should not be made to feel that they are not eligible for services. Further, it is possible that some reactions develop after a delay because of changes in the victim's life or developmental level. For example, sex therapy for an adolescent rape victim may not be appropriate until she is older and/or has developed a relationship. Victims should be made aware that they may receive services whenever they are needed and that recovery may be an ongoing process that may occur in stages.

REFERENCES

Atkeson, B.M., Calhoun, K.S., Resick, P.A., & Ellis, RM. (1982). Victims of rape: Repeated assessment of depressive symptoms. *Journal of Consulting and Clinical Psychology, 50,* 96-102.

Beck, A.T., Ward, C.H., Mendelsohn, M., Mock, J., & Erbaugh, J. (1961). An inventory for measuring depression. *Archives of General Psychiatry, 41,* 561-571.

Becker, J.V., Abel, G.G., & Skinner, L.J. (1979). The impact of a sexual assault on the victim's sexual life. *Victimology: An International Journal, 4,* 229-235.

Becker, J.V., Skinner, L.J., Abel, G.G., & Cichon, J. (1986). Level of postassault sexual functioning in rape and incest victims. *Archives of Sexual Behavior, 15,* 37-49.

Becker, J.V., Skinner, L.J., Abel, G.G., & Treacy, E.C. (1982). Incidence and types of sexual dysfunctions in rape and incest victims. *Journal of Sex and Marital Therapy, 8,* 65-74.

Brown, O. (1961). The development of a self-report inventory and its function in a mental health assessment battery. *American Psychologist, 16,* 402.

Bulman, R.J., & Wortman, C.B. (1977). Attributions of blame and coping in the real world: Severe accident victims react to their lot. *Journal of Personality and Social Psychology, 35,* 351-363.

Burgess, A.W., & Holmstrom, L.L. (1974). Rape trauma syndrome. *American Journal of Psychiatry, 131,* 981-986.

Burgess, A.W., & Holmstrom, L.L. (1978). Recovery from rape and prior life stress. *Research in Nursing and Health, 1,* 165-174.

Burgess, A.W, & Holmstrom, L.L. (1979a). *Rape: Crisis and recovery.* Bowie, MD: Robert J. Brady.

Burgess, A.W., & Holmstrom, L.L. (1979b). Rape: Sexual disruption and recovery. *American Journal of Orthopsychiatry, 49,* 648-657.

Burnam, M.A., Stein, J.A., Golding, J.M., Siegel, J.M., Sorenson, S.B., Forsythe, A.B., & Telles, C.A. (1988). Sexual assault and mental disorders in a community population. *Journal of Consulting and Clinical Psychology, 56,* 843-850.

Calhoun, K.S., Atkeson, B.M., & Resick, P.A. (1982). A longitudinal examination of fear reactions in victims of rape. *Journal of Counseling Psychology, 29,* 655-661.

Chemtob, C., Roitblat, H.L., Hamada, R.S., Carlson, J.G., & Twentyman, C.T. (1988). A cognitive action theory of post-traumatic stress disorder. *Journal of Anxiety Disorders, 2,* 253-275.

Cluss, P.A., Boughton, J., Frank, L.E., Stewart, B.D., & West, D. (1983). The rape victims: Psychological correlates of participation in the legal process. *Criminal Justice and Behavior, 10,* 342-357.

Derogatis, L.R. (1977). *SCL-90-R manual.* Baltimore: Johns Hopkins University Press.

Ellis, E.M., Atkeson, B.M., & Calhoun, K.S. (1981). An assessment of long-term reaction to rape. *Journal of Abnormal Psychology, 90,* 263-266.

Ellis, E.M., Calhoun, K.S., & Atkeson, B.M. (1980). Sexual dysfunctions in victims of rape: Victims may experience a loss of sexual arousal and frightening flashbacks even one year after the assault. *Women and Health, 5,* 39-47.

Feldman-Summers, S., Gordon, P.E., & Meagher, J.R. (1979). The impact of rape on sexual satisfaction. *Journal of Abnormal Psychology, 88,* 101-105.

Fitts, W.H. (1965). *Manual: Tennessee self-concept scale.* Nashville, TN: Counselor Recordings and Tests.

Foa, E.B., Steketee, G., & Olasov-Rothbaum, B. (1989). Behavior/cognitive conceptualizations of post-traumatic stress disorder. *Behavior Therapy, 20,* 155-176.

Frank, E., & Anderson, B.P. (1987). Psychiatric disorders in rape victims: Past history and current symptomatology. *Comprehensive Psychiatry, 28,* 77-82.

Frank, E., & Stewart, B.D. (1984). Depressive symptoms in rape victims: A revisit. *Journal of Affective Disorders, 7,* 77-95.

Frank, E., Turner, S.M., & Duffy, B. (1979). Depressive symptoms in rape victims. *Journal of Affective Disorders, 1,* 269-277.

Frank, E., Turner, S.M., & Stewart, B.D. (1980). Initial response to rape: The impact of factors within the rape situation. *Journal of Behavioral Assessment, 2,* 39-53.

Frank, E., Turner, S.M., Stewart, B.D., Jacob, J. & West, D. (1981). Past psychiatric symptoms and the response to sexual assault. *Comprehensive Psychiatry, 22,* 479-487.

Frazier, P.A. (1990). Victim attributions and post-rape trauma. *Journal of Personality and Social Psychology, 59,* 298-304.

Friedman, M.J. (1991). Biological approaches to the diagnosis and treatment of post-traumatic stress disorder. *Journal of Traumatic Stress, 4,* 67-91.

Girelli, S.A., Resick, P.A., Marhoefer-Dvorak, S., & Hutter, C.K. (1986). Subjective distress and violence during rape: Their effects on long-term fear. *Violence and Victims, 1,* 35-45.

Hamilton, M. (1960). A rating scale for depression. *Journal of Neurology, Neurosurgery, and Psychiatry, 23,* 56-62.

Hassell, R.A. (1981, March). *The impact of stranger versus nonstranger rape: A longitudinal study.* Paper presented at the 8th Annual Conference of the Association for Women in Psychology, Boston, MA.

Holmes, M.R., & St. Lawrence, J.S. (1983). Treatment of rape-induced trauma: Proposed behavioral conceptualization and review of the literature. *Clinical Psychology Review, 3,* 417-433.

Horowitz, M.J. (1976). *Stress response syndromes*. New York: Jason Aronson.

Horowitz, M.J., Wilner, N., & Alverez, W. (1979). Impact of Event Scale: A measure of subjective distress. *Psychosomatic Medicine, 41,* 209-218.

Janoff-Bulman, R. (1979). Characterological versus behavioral self-blame: Inquiries into depression and rape. *Journal of Personality and Social Psychology, 37,* 1798-1809.

Janoff-Bulman, R. (1992). *Shattered assumptions*. New York: Free Press.

Jones, J.C., & Barlow, D.H. (1990). The etiology of post-traumatic stress disorder. *Clinical Psychology Review, 10,* 299-328.

Kilpatrick, D.G., Best, C.L., Veronen, L.J., Amick, A.E., Villeponteaux, L.A., & Ruff, G.A. (1985). Mental health correlates of criminal victimization: A random community survey. *Journal of Consulting and Clinical Psychology, 53,* 866-873.

Kilpatrick, D.G., Edmunds, C.N., & Seymour, A.K. (1992). *Rape in America: A report to the nation*. Arlington, VA: National Victim Center.

Kilpatrick, D.G., & Veronen, L.J. (1983, December). *The aftermath of rape: A three-year follow-up*. Paper presented at the World Congress of Behavior Therapy, 17th Annual Convention of the Association for the Advancement of Behavior Therapy, Washington, DC.

Kilpatrick, D.G., & Veronen, L.J. (1984, February). *Treatment of fear and anxiety in victims of rape* (Final report, grant #MH29602). Washington, DC: National Institute of Mental Health.

Kilpatrick, D.G., Veronen, L.J., & Best, C.J. (1985). Factors predicting psychological distress among rape victims. In C.R. Figley (Ed.), *Trauma and its wake*. New York: Brunner/Mazel.

Kilpatrick, D.G., Veronen, L.J., & Resick, P.A. (1979a). The aftermath of rape: Recent empirical findings. *American Journal of Orthopsychiatry, 49,* 658-669.

Kilpatrick, D.G., Veronen, L.J., & Resick, P.A. (1979b). Assessment of the aftermath of rape: Changing patterns of fear. *Journal of Behavioral Assessment, 1,* 133-148.

Kilpatrick, D.G., Veronen, L.J., & Resick, P.A. (1982). Psychological sequelae to rape: Assessment and treatment strategies. In D.M. Doleys, R.L. Meredith, & A.R. Ciminero (Eds.), *Behavioral medicine: Assessment and treatment strategies* (pp. 473-497). New York: Plenum.

Kilpatrick, D.G., Veronen, L.J., Saunders, B.E., Best, C.L., Amick-McMullen, A., & Paduhovich, J. (1987, March). *The psychological impact of crime: A study of randomly surveyed crime victims* (Final report, grant #84-IJ-CX-0039). Washington, DC: National Institute of Justice.

Koss, M.P., Dinero, T.E., & Seibel, C.A. (1988). Stranger and acquaintance rape: Are there differences in victim's experience? *Psychology of Women Quarterly, 12,* 1-24.

Lerner, M.J. (1980). *The belief in a just world*. New York: Plenum.

Libow, J.A., & Doty, D.W. (1979). An exploratory approach to self-blame and self-derogation by rape victims. *American Journal of Orthopsychiatry, 49,* 670-679.

MacPhillamy, D.J., & Lewinsohn, P.M. (1976). *Manual for the Pleasant Events Schedule*. Eugene: University of Oregon.

Marhoefer-Dvorak, S., Resick, P.A., Hutter, C.K., & Girelli, S.A. (1988). Single versus multiple incident rape victims: A comparison of psychological reactions to rape. *Journal of Interpersonal Violence, 3,* 145-160.

Mason, J.W., Griller, E.L., Jr., Kosten, T.R., & Yehuda, R. (1990). Psychoendocrine approaches to the diagnosis and pathogenesis of post-traumatic stress disorder. In E. L. Griller, Jr. (Ed.), *Biological assessment and treatment of post-traumatic stress disorder* (pp. 65-86). Washington, DC: American Psychiatric Press.

McCahill, T.W., Meyer, L.C., & Fishman, A.M. (1979). *The aftermath of rape.* Lexington, MA: D. C. Heath.

McCann, I.L., Sakheim, D.K., & Abrahamson, D.J. (1988). Trauma and victimization: A model of psychological adaptation. *The Counseling Psychologist, 16,* 531-594.

McNair, D., Lorr, M., & Droppleman, L. (1971). *Manual, profile of mood states.* San Diego, CA: Education and Industrial Testing Service.

Meyer, C.B., & Taylor, S.E. (1985). Adjustment to rape. *Journal of Personality and Social Psychology, 50,* 1226-1234.

Miller, W.R., Williams, M., & Bernstein, M.H. (1982). The effects of rape on marital and sexual adjustment. *American Journal of Family Therapy, 10,* 51-58.

Moss, M.. Frank, E., & Anderson, B. (1987). *The effects of marital status and partner support on emotional response to acute trauma: The example of rape.* Unpublished manuscript, University of Pittsburgh.

Murphy, S.M., Amick-McMullen, A.E., Kilpatrick, D.G., Haskett, M.E., Veronen, L.J., Best, C.L., & Saunders, B.E. (1988). Rape victims' self-esteem: A longitudinal analysis. *Journal of Interpersonal Violence, 3,* 355-370.

Norris, J., & Feldman-Summers, S. (1981). Factors related to the psychological impacts of rape on the victim. *Journal of Abnormal Psychology, 90,* 562-567.

Orlando, J.A., & Koss, M.P. (1983). The effect of sexual victimization in sexual satisfaction: A study of the negative-association hypothesis. *Journal of Abnormal Psychology, 92,* 104-106.

Orr, S.P. (1990). Psychophysiologic studies of post-traumatic stress disorder. In E. L Griller, Jr. (Ed.), *Biological assessment and treatment of post-traumatic stress disorder* (pp. 135-157). Washington, DC: American Psychiatric Press.

Perloff, L.S. (1983). Perceptions of vulnerability to victimization. *Journal of Social Issues, 39,* 41-61.

Pitman, R.K., Orr, S.P., van der Kolk, B.A, Greenberg, M.S., Meyerhoff, J.L. & Moughey, E.H. (1990). Analgesia: A new dependent variable for the biological study of post-traumatic disorder. In M.E. Wolff & A.D. Mosnaim (Eds.), *Post-traumatic stress disorder: Etiology, phenomenology, and treatment* (pp. 140-147). Washington, DC: American Psychiatric Press.

Popiel, D.A., & Susskind, E.C. (1985). The impact of rape: Social support as a moderator of stress. *American Journal of Community Psychology, 13,* 645-676.

Resick, P.A. (1986, May). *Reactions of female and male victims of rape or robbery* (Final report, grant #MH 37296). Washington, DC: National Institute of Mental Health.

Resick, P.A. (1988). *Reactions of female and male victims of rape or robbery* (Final report grant #85-IJ-CX-0042). Washington, DC: National Institute of Justice.

Resick, P.A, Calhoun, K. S., Atkeson, B.M., & Ellis, E.M. (1981). Social adjustment in victims of sexual assault. *Journal of Consulting and Clinical Psychology, 49,* 705-712.

Resick, P.A., Churchill, M., & Falsetti, S. (1990, October). *Assessment of cognitions in trauma victims: A pilot study.* New Orleans, LA: International Society for Traumatic Stress Studies.

Resick, P.A., Jordan, C.G., Girelli, S.A., Hutter, C.K., & Marhoefer-Dvorak, S. (1988). A comparative outcome study of behavioral group therapy for sexual assault victims. *Behavior Therapy, 19,* 385-401.

Resick, P.A., & Schnicke, M.K. (1990). Treating symptoms in adult victims of sexual assault. *Journal of Interpersonal Violence, 5,* 488-506.

Resick, P.A., & Schnicke, M.K. (1992a). Cognitive processing therapy for sexual assault victims. *Journal of Consulting and Clinical Psychology, 60,* 748-756.

Resick, P.A., & Schnicke, M.K. (1992b, October). Cognitive processing therapy for sexual assault victims. In E.B. Foa (Chair), *Treatment of PTSD: An update.* Symposium conducted at the 8th Annual Meeting of the International Society for Traumatic Studies, Los Angeles.

Resick, P.A., Schnicke, M.K., & Markway, B.G. (1991, October). The relationship between cognitive content and PTSD. *Post-traumatic stress disorder after an assault.* Symposium conducted at the 25th Annual Convention of the Association for the Advancement of Behavior Therapy, New York.

Robins, L.N., Helzer, J.E., Croughan, J., & Ratcliff, K.S. (1981). The NIMH Diagnostic Interview Schedule: Its history, characteristics, and validity. *Archives of General Psychiatry, 38,* 381-389.

Rothbaum, B.O., Foa, E.B., Murdock, T., Riggs, D.S., & Walsh, W. (1992). A prospective examination of post-traumatic stress disorder in rape victims. *Journal of Traumatic Stress, 5,* 455-475.

Ruch, L.O., & Chandler, S.M. (1980, September). *The impact of sexual assault on three victim groups receiving crisis intervention services in a rape treatment center: Adult rape victims, child rape victims and incest victims.* Paper presented at the American Sociological Meeting, New York.

Ruch, L.O., Chandler, S.M., & Harter, R.A. (1980). Life change and rape impact. *Journal of Health and Social Behavior, 21,* 248-260.

Ruch, L.O., & Hennessy, M. (1982). Sexual assault: Victim and attack dimensions. *Victimology: An International Journal, 7,* 94-105.

Ruch, L.O., & Leon, J.J. (1983). Sexual assault trauma and trauma change. *Women and Health, 8,* 5-21.

Sales, E., Baum, M., & Shore, B. (1984). Victim readjustment following assault. *Journal of Social Issues, 40,* 117-136.

Schepple, K.L., & Bart, P.B. (1983). Through women's eyes: Defining danger in the wake of sexual assault. *Journal of Social Issues, 39,* 63-81.

Schnicke, M.K., & Resick, P.A. (1990, October). *Self-blame in rape victims.* Paper presented at the 6th Annual Meeting of the Society for Traumatic Stress Studies, New Orleans, LA.

Silver, R.L., Boon, C., & Stones, M.H. (1983). Searching for a meaning in misfortune: Making sense of incest. *Journal of Social Issues, 39,* 81-101.

Silver, R., & Wortman, C. (1980). Coping with undesirable life events. In J. Garber & M. Seligman (Eds.), *Human helplessness* (pp. 279-375). New York: Academic Press.

Spielberger, C.D., Gorsuch, R.L., & Luchene, R.E. (1970). *The state-trait anxiety inventory.* Palo Alto, CA: Consulting Psychologists Press.

Stewart, B.D., Hughes, C., Frank, E., Anderson, B., Kendall, K., & West, D. (1987). Profiles of immediate and delayed treatment seekers. *Journal of Nervous and Mental Disease, 175,* 90-94.

Thornhill, N.W., & Thornhill, R. (1990a). An evolutionary analysis of psychological pain following rape: I. The effects of victim's age and marital status. *Ethology and Sociobiology, 11,* 155-176.

Thornhill, N.W., & Thornhill, R. (1990b). An evolutionary analysis of psychological pain following rape: III. Effects of force and violence. *Aggressive Behavior, 16,* 297-320.

Thornhill, N.W., & Thornhill, R. (1990c). An evolutionary analysis of psychological pain following rape: II. The effects of stranger, friend, and family-member offenders. *Ethnology and Sociobiology, 11,* 177-193.

Veronen, L.J., & Kilpatrick, D.G. (1980). Self-reported fears of rape victims: A preliminary investigation. *Behavior Modification, 4,* 383-396.

Veronen, L.J., Kilpatrick, D.G., & Resick, P.A. (1979). Treatment of fear and anxiety in rape victims: Implications for the criminal justice system. In W.H. Parsonage (Ed.), *Perspectives on victimology.* Beverly Hills, CA: Sage.

Weissman, M.M., & Paykel, C.S. (1974). *The depressed woman: A study of social relationships.* Chicago: University of Chicago Press.

West, D.G., Frank, D., Anderson, B., & Stewart, B.D. (1987). *Social support and post-rape symptomatology.* Unpublished manuscript, Western Psychiatric Institute, Pittsburgh, PA.

Wirtz, P.W., & Harrell, A.V. (1987). Victim and crime characteristics, coping responses, and short- and long-term recovery from victimization. *Journal of Consulting and Clinical Psychology, 55,* 866-871.

Wortman, C.B. (1976). Casual attributions and personal control. In J. H. Harvey, W. J. Ickes, & R. F. Kidd (Eds.), *New directions in attribution research.* Hillsdale, NJ: Lawrence Erlbaum.

Yehuda, R., Southwick, S.M., Perry, B.A., Mason, J.W., & Griller, E.L., Jr. (1990). Interactions of the hypothalamic-pituitary-adrenal axis and the catecholaminergic system in post-traumatic stress disorder. In E. L. Griller, Jr. (Ed.), *Biological assessment and treatment of post-traumatic stress disorder* (pp. 115-134). Washington, DC: American Psychiatric Press.

Patricia A. Resick received her doctorate in clinical psychology from the University of Georgia in 1976. She is currently professor of psychology and director for the Center for Trauma Recovery at the University of Missouri—St. Louis. Her research has focused on assessment and treatment of victims of crime, with emphasis on posttraumatic stress disorder and depression in rape victims. She has been the recipient of several grants from the National Institute of Mental Health and the National Institute of Justice.

Chapter 6

A Contemporary Look at the Effects of Rape Law Reform: How Far Have We Really Come?*

*Ronet Bachman, Ph.D.***
*Raymond Paternoster, Ph.D.****

I. INTRODUCTION

The reform of state and federal rape statutes has been the product of a fragile alliance among feminist groups, victim's rights groups, and organizations promoting more general "law and order" themes.[1] As can be expected from such a diverse coalition, the intended goals of rape law

* An earlier version of this Article was presented at the 1992 meeting of the American Society of Criminology in New Orleans, Louisiana. Points of view and opinions expressed herein are those of the authors and do not necessarily represent the official position or policies of the United States Department of Justice. The authors would like to thank Patsy Klaus for providing a supportive environment in which to work on this project, Pat Langan for supplying data from the National Prisoner Statistics reporting program, and Lawrence Greenfeld for assistance with the prison survey data.

** Bureau of Justice Statistics, United States Department of Justice; Ph.D. University of New Hampshire, 1989.

*** Institute of Criminal Justice and Criminology, University of Maryland; Ph.D. Florida State University, 1978.

[1] *See generally* JEANNE C. MARSH ET AL., RAPE AND THE LIMITS OF LAW REFORM (1982); Ronald J. Berger et al., *The Social and Political Context of Rape Law Reform: An Aggregate Analysis,* 72 SOC. SCI. Q. 221 (1991); Leigh Bienen, *Rape III – National Developments in Rape Reform Legislation,* 6 WOMEN'S RTS. L. REP. 170 (1980); Vicki M. Rose, *Rape as a Social Problem: A By-product of the Feminist Movement,* 25 SOC. PROBS. 75 (1977).

reform have not always been clear, and different reform groups have had somewhat different agendas. For example, feminist groups were largely motivated by ideological issues. These organizations focused on societal perceptions about rape and rape victims.[2] Such perceptions included: (a) the belief that rape was not a serious and violent offense; (b) the notion that acquaintance rapes or rapes perpetrated by intimates[3] were less serious than and different from "real rapes"—those that fit a cultural stereotype involving a stranger jumping out from a place of hiding and violently raping a physically resisting woman; and (c) the various "rape myths" which suggested, among other things, that rape victims were somehow partially to blame for their own victimization.[4] For feminist groups, then, a very important intended consequence of rape law reform was largely symbolic and ideological—to educate the public about the seriousness of all forms of sexual assault, to reduce the stigma experienced by victims of rape, and to neutralize rape myth stereotypes.[5]

Different concerns motivated victim's rights and "law and order" groups. Their intentions were somewhat more pragmatic and instrumental. The problem with extant rape statutes for these groups was that, too frequently, rape offenders were not arrested for their crime because many victims were reluctant to report the offense. These groups also believed that many offenders arrested for rape were not convicted or were convicted of a less serious offense because frequently the victim rather than the offender was put on trial.[6] For instance, the defense would use the victim's own sexual history to question her lack of consent. Further, they perceived that many offenders who were convicted of rape or sexual assault did not receive prison sentences because the sexual assaulter was known to the victim, and that therefore the public did not view the victimization by an acquaintance or intimate as real rape.[7] In addition to changing the public's conceptualization of the crime of rape and of the victims of sexual assault, rape law reformers also intended to modify existing criminal justice practices.

Although differing in emphasis, the impact of the symbolic and instrumental effects of rape law reform were intended to be complementary. Changes in public conceptions about what rape "really is" and who rape "really victimizes" were expected to lead to more reports of rape. Simultaneously, jurors were expected to become more sensitive to

---

[2] *See* Rose, *supra* note 1, at 76.

[3] "Intimates," as used in this Article, refers to either husbands, common-law spouses or boyfriends.

[4] *See* Rose, *supra* note 1, at 78.

[5] *Id.* at 78-79; *see generally* Mary Ann Largen, *Rape-law reform: An Analysis, in* RAPE AND SEXUAL ASSAULT II 271 (A.W. Burgess ed., 1988).

[6] *See* Julie Horney & Cassia Spohn, *Rape Law Reform and Instrumental Change in Six Urban Jurisdictions,* 25 LAW & SOC'Y REV. 117, 119-21 (1991*). See generally* MARSH ET AL., *supra* note 1; Berger et al., *supra* note 1; Bienen, *supra* note 1.

[7] *See* SUSAN ESTRICH, REAL RAPE 8-26 (1987).

both the victimization and stigmatization of rape victims. Consequently, rape reports, arrests, convictions and rates of imprisonment (especially for "non-stereotypical" acquaintance rapes) were all expected to increase.[8]

Significant questions still exist, however, regarding the extent to which the reporting and handling of rape cases has actually changed within the legal system subsequent to rape law reforms. That is, questions remain as to whether rape law reforms have actually produced the more instrumental public policy reforms that their proponents envisioned. At least four important public policy questions exist. First, are victims of sexual assault more likely to report their victimization now than they were in the past? Second, has there been an increase in the number of rape arrests and convictions from pre- to post-reform years? Third, are those convicted of rape more likely to do some prison time? Finally, are non-stereotypical rapes being handled as seriously as those rapes which more closely approximate a stereotypical sexual assault by a stranger?

Surprisingly, there has been little research to address these important public policy issues, and the results of the few studies which have been undertaken remain somewhat equivocal. Many of these studies find weak and inconsistent support for the assumption that rape law reform has had a significant impact on the criminal justice system's processing of rape cases. In Michigan, for example, where the first and most comprehensive reforms were implemented, researchers have found increases in the number of arrests and convictions for rape, but no change in the number of rapes reported to the police.[9] Statistics from other jurisdictions have shown even less of an impact for rape law reform. In fact, except for a few jurisdictions that experienced extremely zealous reforms, research has demonstrated that in the vast majority of jurisdictions, legal reforms have *not* been followed by significant increases in either the reporting of rape cases or the arrest and conviction probabilities for rape.[10]

---

[8] For a detailed discussion of rape law reform, see generally CASSIA SPOHN & JULIE HORNEY, RAPE LAW REFORM: A GRASS ROOTS REVOLUTION AND ITS IMPACT (1992).

[9] Marsh et al. performed an interrupted time-series analysis for data before and after rape law reforms were implemented in Michigan. These investigators found increases in the number of arrests and convictions for rape, but found no change in the number of rapes that were reported to the police. MARSH ET AL., *supra* note 1. Susan Caringella-MacDonald compared pre- and post-reform attrition (the extent to which cases were dropped) and conviction rates from two jurisdictions in Michigan (Kalamazoo county and Detroit). She found decreases in rates of attrition and increases in rates of conviction for both Michigan jurisdictions after reforms had been implemented. Susan Caringella-MacDonald, *Sexual Assault Prosecution: An Examination of Model Rape Legislation in Michigan*, 4 WOMEN & POL. 65 (1984).

[10] Polk examined data for the entire state of California from 1975 to 1982. Although he found an increase in the probability that those convicted of rape would be sentenced to a state institution, his data revealed that police clearance rates for rape and the rate of court filings for rape remained relatively unchanged during this time period. *See* Kenneth Polk, *Rape Reform and Criminal Justice Processing*, 31 CRIME & DELINQ. 191 (1985). Horney and Spohn studied the impact of rape law reforms in six jurisdictions: Detroit, Chicago, Philadelphia, Atlanta, Houston, and Washington, D.C. Only two jurisdictions displayed significant increases in rape adjudication outcomes. Detroit data showed increases in reports and indictments of rape, and Houston data revealed slight increases in reporting and sentence lengths for rapes. *See* Horney & Spohn, *supra* note 6, at 117. In another

Horney and Spohn conducted the most recent and perhaps most extensive study to date to address these issues.[11] After evaluating the impact of rape law reforms on reports of rape and on the processing of rape cases in six urban jurisdictions, these authors pessimistically concluded that, "[o]ur primary finding was the overall lack of impact of rape law reforms. . . . [w]e have shown that the ability of rape reform legislation to produce instrumental change is limited."[12] While this study and others have provided important information regarding the effects of rape law reform in particular jurisdictions, they all have several limitations. Perhaps the foremost limitation is the fact that, except for Horney and Spohn, who investigated six jurisdictions, all the others have relied on single states or jurisdictions. The available knowledge base, therefore, is very restricted and precludes any general conclusion about the effects of rape law reform. In addition, all of the studies have confined their inquiries to data from the late 1970s or early 1980s, thereby leaving a large gap in our understanding about what has occurred with rape reporting and processing during the last decade. Finally, all of the above studies have examined changes in rape reporting and adjudication in isolation, not in comparison to other violent crimes.[13] Necessarily, one must examine rape in relation to other crimes of violence in order to control for extraneous factors, such as an increase in the general efficiency or punitiveness of the criminal justice system. These and other extraneous factors may be affecting the reporting and processing of *all* crimes, not simply the crime of rape. Only if the reporting and adjudication of rape increases relative to other violent crimes can any researcher attribute this trend to the influence of rape law reforms.

For these reasons, it is clear that, in order to advance our understanding of the effects of rape law reforms, it is necessary to conduct a national accounting of the *recent* trends in rape reporting and adjudication *relative* to other crimes of violence. Horney and Spohn adopted this very position after their recent review of the rape reform literature. "These empirical studies provide some evidence of the impact of rape law reforms in four jurisdictions but leave many unanswered questions about the *nationwide* effect of the reforms."[14]

This Article both contributes to and extends the previous literature on the effectiveness of rape law reforms in this country. Using a number of national data sources, we investigate the degree to which there has been a change in three aspects of the rape adjudication process relative

---

study, Loh found no significant changes in conviction rates for rape in King County, Washington (Seattle). *See* Wallace D. Loh, *The Impact of Common Law and Reform Rape Statutes on Prosecution: An Empirical Study*, 55 WASH. L. REV. 543 (1981). *See also* Largen, *supra* note 5.

[11] Horney & Spohn, *supra* note 6.

[12] *Id.* at 149-50.

[13] *See supra* notes 9-13 and accompanying text for a brief overview of previous rape reform studies.

[14] Horney & Spohn, *supra* note 6, at 122 (emphasis added).

to two other crimes of violence—robbery and aggravated assault. We will address three questions regarding rape: (a) to what extent has reporting rape to the police changed from the 1970s to the present; (b) to what extent has the probability of going to prison for rape (conditioned on arrest) changed from the 1970s to the present; and (c) to what extent does the victim/offender relationship composition of rape victimizations reflect the composition of offenders going to prison for rape, and to what extent has this composition changed from the 1970s to the present? Specifically, has there been an increase in the number of "date" or "acquaintance" rape offenders who have been imprisoned?

II. RAPE LAW REFORM

Perhaps the most illuminating characterization of rape laws in this country was provided by Sir Matthew Hale, Lord Chief Justice of the King's Bench: "'rape is an accusation easy to be made, hard to be proved, and harder to be defended by the party accused though ever so innocent.'"[15] This concern with protecting men from false accusations of rape went beyond the "not guilty until proven innocent" standard, and led to arguments for nearly unlimited admissibility of evidence regarding the accused's character.[16] This, combined with cultural conceptions of rape and early rape laws, placed serious impediments on the adjudication of rape cases.[17] Such offender-bias affected the entire adjudication sequence of rape cases, from the victim's reporting of the attack to the state's prosecution of the event.

Pressure from various organizations in the early seventies led to a growing societal awareness that rape laws in this country were antiquated at best.[18] This awareness, in turn, provided the impetus for the enactment of some form of rape law reform in all fifty states.[19] Michigan was the first state to modify its rape statute when it enacted a comprehensive criminal sexual assault law in 1974.[20] Several other states soon followed by reforming their own rape statutes. The reform of state

---

[15] MATTHEW HALE, THE HISTORY OF THE PLEAS OF THE CROWN 634-35 (1847), *quoted in* Andrew Z. Soshnick, Comment, *The Rape Shield Paradox: Complainant Protection Amidst Oscillating Trends of State Judicial Interpretation*, 78 J. CRIM. L. & CRIMINOLOGY 644, 650 (1987).

[16] *See* I.A. JOHN HENRY WIGMORE, EVIDENCE 62 (Tiller's rev. ed. 1983).

[17] *See* Andrew Z. Soshnick, Comment, *The Rape Shield Paradox: Complainant Protection Amidst Oscillating Trends of State Judicial Interpretation*, 78 J. CRIM. L. & CRIMINOLOGY 644, 649 (1987).

[18] *Id.* at 651.

[19] *See id.* at 644 nn. 1-3; Vivian Berger, *Man's Trial, Woman's Tribulation: Rape Cases in the Courtroom*, 77 COLUM. L. REV. 1, 22-39 (1977); Abraham P. Ordover, *Admissibility Patterns of Similar Sexual Conduct: The Unlamented Death of Character for Chastity*, 62 CORNELL L. REV. 90, 95-102 (1977).

[20] *See* Act of August 12, 1974, Pub. L. No. 266, 1974 Mich. Pub. Acts 1025 (codified as amended at MICH. COMP. LAWS ANN. §§ 750.520a-.5201 (West Supp. 1987).

rape statutes also had a "spill over" effect on procedural law, as evidenced by Congress' 1978 enactment of Rule 412 of the Federal Rules of Evidence.[21] This rule excluded from evidence all reputation and opinion testimony concerning a rape complainant's prior sexual conduct, but still allowed for the limited admissibility of evidence of a complainant's specific prior sexual acts.[22]

Although the nature of rape law reforms varied across jurisdictions in comprehensiveness and specific detail,[23] Horney and Spohn identified four common reform themes:

(1) Many states replaced the single crime of rape with a series of offenses graded by seriousness and with commensurate penalties . . . . Traditional rape laws did not include attacks on male victims, acts other than sexual intercourse, sexual assaults with an object, or sexual assaults by a spouse [or an intimate]. The new crimes typically are gender neutral and include a range of sexual assaults.

(2) A number of jurisdictions changed the consent standard by modifying or eliminating the requirement that the victim resist her attacker. Under traditional rape statutes, the victim, to demonstrate her lack of consent, was required to 'resist to the utmost' or, at the very least, exhibit, 'such earnest resistance as might reasonably be expected under the circumstances. Reformers challenged these standards, arguing not only that resistance could lead to serious injury but also that the law should focus on the behavior of the offender rather than on that of the victim.

(3) The third type of statutory reform was elimination of the corroboration requirement—the rule prohibiting conviction for forcible rape on the uncorroborated testimony of the victim. Critics cited the difficulty in obtaining evidence concerning an act that typically takes place in a private place without witnesses. They also objected to rape being singled out as the only crime with such a requirement.

(4) Most states enacted rape shield laws that placed restrictions on the introduction of evidence of the victim's prior sexual conduct. Under common law, evidence of the victim's sexual history was admissible to prove she had consented to intercourse and to impeach her credibility . . . . Critics argued that the rule was archaic in light of changes in attitudes

---

[21] The Privacy Protection for Rape Victims Act of 1978, Pub. L. No. 95-540, 92 Stat. 2046, was signed into law on October 28, 1978, and as FED. R. EVID. 412 applies to all trials conducted after November 29, 1978.

[22] FED. R. EVID. 412.

[23] *See generally* Berger et al., *supra* note 1; Jack E. Call et al., *An Analysis of State Rape Shield Laws*, 72 SOC. SCI. Q. 774 (1991); Harriet R. Galvin, *Shielding Rape Victims in the State and Federal Courts: A Proposal for the Second Decade*, 70 MINN. L. REV. 763 (1986); Horney & Spohn, *supra* note 6.

toward sexual relations and women's role in society . . . . [S]tate legislatures enacted rape shield laws designed to limit the admissibility of
evidence of the victim's past sexual conduct.[24]

Advocates of the new statutes expected a number of positive outcomes
from the reforms. First, they expected the treatment of rape victims to
improve and, in turn, increase the reporting of rape. Second, they expected an increase in the arrest, conviction and imprisonment rates of all types
of rape, including date and marital rape. As noted earlier, however, there
is a paucity of research attempting to measure the success of these reforms,
but the literature which does exist remains somewhat equivocal.[25]

The primary objective of this Article is to provide a national
accounting of the extent to which rape reforms have succeeded in producing three expected outcomes. First, if such procedural reforms as
rape shield laws have reduced the reluctance of victims of rape to report
their victimizations to the police, then we should see an increase in the
number of these victimizations reported to police during the past decade.
Second, if statutes aimed at eliminating the resistance and corroboration
requirements have indeed increased the probability that rapists will be
convicted and sent to prison, then the probability of going to prison for
rape should have increased relative to other violent crimes over the past
twenty years. Third, if new criminal codes which replaced the single
crime of rape with a series of offenses have indeed increased the probability that rape offenders who victimize intimates or acquaintances will
be convicted and go to prison, then we should see an increased incarceration rate for these types of rapists as compared to the late seventies
and early eighties.

III. Methods

To address the research questions posed above, this study relies on
several data sources: the National Crime Victimization Survey
("NCVS"),[26] the Uniform Crime Reports ("UCR"),[27] the National Pris-

---

[24] Horney & Spohn, *supra* note 6, at 118-19 (citations omitted).

[25] *See supra* notes 9-13 and accompanying text.

[26] Bureau of Justice Statistics, National Crime Victimization Survey (1991). The Bureau of
Justice Statistics ("BJS") sponsored and the U.S. Census Bureau conducted both the NCVS and
prison inmate surveys. For a more detailed discussion of the methodologies employed in the NCVS,
see Bureau of Justice Statistics, Criminal Victimization in the United States (1973-91).

[27] Federal Bureau of Investigation, Uniform Crime Reports (1991). The Uniform Crime
Reporting program is sponsored by the Federal Bureau of Investigation ("FBI"). For a detailed
description of this data, see Federal Bureau of Investigation, Crime in the United States (1990).
For a critical evaluation of the UCR data, see Larry Baron & Murray A. Straus, Four Theories
of Rape in American Society 26-32 (1989).

oner Statistics program ("NPS"),[28] and the National Corrections Reporting Program ("NCRP").[29] While we are primarily interested in the extent to which there has been a change in rape reporting and rape case adjudication, it is important to control for other factors which may also affect trends in these outcomes, such as the increased efficiency or punitiveness of the criminal justice system over time. To control for these factors, rape data will be compared to both robbery and assault data in all analyses. If rape law reforms have increased the effectiveness of the criminal justice system's handling of rape cases and of rape victims' willingness to report to the police, then we should expect to see increases in these measures for rape, over and above those increases observed for robbery and assault.

IV. DEPENDENT VARIABLES

A. POLICE REPORTS

This study focused on two indicators to examine trends in the reporting of rape, robbery and assault incidents to the police: the NCVS tally of victims who reported their victimization to the police, and the UCR tally of the same group. Both of these reporting trends are traced from 1973-1990.[30]

---

[28] BUREAU OF JUSTICE STATISTICS, NATIONAL CRIME REPORTS (1991). The collection of admissions data for the NPS is also sponsored by BJS. For a more detailed discussion of this program, see PATRICK A. LANGAN, U.S. DEP'T OF JUSTICE, NCJ-125618, RACE OF PRISONERS ADMITTED TO STATE AND FEDERAL INSTITUTIONS, 1926-86 (1991).

[29] BUREAU OF JUSTICE STATISTICS, NATIONAL CORRECTIONS REPORTING PROGRAM (1991). Data tapes and technical documentation for each of the data sets utilized in this Article can be obtained from the National Archive of Criminal Justice Data at the University of Michigan, Ann Arbor.

[30] It is important to note that the definitions of rape used by the UCR and the NCVS are not the same. The UCR defines rape as "carnal knowledge of a female against her will." UNIFORM CRIME REPORTS, supra note 27, at 23. The NCVS, for the time period studied here, relied on a respondent's self-classification of an incident as rape. That is, in response to a series of questions related to being attacked, threatened, or harmed, those women who voluntarily reported that they had been raped comprise the NCVS sample. RONET BACHMAN, U.S. DEP'T OF JUSTICE, NCJ-145325, VIOLENCE AGAINST WOMEN 1 (1994).

The accuracy of both data sources have been criticized for the extent to which they estimate incident rates of rape in this country. See Mary P. Koss, The Underdetection of Rape: Methodological Choices Influence Incidence Estimates, 48 J. SOC. ISSUES 61 (1992). This Article, however, does not purport in any way to estimate incidence rates of rape victimization in the United States. Because the objective of this study was to discern national trends in rape reporting behavior and in the adjudication process of rape cases by the criminal justice system, it was important to utilize consistent sources of data that were available at the national level. We believe these data are reasonably consistent over time.

It should also be noted that the NCVS procedures for measuring rape have changed as a result of a 10-year redesign project. The survey now asks direct questions about sexual assault, including rapes involving family members or other intimates. For example, NCVS interviewers now ask the following screening question: "Incidents involving forced or unwanted sexual acts are often difficult to talk about. Have you been forced or coerced to engage in unwanted sexual activity by (a) someone you didn't know before, (b) a casual acquaintance, or (c) someone you know well?" This,

B. PROBABILITY OF GOING TO PRISON

To estimate the probability of going to prison for rape, robbery and assault, this study divided the number of individuals admitted to prison for each of the three crimes by the number of individuals arrested for that same crime during a given year. In making this probability estimate we utilized two sources of data: admission series data from the NPS and arrest data from the UCR. As part of the NPS data, the admission series obtains information on each individual admitted to prison during a given year. Because of budgetary concerns, however, the federal government sporadically collected this data during the 1970s. Consequently, for that decade we can only estimate the probability of going to prison for the years 1970, 1974, 1978 and 1979. Thereafter, however, we have continuous trend data from 1981 to 1989.

C. VICTIM/OFFENDER RELATIONSHIP FOR THOSE COMMITTNG OFFENSES AND THOSE IMPRISONED

In order to investigate the extent to which the relationship between the victim and offender for the crimes of rape, robbery and assault reflects the victim/offender relationship for those offenders in prison for these same crimes, and to determine whether there has been increased correspondence between these two measures during the past decade, we have utilized two sources of data: the NCVS for the time periods of 1979-1986 and 1987-1990, and a survey of inmates in state correctional facilities conducted in 1986 and in 1991 as part of the NCRP. In both sources, analysis was restricted first to female victims and victimizations; second, to those incidents which involved single offenders and single victims; and third, to those victimizations involving adults over 18 years of age.[31]

---

along with other questions that specifically address sexual assault victimization, were implemented into 100% of the NCVS sample in July of 1993. Estimates of rape and sexual assault from these new questions will be available in the fall of 1994.

[31] Analyses were restricted in these ways to obtain the purest sample possible. While many sexual assault statutes today are written in gender-neutral terms, the vast majority of victims still remain female. Throughout this Article, the male gender will be used to refer to the perpetrator and the female gender will be used to refer to a victim of rape. The sample was restricted to adult victims as well because crimes of rape involving juveniles are also much different in circumstance, for example incest, compared to rapes involving adults.

In addition, because there may have been differential proportions of strangers and acquaintances in prison due to the fact that victims differentially report these types of victimizations to the police, analyses were replicated using *only* those victims from the NCVS who reported their victimization to the police. As there were no significant differences between analyses in which only reported cases were used and the total sample, results presented in this Article are those obtained for the total sample. The fact that the victim/offender relationship does not have a significant effect on reporting behavior of rape victims is supported by recent research as well. *See* Ronet Bachman, *Predicting the Reporting of Rape Victimization: Have Rape Reforms Made a Difference?*, 20 CRIM. JUST. & BEHAV. 254 (1993).

D. TIME PERIODS

Constructing a perfect interrupted time-series model to evaluate the national impact of rape law reforms was virtually impossible for several reasons. Most important, perhaps, is the fact that even though most state level statutes were enacted during the late seventies,[32] the majority of these statutes have undergone numerous revisions based on appellate court decisions in virtually every state. In fact, these revisions and amendments to original reform statutes continue in states across the country today.

Some have noted that this proliferation of litigation has been necessary because most statutes were hastily enacted by state legislatures in response to constituent pressures.[33] As a result of their hasty construction, many statutes were ambiguous and vague, if not incomprehensible. As Galvin explains, "[u]nder pressure from powerful interest groups to proceed with haste and to embrace a symbol of sexual autonomy and equality with one quick stroke of the legislative pen, drafters of rape-shield legislation failed to approach the task of evidentiary reform functionally."[34] Perhaps the most noteworthy example of these reformulations occurred in 1989 when Steven Lord was acquitted of rape and kidnapping charges in Broward County, Florida. During Mr. Lord's trial, the jury was repeatedly shown the clothes worn by the alleged victim: a lacy white miniskirt with no underwear and a green tanktop. Newspapers nationwide published accounts of this trial, including the following statement made by the jury foreman: " '[w]e all felt she asked for it, the way she was dressed.' "[35] After this trial, Florida revised its existing rape shield statute to preclude the presentation of evidence at trial which suggests that an alleged victim's manner of dress incited a sexual assault.[36]

---

[32] For a detailed account of these early state reform statutes, see HUBERT S. FEILD & LEIGH B. BIENEN, JURORS AND RAPE: A STUDY OF PSYCHOLOGY AND LAW (1980).

[33] Soshnick, *supra* note 17, at 646.

[34] Galvin, *supra* note 23, at 776.

[35] Elinor J. Brecher, *The Whole Story,* MIAMI HERALD, Nov. 26, 1989, at 10.

[36] *See* FLA. STAT. ANN. § 794.022 (West 1993). A glance through virtually every state's penal and evidentiary codes will reveal numerous changes to original rape and sexual assault statutes. It is not our purpose to delineate them all here; a few examples will suffice.

Pennsylvania did not address the proper interpretation of its rape shield statute until 1983 in Commonwealth v. Majorana, 470 A.2d 80 (Pa. 1983). In that case, the defense counsel sought to introduce evidence that the alleged victim had engaged in consensual intercourse with a codefendant two hours prior to the alleged incident. The Commonwealth of Pennsylvania objected on the ground that the evidence was inadmissible under Pennsylvania's rape shield statute. *Id.* at 82. After a lower court sustained the Commonwealth's objection, the Supreme Court reversed the trial court's decision that "evidence which directly contradicts the act or occurrence at issue is not barred by [the rape shield] statute." *Id.* at 83, *cited in* Soshnick, *supra* note 17, at 681. More recently, in Commonwealth v. Johnson. 566 A.2d 1197 (Pa. Super. Ct.), *appeal granted,* 581 A.2d 569 (Pa. 1990), the appellate court ruled that a trial court should conduct an in camera hearing to determine whether the probative value of exculpatory evidence of prior sexual conduct involving the victim outweighs the prejudicial effect. *Id.* at 1202.

Because most state rape reform statutes have undergone so many reformulations since their implementation, it would be virtually impossible to establish a single time point by which to distinguish between pre- and post-reform periods. Therefore, we refer to pre- and post-reform periods in the sections that follow very loosely. Keep in mind that we are simply assuming that, over the time period analyzed, there should be increases in the reporting, convicting and incarcerating of rape offenders, particularly those who rape someone known to them.

It should also be noted that, because the data we utilized were taken from several different nationally representative samples, we were not able to make pre- and post-periods completely consistent across all sources. With these data limitations in mind, however, we believe the important information to be gained from the analyses reported in this Article is a contemporary picture of the criminal justice system as it relates both to rape victims and to the adjudication of rape offenders since the years of reform.

V. RESULTS

A. POLICE REPORTS

This Section will examine the extent to which rape law reforms such as rape shield laws and modifications in the consent standard have, in fact, increased the probability that victims of rape will report their victimization to the police. To investigate this question, we will first examine the NCVS' violent crime victimization data for the years 1973 to 1990. Figure 1 displays the proportion of rape, robbery and assault victims who reported their victimization to the police. As this figure demon-

---

Other states, such as California, have made recent changes in their rape reform statutes through legislation. For example, the following changes were made to the California Penal Code § 1127d in 1990:

(a) In any criminal prosecution for the crime of rape, or for violation of Section 261.5, or for an attempt to commit, or assault with intent to commit, any such crime, the jury shall not be instructed that it may be inferred that a person who has previously consented to sexual intercourse with persons other than the defendant *or with the defendant* would be therefore more likely to consent to sexual intercourse again. *However, if evidence was received that the victim consented to and did engage in sexual intercourse with the defendant on one or more occasions prior to that charged against the defendant in this case, the jury shall be instructed that this evidence may be considered only as it relates to the question of whether the victim consented to the act of intercourse charged against the defendant in the case, or whether the defendant had a good faith reasonable belief that the victim consented to the act of sexual intercourse. The jury shall be instructed that it shall not consider this evidence for any other purpose.*

(b) A jury shall not be instructed that the prior sexual conduct in and of itself of the complaining witness may be considered in determining the credibility of the witness . . . .

CAL. PENAL CODE 1127d (West 1988) (emphasis indicates amendments).

strates, the proportion of victims who reported to the police is far more variable for rape than for both robbery and assault. One reason for this may be the relatively small sample size of rapes in the NCVS. With such small numbers, minor variations in reporting will produce seemingly large effects. To reduce the influence of extreme annual fluctuations, we smoothed the proportion of police reports by rape victims using a moving average span of three.[37] Both the original data proportions of rape victimizations reported to the police and the computed smoothed proportions are presented in Figure 2.

Figure 1
Proportion of NCVS Rape, Robbery and Assault Victims
Who Reported Their Victimization to Police, 1973-90

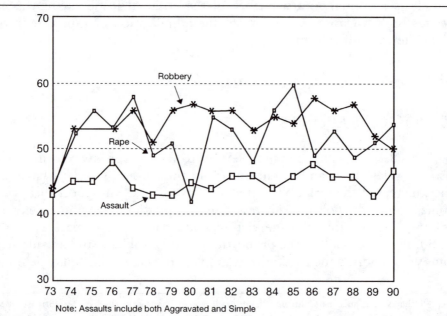

From both Figures 1 and 2, it appears that the proportion of rape victims who reported their victimization to the police has increased slightly since 1980. Looking at the original data points, there was a 28% increase in rape victims who reported to the police from 1980 to 1990.

---

[37] Smoothing is a technique often done to time series data in order to detect visual patterns in data from original data points which change in a rapid and sporadic fashion. We adopted a moving average span of three. After basing both axes at their true values, a moving average span of three involves replacing each year value with the average of the previous year, the current year and the next year. For example, the smoothed data point for the year 1981 would be ascertained by computing the average of the proportion of police reports for the years 1980, 1981 and 1982. For a detailed explanation of smoothing techniques, see LAWRENCE C. HAMILTON, MODERN DATA ANALYSIS (1990).

When these data are smoothed, however, the increase in victim reporting is only 10%. In spite of this small increase, it is greater than the increases for assault (4%) and robbery (a 12% decrease). On the basis of NCVS data, then, it appears that rape reform legislation may have slightly increased the willingness of rape victims to report their victimization to the police. UCR data corroborates this small increase of 10% in rape victim reporting.

Figure 2
Raw and Smoothed Proportion of NCVS Rape Victims
Who Reported to Police, 1973-90

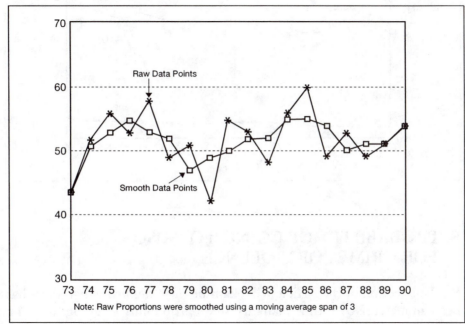

Figure 3 displays UCR data on the rates of rape, robbery, and assaults reported to police departments for the years 1973-1990. The UCR data reveals a 13% increase in rape reporting from 1980 to 1990. Rates of reported robbery increased by only 6% over the same time period, while assault reports increased 46%. Thus, the NCVS and UCR data together paint a comparable picture concerning the impact of rape reform legislation on rape reporting. Both data sources show that rape victims were slightly more likely to report their victimizations after statutory reforms were in place.

Figure 3
Rape, Robbery and Aggravated Assault
Reports to the UCR per 100,000 Population, 1973-90

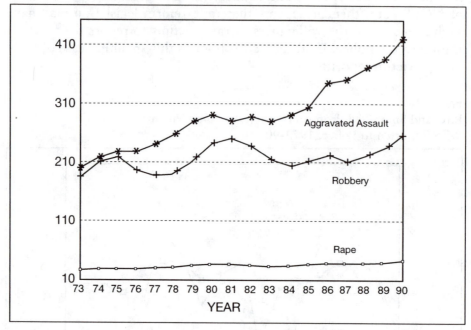

B. PROBABILITY OF GOING TO PRISON FOR CRIMES OF VIOLENCE

This section of the Article will examine the extent to which there has been an increase over time in an arrestee's probability of going to prison for rape, robbery or assault. If rape law reforms have achieved their intended goal, we should observe an increase over time in the probability that arrested rape offenders will serve time in prison relative to either robbery or assault offenders.

Recall that the probabilities used here were computed at the national level by dividing the number of individuals admitted to prison for rape, robbery and assault (NPS) by the number of individuals arrested for that same crime during a given year (UCR). The estimated probabilities of going to prison for rape, robbery and assault are presented in Figure 4.

It appears from Figure 4 that the probability of going to prison for rape has increased over the 1970 to 1989 period. In fact, with only a few exceptions, there has been a monotonically increasing probability of imprisonment for arrested rapists since 1981. It also appears that the greater probability of imprisonment for arrested rapists over time is not due to the growing general punitiveness of the criminal justice system, since the likelihood of imprisonment for arrested rapists has increased at a faster rate than that for either robbery or assault. In fact, since 1981 the probability that an arrested rapist will go to prison has increased by over 200% compared with a 9% increase for robbery and a 25% increase for assault.

Figure 4
Probability of Going to Prison if Arrested for Rape, Robbery and Assault, 1970-1989

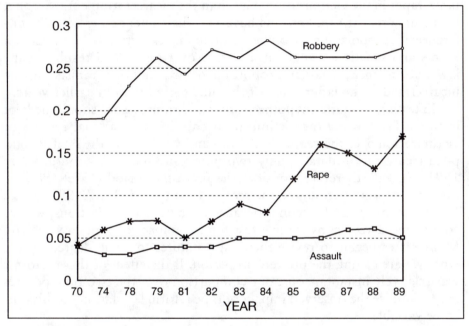

C. VICTIM/OFFENDER COMPOSITION OF CRIMINAL ACTIVITY VERSUS COMPOSITION OF PRISON POPULATION

Earlier we alluded to the symbolic impact of rape law reform. One dimension of this was the expectation that persons would begin to consider "non-traditional" or non-stereotypical forms of sexual assault as real rape.[38] One type of "non-traditional" sexual assault is an assault occurring between acquaintances. If the educational purpose of rape law reform has been successful, rapists who victimized acquaintances should be as likely to be imprisoned as those who victimized strangers (the stereotypical rape). The final issue to be examined here is the extent to which rape law reforms have increased the probability that those who rape acquaintances will be sent to prison relative to those who rape strangers.

---

[38] *See* Estrich, *supra* note 7, at 826.

Our inquiry focuses on the correspondence between crime victims' descriptions of their relationships with their respective attackers (NCVS) and imprisoned violent crime offenders' descriptions of their relationships with their respective victims (NCRP). We make a few assumptions. First, because acquaintance rapes have historically been treated by the legal system as less serious than those involving strangers, we first assume that rape events (victimization incidents) will involve a larger proportion of acquaintance relationships than sanction events (incarcerations). Thus, we would expect to see a higher proportion of acquaintance rapes in the victimization data than the incarceration data. Second, we assume that if rape reforms have had their intended effect, this difference in proportions involving acquaintances between victimization events and sanction events will decrease over time. As a result of rape law reform, then, a larger proportion of acquaintance rapists will be incarcerated in the latter years of the time period than in earlier years.

In testing this latter hypothesis, two additional issues should be kept in mind. First, while the victimization data includes annual reports of victimization over the years 1979-1986 and 1987-1990, the NCRP compiled incarceration data at only two points in time, 1986 and again in 1991. We will, therefore, consider the first time period (1979-1986) as the "pre-reform" period and the second time period (1987-1992) as the "post-reform" period. Second, because of these data limitations, we are conducting a very conservative test for the impact of rape law reform. Many states began to revise their rape statutes to some degree during what we are calling the pre-reform period. If the effect of these reforms was relatively instantaneous, our comparison over the two time periods may minimize the observed impact of rape reform legislation on this outcome variable.

Table 1 compares the proportion of rape, robbery and assault victimizations who were strangers, acquaintances or relatives/intimates as reported by crime victims to the same proportions for the crimes committed by incarcerated offenders.

Table 1 indicates that in the pre-reform period (1979-1986) the proportion of rape crimes that involved a victim who was acquainted with her offender was higher (41%) than the proportion found for those offenders who were incarcerated (29%). Given their proportion in offense data, then, we find an underrepresentation of rapists who victimized acquaintances in the incarceration data. There is a corresponding overrepresentation of rapes involving stranger victims in the incarceration data (56%) relative to their proportion in the victimization data (45%). It is probable that juries during this period did not view acquaintance rapes to be as serious as rape by strangers, and were therefore less likely to send an acquaintance to prison. This is precisely the understanding of sexual assault that rape law reform attempted to modify. A similar and comparable "acquaintance discount" seems to be at work for assault. Acquaintance victims are more likely to be found in the victimization data (46%) than the incarceration data (36%).

Table 1
Percentage of Stranger, Acquaintance and Relative Offenders Based On Victim's Reports to the NCVS Compared With the Percentage of Stranger, Acquaintance and Relative Offenders in Prison According to National Prisoner Statistics

Crime	NCVS Proportion*			NPS Proportion		
	Years: 1979-1986 - "Pre-Reform" Period			Year: 1986 - "Pre-Reform" Period		
	Stranger	Acquaintance	Relative	Stranger	Acquaintance	Relative
Rape	45%	41%	14%	56%	29%	15%
Robbery	70	18	12	85	14	1
Assault	38	46	16	45	36	19
	Years: 1987-1990 - "Post-Reform" Period			Year: 1991 - "Post-Reform" Period		
	Stranger	Acquaintance	Relative	Stranger	Acquaintance	Relative
Rape	36%	48%	16%	43%	40%	17%
Robbery	83	13	4	86	12	1
Assault	52	36	12	48	32	20

*Proportions for the NCVS are based on all single-offender victimizations.

The fact that rapists who victimize acquaintances are less likely to be incarcerated than those who victimize strangers may not be due to the fact that the former are perceived to be less serious than the latter. Rather, it may be that objectively *they are* less serious. Rapes committed against acquaintances may be less brutal and violent and less likely to involve another felony (such as kidnapping) than those committed against strangers. These factors may explain the underrepresentation of acquaintance rapists in the incarceration data. If, however, the underrepresentation of acquaintance rapists declines subsequent to rape reform legislation, we may speculate that such crimes are, more likely than in the past, being viewed by juries as "real rape"—in other words, viewed as comparable in seriousness to those rapes involving strangers.

The second panel of Table 1 shows the representation of acquaintance rapists in victimization and incarceration data during the post-reform period. In comparison to pre-reform years (1979-1986), the correspondence between victimization data and incarceration data with regard to acquaintance rapes is slightly closer in the post-reform period

(12% as opposed to 8%). In the latter years, 48% of rape victims identified their offender as an acquaintance, as did 40% of those incarcerated. Another indication that rape law reform may have had an impact on how acquaintance rapes were being handled by the legal system can be seen in the increase in acquaintance rapists in prison from pre- to post-reform years. In 1986, 29% of those incarcerated for rape victimized an acquaintance. In 1991, this had grown to 40%. There was, then, an 11% increase in the number of acquaintance rapists who were in prison while the number of acquaintance rape victimizations increased by only 7% (41% versus 48%) over this same period. Correspondingly, the proportion of incarcerated offenders who victimized acquaintances in robberies and assaults declined by 2% and 4% respectively, while the proportion victimized by acquaintances for these same two offenses declined by 5% (robbery) and 10% (assault). At the end of the reform period, then, there is some evidence to indicate that those who raped acquaintances were treated more comparably to those who victimized strangers. Although consistent, we must note that the observed changes are not very substantial.

There is yet another way to examine whether acquaintance rapists are being incarcerated with the same consistency as stranger rapists. Using a demographer's technique which Blumstein introduced to criminological research in 1982 and which Langan reinforced in 1985,[39] we explored the extent to which the criminal justice system differentially handles cases of stranger and acquaintance rape by calculating the proportion of acquaintance rapists expected to be in prison based on the probability of a stranger rapist being in prison. Table 2 describes these expected proportions and the supporting mathematical calculations.

For both pre- and post-reform periods, the observed proportion of incarcerated offenders who had raped an acquaintance was significantly lower (.01 level, two-tailed) than the proportion expected. In what we have termed the pre-reform period (1979-1986), the expected proportion of imprisoned acquaintance rapists was 49%, but the proportion of those incarcerated who actually did victimize an acquaintance was only 29%. This difference of 20% between expected and observed proportions is much greater for rape than for both robbery (7%) and assault (14%).

More importantly, however, is whether the difference between the expected and observed proportion of acquaintance offenders in prison narrowed at the end of the reform period. The bottom half of Table 2 demonstrates that the discrepancy for robbery and assault offenses has improved and, in fact, has almost disappeared. In other words, for these two offenses, the observed proportion of acquaintance offenders in

---

[39] Alfred Blumstein, *On the Racial Disproportionality of United States Prison Populations*, 73 J. CRIM. L. & CRIMINOLOGY 1259 (1982); Patrick A. Langan, *Racism on Trial: New Evidence to Explain the Racial Composition of Prisons in the United States*, 76 J. CRIM. L. & CRIMINOLOGY 666 (1985)

prison nearly matches the expected proportion. In contrast, there is still a large discrepancy between expected and observed proportions for the offenses of rape. Of those incarcerated for rape in 1991, 58% should have involved acquaintance rapes, but only 40% of them actually did. This 18% difference is only slightly lower than the 20% difference observed during the pre-reform period. In spite of legal reforms, then, a strong "acquaintance discount" continues to exist for those who rape.

Table 2
Expected Versus Observed Proportion of Acquaintance Offenders
in the Nation's State Prisons Based On the Probability of Going to Prison
if the Offender is a Stranger

Years: 1979-1986 - "Pre-Reform" Period						
	(a)	(b)	(c=b/a)	(d)	(e=c × d)	(f)
Type of Crime	% of Stranger Offender	% of Stranger Offenders in Prison	Probability of a Stranger Going to Prison	% of Acquaint. Offenders	Expected % of Acquaint. Offenders in Prison	Observed % of Acquaint. Offenders in Prison
Rape	45%	56%	1.2	41%	49%	29%
Robbery	70	85	1.2	18	21	14
Assault	38	45	1.1	46	50	36

Years: 1987-1991 - "Post-Reform" Period						
	(a)	(b)	(c=b/a)	(d)	(e=c × d)	(f)
Type of Crime	% of Stranger Offender	% of Stranger Offenders in Prison	Probability of a Stranger Going to Prison	% of Acquaint. Offenders	Expected % of Acquaint. Offenders in Prison	Observed % of Acquaint. Offenders in Prison
Rape	36%	43%	1.2	48%	58%	40%
Robbery	83	86	1.0	13	13	12
Assault	52	48	.92	36	33	32

VI. DISCUSSION

Proponents of rape law reform intended that revisions of state rape statutes would produce a number of specific outcomes.[40] Our empirical examination of the extent to which these expected outcomes have been achieved reveals mixed results. The most obvious impression from these data is that statutory rape law reform has not had a very substantial effect on either victim behavior or actual practices in the criminal justice

---

[40] See *supra* notes 2-7 and accompanying text.

system. We found no large increase over time in the proportion of victims who reported being raped, and a very small change in the likelihood that individuals who raped an acquaintance would be imprisoned. In this regard, our generally null findings are consistent with other research concerning the impact of rape law reform.[41]

We would like to emphasize, however, that we observed some partial success. Although not dramatic, both victim-based (NCVS) and law enforcement (UCR) data suggest that from the 1970s to 1990 there was a slight (approximately 10%) increase in the proportion of women who reported being the victim of a rape. One symbolic effect that rape law reform may have had, then, is a reduction in rape victims' perceptions that the legal process would stigmatize them, which in turn made them more likely to report their victimization. We also found that, subsequent to rape law reforms, rape offenders were more likely to be sent to prison. This increased probability of incarceration in recent years was not due to the general punitiveness of the criminal justice system, because we did not observe comparable increases for robbery or assault. Finally, we also found a small increase in the likelihood that the legal system would sanction acquaintance rapes and stranger rapes similarly. While there continues to be a large "acquaintance discount," treatment of rapes committed against an acquaintance in the post-reform period more closely approximate the treatment of stranger-perpetrated cases of rape.

There is, then, a silver lining to the general clouds revealed by our empirical analyses. In spite of this partial success, however, proponents of rape law reform must be disappointed with the results of our study and those of others before us. Although attitudes about rape and rape victimization may have become more enlightened over the past two decades, there is little evidence to suggest that these attitudes have been translated into significant performance changes in the criminal justice system. Our generally null findings, however, may in part be due to methodological imperfections. For example, our examination of national data over a long period of time may somewhat confound "pre-reform" and "post-reform" periods. In addition, this national analysis may also mask any impact reforms may have had at state-specific levels. The consistency of our findings with previous research, however, would suggest that although statutory revisions of rape laws have had some effect, significant progress still awaits us.

---

[41] See *supra* notes 9-13 and accompanying text.

Section 4
FAMILY VIOLENCE

Family violence affects children, spouses, siblings, parents, and grandparents of every socioeconomic and racial and ethnic background in the United States. It is not a new phenomenon, but it has received significant public attention only relatively recently. For a long time, the formal or informal characterization of women and children as the "property" of their husbands and fathers, and thus subject to whatever treatment was deemed appropriate or necessary, inhibited public interference with acts of violence committed on family members by these men. Even when such norms were abandoned, the fact that most violence by *any* family member (male or female) occurred behind closed doors without any report to the authorities made it difficult to address.

Beginning in the 1960s, family violence came "out of the closet." Although there had been previous periods of attention to individual acts or specific problems regarding child abuse, beginning in the 1960s, child advocates and medical personnel identified characteristics of a battered child syndrome and initiated a still ongoing professional, research, and advocacy response to child abuse and neglect. Also during this period, many of the initial concerns of the emerging victims' movement grew out of the still-evolving women's movement concerns about the criminal justice system's treatment of the mostly female victims of sexual assault and domestic violence. Domestic violence issues remain a central concern of the victims' movement. Finally, the acceleration of the "graying" of the American population, and its related challenges, has increased the occurrence of and the attention to intrafamilial elder abuse.

The definition—and, consequently, the estimates of the extent—of family violence are matters of dispute. Some researchers limit the term *family violence* to acts involving physical injury only. Some include acts of physical or sexual violence in this term, regardless of injury. Others include acts of verbal or psychological abuse or financial coercion. Researchers also vary in their definitions regarding which individuals are included in the concept of "family" violence. Moreover, estimates regarding the extent of family violence differ based on whether they have been compiled in clinical populations (e.g., through hospital, police,

149

or social service contacts) or from the general population, as well as the standard methodological disputes regarding research methods used in compiling the estimates. As a result, estimates of the extent of family violence range from a few million to tens of millions of victims each year, as illustrated by Chapter 7, the Straus selection. Although the actual numbers may be in dispute, there is no dispute that family violence is a serious problem in this country.

The severity of the problem has prompted theorists to search for causal explanations for this distinct form of victimization. At the outset, researchers have recognized that family violence is not a homogeneous form of victimization. The diversity of family violence has fostered a diversity of theories that seek to explain it. Some theories are more socially or culturally based, such as those that focus on the high level of conflict inherent in families, societal norms that condone at least some degree of violence by parents and spouses, and continuing inequality between men and women. Other theories are more individually based, such as social learning theories that emphasize an abuser's early experiences with family violence, an abuser's individual needs to assert power or domination, an abuser's individual psychological abnormalities, or individual characteristics that render a victim especially vulnerable to family violence. Still others point to such non–family-related contributing factors as alcoholism, poverty, and the level of violence in the larger society. As the Straus selection suggests, however, it is unlikely that any *single* factor causes family violence, but rather that *multiple* risk factors interact and increase the likelihood of family violence.

The response to family violence has not been limited to theoretical research. Prompted by victims' movement advocates, there have been significant actions responsive to family violence throughout the American criminal and civil justice systems. Family violence is now typically treated as a criminal justice matter—not a private, family matter. Not only are acts of family violence treated as criminal acts, but they are sometimes pursued more aggressively than other criminal cases through laws or policies requiring mandatory arrest or "no-drop" prosecutions. New laws have been enacted, such as those expanding warrantless arrest authority in family violence situations, enhancing penalties for family violence, and criminalizing stalking behavior (which often occurs in a family context). Some jurisdictions have established specialized police and prosecution units, and even courts, to handle family violence matters. Family violence punishment sanctions now often include batterer treatment requirements. On the civil side, most jurisdictions have enacted family violence protective or restraining order provisions, many of which have criminal sanctions for violations. Reporting requirements leading to the detection of family violence, especially child abuse, have been enhanced. Thus, many of the innovations in family violence policy that are predicted in Chapter 8, the Ford et al. selection, have already been implemented.

Yet in the rush to respond to the very real problem of family violence, some researchers and policy analysts have questioned whether the responses that have been implemented are the most appropriate ones to address the problem. For example, some strategies, such as mandatory arrest policies in spousal violence cases and certain types of batterer treatment programs, have been implemented and maintained, despite equivocal empirical evidence regarding their efficacy in reducing family violence. Moreover, as discussed in the Ford et al. selection, few jurisdictions attempt to coordinate the broad array of criminal, civil, and social service responses to family violence that sometimes lead to conflicting results. Thus, the challenge in the years ahead will be not simply to do *something* to address family violence, but to identify the strategies best suited for reducing the occurrence of family violence, appropriately sanctioning its perpetrators, and protecting its victims.

LEARNING EXPERIENCES

1. The National Family Violence Survey that was discussed in Chapter 7, the Straus selection, was conducted in 1985. Locate information regarding the current incidence and prevalence of family violence. Have the trends Straus reported continued? What factors have changed or remained the same since the 1985 survey?

2. In Chapter 8, Ford et al. make many predictions about how family violence cases will be handled in the years ahead. Many of these predictions have already been implemented in various places throughout the country.

   a. For example, many police departments have special units of officers that handle family violence incidents. If your community has such a unit, find out the way(s) these officers handle domestic violence complaints that may be different from those used by regular patrol officers. If your community does not have such specialized officers, find out what kind of specialized training, if any, officers receive regarding domestic violence.

   b. Most states have procedures for implementing family violence protective or restraining orders. Find out your state's procedures for obtaining and enforcing such an order, as well as what protections the order can provide. Attend a court proceeding in which such a protective or restraining order is sought.

   c. Find out your state's other civil and criminal laws and your community's prosecution and judicial policies regarding domestic violence cases.

3. Identify the family violence shelters and related services in your community. What services are available for victims of family violence? What needed services are not available?

4. Interview a police officer who works with family violence cases, a staff member at a family violence shelter, or a child protective services staff member about family violence in your community.

BIBLIOGRAPHY

Ammerman, R.T., & Hersen, M. (Eds.). (1990). *Treatment of family violence: A sourcebook*. New York: Wiley.

Ammerman, R.T., & Hersen, M. (Eds.). (1991). *Case studies in family violence*. New York: Plenum.

Bachman, R., & Taylor, B.M. (1994). The measurement of family violence and rape by the redesigned National Crime Victimization Survey. *Justice Quarterly, 11*, 499-512.

Bachman, R., & Carmody, D.C. (1994). Fighting fire with fire: The effects of victim resistance in intimate versus stranger perpetrated assaults against females. *Journal of Family Violence, 9*, 317-331.

Belknap, J. (1995). Law enforcement officers' attitudes about the appropriate responses to woman battering. *International Review of Victimology, 4*, 47-62.

Browne, A. (1987). *When battered women kill*. New York: Free Press.

Buzawa, E.S., & Buzawa, C.G. (1990). *Domestic violence: The criminal justice response*. Newbury Park, CA: Sage.

Buzawa, E.S., & Buzawa, C.G. (Eds.). (1996). *Do arrests and restraining orders work?* Thousand Oaks, CA: Sage.

Cardarelli, A.P. (Ed.) (1997). *Violence between intimate partners: Patterns, causes, and effects*. Boston: Allyn and Bacon.

Cicchetti, D., & Carlson, V. (Eds.). (1989). *Child maltreatment: Theory and research on the causes and consequences of child abuse and neglect*. New York: Cambridge University Press.

Courtois, C.A. (1988). *Healing the incest wound: Adult survivors in therapy*. New York: Norton.

Davis, R.C., & Smith, B. (1995). Domestic violence reforms: Empty promises or fulfilled expectations? *Crime & Delinquency, 41*, 541-552.

Davis, R.C., & Taylor, B.G. (1997). A proactive response to family violence: The results of a randomized experiment. *Criminology, 35*, 307-333.

Dobash, R.E., & Dobash, R. (1979). *Violence against wives: A case against the patriarchy*. New York: Free Press.

Dobash, R.P., Dobash, R.E., Wilson, W., & Daly, M. (1992). The myth of sexual symmetry in marital violence. *Social Problems, 39*, 71-91.

Dunford, F.W. (1990). System-initiated warrants for suspects of misdemeanor domestic assault: A pilot study. *Justice Quarterly, 7*, 631-653.

Dunford, F.W., Huizinga, D., & Elliott, D.S. (1990). The role of arrest in domestic assault: The Omaha experiment. *Criminology, 28*, 183-206.

Dutton, D.G. (1995). *The domestic assault of women: Psychological and criminal justice perspectives* (2nd ed.). Boston: Allyn and Bacon.

Dutton, D.G. (1998). *The abusive personality: Violence and control in intimate relationships*. New York: Guilford.

Edleson, J.L., & Tolman, R.M. (1992). *Intervention for men who batter: An ecological approach*. Newbury Park, CA: Sage.

Ewing, C.P. (1997). *Fatal families: The dynamics of intrafamilial homicide*. Thousand Oaks, CA: Sage.

Fagan, J. (1988). Contributions of family violence research to criminal justice policy on wife assault: Paradigms of science and social control. *Violence and Victims, 3*, 159-186.

Fagan, J. (1995). *The criminalization of domestic violence: Promises and limitations*. Washington, DC: U.S. Department of Justice.

Finkelhor, D. (1984). *Child sexual abuse: New theory and research*. New York: Free Press.

Finkelhor, D. (1997). The victimization of children and youth: Developmental victimology. In R.C. Davis, A.J. Lurigio, & W.G. Skogan (Eds.), *Victims of crime* (2nd ed., pp. 86-107). Thousand Oaks, CA: Sage.

Finkelhor, D., & Dziuba-Leatherman, J. (1995). Victimization prevention programs: A national survey of children's exposure and reactions. *Child Abuse & Neglect, 19*, 129-139.

Finkelhor, D., Gelles, R.J., Hotaling, G.T., & Straus, M.A. (Eds.). (1983). *The dark side of families: Current family violence research*. Beverly Hills, CA: Sage.

Ford, D.A. (1991). Prosecution as a victim power resource: A note on empowering women in violent conjugal relationships. *Law and Society Review, 25*, 313-334.

Ford, D.A., Reichard, R., Goldsmith, S., & Regoli, M.J. (1996). Future directions for criminal justice policy on domestic violence. In E.S. Buzawa & C.G. Buzawa (Eds.), *Do arrests and restraining orders work?* Thousand Oaks, CA: Sage.

Garner, J., & Fagan, J. (1997). Victims of domestic violence. In R.C. Davis, A.J. Lurigio, & W.G. Skogan (Eds.), *Victims of crime* (2nd ed., pp. 53-85). Thousand Oaks, CA: Sage.

Garner, J., Fagan, J., & Maxwell, C. (1995). Published findings from the spouse assault replication program: A critical review. *Journal of Quantitative Criminology, 11*, 3-28.

Gelles, R.J. (1987). *The violent home*. Newbury Park, CA: Sage.

Gelles, R.J. (1997). *Intimate violence in families* (3rd ed.). Thousand Oaks, CA: Sage.

Gelles, R.J., & Straus, M.A. (1988). *Intimate violence*. New York: Simon and Schuster.

Gondolf, E.W. (1990). *Psychiatric response to family violence: Identifying and confronting neglected danger*. Lexington, MA: Lexington.

Greven, P. (1991). *Spare the child: The religious roots of punishment and the psychological impact of physical abuse*. New York: Knopf.

Hamberger, L.K., & Hastings, J.E. (1989). Counseling male spouse abusers: Characteristics of treatment completers and dropouts. *Violence and Victims, 4*, 275-286.

Hegar, R.L., Zuravin, S.J., & Orme, J.G. (1994). Factors predicting severity of physical child abuse injury: A review of the literature. *Journal of Interpersonal Violence, 9*, 170-183.

Herzberger, S.D. (1996). *Violence within the family: Social psychological perspectives*. Madison, WI: Brown & Benchmark.

Hirschel, J.D., Dean, C.W., & Lumb, R.C. (1994). The relative contribution of domestic violence to assault and injury of police officers. *Justice Quarterly, 11*, 99-117.

Hirschel, J.D., Hutchinson, I.W., III, & Dean, C.W. (1992). The failure of arrest to deter spouse abuse. *Journal of Research in Crime and Delinquency, 29*, 7-33.

Hudson, M.F. (1989). Analyses of the concepts of elder mistreatment: Abuse and neglect. *Journal of Elder Abuse & Neglect, 1(1)*, 5-25.

Jaffe, P.G., Wolfe, D.A. & Wilson, S.K. (1990). *Children of battered women*. Newbury Park, CA: Sage.

Jasinski, J.L., & Williams, L.M. (with Finkelhor, D., Giles-Sims, J., Hamby, S.L., Kaufman Kantor, G., Mahoney, P., West, C.M., & Wolak, J.) (Eds.). (1998). *Partner violence: A comprehensive review of 20 years of research*. Thousand Oaks, CA: Sage.

Kaufman Kantor, G., & Jansinski, J.L. (Eds.). (1997). *Out of the darkness: Contemporary perspectives on family violence*. Thousand Oaks, CA: Sage.

Knudsen, D.D., & Miller, J.L. (Eds.). (1991). *Abused and battered: Social and legal responses to family violence*. New York: Aldine de Gruyter.

Kolko, D.J. (1992). Characteristics of child victims of physical violence: Research findings and clinical implications. *Journal of Interpersonal Violence, 7*, 244-276.

Macolini, R.M. (1995). Elder abuse policy: Considerations in research and legislation. *Behavioral Sciences & the Law, 13*, 349-363.

Mann, C.R. (1988). Getting even? Women who kill in domestic encounters. *Justice Quarterly, 5*, 33-51.

McCord, J. (1983). A forty year perspective of effects of child abuse and neglect. *Child Abuse and Neglect, 7*, 265-270.

McCurdy, K., & Daro, D. (1994). Child maltreatment: A national study of reports and fatalities. *Journal of Interpersonal Violence, 9*, 75-94.

Mones, P.A. (1991). *When a child kills: Abused children who kill their parents*. New York: Pocket.

Monson, C.M., Byrd, G.R., Langhinrichsen-Rohling, J. (1996). To have and to hold: Perceptions of marital rape. *Journal of Interpersonal Violence, 11*, 410-424.

Pillemer, K.A., & Wolf, R.S. (Eds.). (1986). *Elder abuse: Conflict in the family*. Dover, MA: Auburn House.

Pleck, E. (1987). *Domestic tyranny: The making of social policy against family violence from colonial times to the present*. New York: Oxford University Press.

Quinn, M.J., & Tomita, S.K. (1997). *Elder abuse and neglect: Causes, diagnosis and intervention strategies* (2nd ed.). New York: Springer.

Riggs, D.S., Kilpatrick, D.G., & Resnick, H.S. (1992). Long-term psychological distress associated with marital rape and aggravated assault: A comparison to other crime victims. *Journal of Family Violence, 7*, 283-296.

Roberts, A.R. (Ed.). (1996). *Helping battered women: New perspectives and remedies*. New York: Oxford University Press.

Rose, S.J., & Meezan, W. (1996). Variations in perceptions of child neglect. *Child Welfare, 75*, 139-160.

Saunders, D.G., & Size, P.B. (1986). Attitudes about woman abuse among police officers, victims, and victim advocates. *Journal of Interpersonal Violence, 1*, 25-42.

Schmidt, J., & Hochstadler Steury, E. (1989). Prosecutorial discretion in filing charges in domestic violence cases. *Criminology, 27*, 487-510.

Sherman, L.W. (with Schmidt, J.D., & Rogan, D.P.). (1992). *Policing domestic violence: Experiments and dilemmas*. New York: Free Press.

Sherman, L.W., & Berk, R.A. (1984). The specific deterrent effects of arrest for domestic assault. *American Sociological Review, 49*, 261-272.

Sherman, L.W., & Cohn, E.G. (1989). The impact of research on legal policy: The Minneapolis domestic violence experiment. *Law and Society Review, 23*, 117-144.

Sherman, L.W., & Smith, D.A. (with Schmidt, J.D., & Rogan, D.P.). (1992). Crime, punishment, and stake in conformity: Legal and informal control of domestic violence. *American Sociological Review, 57*, 680-690.

Stalans, L.J., & Lurigio, A.J. (1995). Public preferences for the court's handling of domestic violence situations. *Crime & Delinquency, 41*, 399-413.

Steinman, M. (Ed.). (1991). *Woman battering: Policy responses*. Cincinnati, OH: Anderson.

Steinmetz, S.K. (1977-1978). The battered husband syndrome. *Victimology, 2*, 499-509.

Steinmetz, S.K. (1988). *Duty bound: Elder abuse and family care*. Newbury Park, CA: Sage.

Stout, K.D. (1991). Intimate femicide: A national demographic overview. *Journal of Interpersonal Violence, 6*, 476-485.

Straus, M.A. (1991). Physical violence in American families: Incidence rates, causes, and trends. In D.D. Knudsen & J.L. Miller (Eds.), *Abused and battered: Social and legal responses to family violence* (pp. 17-34). New York: Aldine de Gruyter.

Straus, M.A., & Gelles, R.J. (1990). *Physical violence in American families: Risk factors and adaptations to violence in 8,145 families*. New Brunswick, NJ: Transaction.

Straus, M.A., Gelles, R.J., & Steinmetz, S.K. (1980). *Behind closed doors: Violence in the American family*. Garden City, NY: Doubleday.

Straus, M.A., Kaufman Kantor, G., & Moore, D.W. (1997). Change in cultural norms approving marital violence from 1968 to 1994. In G. Kaufman Kantor & J.L. Jasinski (Eds.), *Out of the darkness: Contemporary perspectives on family violence* (pp. 3-16). Thousand Oaks, CA: Sage.

Tolman R.M., & Weisz, A. (1995). Coordinated community intervention for domestic violence: The effects of arrest and prosecution on recidivism of woman abuse perpetrators. *Crime & Delinquency, 41,* 481-495.

Viano, E.C. (Ed.). (1992). *Intimate violence: Interdisciplinary perspectives.* Bristol, PA: Taylor & Francis.

Walker, L.E. (1979). *The battered woman.* New York: Harper & Row.

Wallace, H. (1996). *Family violence: Legal, medical, and social perspectives.* Boston: Allyn and Bacon.

Widom, C.S. (1989). Child abuse, neglect, and violent criminal behavior. *Criminology, 27,* 251-271.

Willis, C.L., & Wells, R.H. (1988). The police and child abuse: An analysis of police decisions to report illegal behavior. *Criminology, 26,* 695-716.

Wolf, R.S., & Pillemer, K.A. (1989). *Helping elderly victims: The reality of elder abuse.* New York: Columbia University Press.

Zellman, G.L. (1990). Child abuse reporting and failure to report among mandated reporters: prevalence, incidence, and reasons. *Journal of Interpersonal Violence, 5,* 3-22.

Zorza, J. (1992). The criminal law of misdemeanor domestic violence, 1970-1990. *Journal of Criminal Law & Criminology, 83,* 46-72.

Chapter 7

Physical Violence in American Families: Incidence Rates, Causes, and Trends

Murray A. Straus

I. Introduction

Violence is not the exclusive property of a few cruel or mentally ill parents or spouses. It occurs in millions of "normal" families. As long as the general public and legislators perceive family violence as a problem of a few "sick" persons, however, the financial support for the effort needed to end family violence will be inadequate. In addition, the risk— almost the certainty—of serious policy errors or omissions is increased by the lack of information on incidence and prevalence rates of violence among families in general. Research findings based on clinical samples of abused children aided by child protective services or family violence victims in a battered-women's shelter are indeed necessary. However, information obtained from studies of clinical populations may not apply to other abused children or spouses.

The difference between the implications of empirical findings based on a clinical population and those based on a cross section of the general population is illustrated by research on gender differences in domestic assaults. Findings from studies conducted in shelters for battered women or from studies of police reports indicate that physical abuse of spouses is overwhelmingly an act of *male* violence. Studies of the general population, however, show that wives hit husbands about as often as husbands hit wives. Women also initiate assaults just as often as men do

Source: Straus, M.A. (1991). Physical violence in American families: Incidence rates, causes, and trends. In D.D. Knudsen & J.L. Miller (Eds.), *Abused and battered: Social and legal responses to family violence* (pp. 17-34). New York: Aldine de Gruyter. Reprinted by permission of Dr. Murray A. Straus, Family Research Laboratory, University of New Hampshire.

(Stets and Straus 1990; Straus 1989), a fact unknowable from shelter statistics or police statistics.

When men are assaulted, they are *less likely* than women to be injured (Stets and Straus 1990). The police tend to record only those abuse cases in which there is an injury. In addition, men have greater economic resources than women, and therefore do not as often need the equivalent of a battered-women's shelter. Finally, male pride in physical strength and the shame in not being able to "handle the situation" inhibits filing a complaint with the police. The high level of domestic assaults by women is critically important information for primary *prevention* (Straus 1990b; Straus and Smith 1990), although it does not appear in shelter statistics or police statistics. Victim services and treatment efforts must continue to respond to violence by men. In addition, women must be alerted to the criminality and the danger to themselves that comes from assaulting a spouse.

II. What is Violence?

The question, How much violence takes place behind the closed doors of American households? is obscured by the principle of family privacy, and by certain paradoxes regarding the family.

A. Obstacles to Perceiving Family Violence

The family is a loving and supportive group, but—paradoxically—it is an extremely violent group. That does not mean that all families are loving and supportive, nor does it mean that all families are violent. Typically, love is most likely to be experienced in the context of one's family. Similarly, violence is more likely to occur at the hands of a family member than it is at the hands of anyone else. The likelihood of a man's being assaulted by a member of his family is more than 20 times greater than by someone who is not a family member. For women, the risk is more than 200 times greater (Straus et al. 1980:49).[1]

Even though the world outside the family is less violent than the world inside the family, paradoxically, the loving and supportive aspects of the family obscure an ability to perceive the violent aspect of family life and to face up to how much violence exists.

B. Definition and Measurement of Violence

Family violence estimates vary tremendously, depending on how the problem is defined and on the method used to measure it. The definition of violence used for the research reported in this chapter is derived from

Gelles and Straus (1979:554): an act carried out with the intention or perceived intention of causing physical pain or injury to another person.

There are two elements in this definition: act and intention. The first, the act, is clear. One only has to imagine a husband who aims and shoots a gun at his wife. Fortunately, most men are bad shots and usually miss. Nonetheless, the shooting is a serious act of violence, even though no one is injured. Using the act as a defining criterion of violence results in a higher incidence rate than one based only on assaults that actually result in injury.

Consider intention—the second element of the definition. Suppose a husband and wife are moving a piece of furniture. It slips and breaks the wife's toe. This is not violence as defined above, because there is no intent to cause pain or injury.

1. Acts versus Injuries. Child protection workers and staff members working in shelters for battered women often define violence in terms of the injuries sustained. A battered child means an injured child. For some purposes, measuring violence by injuries is appropriate, e.g., if the purpose is to estimate the need for medical services. However, such a measure greatly underestimates the total number of violent incidents. Only about 5% of physically abused children and 3% of physically abused women are injured severely enough to require medical care (Stets and Straus 1990; Straus 1980). Victims are suffering, both from the psychological impact and from the physical blows, but if injury alone were used as the basis for defining and measuring intrafamily violence, the rates of child abuse and wife abuse would be very low. These rates would fail to capture over 95% of the actual cases of violence.

2. Other Aspects of Violence. One dimension that needs to be considered in order to understand violence is whether the violent act is legitimate according to either the legal norms (a parent slapping a child, for example), or the informal norms of society. Some violence is legitimate, whereas some (slapping a spouse, for example) is illegitimate. Another dimension is whether the violence is instrumental (to coerce someone to do or not do something), or expressive (to see the other person in pain).

3. Physical Violence is not the Only Type of Abuse. The focus of this chapter is on physical violence, which does not imply that physical assaults are the only, or even the worst, types of abuse in families. A child or a spouse can be terribly hurt by verbal assaults (Straus et al. 1989; Vissing and Straus 1990). Some children and wives are sexually assaulted (Finkelhor 1986; Finkelhor and Yllo 1985), and theft by a family member is more common than theft by a stranger (Straus and Lincoln 1985).

III. How Violent Are American Families?

The incidence rates for two types of family violence have been known for many years—physical punishment of children and murder of a family member.

A. *Physical Punishment and Murder*

Child development researchers have studied the rate of physical punishment since the 1920s. These studies leave no doubt that physical punishment is nearly universal in American society. While it may seem inappropriate to include physical punishment as violence, it is an act *intended* to cause the child a certain degree of physical pain.

The Federal Bureau of Investigation has compiled statistics for murders of family members since the 1930s. Data are also available from other nations as well. In the United States, within-family killings account for about 25% of all homicides. In Canada, the figure is about 50%, and in Denmark about 66%. These data make it clear that an individual is far more likely to be murdered by a member of one's own family than by anyone else (Straus 1986, 1988).

In Denmark, the few family homicides that do occur are a large slice of a very small pie. On the other hand, the rate of within-family homicides in the United States is low partly because the U.S. murder rate is extremely high. However, even in Denmark, where homicide has nearly been eliminated, the one place where it tends to persist is within the family.

B. *The National Family Violence Surveys*

Information about physical punishment and homicide has been available for a number of years, but little has been known about the rates of violent acts that are more serious than physical punishment, but less serious than murder. To help fill that gap, the first National Family Violence Survey was conducted in 1975 (Straus et al. 1980), based on a nationally representative sample of 2143 American couples. A second survey was conducted in 1985. A representative sample of 6002 couples was surveyed, sufficiently large to allow a 20% change between the survey years to be statistically significant. The 1985 survey corrected for certain 1975 omissions by including single parents, and separated or divorced individuals if the marriage had ended within the previous two years.

Detailed information on how the 1985 study was conducted is given elsewhere (Straus and Gelles 1990), including information showing that the sample accurately represents the U.S. adult population. Some respondents from the National Family Violence Surveys withheld information about violent incidents, and even more respondents did not recall incidents. Consequently, the figures pertaining to violence are minimum rates. The true rates of family violence are higher by some unknown amount.

C. The Conflict Tactics Scales

Both the 1975 and the 1985 National Family Violence Surveys used the Conflict Tactics Scales or CTS (Straus 1979, 1990a) to measure violence, including subscales for both minor and severe violence. The items in the minor-violence scale are pushing, grabbing, shoving, throwing something, and slapping or spanking the spouse or child. The severe-violence scale consists of items that are more likely to cause an injury that needs medical treatment: kicking, biting, punching, beating up, choking, burning, threatening with a knife or gun, and using a knife or gun.

D. Incidence Rates

Table 1 shows the violence rates from the 1985 National Family Violence Survey. These rates are discussed in detail elsewhere (Straus and Gelles 1986, 1990). Thus, only a few key items are elaborated here.

1. Marital Violence. The rates for physical assaults between partners in a married or cohabiting relationship are shown in panel A of Table 1.[2] Sixteen of every hundred couples reported a violent incident during the year of the survey. If this statistic is accurate, an estimated 8.7 million couples experienced violence that year. However, these are lower-bound estimates, and the true figure is much greater—perhaps as high as one-third of American couples in any one year [see Straus et al. (1980:34-35) for an explanation]. On the other hand, 16 per 100 may overstate the situation, because as Table 1 shows, 3.4 million incidents were "severe" assaults that carry a high risk of causing an injury, such as kicking, punching, choking, or use of weapons.

2. Prevalence Rate. In contrast to the one-year incidence rates, prevalence rates are used to indicate the proportion of couples who, *over the course of the marriage,* experienced a violent altercation. The exact figure from the 1985 survey is 30%. However, that is probably even more of an underestimate than the incidence rates are, because violent events are often forgotten, particularly if they occurred only once and a long time ago. Again, assuming that the true rate is much higher, perhaps 60% of American couples experienced at least one physical assault over the course of the marriage.

Table 1.   1985 National Family Violence Survey: Annual Incidence Rates
           for Family Violence and Estimated Number of Cases Based on
           These Rates

Type of intrafamily violence[a]	Rate per thousand couples or children	Number assaulted[b]
A. Violence between husband and wife		
Any violence during the year (slap, push, etc.)	161	8,700,000
Severe violence (kick, punch, stab, etc.)	63	3,400,000
Any violence by the husband	116	6,250,000
Severe violence by the husband (wife beating)	34	1,800,000
Any violence by the wife	124	6,800,000
Severe violence by the wife	48	2,600,000
B. Violence by parents: child aged 0-17		
Any hitting during the year	Near 100% for young child[c]	
Very severe violence (child abuse 1)	23	1,500,000
Severe violence (child abuse 2)	110	6,900,000
C. Violence by parents, child aged 15-17		
Any violence during the year	340	3,800,000
Very severe violence	21	235,000
Severe violence	70	800,000
D. Violence by children aged 3-17 (1975 sample)		
Any violence against a brother or sister	800	50,400,000
Severe violence against a brother or sister	530	33,800,000
Any violence against a parent	180	9,700,000
Severe violence against a parent	90	4,800,000
E. Violence by children aged 15-17 (1975 sample)		
Any violence against a brother or sister	640	7,200,000
Severe violence against a brother or sister	360	4,000,000
Any violence against a parent	100	1,100,000
Severe violence against a parent	35	400,000

[a] Rates for part A are based on the entire sample of 6,002 currently married or cohabiting couples interviewed in 1985. [Note: These rates differ from those in Straus and Gelles (1986) because these are computed in a way that enabled the 1985 rates to be compared with the more restricted sample and more restricted version of the CTS used in the 1975 study.] Rates for part B are based on the 1985 sample of 3,232 households with a child age 17 and under. [Note: These rates differ from those in Straus and Gelles (1986) for the reasons given above.] Rates for parts C and D are based on the 1975 study because data on violence by children were not collected in the 1985 survey.

[b] These figures were computed by multiplying the rates in this table by the 1984 population figures as given in the 1986 Statistical Abstract of the United States. The population figures (rounded to millions) are 54 million couples, and 63 million children aged 0-17. The number of children aged 15-17 was estimated as 11.23 million, by taking 75% of the number of aged 14-17.

[c] The rate for three-year-old children in the 1975 survey was 97%.

3. *Gender Differences in Marital Assaults.* Wife battering has been the aspect of marital violence of most public concern. Women are the major victims when physical, economic, and psychological injury are examined (Straus et al. 1980; Stets and Straus 1990). Nevertheless, the data in Table 1 show that women assault their partners as often as men assault theirs. This is a serious problem, not only because violence is morally wrong, but because it vastly increases the risk of women being attacked in retaliation (Straus 1989).

4. *Chronicity of Assaults on Women.* The annual incidence rates and the marital prevalence rates indicate how many couples experience an assault. The chronicity of violence—how often the violent acts occur—is also important. Among those women who reported an incident involving a severe assault by the husband, one-third reported only one incident. However, the distribution is very skewed; the average is five assaults during the year. These are very violent couples, but they are less violent than the couples in which the female partners sought help from a battered-women's shelter. Two studies of shelter population women using the CTS have found approximately 60 assaults during the year (Giles-Sims 1983; Okun 1986).

5. *Community Samples and Clinical Samples.* The substantial difference in the chronicity of violence between the violent couples in the National Family Violence Survey and the frequency of violence to which women in shelters have been exposed suggests that there is not only a "clinical fallacy," but probably a "representative sample fallacy" as well (Straus 1990b). The "battered women" in this sample are not as frequently battered as the women in shelters. The average of five incidents per year among the cross section of battered women in the National Family Violence Survey suggests that it is equally hazardous to generalize from a representative sample to a clinical population.

6. *Child Abuse.* Panel B of Table 1 shows the rates of physical abuse of children, using two related measures of child abuse. The Child Abuse 1 measure (very severe violence) includes only those acts that are undeniably abusive: kicking, biting, punching, beating up, choking, and attacking a child with a knife or gun. Table 1 shows that 2.3%, or an estimated 1.5 million American children, were physically abused in 1985. Moreover, these attacks occurred an average of seven times (median = 3.5 times).

The Child Abuse 2 measure (severe violence) includes the same acts measured in Child Abuse 1, and in addition includes hitting with an object. The incidence of child abuse derived using this measure is 11 out of every 100 children, or an estimated 6.9 million abused children. The Child Abuse 2 statistic is almost five times greater than the Child Abuse 1 statistic. Which measure is correct?

Many people object to "hitting with an object" as a measure of abuse because it includes traditionally approved objects, such as a paddle, hairbrush, or belt. If child abuse is the use of force beyond what is normatively permitted, then this is not child abuse. On the other hand, it can be argued that such violence is no longer normatively permissible. Sweden and other European countries have made any use of physical punishment illegal, and in the United States, a national committee with that goal was formed in January 1989. The resolution of this issue may depend on research that can identify what the norms really are.

7. *Summary.* The statistics presented provide evidence that the family is preeminent in violence. The risk of assault within the family is many times greater than the risk of stranger assault. This is particularly true for women. Using the figures on assaults from the FBI, the rate of non-family physical assault on women is less than 20 per 100,000 women, but the rate of intrafamily severe assaults on women is about 4,000 per 100,000 women, or about 200 times greater. If one were to count all the instances in which he "slapped" her, the figure would be much higher. The puzzle remains: How can the family be both a loving and supportive group, and at the same time such a violent group?

IV. The Social Causes of Family Violence

This chapter examines only a few of the multiple social causes of family violence, not because other types of causes, especially psychological causes, are unimportant. Rather, the division of labor in science and social science and constraints of space make such limitations necessary.

A. *The High Level of Conflict Inherent in Families*

The first of the social causes of family violence is the inherently high level of conflict that is characteristic of families. Conflict can be observed in all human groups, but it is especially prevalent in certain types of groups, and the family is one of them. There are several reasons for this.

1. *Wide Range of Activities.* First, the family is concerned with the entire range of activities and interests of its members, the "whole person" as the phrase goes. This is what most people want and value in family relationships. The difficulty is that it means that nothing is off limits, and therefore anything can be the focus of a conflict; the greater the number of issues of mutual concern, the greater the probability of conflict.

2. *Gender and Age Differences.* The family usually consists of both men and women, both the young and the old. Differences among them, which are rooted in traditional cultural orientations as well as in the historical experience of each generation, are a potent source of conflict. To a certain extent, men and women have different values and cognitive orientations, different conceptions of power, and different world views (Gilligan 1982). The "battle of the sexes" is built into the family, in fact, in its most acute form. The generation gap is also most acute within the family. It expresses itself in many ways, for example, in clothing styles and whether rock or Bach is going to be played on the family stereo.

3. *Shared Identity.* The rock vs. Bach example also illustrates another reason why conflict is so frequent and so severe within the family—the shared identity of family members, and the resulting intensity of involvement. In addition, there is a presumed right to influence other family members. If one spouse comments that the other one's shirt and jacket colors do not go well together, he or she usually does it out of concern for the other and because they have a "shared fate." Moreover, the comment about clashing colors is not just an abstract esthetic judgment—there is an implicit expectation that a shirt or jacket of a different color will be chosen.

4. *Involuntary Membership.* Membership in the family is, to a considerable extent, not a matter of choice. A parent cannot order children out of the home, and children cannot just leave, even though most have probably thought about doing that at one time or another. The involuntary membership therefore blocks using one of the most frequent solutions for human conflicts—leaving.

Leaving a martial [sic] relationship continues to be difficult for spouses, even in this era of high divorce rates: It is expensive; there is guilt; there are still some good things about the marriage; one must tell parents, friends, and other relatives, and, finally, there is the well-being of the children. So even when the conflict seems to be unresolvable, people stay and put up with conflict that they would otherwise stop by leaving.

5. *Family Privacy.* Another characteristic of the family that accounts partially for the high level of conflict is family privacy. Privacy insulates conflicts within the family from both social controls and social supports that can serve to reduce or resolve the conflict. For example, family members say nasty things to each other in private that they would never say in public.

6. *Conflict and Violence.* Hotaling and Straus (1980) describe a number of other characteristics of the family that engender a high level of conflict (e.g., stress, organizational features of marriage, sexist atti-

tudes). All of these add up to produce a high level of conflict, which in turn increases the risk that one or another member of the family will try to win the conflict by hitting, or will just hit out of anger over the conflict. As the amount of conflict increases, the assault rate also increases dramatically.

B. Gender Inequality

A second major cause of family violence is gender inequality, particularly, male dominance (Straus 1977; Coleman and Straus 1986). Male dominance is manifested in many obvious and subtle ways, such as the fact that men earn more than women in the United States and that the husband is usually considered the head of the household.

The idea of the husband as the head of the household is at the root of a great many assaults on wives. It frequently means that when the couple cannot agree, the husband will have the final say. There are millions of women who believe in that principle—more women than men opposed the Equal Rights Amendment. However, sooner or later within the marriage, an issue will arise that, principle or not, is so important for the wife that her way must prevail. This is double trouble: there is the issue at hand, and, according to the husband, the wife is reneging on the implicit terms of their marriage contract.

The issue then becomes transformed into a moral question for this hypothetical man. This rationale produces moral indignation on the part of men, and provides a powerful justification for violence. In fact, most violence in the family or elsewhere is carried out for what the violent person thinks is a morally correct purpose. This happens, for example, in the stereotypical movie Western, where someone "insults my girl" and is justifiably hit on the head with a whiskey bottle. Or it is seen on the television daytime soap opera, where her husband says something outrageous and she "slaps the cad."

The direct, linear relationship found between inequality and violence in the National Family Violence Survey analysis (Straus et al. 1980:192) indicates that the greater the departure from gender equality, the greater the risk that physical force will be used to maintain the power of the dominant person.

Egalitarian couples have the lowest rates of violence, and husband-dominated couples have the highest rate of spouse abuse. As Coleman and Straus (1986) have shown, male dominance is related to violence even when the wife believes—sometimes fervently—that the husband should be the head of the family. The violence rates in wife-dominant couples are also higher than the rate in egalitarian couples, but not as high as in husband-dominant couples.[3] In addition, one has to keep in mind that there are fewer wife-dominant than husband-dominant couples.

C. Norms That Permit Intrafamily Violence

Almost all human behavior is influenced by the rules of society that specify appropriate behavior in specific situations—what anthropologists and sociologists call *cultural norms*. Every society also has its rules about violence. As with other rules, those regulating violence vary from situation to situation.

1. Violence by Parents. In American society, violence by parents is permitted, and to a certain extent required (Carson 1986). Parents not only have the legal right to hit, but they are expected to do so if the child persistently misbehaves. This right was reaffirmed when a number of states passed child abuse laws. Those statutes say that nothing in the law should be taken as denying the right of parents to use ordinary physical punishment. A certain irony exists here: legislation that was passed to protect children from assault simultaneously puts the weight of the state on the side of hitting children "when necessary."

These laws are not merely obsolete statutes. Most American parents support the use of physical punishment and almost all administer it, at least to small children. Ninety percent of the parents who participated in the National Family Violence Survey approved of physical punishment. These findings are consistent with those from two other recent national surveys (Lehman 1989).

2. Violence by Spouses. The marriage license also is a hitting license. This right was a formal part of the common law until just after the Civil War in the United States (Calvert 1974). Blackstone's (1778) definitive codification of the English common law gave husbands the right to physically "chastise" an errant wife. This rule has not been recognized by the courts for more than a century, but it has lived on de facto in the actions (and nonactions) of the police, prosecutors, and victims. Until it was changed in 1977, the training manual for domestic-disturbance calls published by the International Association of Chiefs of Police essentially recommended that hitting a spouse be treated as a "private matter" and that arrests should be avoided.

Despite the new laws passed during the 1980s, and despite increased police action, the implicit hitting license remains. The major change has been a reduction in the severity of violence that is tolerated.

The informal social norms have changed much less than the law has. Almost a third of American men and a quarter of American women perceive that it is normal for a husband or wife to slap the other "on occasion" (Straus et al. 1980:47), admittedly under very general or unspecified circumstances. If we had specifically asked whether it would be all right to slap a spouse because the dinner was not prepared correctly, the percentage of those approving would probably have dropped to near zero. Conversely, if we had asked about a wife slapping a husband if she came home and found him in bed with another woman, approval would probably increase to at least 60-70%.

Since everyone is against violence "in principle," it is often difficult to perceive that there are norms permitting violence between a couple, as the following example demonstrates. After a lecture, a prominent sociologist objected to my claim that the family is an extremely violent group. He argued that figures showing a 16% violence rate indicate that 84% are *not* violent. In response, I said that if "only" 16% of the faculty had hit other faculty members or students that year, it would be sufficient to conclude that there is *much* violence on campus. The questioner naturally rejected my conclusion. He was implicitly using a different set of norms for families than for universities. The norms of American society absolutely prohibit violence in one setting and tolerate it in the other. This is extremely important because violence, like other crimes, is more likely to occur when the offender believes that detection, arrest, or sanction is unlikely (Gelles 1983; Gelles and Straus 1988).

The distinctiveness of the cultural norm that makes the marriage license a hitting license is illustrated by a recognition that more conflict does not necessarily lead to more violence in all situations. There is a huge amount of conflict in academic departments—novels have been written about it—but neither in novels nor in real life is there physical violence. Yet physical violence occurs in 45% of high-conflict families. There are some very rare exceptions to the rule, but violence does not occur in 45% of high-conflict academic departments. An occasional slap of one professor by another would simply not be tolerated, but an occasional slap within the family is likely to be tolerated. This tolerance is a partial explanation the persistence of family violence.

D. Family Training in Violence

A limitation to the theory presented so far is that it does not explain why the norms for families permit violence, whereas the norms for other groups prohibit it. Part of the explanation lies in the fact that in the family there is a "hidden curriculum" that teaches violence. It starts in infancy with physical punishment. Over 90% of parents surveyed by the National Family Violence Survey report that they hit toddlers in the 3-4 year group (Wauchope and Straus 1990). Over 20% of the parents surveyed report hitting an infant, and approximately 33% continue hitting even when the children are aged 15-17. Again, these are lower-bound estimates, once more illuminating the notion that being hit by a parent is an almost universal experience of children in the United States.

Most of this violence is ordinary physical punishment carried out by a loving and concerned parent. A ten-month old child picks up a stick and puts it in his mouth. The parent takes it away and says, "No, no, don't do that. You'll get sick. Don't put dirty things in your mouth." Unfortunately, children crawling on the ground are almost certain to do it again! Eventually, the parent is likely to come over to the child and gently slap his hand, again saying, "No, don't do that."

The problem is that these actions also teach the child the principle that those who love you are those who hit you. This lesson starts in infancy, when the deepest layers of personality are presumably being formed. It continues for half of all American children until they physically leave home. Moreover, the principle is easily reversed to "those you love are those you can hit." Ironically, the fact that hitting is done by a loving and careful parent makes it worse. Not only do children learn that those who love you hit you, but that it is morally right for them to do so. In one pilot study we found that toddlers have a clear conception of the moral rightness of hitting. The children were shown pictures of an adult hitting a child and were asked to say what was happening. Without exception they said it was because the child in the picture had done something wrong.

The important point for understanding family violence is that this principle extends into adult life. It is a direct transfer from the script learned early in life, through physical punishment.

The hypothesis that the more physical punishment experienced as a child, the greater the probability of hitting one's spouse, was tested with data from the National Family Violence Survey. Each respondent was asked how often he/she was physically punished at about age 12 or 13. The results support the hypothesis. The more a husband was physically punished as a child, the greater was the probability he would assault his wife as an adult. The same effect of physical punishment is also found among wives (Straus 1983).

E. Violence Has Multiple Causes

As developed thus far, the family violence theory has pointed to the high level of conflict in families, the inequality between men and women, cultural norms that permit intrafamily violence, and family training in violence as the risk factors that increase the probability of violence. A number of other risk factors need to be incorporated, such as alcoholism (Kaufman-Kantor and Straus 1987), poverty, and other types of stress (Straus 1980b). The level of violence in the larger society also has a potent influence (Baron et al. 1988).

No single risk factor by itself puts a family at high risk of violence. The weakness of any one factor is illustrated by the finding that individuals who experienced frequent physical punishment as children are more than twice as likely to assault their spouse than those who did not

(11 vs. 5%). At the same time, the 11% figure also indicates that 89% of spouses who *did* experience a great deal of physical punishment at age 13 did *not* assault their spouse during the year of the survey. The same type of interpretation applies to each of the other risk factors. For example, more violence occurs in male-dominant marriages, but most male-dominant marriages are not physically violent.

None of the elements in this theory (or in anyone else's theory) is by itself determinative. It takes the combined effect to produce a high probability of violence. This can be illustrated by reflecting upon some of the risk factors discussed above. Let us envision a hypothetical family in which the husband grew up experiencing a lot of physical punishment. That is one risk factor. If the wife had a similar experience, it is another risk factor. If the husband observed his parents engaging in physical fights, that adds to the risk. If he believes he ought to have the final say in family decisions, that further adds to the risk. Suppose he also drinks heavily and is unemployed and therefore under stress. In combination, these factors add up to a prescription for violence.

Figure 1
Couple violence rate by checklist score

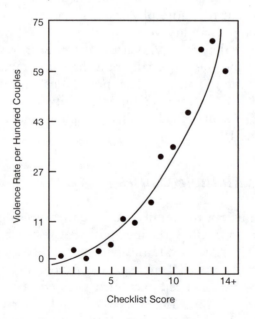

The statistical analysis that demonstrates this theory was conducted by creating a simple (unweighted) checklist score for each of the 2,143 couples in the 1975 National Family Violence Survey. One point was assigned for the presence of any of the six risk factors in the example of the preceding paragraph, and also for the presence of 13 other risk factors. Figure 1 (from Straus et al. 1980:204) shows for each risk factor score group the percentage of couples who reported a violent incident during the year. The horizontal axis is the checklist or risk factor score; the vertical axis is the rate of couple violence.

As Figure 1 shows, couples with low risk factor checklist scores have a violence rate that is nearly zero. Thereafter, as the checklist scores increase, the rate of violence increases exponentially. About 70% of the couples in the highest risk categories reported a violent incident during the year. Similar results were obtained using a checklist of risk factors found to be associated with physical abuse of children (Straus et al. 1980:212). These are truly remarkable findings.[4]

V. Trends in Family Violence

One of the fortunate outcomes from the last 15 years of research on family violence is that it has revealed causal factors that, for the most part, can be changed if society is so inclined.

A. The Campaign against Child Abuse and Wife Beating

On the remedial side of the change effort, we have created a vast network of child protective services (CPS). To be sure, these services are not nearly enough, but they are far greater than what existed in 1960 when state-funded CPS departments did not even exist as a separate entity. Also, there are now about a thousand shelters for battered women in the United States. Most shelters are underfunded and inadequately staffed, but the situation is better than in 1973, when no shelters existed. Arrest and prosecution of wife batterers are now common, even though most cases are still ignored (Kaufman-Kantor and Straus 1990).

B. Changes That Help Prevent Family Violence

On the primary prevention side of the effort (Straus and Smith 1990), parent education programs have continued to grow throughout the past 50 years, even though at a snail-like pace. Gender inequality is being reduced, but at a rate that can be gauged by the fact that the wages of women with full-time employment are about a third less than men's. There has been a tremendous growth in family counseling and therapy. This has no doubt aided couples in resolving the inevitable conflicts of married life, but these services still reach only a fraction of the population, and hardly any of the low-income population, where the known incidence of wife beating is relatively high. Racial segregation is now legally dead, informal discrimination has been reduced, and there is a growing Afro-American middle class. But, there is also a growing Afro-American underclass whose situation is worse than ever. Contraception is now widespread, so there are fewer unwanted children, who are at high risk of abuse, but the United States still has the highest teen pregnancy rate of any industrial country. These and other changes have implications for violence reduction (Straus and Gelles 1986, 1990).

C. Changes in Six Measures of Violence

Clearly, the existing treatment and prevention programs leave much to be desired. Nevertheless, writing in 1981, I suggested that the cumulative effect of the changes discussed above was likely to be a reduction in the incidence of child abuse and wife beating (Straus 1981). In 1985 the second National Family Violence Survey provided an opportunity to test that idea. Somewhat to our surprise, it revealed evidence consistent with the hypothesized decrease (Straus and Gelles 1986).

Figure 2 shows the percentage change in six measures of violence from the National Family Violence Survey, and changes in two other measures of violence that occurred between 1975 and 1985.

The data on child abuse show that the rate of physical abuse of children decreased by 47% between 1975 and 1985. That decrease is exactly opposite to what has been the experience in CPS during this same period. Cases *increased* threefold between 1976 and 1985. The two figures do not contradict each other. The increased rate of cases reported to CPS is a measure of public *intervention* intended to help children. It indicates that between 1976 and 1985, three times as many Americans took the major step of reporting a suspected case of child abuse, a sign that more Americans are starting to do something to reduce this phenomenon. To the extent that those efforts are successful, this could be one of the factors that accounts for the lower rate of child abuse found in the 1985 National Family Violence Survey.

Intrafamily homicides are also plotted in Figure 2 (from Straus 1986) and show a similar decrease during this period. This consistency with the decrease in child abuse is important because homicides are the most accurate of all statistics on violence. The third largest decrease was the number of severe assaults by husbands of their wives—what is often called wife beating. Next is the rate of violent crime, as measured by the National Crime Survey (NCS), conducted each year by the U.S. Department of Justice.

Figure 2
Percentage increase or decrease in violence rates from 1975 to 1985

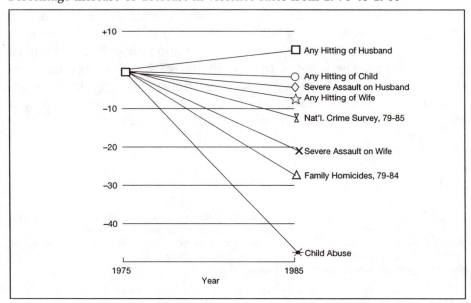

None of the trend lines for other types of violence show changes large enough to be statistically significant. However, the very fact that they did not change much is extremely important. Part of the reason is that none of those forms of violence have been the object of the extensive and sustained effort that has been focused on child abuse and wife beating (Straus and Gelles 1986). The campaign against child abuse has been in place the longest (since the mid-1960s) and has had the most resources directed to it. The campaign against wife beating started a decade later, and has had fewer resources. Consistent with this, the rate of wife beating has declined, but not as much as the rate of child abuse has. Figure 2 shows the rate of assault by wives of husbands and the rate of physical punishment of children. Neither of these has been the object of an extensive public campaign and, consistent with that, neither has declined.[5]

Figure 2 documents impressive gains, and also many aspects of family violence for which no progress has been made. Moreover, even child abuse and wife beating—two forms of violence where large reductions seem to have occurred—remain tremendous problems. The rates for 1985 (shown in Table 1), i.e., the rates *after* the presumed decrease, indicate that more than one of six American couples engaged in a physical assault during the year of the survey—an estimated total of 8.7 million couples, of which 3.4 million made severe assaults (kicking, punching, choking, attacks with weapons). Despite the large decrease in child abuse, more than one out of ten children were *severely* assaulted by a parent that year, a total of 6.9 million children. Clearly, violence is still endemic in the American family. The task ahead remains formidable.

Acknowledgments

This chapter is a publication of the Family Violence Research Program of the Family Research Laboratory, University of New Hampshire, Durham, NH 03824. A program description and publications list will be sent on request. The work of the Family Research Laboratory has been supported by grants from several organizations, including the National Institute of Mental Health (ROlMN40027 and T32MN15161), a National Science Foundation (SES8520232), and the University of New Hampshire.

Notes

1.   These estimates are based on comparing the National Family Violence Survey rate with the National Crime Survey (NCS) rate. They probably exaggerate the greater risk of intrafamily assault for men because the NCS vastly underestimates assaults by intimates inside the family and by friends and acquaintances outside the family. For example, most barroom brawls and street fights that young men get into are not included in the NCS data.

2.   Table 1 combines married couples and unmarried cohabiting couples. The violence rates for the latter are much higher (Yllo and Straus 1981; Stets and Straus 1990). However, since the cohabitors are only a small part of the total, it does not importantly affect the rates shown in this table.

3.   The tendency of men in male-dominant relationships to use violence even more than do women in female-dominant relationships results from the combination of several factors. First, it is more practical for men to use physical force to back up their position because of their greater average physical size and strength. Second, male dominance is often a normatively approved type of couple relationship (Coleman and Straus 1986), whereas female dominance is rarely held to be the desirable state of affairs. Thus, when a man is challenged, he is more likely not only to be frustrated, but as noted above, also to have the moral indignation that is typically used to justify violence. Third, male values in American society make men more amenable to the use of force to achieve some desirable end.

4.   However, the 70% violent figure conversely means that 30% of those with a larger number of risk factors were not violent. This is partly because of the inevitability of measurement error, and partly because the risk factors included in the figure represent a test of a theory concerning the social causes of family violence. If psychological factors had also been included among the risk factors, the prediction of violence might have been even greater.

5.   In addition to the public campaigns and provision of services for children and battered women, many other changes in American society between 1975 and 1985 probably also contributed to the decrease in child abuse and wife beating. These are discussed in Straus and Gelles (1986).

Chapter 8

Future Directions for Criminal Justice Policy on Domestic Violence

David A. Ford
Ruth Reichard
Stephen Goldsmith
Mary Jean Regoli

One can project the future course of criminal justice policy toward domestic violence[1] cases by examining the historical trends of the past three centuries. Many policies foreseen for the next century are already in place in jurisdictions around the United States, Canada, and elsewhere. Others will emerge with the growing awareness of violence as a problem to be addressed through law enforcement in concert with preventive, rehabilitative, and victim-assistance initiatives. The coordination of criminal justice and social service interventions is the guiding principle shaping policy for the year 2000 and beyond.

We first briefly trace the historical events most relevant to future policies. Then, we discuss the current state of criminal justice and domestic violence, especially as influenced by recent research findings. In the remainder of the chapter, we sketch our thoughts on policies likely to be implemented by increasing numbers of police departments, prosecutors, criminal courts, and corrections agencies.

HISTORY

The U.S. criminal justice system's response to wife battering has shifted during the past 200 years from a victim-initiated system of dispute resolution to a formal, state-sponsored system dominated by police and prosecutors intervening on behalf of victim-witnesses. The change parallels a shift in society's stance toward women, morality, and violence. Three periods in U.S. history mark significant efforts to reform legal policies toward domestic violence.[2]

In the mid-17th century, the Massachusetts Bay and Plymouth colonies enacted laws prohibiting wife beating so as to preserve the peace and to uphold the sanctity of the family. There were no formal roles for police and prosecutors as we currently know them. Enforcement rested with community surveillance and complaints adjudicated by either church courts or secular magistrates. Few cases were prosecuted under colonial laws, and as the 17th century came to an end, state interest in family disharmony waned (Pleck, 1987).

Some 200 years later, the state's interest in violence against women rekindled with the growth of the 19th-century's women's rights movement. Although few states passed laws to protect women from violent husbands, the expanded domains of state prosecutors and police enabled the state to bring more men to justice. The efforts resulted in limited policy reforms.[3] But the combination of public attention, emerging feminist ideology, and attempted reforms contributed to a new level of awareness that, like the equal rights movement of the era, nurtured the dramatic changes of the 20th century.

Violence against women was rediscovered as a significant social concern in the 1970s. The role of the criminal justice system with respect to domestic violence shifted from maintaining social order and a family ideal to explicit protection for victims, with the recognition of women as entitled to legal redress despite traditional male dominance of American social institutions. During the past two decades, the criminal justice interest has focused on preventing repetitive violence, initially through a rehabilitative orientation and, more recently, through a control perspective. Wife battery has come to be recognized as a criminal offense deserving of prosecutorial and judicial attention.[4]

TODAY

Recent policy changes bearing on domestic violence have been guided, in part, by research demonstrating the effectiveness of criminal justice practices in preventing continuing violence by a man against his conjugal partner. The most influential of such research projects was the Minneapolis Domestic Violence Experiment (Sherman & Berk, 1984), funded by the National Institute of Justice (NIJ). The researchers found that when police arrested a suspected wife batterer, he was less likely than others to again batter the same partner within 6 months. This finding crowned advocacy for a more vigorous law enforcement reaction to wife battering,[5] and it reinforced two political movements calling for a punitive stance toward criminals. The "law and order" movement pushed for harsh sanctioning to control criminals in general. The feminist movement called for sanctioning wife battery to affirm its seriousness as a criminal offense.[6] Notwithstanding its limitations (e.g., see Binder & Meeker, 1988), the Minneapolis experiment's results instigated legislation and policy reforms throughout the United States and thus made arrest a preferred and, in some jurisdictions, mandated, police response to alleged wife battery (Sherman & Cohn, 1989).

Nonetheless, arrest is not universally effective. NIJ funded additional research projects, known collectively as SARP (Spouse Abuse Replication Program) experiments, designed to test the impact of warrantless arrests elsewhere. In Omaha, Dunford, Huizinga, and Elliott (1989) replicated the Minneapolis experiment and found no support for arrest as a uniquely effective intervention. Similarly, experiments in Charlotte (Hirschel, Hutchison, & Dean, 1992), Milwaukee (Sherman et al., 1992), and Colorado Springs (Berk, Campbell, Klap, & Western, 1992) found no significant reduction in the prevalence of new violence following on-scene arrest of offenders. Only in Dade County (Pate & Hamilton, 1992) did arrest have a significant deterrent impact, but only when measured by victim interview data, as opposed to official records.

Regardless of other limitations, an on-scene warrantless arrest cannot be effected if a suspect flees prior to police contact, as may occur in the majority of police runs on domestics. The Omaha study addressed this in an "offender absent" experiment (Dunford, 1990). When Omaha police officers initiated warrants for the arrest of suspected batterers, those arrested were significantly less likely to repeat their violence against the same victims over the next 12 months.

That any sort of police intervention, by itself, can deter violence is remarkable. But we usually expect judicial outcomes to prevent continuing crime. Prosecution can result in both punitive and rehabilitative sanctions specifically meant to reduce the chance of continuing violence. The Indianapolis Domestic Violence Prosecution Experiment found no evidence to suggest that rehabilitative outcomes are any more effective than other adjudicated outcomes in preventing repeat violence, regardless of whether a man was arrested by the police or identified by a victim-initiated complaint to the prosecutor's office (Ford, 1993; Ford & Regoli, 1992). In victim-complaint cases, however, if a victim is simply told that if she wants, she may have charges dropped following a suspect's arrest on a warrant, that man is significantly less likely to again batter the woman within 6 months of case settlement (Ford, 1993; Ford & Regoli, 1993).

CHANGING ATTITUDES TOWARD
WIFE BATTERING AND CRIMINAL JUSTICE

We do not foresee any weakening of the current trend toward recognizing wife battering as a criminal offense to be treated at least as vigorously as violence against others. Indeed, the 1994 Violence Against Women Act (VAWA) has stimulated considerable activity addressing domestic violence against women, including training and technical assistance, community-based interventions, and research.[7] Underlying the legal and policy changes are changes in social norms and values, reflected in the attitudes of criminal justice personnel, that will give certainty to a vigorous criminal justice response in the future. During the 1980s, several significant normative changes began to influence prosecutorial responses to domestic violence. In the future, the widespread acceptance of these changes will result in continuing progressive policy developments.

First, police officers, prosecutors, judges, and legislators have begun to discard gender stereotypes relating to domestic violence and are coming to recognize the rights of a woman in her home.[8] Greater numbers of women in criminal justice agencies and legislatures have accelerated this change. Second, there is a growing awareness that all domestic violence, even acts that do not leave the victim bloodied, is harmful because it subjugates women and instills in children a sense that violence is normal in conjugal relationships.

Third, and probably the least recognized of the normative changes, traditionally intransigent agencies are no longer reluctant to intervene in the family. In fact, this attitude has changed so much that the current new concern is over how multiple interventions, for various reasons, can be coordinated and controlled. Also, a strong base of applied research, begun with the recommendations of the Attorney General's Task Force on Family Violence and reinvigorated with the VAWA, will continue to cause thoughtful consideration of policy impacts.

Finally, more than in almost any other criminal justice area, officials have considerable information available on the scope, effectiveness, and potential for addressing a broad range of associated problems through domestic violence policy, as contrasted with the more simplistic view of prosecution as a simple case management response to police initiatives. In particular, limitations of prison capacity remove incapacitation as an easy answer and thus force more thoughtful intermediate sanctioning—this with the apparent possibility that results can be accomplished for many offenders and their victims even without significant incapacitation.

The simultaneous development of aggressive victim assistance units and individual advocates against domestic violence has accelerated. Currently, victims and their advocates are forcing criminal justice officials to pay attention to the problem and to possible solutions. Advocates will continue to use litigation on behalf of victimized women to compel changes in criminal justice policies. With society continuing to express its disapproval of wife battery, advocacy groups and victim's rights spokespersons will force attention to domestic violence in efforts to reform criminal justice interventions.

One problem with this generally optimistic picture of criminal justice concern for domestic violence is a conflict between the goal of protecting individual victims seeking help and the state's interest in sanctioning domestic violence as a crime against the state whereby the victim is treated as a mere witness, but one whose security could be compromised by aggressive state actions. For example, in some jurisdictions, police are mandated to arrest a suspected batterer if they find probable cause that a crime has been committed. Some officers elect to ignore a victim's right to defend herself and take injury to the perpetrator as evidence of "mutual combat" and arrest the victim as well as the criminal batterer. Another example occurs with prosecution. Some prosecutors adhere to a strict "no drop" policy to ensure that batterers are impressed by the state's resolve to prosecute, even when doing so may put the victim at greater risk (Ford, 1991, 1993; Ford & Regoli, 1993). Future reforms in policy will have to confront the potential harm of what seems appropriate in response to domestic violence.

BEYOND THE YEAR 2000

In the remainder of this chapter, we "predict" the state of criminal justice policy on domestic violence as the world moves into the next century. We see little in the future that has not already been implemented somewhere. Trends are evident not only in current practices but also in guidelines from such influential documents as the *Attorney General's Task Force on Family Violence Final Report* (U.S. Department of Justice, 1984) and the Violent Crime Control and Law Enforcement Act of 1994. What we describe here are policies likely to gain widespread acceptance as standards for criminal justice practice beyond the year 2000.

Law

We expect state legislatures to continue the trend, begun in the 1980s, of criminalizing wife battering as any other crime of violence. But policymakers, recognizing that domestic violence is a crime involving special and complicated relationships, will be forced to "customize" their interventions (Friedman & Shulman, 1990). We foresee a continuation of the proliferation of laws designed to protect victims, to increase the number of meaningful civil remedies for victims who are not participating in the criminal justice system, and to hold law enforcement officers accountable for their decisions—even if that means eliminating some of their historically unlimited discretion. More state legislatures and voters will consider adding what are known as "victims' bills of rights" to their state constitutions, thus giving victims of all crimes rights such as the right to be kept informed of the progress of a criminal case, the right to be notified of hearings, and the right to consult with the prosecutor concerning possible dispositions of the case.

New laws will enable the criminal and civil processes to operate more efficiently together. Legislators will increase the options for both battered women and officials by expanding the authority of civil courts to intervene and protect women. For example, lawmakers will criminal-ize the violation of traditional civil protections, such as orders of pro-tection and restraining orders. State courts will also honor such orders even if they were issued by other jurisdictions; and federal prosecutors will opt to charge offenders who cross state lines while violating civil orders of protection.[9] "Federalization" of domestic violence crimes under VAWA will mean that, in certain instances, batterers may also face federal prosecution if they are subject to protective orders and exchange firearms.[10] State lawmakers will also adopt criminal laws designed to protect victims from "habitual batterers" in three primary areas. First, batterers will face a higher level of charges (and thus stiffer penalties) for their second battery on the same victim. Second, lawmakers will include the concept of "serial batterers" in the definition of *habitual battering* to account for new victims of one violent offender. Third, more states will enact legislation making stalking behavior a criminal offense.

State legislatures will endeavor to protect municipalities from equal protection litigation by enacting laws mandating training on domestic violence under a certified curriculum, by requiring police reports and data collection, and by mandating arrest for battery when probable cause exists under narrowly defined circumstances.[11] We further expect legislative action empowering police officers to initiate arrest warrants when suspected batterers are not on-scene when the officers respond, a practice found to have a preventive impact in the Omaha experiment (Dunford, 1990).

Finally, we foresee legislatures passing comprehensive "family vio-lence prevention acts"[12] to expand the array of coordinated criminal and civil remedies available to victims of wife battering and their children and to consolidate statutes involving divorce, orders of protection, cus-tody, visitation, and the like. Increasingly, public officials recognize that the difficult problems of reducing crime and poverty and of improving the health and well-being of families need solutions that stretch beyond popular rhetoric and quick fixes. Patchwork remedies often are ineffec-tive because they are narrowly limited to addressing a specific event rather than the complex problem. The prevalence of habitual domestic violence demands interventions by more than criminal justice agencies. But too often, other relevant agencies are not incorporated as part of a coordinated response.

For example, a family may be involved with a number of separate governmental agencies in inconsistent ways. The wife may be receiving help with domestic violence and child support, the delinquent child may be involved with a probation worker, an abused sibling could be involved with the social welfare department, and the school may have assigned a social worker or truancy officer. Policies implemented by one professional may cause counterproductive results in another area. An understanding of applicable policy research will facilitate organized efforts to develop successful, integrated strategies. The VAWA provides for funded demonstrations and evaluation of coordinated, community-based interventions with representation of multiple community sectors, in addition to criminal justice.

Most notably, these functions will be adopted by specialized courts designed to replace the current "compartmentalized" approach under which in two or even three courts may issue separate orders with contradictory provisions regarding contact between victims, defendants, and their children. (Such "family courts" are described in the section "Judicial Policy in this chapter.)"

Police Policy

"To Protect and to Serve"

The next decade will see police departments across the United States implement policies acknowledging both their capacity and their responsibility to protect victims of domestic violence from continuing abuse. Research findings have shown that police intervention in domestic disturbances can reduce the chance of repeat violence, at least in the short term. These findings have reinforced public and political sentiment expecting more of the police in providing security for victims of domestic violence. During the 1980s, several celebrated lawsuits against police for failing to take action to protect victims have forced police departments to evaluate their policies for responding to violent domestic disturbances. We foresee the implementation of policies mandating a vigorous police response to domestic violence, including reporting, providing immediate assistance to victims (as in finding shelter or other protective services), giving victims information on legal remedies, making referrals to social service agencies, and making reports to document victim complaints. Departments will collect data for detecting violent relationships as they set up specialized investigative units to coordinate law enforcement with other agencies oriented toward assisting victims of domestic violence.

Probable Cause Arrest

Policies encouraging officers to arrest suspects will provide a continuing emphasis on the duty of police to provide immediate security to victims of interpersonal violence. Many departments now promote arrest as a decisive and preferred action to prevent the short-term recurrence of violence. We expect to see such policies adopted universally. But policy reforms will be less oriented toward mandating specific police practices than toward mandating action under guidelines favoring officer discretion in the interest of protecting victims. This emphasis on arrest and on the officer's own "judgment call" will entail new attention to training officers on the dynamics of domestic violence and the consequences of alternative actions.

Police officers will also be expected to act decisively in those disturbances where violence may not yet have occurred but where it is likely, as given a prior history of police intervention for alleged violence. When appropriate, arrest for such crimes as disorderly conduct, public intoxication, and criminal trespass will be expected to head off eventual violence. Alternatively, police will assist victims in securing shelter from their abusers.

Police-Initiated Arrest Warrants

Violent men seeking to avoid arrest do not remain at the scenes of their crimes to await the police. When offenders are absent, police officers may advise victims on how to protect themselves for the moment, as well as how to initiate charges with the prosecutor's office. The Omaha experiment demonstrates that officers can themselves take further action to protect victims by initiating warrants independent of the victim actions. Although the Omaha findings may not hold in all jurisdictions, just as on-scene arrest provides a discretionary tool for officers, police-initiated warrants will enhance an officer's capacity to prevent violence.

Specialized Domestic Violence Investigative Units

Future police participation in a coordinated system response to domestic violence will center on specialized investigative units working closely with social service agencies as well as other criminal justice agencies. Such units have several areas of responsibility. First, the unit oversees the implementation of departmental policies for domestic violence, including the investigation of reported violence. Second, it coordinates the service of warrants and orders of protection. Third, it joins with other agencies in detecting relationships at risk, including those involving children of violent adults. Finally, the unit collects data for analyzing domestic violence and for identifying "hot spots" for proactive intervention by either law enforcement or social service agencies.

Currently, police shoulder public expectations for criminal justice intervention to prevent recurring violence against women. In the future, however, the onus of protecting victims will shift to prosecutors and courts. Police patrol officers will act primarily as crisis intervenors with responsibility for immediate victim protection. Their actions will be judged on their effectiveness in removing suspects from violent settings and initiating judicial processes for long-term assistance to victims rather than short-term deterrence from arrest.

Prosecution Policy

Prosecution policy for the next century will be more attentive to the needs of battered women seeking relief from violence. Changing social norms and values, along with significant policy research, will challenge prosecutors to implement procedures acknowledging the public's ownership of the criminal justice system and checking prosecutorial discretion. Policies meant to support victims' individual efforts to find security will bolster those with direct preventive effects. Prosecutors will carefully calibrate their official responses to produce specific preventive outcomes. Here, we note some of the major changes signaling model policies for the future.

Central Role of the Victim

Breaking the victim's cycle of violence and responding to her needs will be central to future prosecutorial policy. Although this perspective seems obvious, the traditional system has not generally pivoted around the victim and what is best for her. A strong victim orientation will guide new policies.

In the previous few years, criminal justice initiatives for domestic violence victims emphasized on-scene arrests. But equally dramatic changes have not occurred for the woman who files her own complaint or does not present a legal request at all. Increasingly, prosecutorial responses will involve a range of services extending more aggressively to the point at which the battery occurs, regardless of police intervention. Prosecutors' citizen intake bureaus will become more open to filing charges against batterers based on complaints from abused women. At the same time, prosecutors will undertake a conscientious effort to fashion effective immediate sanctions comparable to those following an on-scene police arrest. Accused batterers will be arrested on warrants and ordered to stay away from the complaining victims. In essence, we foresee citizen complaint cases being treated more like outright arrests in terms of prosecutor response. The practice of prosecutors simply passing cases from the police to a court, without attending to victim needs at the time, will cease.

The victim orientation will result in an expressed effort to empower battered women. Officials will come to understand their responsibility to balance the differences in power between an aggressor and his female victim; this task involves both an awareness of the system's capacity for supporting victims' self-protective actions and an understanding that her actions may be ineffective if she is denied control over the process (Ford, 1991). Thus, whether the victim is allowed to "drop charges" or to participate in determining the case outcome, and how that information is communicated to the defendant, will be increasingly important.[13] A guiding principle for empowering battered women is that prosecutors stand in alliance with victims. The future impact of criminal justice will be gauged, in part, by the reliability of that alliance—what services it can mobilize for victims and how vigorously it responds to continuing abuse by a suspect.

Case Monitoring

Expanding technological advances for computer-assisted case management enable prosecutors to more closely supervise cases. Technology will facilitate the monitoring of defendants—detecting those with previous complaints by the same or another victim, supervising defendants who are diverted to counseling programs—and will aid in keeping readily available information on victims (e.g., names, addresses, complaints/affidavits, contacts and notifications, special interests or desired criminal justice outcomes).

Through computer tracking systems, especially those that integrate police and prosecutor databases, prosecutors' offices will be able to reach all victims known to the system, even without formal processing. These contacts may be in person—through advocate outreach, through hospital social workers in emergency rooms, in conjunction with shelters—or by letters from the prosecutor's office. Tracking information will enable officials to initiate multiple agency interventions to protect those at risk, especially where instances of repeated abuse occur.

A Wider and Integrated Range of Official Actions

The coordination of functions and the merging of sanctions is readily apparent in efforts to prevent contact between the abuser and his victim. We expect to see a fruition of those efforts, with civil courts having sweeping authority to grant protective orders denying the abuser contact with the victim and her family and excluding him from the victim's premises and nearby areas. Those orders will be centrally registered and their violation criminalized, so as to enable intervention even before a violent act is committed. Prosecutors will more frequently and routinely secure "no contact" orders at the preliminary hearings after a battery, affording similar protection as that offered by a civil order.

The debate about the efficacy of various sanctions will continue. We expect new research fashioned after the Indianapolis Prosecution Experiment; however, we do not expect new criminal justice research to be definitive or consistent from city to city. Effective prosecution policies will occur only after rigorous evaluations of rehabilitative interventions, such that effective treatment can be mandated under the threat of criminal sanctions. The uncertainty concerning the relative sanctions' effects on recidivism, coupled with pressure to avoid jail overcrowding, will result in prosecutors diverting increasing numbers of defendants out of the criminal justice system. Men who have been diverted will enter treatment under carefully negotiated contracts. And, as realistic criteria for treatment success are identified, prosecutors will use such rehabilitative counseling agreements as a strategy for assuaging victims who might otherwise not prosecute.

Judicial Policy

Judges have a greater role in the criminal justice system's response to wife battering than has been acknowledged in recent literature. They are involved at virtually all critical points in the process: They approve warrants and affirm probable cause for arrests; they set bond and issue protective orders; they approve pretrial diversion agreements; they adjudge guilt and sentence offenders; and ultimately they rule on violations of probation. Yet, judges have received little attention in discussions of wife battery and criminal justice. Perhaps this is because they hear only a small proportion of the cases identified by the police and prosecutors. Or perhaps they are sufficiently responsive to the plight of battered women that they are not associated with the insensitivity and recalcitrance noted in other agencies. In our experience, however, judges have generally been slow to recognize wife battering as a serious criminal issue that they might control.

Discretion and Judgments

Judges will become more responsive to the problem of battered women as society grows more disposed toward criminal justice solutions. Prodded by increasing numbers of women on the bench, by community sentiment, by legislative mandate, and by the demands of cases presented by police and prosecutors, judges will exercise their powers in ways consistent with ensuring victim safety while protecting the rights of the accused. Specifically, judges will routinely support police intervention by approving warrantless on-scene arrests for battery based on probable cause (rather than on the direct observation of a law enforcement officer). Judges will also approve warrants on charges initiated by victims and will see that they result in arrests.

As society comes to expect more concern on the part of the judiciary, judges will find themselves under greater scrutiny by victim advocates and, where relevant, by an intolerant electorate. Communities will hold judges accountable for pretrial release decisions, as well as for sentencing decisions. Legislation may serve to "regulate" judges by replacing some of their discretion with guidelines for pretrial release and postconviction sentencing in areas related to family violence. For example, statutes may specify certain factors to be weighted (and certain factors that should *not* be weighted) by judges when making release and sentencing decisions. Judges will receive training in adjudication oriented toward preventing domestic abuse at their continuing judicial education seminars, as encouraged by the VAWA.

Bail Decisions

Because of a growing recognition of the lethality of domestic violence, as well as the fact that it frequently escalates in severity, judges or court administrators will alter their bail policies in a number of ways. Some will include the imposition of a fixed "holding period" (e.g., 12 hours) for individuals arrested for crimes involving domestic violence, as a means of controlling those offenders who would otherwise be released and immediately commit new violence. Other policies will affect bail commissioners, requiring them to contact victims during the offenders' bail interviews in order to develop pretrial release plans that ensure the victims' safety after an initial police arrest or warrant arrest. Although most offenders will eventually be released pending trial, there are advantages to holding wife-battery offenders overnight at least until their initial hearing. This short pretrial incapacitation of a batterer provides an opportunity for the victim to safeguard her belongings and to seek shelter elsewhere. Criminal justice and social service agencies have the opportunity to contact the victim to provide information on what she can expect to happen and her options. If a batterer has not been immediately released, the prosecutor and the victim can provide important information to the judge to guide the decision whether release on recognizance should be granted, what bail should be set, and what conditions should be placed on this release, including protective orders.

State legislators and voters may also approve changes in state constitutions and statutes allowing judges to consider a defendant's dangerousness to both the individual victim and the public at large; this mirrors recent federal developments. Currently, judges in most states may consider only the likelihood a defendant will reappear for future court proceedings when making bail decisions.

Protection Orders

The process for obtaining orders of protection[14] will become more accessible than ever for victims. The procedures will be streamlined for victims who, often acting without legal counsel, need a user-friendly court system. Orders will be available on an emergency basis, even at times when courts are traditionally closed. Victims will also find it easier to proceed without paying any fees or court costs, as policymakers take a more realistic view of victims' economic dependence on their abusers. With legislative changes supporting a coordinated criminal and civil intervention process, victims will enjoy access to a wider array of remedies—remedies that were traditionally available only to married persons getting a divorce. For example, victims will be able to obtain evictions of their abusers, child support, and visitation, in addition to gaining the no-contact provisions historically available in orders of protection. Finally, with the criminalization of the violations of these orders, judges will be able to provide more effective sanctions.

Sentencing Alternatives

Domestic violence is one of the few crimes in which victim and offender share an intimate relationship, often living together. Many victims are understandably reticent about making sentencing recommendations when in the presence of their abusers. The advent of victims' bills of rights may pose a solution to the potential Sixth Amendment problem that is created if judges elect to obtain a recommendation from a victim outside the defendant's presence; many statutes allow judges to appoint "victim representatives" to speak on behalf of individual victims during the sentencing phase of a case.

Incarceration is the one sentence clearly conveying the seriousness of wife battering as a criminal offense. But, for a variety of reasons, including jail and prison overcrowding, the relative ineffectiveness of incarceration for preventing further violence, and victim reluctance to have their batterers incarcerated, judges will impose alternative sanctions, as described in the "Corrections" section below.

Judges will also endeavor to find rehabilitative alternatives for preventing continuing abuse of the original victim, as well as of women in future relationships. Thus, court-mandated treatment of batterers will increase, but the efficacy of the treatment may be influenced by three factors: First, new research on the relative effectiveness of treatment alternatives for different types of batterers will point to preferred options; second, judges or their staff must employ reliable assessment tools to match individual offenders with appropriate treatment programs; third, policymakers must make certain that the assessment tools screen for those individuals for whom treatment is *not* appropriate ("pathological" batterers).

Finally, judges will enforce conditions of probation and impose meaningful sanctions for violations of probation, in recognition of the importance of holding batterers accountable for their behavior. With prison overcrowding, probation violators may not be jailed for the full term of their original sentences. Instead, judges will impose incrementally longer sentences for each violation.

Specialized Courts

We foresee widespread development of courts empowered to hear both criminal and civil issues pertaining to couples in violent relationships. These family courts have jurisdiction over not only criminal family violence cases but also dissolutions of marriages, paternity establishment and child support enforcement actions, child protective services cases and some delinquency cases, and orders of protection. Such specialized courts provide a coordinated, holistic approach to ending family violence and to ensuring victim safety by facilitating information sharing and coordination among all of the different agencies that might encounter a particular family.

Specialized courts will support "vertical prosecution," whereby a single prosecutor manages a case from screening through adjudication and, when necessary, probation hearings. These courts will help prosecutors monitor each offender more closely and keep in contact with each victim, thus reducing victim attrition. Where comprehensive family courts are impractical for some jurisdictions because of a high volume of cases, policymakers in those areas may opt for specialized courts that hear criminal cases involving domestic violence only and mandate information sharing among all the relevant agencies and courts.

Corrections

Corrections agencies play a critical part in protecting a victim because they implement court-imposed sanctions. They will assume greater responsibility in the future for closer supervision of convicted batterers, for overseeing the effectiveness of counseling/rehabilitative agencies, for hearing victims' reports of probation/parole violations and acting on them, and for notifying victims of release or escape.

Incarceration

Jails and prisons are unlikely to play a major direct role in the future criminal justice response to wife battering, for reasons cited above. These institutions will be used selectively and in innovative ways as the final stages in a series of graduated sanctions to deal with wife batterers on the basis of seriousness and nature of the current charge and on the prior record and present circumstances of the offender. Incarceration will figure in future wife-battery policy primarily at the pretrial stage to protect victims, as a coercive trial outcome threatened to ensure other sanctions are fulfilled, and as a response to violations of other sanctions imposed.

Probation

After conviction, corrections will be used in a variety of ways to ensure the success of less intrusive sanctions. The most prevalent will be the use of suspended sentences in which prison terms are assessed but then suspended as long as the offender successfully completes other conditions, such as committing no further violence, paying fines and restitution to the victim, performing community service work, or completing a treatment program. Offenders with a prior record of violence or probation violations or who had trouble keeping conditions of pretrial release may be given split sentences involving a probation term preceded by a short term of incarceration to serve as a reminder to the offender of the consequences of not abiding by the conditions of probation. The incarceration term may be served all at once or intermittently, as on successive weekends, evenings, or vacations. In the future, this short jail term may be served at halfway houses for batterers where group or individual counseling can be combined with incapacitation.

Future policy will also employ corrections within the community in "intensive supervision probation" programs. Intensive supervision will provide more stringent control than usually experienced by men on probation. It allows offenders to maintain employment to pay child support and victim restitution, but still provides a substantial degree of security for the victim. Current programs usually involve some form of curfew or house arrest, with offenders being allowed to leave their homes for such purposes as work, school, community service work, probation and counseling sessions, and religious services. Future restraints on the offender's movements will be enforced by frequent contact with a probation officer and may be enhanced by some type of passive or active electronic monitoring device.

Probation will also be used to force participation in rehabilitative programs. As discussed above, currently there is no conclusive evidence that batterer treatment programs are effective in reliabilitating violent men. But we expect to see considerable research on rehabilitation programs in the near future. The need for evaluation research is obvious. For one, courts currently are sentencing men to unproven rehabilitative programs. At some point, the programs will be held accountable if they cannot demonstrate success. Also, continuing research on batterers will enable programs to tailor their treatments to more refined classifications of batterers for more general use in shaping coordinated services.

Home Detention

The improvement and expansion of electronic monitoring technology may provide the greatest security short of incarceration for victims who face continual threats of violence after separating from their offenders. A central computer stores information on the restrictions to movement for each offender. "Passive" electronic devices do not provide constant monitoring, but rather the computer generates random calls to offenders who must verify their presence through voice identification, via a video image, or by inserting a wristlet into a verification box attached to the telephone. "Active" electronic devices involve placing a transmitter on the ankle, waist, wrist, or neck of the offender. If the offender is not within a 150-foot radius of a receiving device in the home at scheduled times, the probation office is notified (Ball, Huff, & Lilly, 1988; Morris & Tonry, 1990). These technologies will be replaced by continuous-monitoring, satellite tracking systems so that victims can be equipped with portable receivers to detect the presence of a transmitter worn by the batterer anywhere. Victims would be instructed on appropriate measures to take if the signal indicated the batterer was within a certain distance. If necessary, the alarm will not only alert police but also locate the victim and offender anyplace in the nation. This sort of sophisticated electronic monitoring of domestic violence offenders will become commonplace with reduced costs, with the proliferation of anti-stalking laws,[15] and with the shortage of prison space.

Straight prison terms will be reserved for felony battery cases and more serious misdemeanor charges, especially those involving repeat offenders. Special prison programs for violent offenders, including wife batterers, will be developed as effective rehabilitative strategics are identified. These would be therapeutic communities within the prison but with ties to outside social services and perhaps using former batterers as peer counselors.[16]

CONCLUSION

As we presume to look into the future, we are reminded how ethereal policy can be. The best of extant policies may be lost to fiscal cuts or political whim. The best of anticipated policies may never be implemented because of a host of constraints and hindrances—for example, value conflicts, financial crises, officials' recalcitrance, jail overcrowding, and fear of litigation.

Indeed, rapidly changing social conditions and criminal problems will force policy adaptations. The mounting press of cases and workloads, the complicating challenge of drugs in communities, the impotence of the expected social control functions of schools and families, and the failure of law enforcement in other areas cause fundamental shifts in operating styles and strategies of criminal justice agencies.

With respect to family violence, whether it is committed against children, spouses, or elders, criminal justice practitioners sit at a pivotal point in deciding what intervention from arrest, to prosecution, to counseling is most appropriate. Increasingly, urban families face multiple problems with limited resources. The risks to their well-being will force a cooperative and coordinated response by social service agencies, along with police, prosecutors, judges, advocates, and correction officials; for example, court-mandated batterers' groups may be combined with substance abuse programs or drug testing. And child abuse investigators will more frequently make inquiries concerning spousal abuse that result in more frequent and broader based and coordinated interventions involving multiple family members. This will lead not only to more effective criminal case dispositions but also to results that treat underlying problems in a more holistic manner. Informed by important practical research, unburdened by traditional gender stereotypes, and concerned about the deleterious effects of spousal violence, the criminal justice system will join other community institutions in combating abuse through more comprehensive, though more individually tailored, programs.

NOTES

1. The term *domestic violence* is used here as a generic descriptor of violence against women by their conjugal partners. Elsewhere in the chapter, we use *wife battery*, a synonym meant to more precisely convey the criminality of such violence. The violence may range from simple misdemeanor assault and battery through the most serious of felony assaults. Our discussion centers on misdemeanor battery, the crime charged in the vast majority of cases.

2. This historical summary is based principally on Elizabeth Pleck's *Domestic Tyranny* (1987). The general changes in the domains of criminal justice roles are discussed in William McDonald's "The Prosecutor's Domain" (1979).

3. Pleck (1987) reports that antebellum feminists were primarily interested in seeking reforms in divorce laws to protect women from drunken and cruel husbands. Wife beating, however, became a law-and-order issue in the late 19th century as legislatures considered harsh punishments, includ-

ing especially whipping posts, as means of deterring violent men. Only Maryland passed a whipping-post law for wife beating during that period.

4. Domestic violence was so certified with issuance of the final report of the Attorney General's Task Force on Family Violence in 1984 (U.S. Department of Justice, 1984). Currently, however, in some major urban jurisdictions, criminal justice agencies, especially district attorneys' offices and courts, are still unwilling to act on complaints of domestic violence.

5. See, for example, the U.S. Department of Justice (1984).

6. Mederer and Gelles (1989) argue that at least five factors led to the adoption of current control strategies: (a) the feminist movement's concern over criminal justice indifference to violence against women, (b) the findings of the Minneapolis experiment, (c) the publication of the Attorney General's Task Force report, [d] the threat of litigation on the heels of a $2.3 million judgment against the police in *Thurman v. City of Torrington*, and (e) the "control atmosphere" accompanying an era of political conservatism.

7. The Violence Against Women Act (VAWA) is Title IV of the Violent Crime Control and Law Enforcement Act of 1994.

8. The VAWA includes the Civil Rights Remedies for Gender-Motivated Violence Act, which in Section 40302 amends 42 U.S.C. Section 13981 to provide for a new civil right: the right to be free from crimes of violence motivated by gender. Although this language is gender neutral, it is expected that most of the litigation commenced under this new section will involve domestic violence allegations. Of course, favorable judgments, monetary damages, and attorneys' fees may be merely symbolic in nature, depending on the abuser's financial situation. One assumes that it will not be cost efficient for victims to bring lawsuits under this section unless the abusers are wealthy.

9. The VAWA also contains a subsection entitled the "Safe Homes for Women Act of 1994," which amends the United States Code to mandate that state courts honor and enforce protective orders issued by courts of different states (the constitutional term for this is "full faith and credit"). This section of the VAWA also creates federal crimes for violating protective orders when the offender crosses state lines to do so.

10. Title XI of the 1994 Violent Crime Control and Law Enforcement Act contains language prohibiting domestic abusers from receiving and/or disposing of firearms. This legislation is codified in Title 18 of the United States Code.

11. Although mandatory arrest laws have been enacted in response to litigation against the police, we do not think many jurisdictions that do not now mandate arrest will do so in the future without qualification. Contradictory findings on the effectiveness of arrest as a deterrent (Fagan & Garner, 1995) and failures in implementing mandatory policies (Ferraro, 1989) currently favor discretionary arrest powers except in life-threatening circumstances. Through its grants program, however, the VAWA calls for implementation of mandatory or proarrest policies for responding to domestic violence. It remains to be seen which policy orientation is favored in grants.

12. For examples of such acts, see Lerman's "A Model State Act: Remedies for Domestic Abuse" (1984) or the newer, more comprehensive "Family Violence: A Model State Code" (1994), published by the National Council of Juvenile and Family Court Judges. The adoption of such model laws, along with the proliferation of federal laws concerning domestic violence, should help promote much-needed interstate uniformity and eliminate the current situation in which a victim in one state may enjoy greater protection from domestic abuse than her neighbor in the next state.

13. The one prosecution policy found to protect battered women in Indianapolis is to give a woman permission to have charges dismissed, following an initial hearing, while assuring her of continuing support no matter what she decides (Ford, 1993; Ford & Regoli, 1993). Because a woman is least likely to be battered anew if she "follows through" with prosecution, however, the prosecutor's office discourages dropping and grants her a say in the decision to offer a defendant pretrial diversion to counseling or to prosecute him with alternative sentencing options.

14. Orders of protection include what are variously called restraining orders, no-contact orders, stay-away orders, and protective orders.

15. The VAWA contains a "National Stalker and Domestic Violence Reduction" section, which encourages states to forward data about stalkers and domestic violence offenders who violate orders of protection to the National Crime Information Center (NCIC), which is the same national database used by the FBI to track an offender's criminal history on a national scale. State jurisdictions also use the NCIC's records to determine whether an individual has engaged in criminal activity elsewhere in the United States. As the number of states with antistalking laws increases, prosecutors will become more creative with charging decisions and will begin to charge domestic abusers with stalking (in addition to other, more traditional crimes) when they are able to detect clear patterns of intentional harassment, threats, and actual harm.

16. Such a "community" might be modeled after the therapeutic drug treatment programs currently found in prisons (e.g., Wexler, Falkin, & Lipton, 1990).

REFERENCES

Ball, R.A., Huff, C.R., & Lilly, J.R. (1988). *House arrest and correctional policy: Doing time at home*. Newbury Park, CA: Sage.

Berk, R.A., Campbell, A., Klap, R., & Western, B. (1992). A Bayesian analysis of the Colorado Springs Spouse Abuse Experiment. *Journal of Criminal Law and Criminology, 83*(1), 170-200.

Binder, A., & Meeker, J. (1988). Experiments as reforms. *Journal of Criminal Justice, 16*, 347-358.

Dunford, F.W. (1990). System-initiated warrants for suspects of misdemeanor domestic assault: A pilot study. *Justice Quarterly, 7*, 631-653.

Dunford, F.W., Huizinga, D., & Elliott, D.S. (1989). *The Omaha Domestic Violence Police Experiment: Final report*. Washington, DC: National Institute of Justice.

Fagan, J., & Garner, J. (1995). Published results of the NIJ Spouse Assault Replication Program: A critical review. *Journal of Quantitative Criminology, 8*, 1-29.

Ferraro, K.J. (1989). Policing woman battering. *Social Problems, 36*, 61-74.

Ford, D.A. (1991). Prosecution as a victim power resource: A note on empowering women in violent conjugal relationships. *Law & Society Review, 25*, 313-334.

Ford, D.A. (1993). *The Indianapolis Domestic Violence Prosecution Experiment: Final report*. Washington, DC: National Institute of Justice.

Ford, D.A., & Regoli, M.J. (1992). The preventive impacts of policies for prosecuting wife batterers. In E.S. Buzawa & C.G. Buzawa (Eds.), *Domestic violence: The criminal justice response*. Westport, CT: Auburn House.

Ford, D.A., & Regoli, M.J. (1993). The criminal prosecution of wife assaulters: Process, problems, and effects. In N.Z. Hilton (Ed.), *Legal responses to wife assault: Current trends and evaluation*. Newbury Park, CA: Sage.

Friedman, L.N., & Shulman, M. (1990). Domestic violence: The criminal justice response. In A.J. Lurigio, W.G. Skogan, & R.C. Davis (Eds.), *Victims of crime: Problems, policies, and programs*. Newbury Park, CA: Sage.

Hirschel, J.D., Hutchison, I.W., & Dean, C.W. (1992). The failure of arrest to deter spouse abuse. *Journal of Research in Crime and Delinquency, 29*(1), 7-33.

Lerman, L.G. (1984). A model state act: Remedies for domestic abuse. *Harvard Journal on Legislation, 21*, 61-69.

McDonald, W.F. (1979). The prosecutor's domain. In W.F. McDonald (Ed.), *The prosecutor*. Beverly Hills, CA: Sage.

Mederer, H.J., & Gelles, R.J. (1989). Compassion or control: Intervention in cases of wife abuse. *Journal of Interpersonal Violence, 4,* 25-43.

Morris, N., & Tonry, M. (1990). *Between prison and probation*. New York: Oxford University Press.

National Council of Juvenile and Family Court Judges. (1994). *Family violence: A model state code*. Reno, NV: State Justice Institute.

Pate, A.M., & Hamilton, E.E. (1992). Formal and informal deterrents to domestic violence: The Dade County Spouse Assault Experiment. *American Sociological Review, 57,* 691-697.

Pleck, E. (1987). *Domestic tyranny*. New York: Oxford University Press.

Sherman, L. W., & Berk, R. A. (1984). The specific deterrent effects of arrest for domestic assault. *American Sociological Review, 49,* 261-272.

Sherman, L. W., & Cohn, E. G. (1989). The impact of research on legal policy: The Minneapolis Domestic Violence Experiment. *Law & Society Review, 23,* 117-144.

Sherman, L. W., Schmidt, J. D., Rogan, D. P., Smith, D. A., Gartin, P. R., Cohn, E. G., Collins, D. J., & Bacich, A. R. (1992). The variable effects of arrest on criminal careers: The Milwaukee Domestic Violence Experiment. *Journal of Criminal Law and Criminology, 83,* 137-169.

Thurman v. City of Torrington, 595 F. Supp. 1521 (1985).

U.S. Department of Justice. (1984). *Attorney General's Task Force on Family Violence: Final report*. Washington, DC: Author.

Wexler, H.K., Falkin, G.P., & Lipton, D.S. (1990). Outcome evaluation of a prison therapeutic community for substance abuse treatment. *Criminal Justice and Behavior, 17,* 71-92.

Section 5
PROPERTY CRIMES

Although most victimological research and victims' movement advocacy has addressed violent crimes, property crimes are far more prevalent and also have significant financial and psychological effects on their victims. Property crimes can range from the theft of canned goods from a grocery store, to the burglary of a home, to the arson of an insured business establishment, to fraudulent schemes to obtain funds from consumers or investors, to massive "white-collar" conspiracies or environmental crimes. Financial losses can range from a few to billions of dollars.

With regard to the frequency of property crime, the 1997 Uniform Crime Reports listed the crime rate for reported property crimes (i.e., burglary, motor vehicle theft, and larceny-theft) at 4,312 for every 100,000 persons. The 1997 National Crime Victimization Survey estimates that there were almost 250 property crimes (i.e., household burglary and theft and motor vehicle theft) per every 1,000 households. These crime rates translate into approximately 11,500,000 of the reported UCR property crimes and approximately 26,000,000 of the NCVS property crime victimizations. Another almost 82,000 reported arsons can be added to these 1997 figures. As dramatic as these property crime victimization figures are, they are eclipsed by the estimate suggested in Chapter 10, the Titus et al. selection, that 30 percent of the American population (18 or older) are victimized each year by an attempted or successful personal fraud. Moreover, these figures do not include various other property crime categories that are even more difficult to measure.

Significant financial losses accompany these property crimes. Individual property losses from the 1997 UCR property crimes estimate range from an average of $585 for larceny-theft, to $1,305 for residential burglary, to $5,416 for motor vehicle theft, to $11,294 for arson. In the aggregate, the UCR's 1997 estimated stolen property loss for these crimes (excluding arson) was $15 billion. When this figure is added to Titus et al.'s estimated $40 billion in annual personal fraud losses, the annual financial loss from even this incomplete list of property crimes is staggering. Moreover, these figures do not include non-property losses that may result from these crimes.

Despite the enormity of these crimes in terms of both frequency and personal loss, only limited research attention has been devoted to them. For example, contrary to the significant research interest in the psychological impact of violent crime (especially sexual assault) on victims, few researchers have explored the psychological impact of property crime on its victims. As Chapter 9, the Lurigio selection, indicates, burglary victims (as opposed to nonvictims of crime) may experience heightened levels of vulnerability, fear, symptomology, and other effects as a result of their victimization. Moreover, Lurigio's research indicates that burglary victims may even experience higher levels of vulnerability and fear of property crime than do robbery and nonsexual assault victims. Likewise, Chapter 10, the Titus et al. selection, which describes a study of personal fraud victimization, challenges common stereotypes regarding this type of victimization. Research such as this has practical significance for criminal justice practitioners and service providers.

Similarly, limited research attention has been devoted to explanatory theories of property crime victimization. Research, such as the Titus et al. study, that identifies property crime victim characteristics, can contribute to this. Some researchers have focused on physical design factors that may deter offenders from selecting particular targets for crime, including property crime. Extending this concept further, another area of more active research interest has been the application of opportunity and routine activity causal theories to property crime victimization. Exploring variables that reflect the exposure and attractiveness of a potential crime target, the presence or absence of deterring "guardians," the proximity of offenders to a chosen crime target, and the motivations of potential offenders, researchers have attempted to predict the likelihood of property crime victimization. All of these are interesting approaches that merit further exploration.

Finally, just as property crime victimization has received less research attention than violent crime victimization, it has also received less attention from the victims' movement. For example, some of the criminal justice system reforms that expand the victim's role in the criminal justice process, and that were advocated by the victims' movement, apply only to victims of violent crime. Just as significantly, most state victim compensation programs apply only to victims who have experienced some degree of personal injury from the crime and thus exclude property crime victims. In addition, most criminal-justice–related treatment and social services are oriented to violent, but not property, crime victims.

For those involved in victimology research and the victims' movement, the challenge for the next century will be to extend the interest and accomplishments developed regarding victims of violent crime to the more numerous victims of property crime. If this can be achieved, the impact of victimology and the victims' movement will expand exponentially.

LEARNING EXPERIENCES

1. In Chapter 9, the Lurigio study explores the impact of victimization on a number of variables (e.g., vulnerability, fear, protective behaviors, self-efficacy, symptoms, and perceptions of the police). Identify other research that examines the differences between crime victims and nonvictims and between victims of various types of crimes regarding these variables. Focus especially on the research regarding property crime victims.

2. In addition to the relationship between victimization and fear of crime examined in the Lurigio study, there is a substantial body of research that explores the relationship between fear of crime and various demographic characteristics (e.g., gender, age, racial and ethnic background, and economic status). Identify and examine research in these areas.

3. Lurigio's study suggests that victims of robbery, burglary, and non-sexual assault may suffer significant psychological effects from their victimization that the criminal justice system and social service and treatment providers may not be adequately addressing. How, if at all, are the psychological needs of these victims, especially property crime victims, met in your community?

4. Identify which of your state laws expanding the role of crime victims in the criminal justice process apply to property crime victims. Determine whether property crime victims are eligible to participate in your state victim compensation program. If property crime victims are excluded from these provisions, interview a state legislator or a victim rights advocate to determine why property crime victims have been excluded.

5. As a class, complete the survey regarding fraud victimization that appears in the appendix of Chapter 10, the Titus et al. selection. Are your class results consistent with the study findings? Why or why not?

6. Titus et al. identify several areas for additional research regarding fraud victimization. Identify and examine research that has been conducted in these areas since the Titus et al. study.

BIBLIOGRAPHY

Brems, C., & Wagner, P. (1994). Blame of victim and perpetrator in rape versus theft. *Journal of Social Psychology, 134,* 363-374.

Buck, A.J., Hakim, S., & Rengert, G.F. (1993). Burglar alarms and the choice behavior of burglars: A suburban phenomenon. *Journal of Criminal Justice, 21,* 497-507.

Cohen, L.E., & Cantor, D. (1980). The determinants of larceny: An empirical and theoretical study. *Journal of Research in Crime and Delinquency, 17,* 140-159.

Cohen, L.E., & Cantor, D. (1981). Residential burglary in the United States: Life-style and demographic factors associated with the probability of victimization. *Journal of Research in Crime and Delinquency, 18,* 113-127.

Cohen, L.E., Cantor, D., & Kluegel, J.R. (1981). Robbery victimization in the U.S.: An analysis of a nonrandom event. *Social Science Quarterly, 62,* 644-657.

Cohen, L.E., Felson, M., & Land, K.C. (1980). Property crime rates in the United States: A macrodynamic analysis, 1947-1977; with ex ante forecasts for the mid-1980s. *American Journal of Sociology, 86,* 90-118.

Cook, P.J. (1985). Is robbery becoming more violent? An analysis of robbery murder trends since 1968. *Journal of Criminal Law & Criminology, 76,* 480-489.

Cullen, F.T., Maakestad, W.J., Cavender, G. (1987). *Corporate crime under attack: The Ford Pinto case and beyond.* Cincinnati, OH: Anderson.

Cullen, F.T., Mathers, R.A., Clark, G.A., & Cullen, J.B. (1983). Public support for punishing white-collar crime: Blaming the victim revisited? *Journal of Criminal Justice, 11,* 481-493.

Edelhertz, H., & Overcast, T.D. (Eds.). (1982). *White-collar crime: An agenda for research.* Lexington, MA: Lexington.

Edelhertz, H. & Rogovin, C. (Eds.). (1980). *A national strategy for containing white-collar crime.* Lexington, MA: Lexington.

Garofalo, J., & Clark, D. (1992). Guardianship and residential burglary. *Justice Quarterly, 9,* 443-463.

Geis, G., & Stotland, E. (Eds.). (1980). *White-collar crime: Theory and research.* Beverly Hills, CA: Sage.

Hagan, J. (1982). The corporate advantage: A study of the involvement of corporate and individual victims in a criminal justice system. *Social Forces, 60,* 993-1022.

Hannan, T.H. (1982). Bank robberies and bank security precautions. *Journal of Legal Studies, 11,* 83-92.

Hills, S.L. (Ed.). (1987). *Corporate violence: Injury and death for profit.* Totowa, NJ: Rowman & Littlefield.

Hindelang, M.J. (1974). Decisions of shoplifting victims to invoke the criminal justice process. *Social Problems, 21,* 580-593.

Hochstedler, E. (Ed.). (1984). *Corporations as criminals.* Beverly Hills, CA: Sage.

Inciardi, J.A. (1976). The pickpocket and his victim. *Victimology, 1,* 446-453.

Jesilow, P., Klempner, E., & Chiao, V. (1992). Reporting consumer and major fraud: A survey of complainants. In K. Schlegel & D. Weisburd (Eds.), *White-collar crime reconsidered* (pp. 149-168). Boston: Northeastern University Press.

Johnson, K.W., Tamberrino, R.A., Marshall, A.A., & Moyer, A.A. (1978). Consumer protection: Responsiveness of control agents to victims of fraud. *Victimology, 3,* 63-76.

Karmen, A. (1980). Victim facilitation: The case of automobile theft. *Victimology, 4,* 361-370.

Karmen, A. (1980). Auto theft: Beyond victim blaming. *Victimology, 5,* 161-174.

Kaufman, I. (1990). Arson—From creation to destruction. In E.C. Viano (Ed.), *The victimology handbook: Research findings, treatment, and public policy* (pp. 147-157). New York: Garland.

Kruttschnitt, C. (1985). Are businesses treated differently? A comparison of the individual victim and the corporate victim in the criminal courtroom. *Sociological Inquiry, 55,* 225-238.

Levi, M. (1992). White-collar crime victimization. In K. Schlegel & D. Weisburd (Eds.), *White-collar crime reconsidered* (pp. 169-192). Boston: Northeastern University Press.

Leymann, H., & Lindell, J. (1990). Social support after armed robbery in the workplace. In E.C. Viano (Ed.), *The victimology handbook: Research findings, treatment, and public policy* (pp. 285-304). New York: Garland.

Lurigio, A.J. (1987). Are all victims alike? The adverse, generalized, and differential impact of crime. *Crime & Delinquency, 33,* 452-467.

Lynch, J.P., & Cantor, D. (1992). Ecological and behavioral influences on property victimization at home: Implications for opportunity theory. *Journal of Research in Crime and Delinquency, 29,* 335-362.

Massey, J.L., Krohn, M.D., & Bonati, L.M. (1989). Property crime and the routine activities of individuals. *Journal of Research in Crime and Delinquency, 26,* 378-400.

McCaghy, C.H., Giordano, P.C., & Henson, T.K. (1977). Auto theft: Offender and offense characteristics. *Criminology, 15,* 367-385.

Moore, E., & Mills, M. (1990). The neglected victims and unexamined costs of white-collar crime. *Crime & Delinquency, 36,* 408-418.

Osborn, D.R., Ellingworth, D., Hope, T., & Trickett, A. (1996). Are repeatedly victimized households different? *Journal of Quantitative Criminology, 12,* 223-245.

Polvi, N., Looman, T., Humphries, C., & Pease, K. (1991). The time course of repeat burglary victimization. *British Journal of Criminology, 31,* 411-414.

Rand, M. (1998). *National Crime Victimization Survey: Criminal Victimization 1997.* Washington, DC: U.S. Department of Justice.

Schlegel, K., & Weisburd, D. (Eds.). (1992). *White-collar crime reconsidered.* Boston: Northeastern University Press.

Shover, N., Fox, G.L., & Mills, M. (1994). Long-term consequences of victimization by white-collar crime. *Justice Quarterly, 11,* 75-98.

...d, E.H. (1949). *White collar crime*. New York: Dryden.

...M., Heinzelmann, F., & Boyle, J.M. (1995). Victimization of persons by fraud. *Crime & Delinquency, 41*, 54-72.

Trickett, A., Osborn, D.R., & Ellingsworth, D. (1995). Property crime victimisation: The roles of individual and area influences. *International Review of Victimology, 3*, 273-295.

Umbreit, M.S. (1990). The meaning of fairness to burglary victims. In B. Galaway & J. Hudson (Eds.), *Criminal justice, restitution, and reconciliation* (pp. 47-57). Monsey, NY: Criminal Justice Press.

U.S. Department of Justice. Federal Bureau of Investigation. (1998). *UCR press release—Crime in the United States, 1997*. Washington, DC: Author.

Walsh, D. (1986). Victim selection procedures among economic criminals: The rational choice perspective. In D.B. Cornish & R.V. Clarke (Eds.), *The reasoning criminal: Rational choice perspectives on offending* (pp. 31-52). New York: Springer-Verlag.

Warr, M. (1988). Rape, burglary, and opportunity. *Journal of Quantitative Criminology, 4*, 275-288.

Wilcox Rountree, P., & Land, K.C. (1996). Burglary victimization, perceptions of crime risk, and routine activities: A multilevel analysis across Seattle neighborhoods and census tracts. *Journal of Research in Crime and Delinquency, 33*, 147-180.

Winkel, F.W. (1989). Increased fear of crime and related side effects of persuasive communication: The price tag of burglary prevention campaigns? In E.C. Viano (Ed.), *Crime and its victims: International research and public policy issues* (pp. 273-296). New York: Hemisphere.

Winkel, F.W., & Vrij, A. (1993). Facilitating problem- and emotion-focused coping in victims of burglary: Evaluating a police crisis intervention program. *Journal of Community Psychology, 21*, 97-112.

Zimring, F.E., & Zuehl, J. (1986). Victim injury and death in urban robbery: A Chicago study. *Journal of Legal Studies, 15*, 1-40.

Chapter 9

Are All Victims Alike?
The Adverse, Generalized, and
Differential Impact of Crime

Arthur J. Lurigio

Samples of crime victims (burglary, robbery, felonious assault) and non-victims were compared to examine the short-term differential and generalized effects of crime on psychological, behavioral, and attitudinal measures. Victims were more likely to report experiencing higher levels of vulnerability, fear, and symptomology, and lower levels of self-efficacy. Also, victims were more likely to engage in protective behaviors. There were fewer differences, however, among the three groups of crime victims. Burglary victims were more likely to report feeling vulnerable and fearful, while assault victims were more likely to express more negative views of the police.

The existing literature on the psychological effects of criminal victimization is limited in several important respects. One notable gap in our knowledge about the effects of crime is an explicit documentation of its differential impact on victims of different categories of offenses,

ARTHUR J. LURIGIO: is at the Department of Psychology at Northwestern University where he is also a Research Associate at the Center for Urban Affairs and Policy Research. In addition, he is Director of Research for the Cook County Adult Probation Department.

The research described in this article was supported by National Institute of Justice Grant No. 85-IJ-CX-4069. Points of view or opinions expressed in this work are those of the author and do not necessarily represent the official position or policies of the U.S. Department of Justice.

I would like to thank Wesley G. Skogan, Geoffrey T. Fong, and Dennis P. Rosenbaum for their useful comments on an earlier draft of this article.

between the extremes of obviously very serious (e.g., rape) and
ious crimes (e.g., petty theft). Other limitations in our knowl-
from the failure of prior investigations to include a control
group of nonvictims for a baseline comparison of generalized effects, and
to examine the impact of victimization across a variety of dependent variables. In the present study, we sought to overcome these shortcomings.
Our efforts were aimed at exploring both the generalized effects of crime
by comparing victims against a control group of nonvictims and the differential effects of crime by comparing separate groups of burglary, robbery, and nonsexual assault victims. We made these comparisons on a
range of basic psychological, behavioral, and attitudinal measures.

RESEARCH ON THE PSYCHOLOGICAL EFFECTS OF CRIME

A growing literature suggests that criminal victimization, like other
deleterious life events (e.g., paralyzing accidents, fatal illness, natural
disasters), can have profound effects on a person's emotional well-being
and adjustment (e.g., American Psychological Association Task Force
Report, 1984; Greenberg and Ruback, 1984; Janoff-Bulman and Frieze,
1983; Kilpatrick, 1985; Kilpatrick, Resick, and Veronen, 1981). Studies
have shown, for example, that criminal victimization may eventuate in a
host of symptoms, known collectively as posttraumatic stress syndrome
(Steketee and Foa, 1987). These symptoms include difficulties in resum-
ing normal activities, depression, anxiety, a loss of emotional control,
guilt, sleep disturbances, and obsessive thoughts about the crime incident (e.g., Bard and Sangrey, 1979; Burgess and Holmstrom, 1979;
Rifai, 1982a; Waller, 1982). Moreover, the experience of victimization
appears to accentuate victims' fears of personal and property crime and
to heighten their general concern about crime in their neighborhood
(Skogan, 1987).

Other researchers report that crime compels its victims to challenge
basic implicit assumptions and expectations about themselves, others,
and their surroundings (Janoff-Bulman and Frieze, 1983; Lejeune and
Alex, 1973). According to some investigators, many victims are forced
to alter their view of the world as meaningful, optimally benign, trust-
worthy, and predictable as a way to explain sufficiently their suffering
and loss (Bard and Sangrey, 1979). Victims' exaggerated self-awareness
of their own mortality and vincibility may lead to a sense of excessive
vulnerability (Lejeune and Alex, 1973; Perloff, 1983) or a state of
learned helplessness (Peterson and Seligman, 1983).

Reactions to criminal victimization often extend beyond thoughts
and feelings to affect everyday behaviors. In the aftermath of the
episode, crime victims may engage in various preventive or avoidance
measures, such as buying a gun, participating in self-defense courses,

putting new locks on doors, installing alarms, changing their phone number or job, moving, restricting their nighttime activities, or reducing their social contacts (Bard and Sangrey, 1979; Berg and Johnson, 1974; Conklin, 1975; Krupnick, 1980; Lejeune and Alex, 1973; Maguire, 1980; Skogan and Maxfield, 1981).

In contrast to the above findings, there is evidence to suggest that the impact of victimization can be relatively innocuous or ephemeral. Hindelang, Gottfredson, and Garofalo (1978), for example, reported that crime victims altered their lives in only subtle and transitory ways following victimization. Along similar lines, Mayhew (1984) argued that crime in its usual form does not have dire emotional consequences for its victims. To support her assertion, she cited survey results showing that two-thirds of a national random sample of 3,000 "typical" victims in Britain related that they had experienced little or no emotional trauma succeeding the crime incident.

In separate analyses of victimization data, Reiss (1982) and others (e.g., Rifai, 1982b; Sparks, Genn, and Dodd, 1977) have also concluded that criminal victimization is minimally disruptive to peoples' lives inasmuch as most incidents are of the "attempted" variety or occasion little or no hardship on victims with respect to physical injury or lost property. These findings and propositions cast doubt on conceptualizations that inextricably link crime with psychological trauma or crisis.

The Present Study

The lack of consistency that surrounds findings in this area emanates in part from the disparate types of victims included in the studies. Apart from a handful of more recent investigations, psychological studies of crime victims have been limited largely to the adverse effects of rape or sexual assault (Katz and Mazur, 1979). As expected, these studies generated evidence to advance the view of crime as a crisis or trauma-inducing event.

Other research, such as Mayhew's (1984), reached its conclusions from analyses of large aggregate data sets that tend to wash or attenuate the overall effect of crime because they make up a confection of victims ranging from very small numbers of rape and other victims of serious crime to overwhelming numbers of victims of failed or petty offenses. In short, these investigations represent the universe of victims, weighted in number by the relative frequency of their type of encounter. The results of this research are not entirely surprising in the light of victimization data that indicate that in approximately 40% of the "serious" household and personal crimes reported to the police, a vehicle (rather than a person) is the primary target of the offense (Bureau of Justice Statistics, 1984). Thus it appears that past studies on the effects of crime have commonly drawn from the polarities of the victimization experience, and this has produced ostensibly conflictive results: Studies of rape victims suggest that the impact of crime is onerous, whereas studies of victims of attempted or less-serious crime suggest that the impact of crime is trivial.

Between victims of rape and attempted or petty crimes are vast numbers of victims of moderately serious offenses, who may be greatly affected by the episode. These "forgotten victims," who have been relatively neglected by both researchers and service providers (Lurigio and Rosenbaum, in press), are the focus of the current study. By examining victims of different types of crimes that lie broadly across the "mid-range" of seriousness (i.e., nonsexual, personal crimes), we can acquire a greater understanding of the psychological sequelae of criminal victimization. More variation in impact would be expected because there are no anticipated ceiling or floor effects to constrain the breadth of experiences they are likely to report. That is, we would not be studying offenses that are generally so serious that virtually all victims will be traumatized by the episode or are generally so innocuous that virtually none of the respondents will be traumatized by the episode. Another related problem with past research is that numerous investigations have treated criminal victimization as a unitary phenomenon and have made few or no attempts to perform a comparative analysis of the impact of different types of crime. Hence we know relatively little about the robustness or generalizability of the short-term effects of crime across categories of victims. This article addresses the deficiency by comparing groups of burglary, robbery, and nonsexual assault victims.

Many prior studies on the psychological impact of crime have also failed to incorporate a comparison or control group in the design or to control competing factors that confound the causal connection between victimization and outcomes. Data presented in the absence of controls, that is, without baseline measures of the prevalence of these outcomes in similar nonvictim populations, are virtually uninterpretable. Therefore, we included a comparable group of nonvictims in our study. Moreover, in our analyses we controlled for confounding variables so that we could more confidently attribute any differences between victims and nonvictims to the impact of crime, rather than to any rival systematic differences uniquely characterizing one group or the other.

A final problem with past research is that measures of the effects of criminal victimization in a single study have typically been limited to one or two domains, such as symptomolgy, fear, or protective behaviors. It is likely, however, that the actual impact of crime is more multifaceted than those studies suggest. In the present investigation, we included a much broader array of indicators designed to tap respondents' thoughts, emotions, perceptions, symptoms, and behaviors.

METHOD

Respondents

The present analyses are based on telephone interviews with (a) 227 crime victims in Detroit who were victimized during a four-month period of interest (May 1986-August 1986), and (b) 104 randomly selected nonvictims in Detroit, who constituted the subsample of control respondents for the study. Thus the total sample included 331 individuals.

The victim sample was generated through the Detroit police department, which provided us with the names and phone numbers of crime victims who had been victimized during the temporal interval of the study. The victim sample was restricted to three types of victimizations: residential burglary, robbery, and felonious assault. As discussed earlier, our intent was to select a sample of "forgotten victims," which precluded victims of sexual assault and domestic violence as well as victims of less serious offenses such as larceny, auto theft, and vandalism. The sample was also restricted to those cases in which there was no indication that the victim was a friend, relative, or acquaintance of the offender.

Control respondents for the nonvictims sample were selected via a random digit dialing procedure. The nonvictim sample was carefully screened to exclude potential respondents who (a) had been victims of personal or property crime in the preceding twelve months, (b) were not residents of Detroit proper, and (c) were not 18 years of age or older. We also attempted to match the victim and nonvictim samples on race and income by selecting telephone prefixes for the nonvictim sample telephone numbers, which covered roughly the same geographic areas from which the crime victim samples originated.

Demographics of the Sample

The demographic characteristics of the sample are provided in Table 1. As shown, more than half of the victim respondents (56%) were female, 70% were black, and 57% had completed high school or were less educated. There was considerable variation in the crime victim sample's ages, which ranged from 17 to 91. The mean age of the victims was 42 years old. In total, 64% of the sample was employed, full- or part-time, and nearly half (48%) reported an annual income of less than $10,000. Of the crime victims interviewed, 40% were victims of burglary (n = 91), 40% were victims of robbery (n = 91), and 20% were victims of felonious assault (n = 45).

Table 1 also displays the demographic characteristics of the nonvictim sample. Higher percentages of the nonvictims, when compared to the victims, were female (69%) and black (75%). Victims and nonvictims were highly similar with respect to age and educational level. The mean age of nonvictims was also 42 years old, and 53% had obtained a high school education or less. A somewhat lower percentage of nonvictims (40%), when compared to victims, reported an annual income of less than $10,000. Further, it appeared that respondents in the nonvictim sample were also more likely to be retired persons or housekeepers.

TABLE 1

Demographic Characteristics of Victim and Nonvictim Respondent Samples (in percentages)

Characteristics	Victims	Nonvictims
Sex		
Male	44	31
Female	56	69
Age		
17-31 years	35	37
32-46 years	33	29
47-61 years	15	13
62-76 years	13	14
77-91 years	4	7
Race/Ethnicity		
Black	70	75
White	28	22
Other	2	3
Education		
Less than high school (0-8)	5	4
High school (9-12)	52	49
Some college (13-16)	34	33
College graduate	5	6
Some graduate school	1	4
Master's degree or beyond	3	4
Employment		
Full-time	51	42
Part-time	13	14
Housekeeper	6	14
Student	3	3
Retired	12	22
Unemployed	10	5
Disabled	5	0
Income		
Less than $10,000	48	40
$10,000-$14,999	15	12
$15,000-$19,999	8	10
$20,000-$29,999	14	16
$30,000-$49,999	8	15
$50,000-above	3	7

Procedure

All victim respondents were initially sent a letter by the Chief of Police in Detroit that described the study and encouraged them to participate. Crime victims were told that the study was intended to identify crime victims' needs for the purpose of developing services that would be responsive to those needs. They were assured that any information collected during the interview would remain completely confidential. Victims who expressed hesitancy or suspiciousness regarding the study were urged to call a specially assigned police officer in Detroit to verify the legitimacy of the interview.

The nonvictim respondents were informed at the time of the interview that their number was obtained through a random dialing process that identified a representative sample of residents in Detroit. They were told that the purpose of the interview was to ask them about the quality of life in their neighborhood, crime, and other urban problems. The nonvictims were also assured that their answers would remain confidential.

Interviews were conducted at Northwestern University's Survey Laboratory at the Center for Urban Affairs and Policy Research. Both surveys were administered by well-trained and experienced interviewers. Because we were interested in the immediate impact of crime, an effort was made to contact victim respondents within two weeks following their report of the incident to the police. Victims who could not be interviewed within a three-week period were dropped from the study.

Instrumentation. The study employed two interview schedules. The first instrument was the crime victim survey, which was developed primarily to test the effectiveness of two interventions designed to alleviate the adverse psychological impact of criminal victimization, to facilitate victim participation in the criminal justice system, and to increase victim satisfaction with police services (see Rosenbaum, this issue). The second instrument was the nonvictim survey, which was essentially identical to the victim survey save for those items that were expressly designed to (a) describe the crime incident and its direct consequences (e.g., how many offenders were present, did the offender[s] brandish a weapon, what was the extent of victim injury), and (b) elicit the victim's perceptions of the two interventions (e.g., did they feel better after contact with the police, were the police attentive, sensitive, and responsive).

Outcome Variables

Vulnerability. Prior research demonstrates that people maintain an illusion of unique invulnerability when estimating their chances of falling prey to a wide range of negative life events (Perloff, 1983; Perloff and Fetzer, 1986). Unique invulnerability refers to the tendency of persons to see themselves and those close to them as less susceptible than others to tragic occurrences (e.g., illness, accidents). In the domain of crime, for example, past research suggests that people often perceive themselves as less likely than hypothetical targets to become victims of crime, and they often believe that crime in their neighborhood is less serious and prevalent than in other neighborhoods, regardless of actual crime rates (Heath, 1984; Weinstein, 1980). The present study examined two aspects of perceived vulnerability: specific vulnerability to crime and generalized vulnerability to other adverse events. The former assessed respondents' perceptions of the likelihood that they would become victims of any type of future crime, while the latter assessed respondents' perceptions of the likelihood that they would become victims of a future auto accident, fire, or serious illness.

Fear. The relationship between fear and criminal victimization is problematic. Studies on fear of crime have generated mixed findings. Some investigations have shown a marked increase in fear as a consequence of victimization (Krupnick, 1980), whereas others have shown that run-of-the-mill experiences with victimization only rarely eventuate in enhanced fearfulness (e.g., Rifai, 1982b). Indeed, some research suggests that criminal victimization effectively reduces fear by leading victims to the realization that the incident is survivable or not as harmful as they envisioned (Sparks, Genn, and Dodd, 1977).

Vulnerability and fear are related but differentiable constructs. Vulnerability is the perception of one's likelihood or estimated probability of victimization, whereas fear is the affective component often attendant with the perception. They may fit together in predictable ways (e.g., greater estimates of vulnerability being associated with higher levels of fear) or they may be inversely or only weakly related. Young males, for example, whose real or perceived risk of victimization (i.e., vulnerability) may actually be quite high, are one of the groups to express a low fear of crime. Therefore, we measured fear as a separate outcome, which constituted two dimensions: fear of personal crime and fear of property crime (Rosenbaum and Baumer, 1981).

Protective behaviors. It seems reasonable to expect that changes in fear and vulnerability will covary with changes in protective behaviors, which may be consciously adopted to alleviate fear and vulnerability or may be an unconscious by-product of one or both (Bard and Sangrey, 1979; Cohn, 1974; Lavrakas, 1981). We queried respondents about four such protective behaviors. In the context of this study, we made no attempt to relate the activities to fear and vulnerability or to explore the specific mediating factors that induced the activities.

Self-efficacy. Becoming a victim can be associated with a reduced sense of self-efficacy, that is, the belief that one's efforts are effective in producing desired outcomes (Bandura, 1986). Crime victims, especially those who are severely traumatized by the episode or are victims of multiple incidents, may experience feelings of helplessness and depression, which often translate into diminished self-efficacy (Peterson and Seligman, 1983). We were particularly interested in investigating whether victimization or different types of victimization are associated with reduced self-efficacy regarding crime-related avoidance behaviors.

Symptoms. The results of clinical studies suggest that for some victims the episode represents a significant and traumatic event that is accompanied by short- or long-term symptomology (American Psychological Association Task Force Report, 1984). Drawing on this literature, we measured a wide range of potential immediate symptoms, including cognitive, affective, and behavioral reactions to crime. All symptoms were tapped via respondents' self-reports.

Perceptions of police. For crime victims who report the incident, the initial contact with the police may color their overall perceptions of law enforcement and influence their decision to cooperate in the criminal justice system (Bard and Sangrey, 1979). Hence we elicited respondents' judgments concerning police effectiveness, their satisfaction with police services, and their willingness to go to court.

Data Analysis

We performed a series of multiple-regression analyses to investigate whether criminal victimization in general or different types of criminal victimization make an independent (unique) contribution toward explaining the variance in the key outcome variables of the study. This was achieved by equating victims and nonvictims on initial differences such as sex, race, and income and on competing factors, such as prior victimization and vicarious victimization (i.e., knowing about others in the community who have been victimized by crime), which have been found to be associated with crime-related perceptions and behaviors and would therefore confound the interpretation of results regarding the true effects of the victimization experience. Variance in outcome variables attributable to the confounds was removed (controlled for) by entering the factors as a set of covariates, which preceded victimization (coded as a dummy variable) in their order of entry into the analysis. Crime victim categories (burglary, robbery, assault) were collapsed for the purpose of testing generalized differences between victims and nonvictims but were obviously kept separate for testing the differential impact of crime.

RESULTS

Vulnerability

There were highly significant differences between victims and non-victims on all three vulnerability measures relating to future criminal victimization. Victims were significantly more likely to perceive themselves as highly vulnerable to any future crime (p < .002), to perceive their chances of being victimized as significantly greater than similar others living in their neighborhoods (p < .0006), and to perceive their close relatives or friends as highly vulnerable to any future crime (p < .001). Only one of the three generalized vulnerability measures was significant. Victims were more likely than nonvictims to perceive themselves as highly vulnerable to future illness (p < .003). There were no differences between victims' and nonvictims' perceptions of their perceived vulnerability to future fire or auto accidents.

Two marginally significant differences were found among the crime victim groups on the three vulnerability measures relating to future criminal victimization. Burglary victims were more likely than robbery or assault victims to perceive themselves as highly vulnerable to future crime (p < .07), and to perceive their close relatives or friends as highly vulnerable to future crime (p < .07). There were no differences among the three victim groups on any of the generalized vulnerability measures.

Fear

The comparison of victims and nonvictims on fear measures of both property and personal crime revealed highly significant differences. Victims were more likely to report higher levels of fear relating to being attacked or robbed at night (p < .0001) and having their homes burglarized (p < .0001).

There were no differences among the victim groups on the fear of personal crime measure. A highly significant difference emerged, however, when victims were compared on the fear of property crime measure. Burglary victims were more likely than robbery or assault victims to express a high level of fear regarding property crime (p < .003).

Protective Behaviors

The analyses yielded a number of differences between victims and nonvictims on the measures of protective behaviors. Victims were more likely to report adopting three of the four protective behaviors measured in the study: (a) looking out for suspicious people (p < .05); (b) avoiding strangers during walks (p < .01); and (c) checking behind the front door of their apartment or home as they enter (p < .0001). There was no difference between victims and nonvictims on the fourth measure, which involved taking along a dog, whistle, or weapon with them for protection at night. Comparisons among the three victims' groups revealed no significant differences on any of the protective behavior measures.

Self-Efficacy

Highly significant differences appeared between victims and nonvictims on both self-efficacy measures. Results revealed that victims were more likely than nonvictims to report that future criminal victimization was "pretty much beyond their control," that is, that precautions would not help them avoid being victimized in the future (p < .0001), and less likely than nonvictims to report that "making an extra effort would keep them from becoming a victim of crime" (p < .003). There were no differences among the three victims groups on either of the self-efficacy measures.

Symptoms

Victim respondents reported a wide range of symptomology when compared to nonvictim controls. There were highly significant differences between the two groups on reported nervousness (p < .0001), unpleasant thoughts (p < .0001), poor appetite (p < .0001), generalized fearfulness (p < .0001), upset stomach (p < .007), sleep disturbances (p < .0001), uncontrollable urges to retaliate (p < .0001), and a greater need to use prescription drugs (p < .001).

The only marginally significant difference in symptomology among the crime victim groups was alcohol use, with assault victims indicating a greater tendency to experience drinking problems when compared with robbery and burglary victims (p < .07). Also, there was a non-significant but apparent trend in the data showing a greater tendency among burglary victims to experience sleep disturbances.

Perceptions of Police and Willingness to Go to Court

No differences between victims and nonvictims were found on their willingness to go to court, their satisfaction with police services, or their perceptions of police effectiveness. Significant differences were found, however, when comparing the three victim groups on these measures. When compared with burglary and robbery victims, assault victims were less willing to go to court (p < .01), less satisfied with police services in

Detroit (p < .03), and less likely to judge the Detroit police as effective in preventing crime (p < .05).

SUMMARY AND CONCLUSIONS

The present research provides considerable support for the notion that crime victims suffer from adverse, short-term psychological consequences as a result of the incident. When compared to nonvictims, crime victims report higher levels of vulnerability and fear as well as varying manifestations of distressing symptomology (e.g., anxiety, unpleasant thoughts, upset stomach). Moreover, although victims are more likely to engage in protective behaviors, they appear to experience a diminished sense of self-efficacy, that is, the belief that their behaviors will be effective in helping them to avoid future victimization. In contrast, among the three categories of crime victims, there were no patterns of clear or consistent differences. There were, however, some exceptions to this general finding: Burglary victims did seem to be more unfavorably affected, which is reflected in a greater tendency to report specific vulnerability, fear and sleep disturbances, while assault victims seem to express more negative views of the police.

This study leaves a number of unanswered empirical questions that point to viable directions for future research. First, the current investigation does not offer an explication of the specific factors or mediational processes that underlie victim responses. The evidence here suggests that different groups of crime victims are highly similar in their reported reactions to the episode (see Resick, this issue). It would be useful for subsequent studies to identify the common experiential thread that apparently runs through these different instances of criminal victimization (see Janoff-Bulman and Frieze, 1983).

Second, although studying the effects of crime across a variety of offenses is an informative point of departure for elucidating differential impact, it should be noted that crime type is essentially a proxy that "stands for" a multitude of differences lying along numerous other dimensions. An alternative strategy for dicing the data could involve a more precise exploration of these various dimensions or elements that constitute (i.e., characterize) the crime incident, such as seriousness, the victim/offender relationship, the presence of other victims, and the victim's responses during the incident. Our understanding would be fostered by combining episode descriptors with previctimization and postvictimization data in a multivariate framework that predicts victim readjustment or coping (Lurigio & Rosenbaum, in press).

With respect to its practical implications, the current study underscores the importance of criminal justice practitioners and service providers recognizing that victims of nonsexual offenses may also experience adverse effects (see Resick, this issue; Kilpatrick et al., this issue). This demands a recasting of more traditional approaches for the treatment of crime victims, which have been formulated largely to be responsive to victims of rape and sexual assault, but that have assumed, either explicitly or implicitly, that victims of other crimes do not experience many adverse effects. As the present research demonstrates, a much wider range of victims are likely to suffer in the aftermath of crime.

REFERENCES

American Psychological Association. 1984. *Final Report of the Task Force on the Victims of Crime and Violence*. Washington, DC: Author.

Bandura, A. 1986. *Social Foundations of Thought and Action: A Social Cognitive Theory*. Englewood Cliffs, NJ: Prentice-Hall.

Bard, M., and D. Sangrey, 1979. "The crime victim's book." New York: Scribners.

Berg, W. and R. Johnson. 1979. "Assessing the Impact of Victimization: Acquisition of the Victim Role Among Elderly and Female Victims." Pp. 18-36 in *Perspectives on Victimology*, edited by W. Parsonage. London: Sage.

Bureau of Justice Statistics. 1984. "Criminal Victimization in the United States, 1982" (Publication No. NCJ-92820). Washington, DC: Department of Justice.

Burgess, A. and L. Holmstrom. 1979. "Rape: Sexual Disruption and Recovery." *American Journal of Orthopsychiatry* 49:658-669.

Chon, Y. 1974. "Crisis Intervention and the Victim of Robbery." Pp. 11-16 in *Victimology: A New Focus*. Vol. 2. Lexington, MA: Lexington Books.

Conklin, J. 1975. *The Impact of Crime*. New York: Macmillan.

Greenberg, M.S. and R.B. Ruback, eds. 1984. "Criminal Victimizations." *Journal of Social Issues* 40(l).

Heath, L. 1984. "Impact of Newspaper Crime Reports on Fear of Crime: Multi-Methodological Investigation." *Journal of Personality and Social Psychology* 47: 263-276.

Hindelang, M., M. Gottfredson, and J. Garofalo. 1978. *Victims of Personal Crime: An Empirical Foundation for a Theory of Personal Victimization*. Cambridge: Ballinger.

Janoff-Bulman, R. and I. Frieze. 1983. "A Theoretical Perspective for Understanding Reactions to Victimology." *Journal of Social Issues* 39:1-17.

Katz, S. and M.A. Mazer. 1979. *Understanding the Rape Victim: A Synthesis of Research Findings*. New York: John Wiley.

Kilpatrick, D.G. 1985. "Research on Long-Term Effects of Criminal Victimization: Scientific, Service Delivery, and Public Policy Perspectives." Washington, DC: National Institute of Mental Health with the Cooperation of the National Organization for Victim Assistance.

―――――, P.A. Resick, and L.J. Veronen. 1981. "Effects of a Rape Experience: A Longitudinal Study." *Journal of Social Issues* 37: 105-122.

Krupnick, J. 1980. "Brief Psychotherapy with Victims of Violent Crime." *Victimology 5:* 347-354.

Lavrakas, P.J. 1981. "On Households." Pp. 26-44 in *Reactions to Crime,* edited by D. A. Lewis. Newbury Park, CA: Sage.

Lejeune, R. and N. Alex. 1973. "On Being Mugged." *Urban Life and Culture* 2:259-287.

Lurigio, A.J. and D.P. Rosenbaum. In press. "The Psychological Effects of Criminal Victimization: Past and Future Research." *Victimology.*

Maguire, M. 1980. "The Impact of Burglary on Victims." *British Journal of Criminology* 20:261-275.

Mayhew, P. 1984. "The Effects of Crime: Victims, the Public, and Fear." Paper presented at the 16th International Symposium on Criminology, Strasbourg.

Perloff, L.S. 1983. "Perceptions of Vulnerability to Victimization." *Journal of Social Issues* 39:41-61.

—————— and B.K. Fetzer. 1986. "Self-Other Judgments and Perceived Vulnerability to Victimization." *Journal of Personality and Social Psychology* 50:501-510.

Peterson, C. and M.E.P. Seligman. 1983. "Learned Helplessness and Victimization." *Journal of Social Issues* 39:105-118.

Reiss, A.J. 1982. "How Serious is Serious Crime?" *Vanderbilt Law Review* 35:541-585.

Rifai, M.Y. 1982a. "Methods of Measuring the Impact of Criminal Victimization Through Victimization Surveys." Pp. 189-202 in *The Victim in International Perspective,* edited by Hans Joachim Schneider. New York: de Gruyter.

—————— 1982b. "Stress, Trauma, and Crisis: The Theoretical Framework of Victimization Reconsidered." Washington, DC: National Organization for Victim Assistance.

Rosenbaum, D.P. and T. Baumer. 1981. *Measuring Fear of Crime.* Evanston, IL: Westinghouse Evaluation Institute.

Skogan, W.G. 1987. "The Impact of Victimization on Fear." *Crime & Delinquency* 33:135-154.

Skogan, W.G. and M.M. Maxfield. 1981. *Coping with Crime.* Newbury Park, CA: Sage.

Sparks, R.F., H. Genn, and D. Dodd. 1977. *Surveying Victims.* London: John Wiley.

Stekette, G. and E.B. Foa. 1987. "Rape Victims: Post-Traumatic Stress Responses and Their Treatment: A Review of the Literature." *Journal of Anxiety Disorders* 1:69-86.

Waller, I. 1982. "Crime Victims: Needs, Services and Reforms-Orphans of Social Policy." Paper presented at the Fourth International Symposium on Victimology, Tokyo.

Weinstein, N.D. 1980. "Unrealistic Optimism About Future Life Events." *Journal of Personality and Social Psychology* 39:806-820.

Chapter 10

Victimization of Persons by Fraud

Richard M. Titus
Fred Heinzelmann
John M. Boyle

This research focuses on the victimization of persons by personal fraud, which we define as involving the deliberate intent to deceive with promises of goods, services, or other financial benefits that in fact do not exist or that were never intended to be provided. The article presents data based on a national telephone survey involving a representative probability sample of 1,246 respondents aged 18 and older. The survey measured the incidence and prevalence of personal fraud victimization, the characteristics of the victims involved, and the impacts and effects of these offenses. The reactions of victims and official agencies to the victimization experience were also addressed, as well as implications for research and public education.

The FBI's Uniform Crime Reports (UCR), and the Justice Department's National Crime Victimization Survey (NCVS), provide annual tabulations on property and violent crimes, based on crimes reported to the police and surveys of households. However, they do *not* provide information with regard to the victimization of persons by fraud. These types of white-collar/economic crime are targeted against individuals and employ deception for the purpose of obtaining illegal financial gain.

RICHARD M. TITUS: Program Manager, Victims of Crime, National Institute of Justice, U.S. Department of Justice, Washington, D.C. This paper does not represent the official views of the National Institute of Justice nor of the U.S. Department of Justice. FRED HEINZELMANN: Former Director, Crime Prevention and Enforcement Division, National Institute of Justice. JOHN M. BOYLE: Senior Vice President, Schulman, Ronca, and Bucuvalas, Inc.

Source: Titus, R.M., Heinzelmann, F., & Boyle, J.M. (1995). Victimization of persons by fraud. *Crime & Delinquency*, 41, 54-72. Copyright © 1995 by Sage Publications, Inc. Reprinted by permission of Sage Publications, Inc.

They involve the misrepresentation of facts and the deliberate intent to deceive with the promise of goods, services, or other financial benefits that in fact do not exist or that were never intended to be provided. This includes various forms of telemarketing fraud, frauds involving consumer goods and services, and frauds dealing with financial advice, insurance coverage, and investment or business schemes. Examples include offers of "free" prizes that in fact incur unwanted costs, scams involving credit assistance or loan consolidation, unauthorized use of credit card or bank account numbers, charity scams in which victim contributions are obtained deceptively, worthless warranties, fraudulent health or beauty products, and scams involving the provision of unnecessary or useless goods, services or repairs. The appendix indicates how these frauds were defined for the respondents in this survey.

Both criminal justice professionals and researchers have highlighted the need for systematic information on the nature and extent of various economic crimes including personal frauds, to influence both the actions of potential victims and the policies and practices of the criminal justice system (Benson, Cullen, and Maakestad 1990; Geis and Stotland 1980; Moore and Mills 1990). Moreover, the needs of the victims of these crimes have not been adequately addressed by researchers and policymakers. The focus of legislation and victim assistance programs has been on victims of interpersonal violence and street property crimes, not on the victims of economic crimes including personal fraud.

At present, research on the nature of personal frauds is limited and statistical data on these crimes and their victims is scarce (Kusic 1989; Moore and Mills 1990). Although some case studies or special surveys have been carried out, these are usually not comprehensive and often focus on a limited number of victims. For example, there have been studies of Ponzi schemes using convenience samples of victims who were willing to report these offenses to a law enforcement agency (Ganzini, McFarland, and Bloom 1990), as well as case studies of victims of various types of consumer frauds (McGuire and Edelhertz 1980).

A survey by Harris and Associates addressed public knowledge of, attitudes toward, and experiences with several types of telemarketing fraud (Bass and Hoeffler 1992). This survey found that nearly one in three Americans have, at one time or another, been cheated out of money through various deceptive means, including receiving a lower quality product than they paid for or never receiving items that were ordered. Fewer than one third of those persons who had been victimized reported the incident to anyone, and nearly two thirds of the American public would not know where to call to find out if some offer or promotion is legitimate. A Princeton survey of the behavior of consumers (American Association of Retired Persons 1994) also found that three quarters of the respondents claimed that at least once during the past year they were deceived or defrauded through various telemarketing or other direct personal marketing schemes. In addition, one person in seven reported being the victim of a major fraud at some point in his or her lifetime.

These last two studies were limited in that the first focused on only one type of personal fraud victimization: telemarketing; whereas the other study focused on consumer transactions, only some of which were fraudulent, and on knowledge and attitudes more than on victimization. The studies do not yield data on victimization by personal fraud that will allow comparison with NCVS data on victimization by such crimes as burglary, vehicle theft, robbery, assault, and larceny, in terms of the number and characteristics of personal fraud victims, and the financial and other forms of harm caused. In addition, we need to know which types of personal fraud are most prevalent and how victims and official agencies respond to them. This information will make it possible to develop improved programs for controlling these crimes and responding to the needs of their victims.

The study reported here was conducted by two staff members of the National Institute of Justice, with the survey research firm of Schulman, Ronca, and Bucuvalas, as an exploratory effort to (a) determine whether valid measures of personal fraud victimization could be obtained, (b) obtain measures of incidence and prevalence, and (c) examine the nature of fraud incidents. Comparisons with the forms of victimization captured by the NCVS should provide useful information to citizens, as well as public and private agencies, concerned with this form of crime.

METHOD

Following a review of the literature on personal fraud victimization, a national focus group of fraud investigators and prosecutors was convened to outline key issues in personal fraud victimization. A draft survey instrument was developed based on the issues raised in the literature and by the expert focus group. Next, a focus group of ordinary citizens was convened to critique the draft instrument in the light of their own experiences with personal fraud; the instrument was revised appropriately. A pilot test of the instrument was conducted, and the instrument revised appropriately.

This instrument was used in a survey that was administered in November 1991 by the survey research firm of Schulman, Ronca, and Bucuvalas. The sample was constructed as a national random digit dialing sample of telephone households in the United States. The designated respondent within each sampled household was chosen as the individual 18 years or older having the most recent birthday. Computer-Assisted Telephone Interviewing (CATI) was used in the survey. The participation rate was 66.1%; a total of 1,246 usable interviews was completed. The achieved sample was first weighted to correct for unequal probability of selection of households (number of telephones), and of eligible respondents within households (number of adults). It was next weighted for nonparticipation. The weighting required was minimal.

The first six screener questions of the survey instrument were adapted from the NCVS and dealt with victimization within the last year of the respondent by robbery or assault, or of the household by burglary or motor vehicle theft. These NCVS questions were intended to orient the respondent's thinking from the outset to events that were criminal in nature. The emphasis on criminal activity and criminal intent was continued in the interviewer's introduction to the fraud screener questions, which emphasized criminal activity involving clear elements of deception, false and misleading information, impersonation, misrepresentation, abuse of trust, and failure to deliver. These elements were emphasized again in the wording of each individual fraud screener item (see appendix).

In the screener portion of the survey instrument, respondents were asked if they had ever been victimized, or if an attempt had ever been made to victimize them, by 21 specific types of fraud, plus any other type of fraud. This yielded 22 fraud screener items on which the respondent could have reported ever having experienced a victimization or attempted victimization. Of the 1,246 respondents, 720 (58%) experienced one or more lifetime victimizations, or attempted victimizations. Respondents were asked how long ago the events happened; the five choices ranged from "within the past 12 months" to "five years or longer," plus "not sure." Of the 1,246 respondents, 387 (31%) experienced one or more victimizations or attempted victimizations within the past 12 months (details are presented in Table 1).

Incident reports were taken only for incidents that occurred within the last 12 months to avoid the decrease in accuracy of recall of details over longer time periods. If the respondent had experienced more than one victimization or attempted victimization for a given fraud type within the last 12 months, he or she was asked to report only on the most recent incident. The incident report questions explored characteristics of the crime and the offender, the effects of the crime, whether the crime was reported to an official, and what type of assistance, if any, was received.

Incident reports were taken for no more than five fraud categories per respondent. If more than five types were reported by a respondent, five were selected at random by CATI for that respondent. Only 8% of respondents reported a victimization or attempted victimization for more than five of the 22 fraud categories, so this procedure caused little loss of data and avoided overrepresenting this group of respondents.

Because a sequential-order effect could arise from taking incident reports in the same order of fraud category for all respondents, the order was randomized by CATI for each respondent.

Following the incident report items, a final set of questions focused on characteristics of the respondent and his or her household: age, race, Hispanic, income, education, location, and household size. Respondent sex was entered by the interviewer.

TABLE 1
Prevalence of Fraud Attempts, Successes, and Losses of Money or Property, in Previous Year

	Frequency	Percentage
Past-year fraud experience		
No attempts made	859	69
Attempts	387	31
Total	1246	100
Outcome of attempts		
Not successful	200	52
Successful	187	48
Total	387	100
"Successes": Amount of loss		
No Loss[a]	22	11.8
$1 to $25	38	20.3
$26 to $50	21	11.2
$51 to $100	21	11.2
$101 to $250	29	15.5
$251 to $500	19	10.2
$501 to $1,000	9	4.8
$1,001 to $2,000	11	5.9
$2,001 to $5,000	8	4.3
$5,001 to $10,000	4	2.1
$10,001 to $65,000	5	2.7
Total	187	100.0

[a] Respondent may have subsequently recovered the loss from offender or from others.

A bivariate data analysis was conducted using SPSS/PC+. Unless otherwise noted, any results reported were significant at $p < .05$. Because of conditionals (skip-patterns) in the instrument, for many variables the number of cases is too small for analysis; in those cases only totals are reported.

RESULTS

Characteristics of Personal Fraud Victims

We look first at the person-level data set $(N = 1,246$; see Table 1). In the last 12 months, 31% of the sample had a personal fraud attempt made on them; of these, 48% were reported to have been successful, so that 15% of the total sample were victimized by a successful personal fraud. Almost all (88.2%) of these successful frauds involved the loss of money or property; 13% of the total sample reported such a loss. The number of cases by amount of loss decreases steadily and with minimal discontinuities from $1-$25 to $65,000. Table 2, from the incident data set, expands the high end of the distribution (losses at $1,000 and above). Assuming that the sample itself was properly drawn, we believe that respondents with very high losses were not overrepresented in this data set. Personal fraud appears to be a type of crime in which losses, although typically rather small, in many cases can be quite large.[1] The mean loss for our sample was $216.29. Expanding our sample of 1,245 persons 18 years or older to the 1991 estimated U.S. population of 185,105,441 persons 18 years or older yields an estimated annual loss from personal fraud in excess of $40 billion ($40,036,455,000).

TABLE 2
Estimates of Money Lost: Incidents at $1,000 and Above ($)

Amount of Money Lost	Number Of Incidents
1,000	3
1,200	1
1,400	1
1,500	6
1,800	1
2,000	6
3,000	1
3,800	1
4,300	1
4,700	1
5,000	2
6,000	2
7,400	1
10,000	1
17,000	1
28,000	1
50,000	1
65,000	1

The NCVS shows that victimization by the various forms of crime measured by the NCVS is influenced by demographic and locational factors. Criminal justice system practitioners who specialize in fraud often express a belief that certain groups, such as the elderly, are more vulnerable to victimization by fraud. Table 3 reveals only two demographic variables—age and education—that are significantly associated with the likelihood of fraud attempts and the outcomes of those attempts. Other variables that make a difference for many NCVS crimes do not do so for personal fraud.

TABLE 3
Respondents' Fraud Experience (no attempts/attempts only/success),
by Demographic Variables

Variable	Chi-Square
Age	0.00
Education	0.00
Household size	0.09
Region of the United States	0.11
Household income	0.39
City/suburb/rural	0.56
Race	0.79
Hispanic	0.86
Sex	0.89

Table 4 shows that although age is the demographic variable most significantly associated with fraud victimization, it is a negative relationship. Moreover, we see in Table 5 that the elderly (persons 65 and above), when they are fraud victims, are less likely to lose money or property than those in younger age groups. In our survey, fraud victimization follows the pattern of almost all NCVS crimes: The older one is, the less likely one is to be the victim of fraud. Although fraud investigators and prosecutors often express the opposite opinion, their experience is limited to those victims who report, and in our sample, incidents involving the elderly were much more likely to be reported to the authorities than those involving younger respondents $(p < .031)$.

Table 6 shows that those at the extremes of education (no high school diploma, graduate degree), are least likely to be the victim of fraud, whereas those with some college or a college degree appear to be the most vulnerable. Moreover, if we look at how education affects the likelihood that a fraud attempt will be successful, we find that there is no significant effect $(p < .168)$, and that attempts against those with a graduate degree are slightly more likely to be successful than attempts against those who did not finish high school.

Table 7 shows that, contrary to what one might expect, demographic variables such as education, income, or age do not significantly influence an individual's likelihood of succumbing to a fraud attempt: No demographic indicator approaches significance in predicting whether a fraud attempt, if received, will be successful. The key factor in victimization by personal fraud appears to be whether one receives an attempt; the likelihood of a success given an attempt does not vary significantly across the demographic variables of age, education, household size, region of the United States, household income, urban or rural location, race, Hispanic origin, or gender.

TABLE 4
Fraud Experience in the Past Year, by Age: Observed Values and Expected Values

Age	18-24	25-34	35-44	45-54	55-64	65-74	75+
No attempts	89	186	164	119	106	101	82
	(119)	(200)	(173)	(116)	(98)	(84)	(60)
Attempts	39	53	45	31	17	13	2
	(28)	(47)	(41)	(27)	(23)	(20)	(14)
Successes	44	52	42	19	18	9	3
	(26)	(44)	(38)	(26)	(21)	(18)	(13)
Column total	172	291	251	169	142	122	87
Column %	14	24	20	14	12	10	7

NOTE: Chi-square = 0.00000. Expected values are in parentheses.

TABLE 5
Lost Money or Property in the Past Year, by Age: Observed Values and Expected Values

Age	18-24	25-34	35-44	45-54	55-64	65-74	75+
Did not lose	135	240	215	151	129	115	85
	(149)	(252)	(218)	(147)	(123)	(106)	(76)
Did lose	38	50	37	18	13	7	2
	(23)	(39)	(34)	(23)	(19)	(16)	(12)
Column total	172	291	251	169	142	122	87
Column %	14	24	20	14	12	10	7

NOTE: Chi-square = 0.00001. Expected values are in parentheses.

TABLE 6
Fraud Experience in the Past Year, by Last Year or Grade of School Completed: Observed Values and Expected Values

Education	High Drop out	High School Graduate	Some College	B.A.	M.A.+
No attempts	136	293	205	145	69
	(114)	(295)	(220)	(154)	(65)
Attempts	16	66	55	49	13
	(27)	(69)	(52)	(36)	(15)
Successes	13	70	60	30	13
	(25)	(65)	(49)	(34)	(14)
Column total	166	429	320	225	94
Column %	14	35	26	18	8

Note: Chi-square = 0.00146. Expected values are in parentheses.

TABLE 7
Respondents' Fraud Experience (attempts only vs. successes),
by Demographic Variables

Variable	Chi-Square
Age	0.69
Education	0.32
Household size	0.36
Region of the United States	0.39
Household Income	0.59
City/suburb/rural	0.25
Race	0.62
Hispanic	0.94
Sex	0.76

To summarize the findings from the person-level data set, fraud is more common than many NCVS crimes and shows a highly skewed distribution of monetary losses. The data do not support some common stereotypes about what sort of person is most likely to become a fraud victim: The elderly, those who have less education or income, minorities, females, and those who live in rural areas are no more likely than their opposites to be fraud victims and, in some cases, are less so. We now turn from the examination of persons to the examination of incidents.

Characteristics of Personal Fraud Incidents

As noted earlier, incident reports were taken only for incidents that occurred within the last 12 months and for no more than five fraud categories per respondent; these categories were selected at random for each such respondent. If the respondent had experienced more than one victimization or attempted victimization for a given fraud type within the last 12 months, he or she was asked to report only on the most recent incident.

There were 711 incidents that occurred within the last 12 months. For these incidents, the respondent was asked about contacts with the offender, prior familiarity with the type of fraud involved, prior efforts to investigate it, whether it was reported to authorities, and what action was taken. Respondents were asked if the attempt to defraud them was successful or only an attempt.

Of the 711 incidents, there were 279 successful attempts; for these the respondent was also asked about monetary losses and other forms of harm resulting from the incident. Of these successful incidents, the respondent lost money or property (85%), was caused financial or personal credit problems (20%), suffered health or emotional problems (14%), lost time from work (13%), and was harmed in some other way (5%). Other members of the respondent's household were caused significant harm or loss in 11% of these incidents.

Table 8 examines all 711 fraud incidents, both attempts and successes, and shows how they ranked in terms of frequency and whether the attempts were successful. (For this cross-tabulation, there were 700 incidents distributed over 22 categories of fraud types; cell sizes in many cases were too small for tests of significance and none are reported.) We see that the types of fraud that are frequently mentioned by fraud investigators (pigeon drop, fake bank official, fake ticket, phony inspector, credit repair) are not very common, and others that are frequently mentioned ("free" prize, credit card number scam, fake charity), although more often reported among our sample, are not usually successful.

Looking next at the fraud types that occur more often and that are most likely to be successful (appliance/auto repair, fraudulent price, 900 number swindles, fraudulent subscriptions, and fake warranties), it is clear that these relate to consumer transactions that some might argue simply involve misunderstandings or consumer dissatisfaction. However, it should be remembered that the survey was specifically designed to orient the respondent from the outset to the reporting of events that were criminal and fraudulent, involving the elements of deception, false and misleading information, impersonation, misrepresentation, abuse of trust, and failure to deliver (see appendix). Moreover, the evidence provided by congressional hearings and consumer protection agencies indicates that consumer transactions in fact often do involve deception and abuse of trust for financial gain, which are the hallmarks of economic crimes such as fraud.

In many cases, the more successful types of fraud seen in Table 8 indicate or suggest a nonstranger dimension (Pearson chi-squares are reported):

- Greater success if respondent knew or knew of the offender, than if a stranger $(p < .003)$.
- Greater success if the mode of the initial contact was in person, through a third person, through television or the print media, or initiated by respondent, than if the initial contact was by telephone or mail $(p < .000)$.
- Greater success if the location of the initial contact was at the swindler's home or place of business, at victim's workplace, or in victim's neighborhood, than if at respondent's home $(p < .000)$.

The nonstranger factor is more likely to be present in the business-related types of fraud that Table 8 also shows to be more often successful. However, there were other factors related to whether the fraud attempt would be successful that are probably independent of the business dimension; they may have important implications for fraud prevention programs. These factors are

- Greater success if respondent had not heard of this type of fraud before (p < .000).
- Greater success, approaching significance, if the respondent did not try to investigate the person or proposition before responding (p < .078).

It is curious to note that whether or not the fraud attempt was successful had absolutely no effect on whether it would be reported to the authorities (p < .660). Overall, only 15% of incidents were reported, the majority (62%) to law enforcement, with most of the remainder split between consumer protection agencies and Better Business Bureaus.

Table 9 shows the mean and median loss for each type of fraud. Recall that Table 8 identified certain fraud types that occur more often *and* are frequently successful (appliance/auto repair, fraudulent price, 900 number swindles, fraudulent subscriptions, fake warranty). All of these except subscription swindles have mean losses in excess of $250.00.

TABLE 8
Types of Fraud Incident, and Outcomes

Fraud Type	Total Number of Incidents	Number of Attempts	Number Successful	Percentage Successful
Free prize	131	114	17	13.0
Appliance/auto repair	70	20	50	71.4
Card number	57	48	9	15.8
Price	55	30	25	45.5
900 number	52	31	21	40.4
Other types[a]	50	27	23	46.0
Subscriptions	43	13	30	69.7
Charity	39	32	7	17.9
Warranty	31	11	20	64.5
Work at home	23	19	4	17.4
Health/beauty	23	12	11	47.8
Insurance	20	14	6	30.0
Home repair	18	6	12	66.7
Broker/planner	17	10	7	41.2
Credit repair	16	12	4	25.0
Inspector	13	10	3	23.1
Investment	12	8	4	33.3
Ticket	10	9	1	10.0
Fees/membership	8	0	8	100.0
Pigeon drop	6	5	1	16.7
Training course	5	0	5	100.0
Bank official	1	1	0	0.0
Totals	700	432	268	38.3

[a] Frauds that fit in no other category.

TABLE 9
Types of Fraud Incident, Mean and Median Losses

Type of Fraud	Number of Cases	Mean	Median
Investment	3	$22,175	$1,500
Other types	24	4,180	550
Insurance	5	1,780	1,200
Broker/planner	5	1,564	100
Card number	8	1,321	200
Appliance/auto repair	48	1,039	200
Home repair	8	459	117
Ticket	1	398	
900 number	16	348	35
Price	18	332	100
Warranty	14	281	200
Fees/membership	8	263	150
Free prize	16	261	64
Training course	5	118	100
Credit repair	4	103	80
Health/beauty	11	87	60
Pigeon drop	1	80	
Inspector	2	64	64
Subscriptions	26	42	28
Work at home	4	40	43
Charity	5	32	25
Bank official	0	0	0

There are also fraud types that attract attention because of the very large amounts of money that some of their victims lose. Frauds involving losses of $3,000 or more (with the number of victims in parentheses) are as follows: other types (6), appliance/auto repair (2), fraudulent use of bank or credit card (2), broker/planner (1), insurance (1), investment (1), and 900 number (1).

DISCUSSION

In these data, personal fraud, compared to the NCVS crimes, appears to be very common, and although fraud attempts are typically not successful, losses for some victims can be extreme. Victimization by personal fraud does not vary significantly across the demographic variables of household size, region of the United States, household income, urban or rural location, race, Hispanic origin, or gender. Only age and education make a significant difference, and not in the expected directions: Younger, as well as better educated persons are victimized more often, rather than less often. Moreover, no demographic indicator approaches significance in predicting whether a fraud attempt, if received, will be successful; the key factor in victimization by personal fraud appears to be whether one receives an attempt.

The environmental and geographic variables associated with victimization in the "routine activities" perspective (Cohen and Felson 1979; Lynch 1987; Meier and Miethe 1993), such as convergence of unguarded targets and motivated offenders, appear to be more relevant to NCVS crimes than to victimization by personal fraud. It may be that because con artists can make use of the phone, the mail, the media, and electronic bulletin boards, the demographic variables that are so tied to geographic proximity variables in most NCVS crimes are much less important in personal fraud victimization.

Concerning the elderly, these data suggest that they are far from being the trusting and compliant victims that are commonly portrayed in much of the fraud literature. Part of the explanation may be that the elderly are more likely to report a fraud to authorities, but it is also possible that they are being unfairly stereotyped, and that in addition to getting older, they have also gotten smarter. Looking at this from the other end of the age spectrum, given the typically lower incomes of the young, they may be more receptive to promises of fabulous bargains and spectacular opportunities, especially given their shorter lifetimes in which to have become—personally or vicariously—"sadder but wiser" about such things.

It is curious that education does not appear to be the protective factor that one might expect it to be in a type of crime that can be characterized much more as a battle of wits than most NCVS crimes. For an individual to believe that more education confers greater ability to deal with con artists could prove costly to him or her.

Age and education may work together in that younger, better educated persons may have wider interests and a broader range of activities and purchases and, for this reason, may be more likely to encounter situations, or be on telephone or mailing lists, that result in a fraudulent solicitation.

The study suggests the value of public information programs aimed at the prevention of personal fraud, because fraud attempts were less likely to be successful if the intended victim had heard of the fraud before. Information programs need to highlight the fact that victimization by personal fraud is a pervasive threat to all segments of the society, identify the types of fraud that are current, and the kinds of action that can help persons to detect and prevent fraud. This includes 1-800 telephone numbers and other services providing the public with information dealing with fraud prevention and control and with directions to useful sources of information and assistance.

It appears from our data that victims of personal fraud, who report to authorities, receive few positive results, monetary or otherwise, from doing so. Based on our estimate of the annual losses incurred by fraud victims, and the relative frequency of these frauds, fraud victims may merit more attention than they are now receiving.

Although we believe that our survey produced accurate estimates of the incidence and prevalence of personal fraud victimization and the magnitude of its dollar losses, it was not designed to provide great detail on the subject. Future research could take three directions:

- Analysis of the information available from public and private agencies that deal with fraud. However, as we have noted, reporting rates are low and not representative.
- A comprehensive approach that draws together, for a representative sample of specific cases, information from the victim, agencies to whom the victim reported (if any), and CJS courts and corrections personnel to yield a fuller picture of how these crimes are perpetrated, investigated, prosecuted, and punished, along with detailed profiles of the offenders and their modus operandi.
- Larger national fraud victimization surveys that might include the incorporation of fraud items into the NCVS.

The current study raised, but could not explore, some questions because of the size of its sample, including the following: (a) why certain persons are more likely to be selected as targets of fraud, (b) why some persons are more effective in resisting attempts to defraud them, (c) how law enforcement and regulatory agencies can more proactively detect and respond to emerging fraud schemes with less reliance on reporting by victims, and (d) how the CJS can develop and use more appropriate sanctions for deterring personal fraud.

APPENDIX

STUDY OF FRAUD VICTIMIZATION: SURVEY INSTRUMENT

INTRODUCTION:
Hello, I'm _____ from SRBI, the national research organization in New York City. We are conducting a national assessment of public attitudes toward and experience with crime. We would like to speak to the person in this household, aged 18 or older, *WHO HAS HAD THE MOST RECENT BIRTHDAY*.

We would like to conduct a short interview with you, as part of a nationally representative sample of Americans. Your answers are strictly confidential. Your participation is voluntary, but it would really help us in planning for programs to control crime and increase public safety.

QUESTION #1
First we'd like to ask you a few questions about some of the more common types of crime that happen to people. These questions refer only to things that happened to you, personally, within the last twelve months that is since (MONTH) of last year.

In the last twelve months, did anyone ROB you by using force or threatening to harm you?

QUESTION #2
Did anyone BEAT YOU UP, attack you or hit you with something (not counting anything you've already told me about)?

QUESTION #3
Did anyone THREATEN to beat you up or THREATEN you with a knife, gun or some other weapon, NOT including telephone threats (not counting anything you've already told me about)?

QUESTION #4
During the last 12 months, did anyone BREAK INTO or somehow illegally get into your home (not counting anything you've already told me about)?

QUESTION #5
Did anyone steal or use without permission any car, truck, motorcycle or other motor vehicle belonging to you?

QUESTION #6
Did anyone steal anything FROM any car, truck, motorcycle or other motor vehicle belonging to you such as the battery, tires, tape deck and so on (not counting anything you've already told me about)?

QUESTION #8
Now we'd like to ask you about some other types of crime that happen to people. But this time now we want to know whether these things have EVER happened to you, personally, at any time in your life.

These other types of crime include someone cheating you, or attempting to cheat you out of money or property by deliberately lying to you or giving you false information or phoney promises about a product or service, or getting you to pay for something that you never received, or swindling you in some other way.

The person could have been a relative, a neighbor, a friend or acquaintance, someone you do business with, or a total stranger. You may have been contacted in person, on the telephone, by mail, or you may have contacted them after reading or hearing about it.

Since there are a lot of ways in which a person might be swindled, I am going to read you a list of some of the ways in which people are sometimes cheated. Please tell me which of these things, if any have EVER HAPPENED to you, personally, or if someone EVER TRIED to do these things to you at any time in your life.

QUESTION #9
Has anyone ever sold or tried to sell you what they claimed was a lottery ticket, or a ticket of admission which turned out to be fake?

QUESTION #10
Has a stock broker, a financial planner or someone like that ever given you false, deceptive or deliberately misleading information or advice in order to swindle you out of money or property?

QUESTION #11
Has anyone ever gotten or tried to get money from you by promising to share some money they'd found?

QUESTION #12
Has anyone ever pretended to be the police or a bank official, in order to get you to withdraw money from your bank and give it to them?

QUESTION #13
Not counting lost or stolen cards, has anyone ever tricked you or tried to trick you into giving them your credit card number, your checking or bank account number, or your telephone card number so that they could make charges or withdrawals without your knowledge or permission?

QUESTION #14
Has anyone ever pretended to be from a charity or religious organization in order to get money from you that was not really going to a charity?

QUESTION #15
Has anyone ever sold or tried to sell you life insurance, medical insurance, long-term health care insurance, etc., that turned out to be worthless or didn't cover what they said it would cover?

QUESTION #16
Has anyone ever lied to sell or try to sell you a health, beauty care, or weight-loss product or service that did not work as claimed or was even harmful?

QUESTION #17
Has anyone ever promised you a prize, a free vacation, or a free sample, which later turned out not to be free or ended up costing you more than the prize, vacation or sample was worth?

QUESTION #18
Has anyone gotten or tried to get you to put money into a business venture such as a work-at-home plan, a franchise, or a business opportunity that you found out was a fraud or a fake?

QUESTION #19
Have you ever given someone money for advance fees or lifetime membership in a health club, spa, dance studio, or other place, which never existed or went out of business without giving you your money back?

QUESTION #20
Have you ever paid for a training course, correspondence course, or diploma-by-mail that turned out to be worthless or a fake?

QUESTION #21
Has anyone ever lied to you to get you involved in an investment deal that turned out to be phony or a scam, not counting anything I've asked you about so far?

QUESTION #22
Has anyone ever promised to help you improve your credit or finances, convert the equity in your home, or prepare you financially for retirement, but actually cheated, or tried to cheat you, out of your money or property?

QUESTION #23
Has anyone ever lied to you about the price of a product or service when you were buying it and then when you got it they charged you a lot more than they originally told you it would cost?

QUESTION #24
Has anyone ever gotten you to purchase a product or service that they said had a good guarantee or warranty, which you later found out would not cover the things they said it would?

QUESTION #25
Has someone pretending to be an "inspector" or some other kind of official ever gotten or tried to get you to pay for repairs to the plumbing, heating, wiring, roofing or something else at your residence that wasn't really necessary or required?

QUESTION #26
Has someone ever gotten money from you for home remodeling, driveway resurfacing, pest control, lawn care, radon removal or some other kind of home repair or service, and then never did the work or didn't do what they said they would?

QUESTION #27
Have you ever paid for repairs to an appliance or an automobile for work that was never performed or that you later discovered was completely unnecessary?

QUESTION #28
Has anyone used a 900 telephone number or some other special advertised telephone number to cheat or try to cheat you out of money or property, not counting anything I've asked you about so far?

QUESTION #29

Has anyone ever sold you subscriptions to magazines, records, books or something else that you paid for but never received or were charged a lot more for than you had been told when you subscribed?

QUESTION #30

We've been talking about some SPECIFIC ways you might have been cheated or defrauded. Now I'd like you to tell me if there were any OTHER occasions where you felt someone cheated or tried to cheat you out of money or property?

NOTE

1.   See Table 10 [sic] for mean and median losses for each type of fraud incident.

REFERENCES

American Association of Retired Persons. 1994. *A Report on the 1993 Survey of Older Consumer Behavior.* Washington, DC: AARP.

Bass, Ron and Lois Hoeffler. 1992. *Telephone-Based Fraud: A Survey of the American Public.* New York: Louis Harris and Associates, Inc.

Benson, Michael, Francis Cullen, and William Maakestad. 1990. "Local Prosecutors and Corporate Crime." *Crime & Delinquency* 36:356-72.

Cohen, Lawrence and Marcus Felson. 1979. "Social Change and Crime Rate Trends: A Routine Activity Approach." *American Sociological Review* 44:588-608.

Ganzini, Linda, Bentson McFarland, and Joseph Bloom. 1990. "Victims of Fraud: Comparing Victims of White Collar and Violent Crime." *Bulletin of the American Academy of Psychiatry and Law* 18:55-63.

Geis, Gilbert and Ezra Stotland, eds. 1980. *White Collar Crime: Theory and Research.* Beverly Hills, CA: Sage.

Kusic, Jane. 1989. *White Collar Crime Prevention Handbook.* Vienna, VA: White Collar Crime 101.

Lynch, James. 1987. "Routine Activity and Victimization at Work" *Journal of Quantitative Criminology* 3:283-300.

McGuire, Mary and Herbert Edelhertz. 1980. "Consumer Abuse of Older Americans: Victimization and Remedial Action in Two Metropolitan Areas." Pp. 266-92 in *White Collar Crime: Theory and Research,* edited by G. Geis and E. Stotland. Beverly Hills, CA: Sage.

Meier, Robert F. and Terance D. Miethe. 1993. "Understanding Theories of Criminal Victimization." *Crime and Justice: A Review of Research* 17:459-99.

Moore, Elizabeth and Michael Mills. 1990. "The Neglected Victims and Unexamined Costs of White Collar Crime." *Crime & Delinquency* 36: 408-18.

Section 6
THE VICTIM'S ROLE IN THE AMERICAN CRIMINAL JUSTICE PROCESS

Introduction

The earliest criminal prosecutions were primarily private proceedings through which a victim sought retribution against and restitution from the perpetrator of the crime. During medieval times, however, the government asserted itself as the party in interest in criminal prosecutions against alleged offenders. As a result, fines paid to the government and other punishments replaced victim retribution and restitution as the principal outcomes in a criminal proceeding, and the victim became a mere witness in the government's prosecution of the offender. A similar evolution from victim-centered to government-centered proceedings and sanctions took place in the United States following the American Revolution. A principal goal of the victims' movement, which emerged in this country in the 1970s, was to make the crime victim an integral part of the administration of American criminal justice once again. The readings in this section illustrate efforts to achieve this goal by the expansion of the services, assistance, and rights of participation now available to victims in the criminal justice system. The final selection introduces the concept of restorative justice, an even more victim-centered alternative to the current system of justice.

Victim Services and Assistance

Criminal victimization can have significant physical, psychological, and financial consequences. Medical, property, and productivity costs associated with victimization are estimated to exceed $100 billion each year. It is not surprising, therefore, that the earliest efforts of the victims' movement focused on restoring victim entitlement or access to compensation or restitution for losses suffered as a result of crime. In fact, some identify California's enactment, in 1965, of the first state statute providing government-sponsored compensation for victims of violent crime, as the starting point of the victims' movement.

California's victim compensation program represented a recognition that offender restitution was an inadequate remedy to make the victim "whole." Many offenders were never apprehended or convicted; moreover, those that were often were unable to pay restitution. By 1980, 30 states had victim compensation programs. These initial state programs varied considerably, but they typically shared the characteristics of small size, limited funding, restrictive eligibility requirements, and poor visibility. Some of these problems were addressed when Congress enacted the Victims of Crime Act of 1984 (VOCA), in response to a recommendation of the President's Task Force on Victims of Crime, convened by President Reagan in 1982. VOCA established a Crime Victims Fund, consisting primarily of federal offenders' fines and other funds, the proceeds of which were to be used for grants to support victim compensation and assistance programs. The establishment of the fund gave financial stability to existing compensation programs and encouraged the development of new state programs. It also brought a degree of uniformity to state programs by establishing minimum program criteria for funding eligibility. Every state now operates a victim compensation program eligible for VOCA grant funds. As impressive as these achievements have been, however, significant problems in the implementation and utilization of victim compensation programs remain, as discussed in Chapter 11, the McCormack selection.

Although perhaps less dramatic than the rapid expansion of state victim compensation programs, improvements have also been made in the award of restitution to crime victims. The federal system and virtually every state authorize an order of restitution as a condition of an offender's probation. The federal system and a majority of states also authorize restitution as an independent sentence, in addition to or instead of other sentences. Some jurisdictions make restitution mandatory unless the sentencing court explicitly justifies the failure to award it. As a result of these legislative changes, the frequency and size of restitution orders have increased significantly in recent years. Continuing problems with the scope of restitution orders and offender compliance with them, however, mean that restitution is still often an inadequate remedy to recover a victim's financial losses from the crime.

As devastating as financial loss from crime can be, victims also frequently suffer other personal losses as a result of crime. Consequently, the expansion of victim services has been another aim of the victims' movement. Indeed, local grassroots efforts to provide victims with crisis intervention, counseling, and support during the prosecution predated the coalescing of the national victims' movement. Local and state efforts to provide such services have been supported by federal VOCA victim assistance grants and oversight provided by the federal Office for Victims of Crime in the Department of Justice. Currently, both through law enforcement and prosecutors' victim services staff and federally supported private agencies, victims can receive an array of services. A recent national directory of victim service programs identified almost 10,000 such programs. Yet, as McCormack points out, despite the large number of programs, not all victim needs are addressed by such programs and not all programs are available to all victims who need them.

Victim Participation in the Criminal Justice Process

Mirroring the impressive but incomplete expansion of victim services and assistance has been the expansion of victim rights of participation in the criminal justice process in the years since the issuance of the Final Report of the President's Task Force on Victims of Crime. As suggested by Chapter 12, the Kelly selection, many victim advocates have placed as high a priority on the expansion of these rights of participation as they have on the expansion of victim services and assistance. Most of their efforts have focused on the expansion of victim rights to notice of, and presence and hearing at, important stages of the criminal justice process. Their efforts have met with remarkable success.

Prior to the President's Task Force, few states required such victim participation in criminal justice proceedings. The Task Force recommendations addressed to federal and state executive and legislative authorities and criminal justice system agencies proposed actions to provide victim rights to notice of and presence and hearing at important criminal justice proceedings. The Task Force even recommended that the federal constitution be amended to guarantee victim rights of presence and hearing. Although the Task Force's recommendation of a federal constitutional victim rights amendment has not been adopted, more than 30 states have ratified constitutional victim rights amendments, most of which include victim rights of participation to some degree. In addition, the federal government and every state have legislation regarding at least some of the victim participatory rights.

Despite these impressive achievements regarding expanded victim participatory rights, such rights are not universal. At the outset, the federal system and most states restrict their victim participatory rights to victims of certain crimes only. Provisions requiring victim notification of significant proceedings and outcomes in the prosecution are sometimes ambiguous with regard to the subject matter addressed or are conditional in their application. Although the victim right to be present at court and parole proceedings has been significantly expanded, this right typically remains conditional regarding proceedings at which the victim will offer testimony. The victim right to be heard regarding the offender's sentence has been adopted by the federal system and virtually every state by allowing the submission of a written victim impact statement, authorizing oral victim allocution at sentencing, or both. A significant majority of states also authorize victim input regarding plea negotiations and parole decisionmaking. Nevertheless, most victim rights provisions lack enforcement mechanisms or sanctions for rights violations. Finally, as reflected by Chapter 13, the Davis and Smith selection, researchers have been unable to confirm significant increases in victim satisfaction with the criminal justice process or significant impact on sentence outcomes resulting from the implementation of these victim participatory rights.

The absence of significant impact on victim satisfaction or case outcome from this extensive (albeit incomplete) expansion of victim participatory rights has led some researchers to reject this attempt to modify the existing criminal justice process and to advocate an alternative system of *restorative justice*. Chapter 14, the Van Ness and Strong selection, illustrates restorative justice principles that propose the inclusion of the government, victim, offender, and community in an integrated effort to resolve the criminal episode and achieve public safety. The goal of this approach is to prevent or repair the harm caused by crime. Although not totally adopting the restorative justice approach, other researchers have advocated the expansion of victim-offender reconciliation and mediation efforts designed to increase offender accountability to the victim as well as victim involvement in the resolution of the prosecution. There are currently more than 100 such mediation programs in the country, primarily addressing property offenses.

Conclusion

The expansion of victim services, assistance, and participation in the criminal justice process since the emergence of the victims' movement has been remarkable. Although still far from being a victim-centered process, the needs and interests of victims are being addressed in the criminal justice process to a much more significant degree than at any time since the adoption of the public prosecution system. It is therefore an appropriate time for advocates, researchers, and policymakers to assess the strengths and weaknesses of the victim rights and remedies that have been recognized, in order to determine whether these changes have truly been responsive to victims' actual needs and desires, and to analyze whether they have improved the administration of justice in this country. Such a review will help determine the victim's role in the American criminal justice process in the next century.

LEARNING EXPERIENCES

1. Chapter 11, the McCormack selection, describes the history of victim services and assistance in this country as well as the challenges facing them. Identify the types of services and assistance that you feel crime victims need. Design the kind of service delivery system that you feel would most effectively deliver such services and assistance. Compare your list of services and your service delivery system with the services and systems that are available in your community.

2. To acquaint yourself further with the challenges facing victim services that McCormack describes, interview a victim services professional in your community. Identify the strengths and weaknesses in victim services the professional has observed in the course of delivering such services.

3. Many victims suffer financial losses from crime that can be recovered from no source other than their state victim compensation funds. Every state has such a fund. Find the laws establishing and implementing your state's victim compensation fund. Identify the victim losses that are covered and the monetary limits of coverage, the procedures for filing claims, and the restrictions on coverage. Many states prepare an annual report regarding their funds' activities. If your state prepares such a report, obtain it and evaluate how effective the state has been in addressing victims' financial needs. Identify ways in which your state compensation system could be improved.

4. Chapter 12, by Kelly, and Chapter 13, by Davis and Smith, discuss the need for and the results of expanded victim participation in the criminal justice process. As the two selections indicate, expanded rights of victim participation have been a source of controversy. The federal system and every state have constitutional or legislative victim rights provisions (or both) addressing victim participatory or related rights. Locate and compare the proposed federal constitutional victim rights amendment and federal victim rights legislation with the constitutional and/or legislative victim rights provisions of your state. Draft "model" victim rights provisions that you believe effectively address necessary victim rights.

5. Chapter 14, the Van Ness and Strong selection, describes the alternative concept of restorative justice. For what types of crimes or offenders would such a model be most effectively implemented? What problems would arise from such a model of justice? If your community has a victim-offender mediation or reconciliation program, interview one of its staff members to determine the effectiveness of the program's approach.

BIBLIOGRAPHY

Adair, D.N., Jr. (1992). Looking at the law: Recent developments in restitution. *Federal Probation, 56(4)*, 68-72.

Anderson, J.R., & Woodard, P.L. (1985). Victim and witness assistance: New state laws and the system's response. *Judicature, 68*, 221-244.

Andrews, A.B. (1992). *Victimization and survivor services: A guide to victim assistance.* New York: Springer.

Belknap, J. (1995). Law enforcement officers' attitudes about the appropriate responses to woman battering. *International Review of Victimology, 4*, 47-62.

Berman, H.J. (1978). The background of the western legal tradition in the folklaw of the peoples of Europe. *University of Chicago Law Review, 45*, 553-597.

Bernat, F.P., Parsonage, W.H., & Helfgott, J. (1994). Victim impact laws and the parole process in the United States: Balancing victim and inmate rights and interests. *International Review of Victimology, 3*, 121-140.

Brown, J.G. (1994). The use of mediation to resolve criminal cases: A procedural critique. *Emory Law Journal, 43*, 1247-1309.

Cardenas, J. (1986). The crime victim in the prosecutorial process. *Harvard Journal of Law & Public Policy, 9*, 357-398.

Castellano, T.C. (1992). Assessing restitution's impact on recidivism: A review of the evaluative research. In E.C. Viano (Ed.), *Critical issues in victimology: International perspectives* (pp. 233-247). New York: Springer.

Chelimsky, E. (1981). Serving victims: Agency incentives and individual needs. In S.E. Salasin (Ed.), *Evaluating victim services* (pp. 73-97). Beverly Hills, CA: Sage.

Davis, R.C. (1987). Studying the effects of services for victims in crisis. *Crime & Delinquency, 33*, 520-531.

Davis, R.C., Kunreuther, F., & Connick, E. (1984). Expanding the victim's role in the criminal court dispositional process: The results of an experiment. *Journal of Criminal Law & Criminology, 75*, 491-505.

Davis, R.C., & Smith, B.E. (1994). Victim impact statements and victim satisfaction: An unfulfilled promise? *Journal of Criminal Justice, 22*, 1-12.

Davis, R.C., & Smith, B.E. (1994). The effects of victim impact statements on sentencing decisions: A test in an urban setting. *Justice Quarterly, 11*, 453-469.

Davis, R.C., Smith, B., & Hillenbrand, S. (1991). Increasing offender compliance with restitution orders. *Judicature, 74*, 245-248.

Davis, R.C., Smith, B., & Hillenbrand, S. (1992). Restitution: The victim's viewpoint. *Justice System Journal, 15*, 746-758.

Diamond, A.S. (1950). *Primitive law* (2nd ed.). London: Watts.

Doerner, W.G., Knudten, M..S., Knudten, R.D., & Meade, A.C. (1976). An analysis of victim compensation programs as a time-series experiment. *Victimology, 1*, 295-313.

Doerner, W.G., Knudten, R.D., Meade, A.C., & Knudten, M.S. (1976). Correspondence between crime victim needs and available public services. *Social Service Review, 50*, 482-490.

Doerner W.G., & Lab, S.P. (1980). The impact of crime compensation upon victim attitudes toward the criminal justice system. *Victimology, 5,* 61-67.

Dolliver, J.M. (1987). Victims' rights constitutional amendment: A bad idea whose time should not come. *Wayne Law Review, 34,* 87-93.

Eikenberry, K. (1987). Victims of crime/victims of justice. *Wayne Law Review, 34,* 29-49.

Elias, R. (1983). The symbolic politics of victim compensation. *Victimology, 8(1-2),* 213-224.

Elias, R. (1984). Alienating the victim: Compensation and victim attitudes. *Journal of Social Issues, 40,* 103-116.

Elias, R. (1986). Community control, criminal justice and victim services. In E.A. Fattah (Ed.), *From crime policy to victim policy: Reorienting the justice system* (pp. 290-316). New York: St. Martin's.

Erez, E. (1994). Victim participation in sentencing: And the debate goes on. . . . *International Review of Victimology, 3,* 17-32.

Erez, E., & Tontodonato, P. (1990). The effect of victim participation in sentencing on sentence outcome. *Criminology, 28,* 451-474.

Erez, E., & Tontodonato, P. (1992). Victim participation in sentencing and satisfaction with justice. *Justice Quarterly, 9,* 393-415.

Fattah, E.A. (1997). Toward a victim policy aimed at healing, not suffering. In R.C. Davis, A.J. Lurigio, & W.G. Skogan (Eds.), *Victims of crime* (2nd ed., pp. 257-272). Thousand Oaks, CA: Sage.

Fattah, E.A. (1997). From crime policy to victim policy: The need for a fundamental policy change. In M. McShane & F.P. Williams III (Eds.), *Victims of crime and the victimization process* (pp. 75-92). New York: Garland.

Fein, E., & Knaut, S.A. (1986). Crisis intervention and support: Working with the police. *Social Casework: The Journal of Contemporary Social Work, 67,* 276-282.

Finn, M.A., & Stalans, L.J. (1995). Police referrals to shelters and mental health treatment: Examining their decisions in domestic assault cases. *Crime & Delinquency, 41,* 467-480.

Finn, P. (1986). Collaboration between the judiciary and victim-witness assistance programs. *Judicature, 69,* 192-198.

Frank, L.F. (1992). The collection of restitution: An often overlooked service to crime victims. *St. John's Journal of Legal Commentary, 8,* 107-134.

Friedman, K., Bischoff, H., Davis, R., & Person, A. (1982). *Victims and helpers: Reactions to crime.* Washington, DC: U.S. Department of Justice.

Galaway, B. (1988). Restitution as innovation or unfilled promise? *Federal Probation, 52(3),* 3-14.

Galaway, B., & Hudson, J. (Eds.). (1990). *Criminal justice, restitution, and reconciliation.* Monsey, NY: Criminal Justice Press.

Gegan, S.E., & Rodriguez, N.E. (1992). Victims' roles in the criminal justice system: A fallacy of victim empowerment? *St. John's Journal of Legal Commentary, 8,* 225-250.

Gittler, J. (1984). Expanding the role of the victim in a criminal action: An overview of issues and problems. *Pepperdine Law Review, 11,* 117-182.

Goddu, C.R. (1993). Victims' "rights" or a fair trial wronged? *Buffalo Law Review, 41,* 245-272.

Goldstein, A.S. (1982). Defining the role of the victim in criminal prosecution. *Mississippi Law Journal, 52,* 515-561.

Hagan, J. (1982). Victims before the law: A study of victim involvement in the criminal justice process. *Journal of Criminal Law & Criminology, 73,* 317-330.

Hall, D.J. (1975). The role of the victim in the prosecution and disposition of a criminal case. *Vanderbilt Law Review, 28,* 931-985.

Hall, D.J. (1991). Victims' voices in criminal court: The need for restraint. *American Criminal Law Review, 28,* 233-266.

Harland, A.T. (1983). One hundred years of restitution: An international review and prospectus for research. *Victimology, 8(1-2),* 190-203.

Harland, A.T., & Rosen, C.J. (1990). Impediments to the recovery of restitution by crime victims. *Violence and Victims, 5,* 127-140.

Heinz, A.M., & Kerstetter, W.A. (1979). Pretrial settlement conference: Evaluation of a reform in plea bargaining. *Law and Society Review, 13,* 349-366.

Hellerstein, D.R. (1989). The victim impact statement: Reform or reprisal? *American Criminal Law Review, 27,* 391-430.

Henderson, J., & Gitchoff, G.T. (1981). Using experts and victims in the sentencing process. *Criminal Law Bulletin, 17,* 226-233.

Henderson, L.N. (1985). The wrongs of victim's rights. *Stanford Law Review, 37,* 937-1021.

Henley, M., Davis, R.C., & Smith, B.E. (1994). The reactions of prosecutors and judges to victim impact statements. *International Review of Victimology, 3,* 83-93.

Hernon, J.C., & Forst, B. (1984). *The criminal justice response to victim harm.* Washington, DC: U.S. Department of Justice.

Hillenbrand, S.W., & Smith, B.E. (1989). *Victim rights legislation: An assessment of its impact on criminal justice practitioners and victims.* Chicago, IL: American Bar Association.

Hudson, J., & Galaway, B. (Eds.). (1975). *Considering the victim: Readings in restitution and victim compensation.* Springfield, IL: Charles C Thomas.

Hudson, P.S. (1984). The crime victim and the criminal justice system: Time for a change. *Pepperdine Law Review, 11,* 23-62.

Hughes, S.P., & Schneider, A.L. (1989). Victim-offender mediation: A survey of program characteristics and perceptions of effectiveness. *Crime & Delinquency, 35,* 217-233.

Jerin, R.A., Moriarty, L.J., & Gibson, M.A. (1995). Victim service or self service? An analysis of prosecution based victim-witness assistance programs and providers. *Criminal Justice Policy Review, 7,* 142-154.

Karmen, A.J. (1992). Who's against victims' rights? The nature of the opposition to pro-victim initiatives in criminal justice. *St. John's Journal of Legal Commentary, 8,* 157-175.

Kelly, D.P. (1984). Victims' perceptions of criminal justice. *Pepperdine Law Review, 11,* 15-22.

Kelly, D.P. (1984). Delivering legal services to victims: An evaluation and prescription. *Justice System Journal, 9,* 62-86.

Kelly, D.P. (1987). Victims. *Wayne Law Review, 34,* 69-86.

Kelly, D.P., & Erez, E. (1997). Victim participation in the criminal justice system. In R.C. Davis, A.J. Lurigio, & W.G. Skogan (Eds.), *Victims of crime* (2nd ed., pp. 231-244). Thousand Oaks, CA: Sage.

Kennard, K.L. (1989). The victim's veto: A way to increase victim impact on criminal case dispositions. *California Law Review, 77,* 417-453.

Kilpatrick, D.G., & Otto, R.K. (1987). Constitutionally guaranteed participation in criminal justice proceedings for victims: Potential effects on psychological functioning. *Wayne Law Review, 34,* 7-28.

Lamborn, L.L. (1987). Victim participation in the criminal justice process: The proposals for a constitutional amendment. *Wayne Law Review, 34,* 125-220.

Laster, R.E. (1970). Criminal restitution: A survey of its past history and an analysis of its present usefulness. *University of Richmond Law Review, 5,* 71-98.

Lurigio, A.J., & Davis, R.C. (1990). Does a threatening letter increase compliance with restitution orders?: A field experiment. *Crime & Delinquency, 36,* 537-548.

Maguire, M. (1985). Victims' needs and victim services: Implications from research. *Victimology, 10,* 539-559.

McLeod, M. (1987). An examination of the victim's role at sentencing: Results of a survey of probation administrators. *Judicature, 71,* 162-168.

McLeod, M. (1989). Getting free: Victim participation in parole board decisions. *Criminal Justice, 4,* 12-15.

McCormack, R.J. (1991). Compensating victims of violent crime. *Justice Quarterly, 8,* 329-346.

McCormack, R.J. (1994). United States crime victim assistance: History, organization and evaluation. *International Journal of Comparative and Applied Criminal Justice, 18,* 209-220.

McDonald, W.F. (1976). Towards a bicentennial revolution in criminal justice: The return of the victim. *American Criminal Law Review, 13,* 649-673.

Miers, D.R. (1983). Compensation and conceptions of victims of crime. *Victimology, 8(1-2),* 204-212.

Moesteller, R.P. (1997). Victims' rights and the United States Constitution: An effort to recast the battle in criminal litigation. *Georgetown Law Journal, 85,* 1691-1713.

National Network to End Domestic Violence. (1997). *Survey of state laws and constitutional provisions regarding crime victims' rights.* Washington, DC: Author.

National Victim Center. (1996). *1996 victims' rights sourcebook: A compilation and comparison of victim rights laws*. Arlington, VA: National Victim Center.

Norris, F.H., Kaniasty, K.Z., & Scheer, D.A. (1990). Use of mental health services among victims of crime: Frequency, correlates, and subsequent recovery. *Journal of Consulting and Clinical Psychology, 58*, 538-547.

Norris, F.H., & Thompson, M.P. (1993). The victim in the system: The influence of police responsiveness on victim alienation. *Journal of Traumatic Stress, 6*, 515-532.

Parent, D.G., Auerbach, B., & Carlson, K.E. (1992). *Compensating crime victims: A summary of policies and practices*. Washington, DC: U.S. Department of Justice.

Parsonage, W.H., Bernat, F.P., & Helfgott, J. (1992). Victim impact testimony and Pennsylvania's parole decision making process: A pilot study. *Criminal Justice Policy Review, 6*, 187-206.

Polito, K.E. (1990). The rights of crime victims in the criminal justice system: Is justice blind to the victims of crime? *New England Journal on Criminal and Civil Confinement, 16*, 241-270.

President's Task Force on Victims of Crime. (1982). *Final report*. Washington, DC: U.S. Government Printing Office.

Ramker, G.F., & Meagher, M.S. (1982). Crime victim compensation: A survey of state programs. *Federal Probation, 46(1)*, 68-76.

Roberts, A.R. (1990). *Helping crime victims: Research, policy, and practice*. Newbury Park, CA: Sage.

Roberts, A.R. (1991). Delivery of services to crime victims: A national survey. *American Journal of Orthopsychiatry, 6*, 128-137.

Roland, D.L. (1989). Progress in the victim reform movement: No longer the "forgotten victim." *Pepperdine Law Review, 17*, 35-58.

Rubel, H.C. (1985). Victim participation in sentencing proceedings. *Criminal Law Quarterly, 28*, 226-250.

Salasin, S.E. (Ed.). (1981). *Evaluating victim services*. Beverly Hills, CA: Sage.

Sarnoff, S.K. (1996). *Paying for crime: The policies and possibilities of crime victim reimbursement*. Westport, CT: Praeger.

Schafer, S. (1970). *Compensation and restitution to victims of crime* (2nd ed.). Montclair, NJ: Patterson Smith.

Schneider, A.L. (1986). Restitution and recidivism rates of juvenile offenders: Results from four experimental studies. *Criminology, 24*, 533-552.

Shapland, J. (1986). Victim assistance and the criminal justice system: The victim's perspective. In E.A. Fattah (Ed.), *From crime policy to victim policy: Reorienting the justice system* (pp. 218-233). New York: St. Martin's.

Smith, B.E., & Hillenbrand, S.W. (1997). Making victims whole again: Restitution, victim-offender reconciliation programs, and compensation. In R.C. Davis, A.J. Lurigio, & W.G. Skogan (Eds.), *Victims of crime* (2nd ed., pp. 245-256). Thousand Oaks, CA: Sage.

Smith, R.M. (1984). Victim services on a shoestring. *Federal Probation, 48(2)*, 39-42.

Symposium: Perspectives on proposals for a constitutional amendment providing victim participation in the criminal justice system. (1987). *Wayne Law Review, 34*, 1-220.

Tobolowsky, P.M. (1993). Restitution in the federal criminal justice system. *Judicature, 77*, 90-95.

Tobolowsky, P.M. (1997). "Constitutionalizing" crime victim rights. *Criminal Law Bulletin, 33*, 395-423.

Tobolowsky, P.M. (1999). Victim participation in the criminal justice process: Fifteen years after the President's Task Force on Victims of Crime. *New England Journal on Criminal and Civil Confinement, 25*, 21-105.

Tomz, J.E., & McGillis, D. (1997). *Serving crime victims and witnesses* (2nd ed.). Washington, DC: U.S. Department of Justice.

Tontodonato, P., & Erez, E. (1994). Crime, punishment, and victim distress. *International Review of Victimology, 3*, 33-55.

Umbreit, M.S. (1989). Crime victims seeking fairness, not revenge: Toward restorative justice. *Federal Probation, 53(3)*, 52-57.

Umbreit, M.S. (1994). *Victim meets offender: The impact of restorative justice and mediation.* Monsey, NY: Criminal Justice Press.

U.S. Department of Justice. Office for Victims of Crime. (1997). *Victims of Crime Act of 1984 as amended: A report to the President and the Congress.* Washington, DC: Author.

U.S. Department of Justice. Office for Victims of Crime.(1998). *New directions from the field: Victims' rights and services for the 21st century.* Washington, DC: Author.

U.S. Department of Justice. Office of Justice Programs. (1986). *Four years later: A report on the President's Task Force on Victims of Crime.* Washington, DC: Author.

Van Ness, D.W. (1993). New wine and old wineskins: Four challenges of restorative justice. *Criminal Law Forum, 4*, 251-276.

Van Ness, D., & Strong, K.H. (1997). *Restoring justice.* Cincinnati, OH: Anderson.

Victims of Crime Act of 1984, 42 U.S.C.A. § 10601 *et seq.* (West 1995).

Victims' rights symposium. (1984). *Pepperdine Law Review, 11*, 1-182.

Villmoare, E., & Neto, V.V. (1987). *Victim appearances at sentencing hearings under the California Victims' Bill of Rights.* Washington, DC: U.S. Department of Justice.

Walsh, A. (1986). Placebo justice: Victim recommendations and offender sentences in sexual assault cases. *Journal of Criminal Law & Criminology, 77*, 1126-1141.

Weigend, T. (1983). Problems of victim/witness assistance programs. *Victimology, 8(3-4)*, 91-101.

Welling, S.N. (1987). Victim participation in plea bargains. *Washington University Law Quarterly, 65*, 301-356.

Welling, S.N. (1988). Victims in the criminal process: A utilitarian analysis of victim participation in the charging decision. *Arizona Law Review, 30*, 85-117.

Winkel, F.W. (1991). Police, victims, and crime prevention. *British Journal of Criminology, 31,* 250-265.

Wolfgang, M.E. (1965). Victim compensation in crimes of personal violence. *Minnesota Law Review, 50,* 223-241.

Wright, M. (1985). The impact of victim/offender mediation on the victim. *Victimology, 10,* 631-644.

Yaroshevsky, E. (1989). Balancing victim's rights and vigorous advocacy for the defendant. *Annual Survey of American Law, 1989,* 135-155.

Young, M.A. (1997). Victim rights and services: A modern saga. In R.C. Davis, A.J. Lurigio, & W.G. Skogan (Eds.), *Victims of crime* (2nd ed., pp. 194-210). Thousand Oaks, CA: Sage.

Chapter 11

United States Crime Victim Assistance: History, Organization and Evaluation

Robert J. McCormack
Trenton State College

Segments of this article originally were written and presented to an international audience at the meetings of The World Society of Victimology, held in Jerusalem in 1988; other parts of the paper are new. The early material has been expanded and updated to reflect recent changes in assistance to crime victims. The first part of the paper presents a brief history of the victim assistance movement in the United States from the 1960s to the 1990s. The second part discusses the organization and operations of the victim assistance system at the federal, state, and local levels; the final section provides suggestions for evaluation, and perhaps change, in policy and procedure.

Over the past several decades, as a result of dramatic increases in violent crime, concern for the victims of crime has been growing in the United States. A general anxiety about the government's ability to provide a basic level of safety for its citizens has contributed significantly to this concern.

The heightened awareness of crime and victims has been ascribed to several major factors. First was the sheer number of individuals affected by crime during the 1960s, and the apparent inability of the criminal justice system to respond effectively. Second was the initiation of the National Crime Surveys in 1972 by the Law Enforcement Assistance Administration. These surveys showed that the official FBI data signifi-

Source: McCormack, R.J. (1994). United States crime victim assistance: History, organization and evaluation. *International Journal of Comparative and Applied Criminal Justice, 18,* 209-220. Reprinted by permission of the Editor-in-Chief of the *International Journal of Comparative and Applied Criminal Justice.*

247

cantly underestimated actual levels of victimization, and thus increased citizen anxiety. A third factor was the simultaneous resurgence of the feminist movement and its advocacy for the increasing number of female crime victims. The movement highlighted the particular vulnerability of women as a social group to violent crimes such as rape, battering, and other forms of domestic abuse (Schwendinger and Schwendinger, 1983). A final factor was the determination and eventual success of victims' advocates in placing financial responsibility for victim compensation on state governments (Young, 1987:9). I discuss each of these factors briefly.

Crime in America

The beginning of the baby boom in the late 1940s and the concomitant increase in crime in the United States are related to the circumstances surrounding the conclusion of World War II. More than 16 million Americans served in the armed forces from 1940 through 1945. When the war ended, Americans were eager to resume their previous lives. One of the fruits of victory was a return to familism. This traditional orientation was particularly strong during the postwar years; home life had been threatened so seriously that most women (and men) wanted more than anything else to marry and have families (Hunt, 1970:95). During the ensuing years, 1946 through 1964, 76 million Americans were born. In 1946, the year immediately following the end of hostilities, the birth rate was the highest ever for Americans—more than 30 births per 1,000 of the population (Time, 1986:22).

By the mid-1960s an unanticipated by-product of the baby boom developed: the unprecedented increase in teenagers was accompanied by a corresponding increase in the volume of crime. "The crime rate skyrocketed between 1960, when about 3.3 million crimes were reported to police agencies, and 1981, when 13.4 million crimes were recorded" (Seigel and Senna, 1991:28). Concern about crime victims grew steadily during this period. Law-and-order groups began to call for tougher measures against offenders. They criticized civil rights and civil liberties groups for their efforts to control government responses to the crisis, and began to champion a victim-oriented criminal justice system (Karmen, 1990:36).

For the first time in this century, victims began to be included in the criminal justice process in a meaningful way. In the 1970s, prosecutors began to consider their concerns seriously in plea bargains; "impact statements" from victims and/or survivors became a part of the courts' sentencing process; probation and parole conditions included restitution more frequently than in the past. By the mid-1980s, well over half the states had passed victims' rights legislation. By the later part of the decade at least 10 states had introduced legislation to amend the Sixth

Amendment to the U.S. Constitution to guarantee that "the victim, in every prosecution, has the right to be present and to be heard at all critical stages of judicial proceedings" (Task Force Report on Victims of Crime, 1982).

More recently, court decisions at the federal level have supported crime victims and survivors, In June 1991, for example, the United States Supreme Court overruled a state court decision (*Payne v. Tennessee*) that prohibited impact statements in death penalty hearings. Chief Justice William H. Rehnquist found that those prior rulings turned the victim into a "faceless stranger." He concluded that allowing the family and friends of a convicted murderer to testify to a sentencing jury on the offender's behalf while silencing the victim's family "unfairly weighted the scales" of justice.

People still harbor serious doubts about the ability of government or the criminal justice system to significantly reduce current levels of personal violence and property crime, even though the increase in the crime rate has slowed since the early 1980s and the prison and probation populations have doubled.

Crime Reporting and the National Crime Surveys

Although fear of crime has affected the quality of life in the United States since the early 1960s, the true extent of victimization was not known until the National Crime Surveys were initiated in 1972. Before that time, the American public relied on the Uniform Crime Reports (UCR) of the Federal Bureau of Investigation for their information. The accuracy of the UCR had been the subject of much discussion since the creation of the system by Congress in 1930. The data came from local police agencies throughout the country and included only reported crimes. Further, in the early years, the types, numbers, and clearance rates for crimes were false in many cases, and were intended to make police agencies appear more effective than they were.

Many of these reporting problems were corrected over the years as police departments became more professional and crime analysis techniques became more sophisticated. By the 1960s the major issue connected with the use of the UCR was that they measured only "crimes known to police." Many criminologists recognized that for a variety of reasons, many victims did not report incidents to the police, and that the police did not record every criminal act brought to their attention. Until the early 1960s, one could only speculate on the level of under reporting and under recording.

In 1966 a pilot victimization study was conducted under the sponsorship of the Law Enforcement Assistance Administration of the Department of Justice. In 1972, as a result, the United States Bureau of

Census began to conduct the largest survey of crime victimization ever undertaken. The survey involved 60,000 households selected randomly from a pool of 80 million families in the United States. Twice a year for three consecutive years, these families were visited and were interviewed personally about their experiences as victims of crime (currently these victim survey groups are changed every three years). The results showed that "for the crimes measured (rape, robbery, assault, burglary, theft), 36 million victimizations affecting 22 million households (about 25% of all U.S. households) occur each year, a level much higher than indicated by the number of crimes reported to the police" (Cole, 1992:15). The National Crime Surveys (NCS), as these studies are called, indicated that official FBI statistics underestimated actual victimization by 300 to 500 percent (Elias, 1986:38). NCS data, which presented a realistic assessment of the actual level of victimization in the United States, gave additional impetus to advocates of expanded services and financial help for crime victims.

Victims of Crime and the Feminist Movement

After major successes during the late nineteenth and early twentieth century in regard to liberalized divorce laws, property rights for women, birth control clinics, and voting rights, feminists in post-World War II America saw their gains evaporating. In the resurgence of familism, many women gave up the work place for a place at home. As returning servicemen were reemployed, the salary gap widened between those men and the women who continued to work. Fewer women held legislative seats than previously; the number of faculty positions occupied by women in higher education decreased. No in-roads into upper-echelon business and industrial management were made in the two decades after the war (Hunt, 1970:95).

Betty Friedan's *The Feminine Mystique*, published in 1963, sold 1.5 million copies. The book inspired the founding, in 1966, of the National Organization for Women (NOW). The major goal of this contemporary feminist organization was to challenge and remedy the discrimination faced by women in American society, particularly in education and employment. The organization also would have a dramatic impact on the social response to female victims of crime, especially victims of unreported domestic violence and rape (Karmen, 1990:34).

The first grassroots effort to assist sexual assault victims was made in 1972 by a group of feminists in Berkeley, California:

> It was here that the idea of a 24-hour hotline and the belief that victims needed alternative services to the criminal justice, hospital, and the mental health institutions, were born. BAWAR'S (Bay Area Women Against Rape) vision of services incorpor-

ed these ideas and implemented them along with direct counseling, public education, and rape prevention activity. The tiny handful of women . . . was composed of political activists and militant feminists who saw themselves as advocates of rape victims in the established institutions (Schwendinger and Schwendinger, 1983:9).

This program was followed rapidly by programs providing shelters for battered women and by victim assistance programs to deal with child abuse and neglect.

NOW had a significant impact on the treatment of female victims of crime. Its court challenges led to changes in the laws in many states, which make prosecution of offenders more of an option for women than in the past. Its educational work, emphasizing sexual equality, resulted in significant social change in a relatively short period. The impact of NOW on the actual operations of victims' assistance programs, however, has diminished. A current leader in the victims' movement describes the change:

> The feminist movement is responsible for the establishment of rape crisis centers and domestic violence shelters, and out of that I think it is clear that the victims' movement today is made up predominantly of women. But I think the impact of the National Organization for Women fell off sharply after that initial enthusiasm and that initial involvement, so that in today's world it simply does not have the same kind of impact on victims' assistance, per se, although clearly women are still in charge of most programs (Young, 1987:9).

Crime Victim Compensation Programs

One of the most politically significant and dramatic advances in contemporary victim assistance was made in 1965, when the State of California began its own program to compensate crime victims in the absence of any private or governmental programs. Initially the state provided funds to innocent and needy victims of violent criminal acts and to dependents of murder victims. California's initiative was followed quickly by similar programs in New York State (1966), Hawaii (1967), Massachusetts and Maryland (1968), and New Jersey (1971). Miers suggests, in regard to the emergence of violent crime compensation boards (VCCBs), that:

> a significant characteristic of the relationship between government and the individual during this period (the late sixties) was the "politicization" of the victim of crime. By this I mean that through media pressure and the influence of certain individu-

als in public office and elsewhere, victims of crimes of violence
were converted into an identifiable and coherent group, with
evident political potential . . . . There is, in my view, little doubt
but that political factors were the single most important deter-
minant behind the introduction of victim compensation
schemes (Miers, 1978:51).

Another expert on crime victims declares that the importance of the
emergence of VCCBs should not be underestimated: "Although the civil
rights and anti-war movements in the United States, and comparable
movements elsewhere, helped promote a climate for considering victims
generally, not until compensation programs arose in the late 1960's did
crime victims really begin to emerge." (Elias, 1986:19).

By 1991, 45 states had established victim compensation programs
(McCormack, 1991:330). These programs reimburse victims of crime
for their losses, pay significant out-of-pocket medical expenses, provide
for long-term care for seriously injured victims, pay burial expenses, and
provide other services. The programs vary as to fund-raising methods,
eligibility requirements, and the size of the compensation awards.

An Overview of Victim Assistance Programs

To understand the nature of the victims' assistance network in the
United States, it might be helpful at this point to discuss briefly how the
national, state, and local governments interact on behalf of crime victims.

At the national level, the government is headed by a president elect-
ed every four years. A bicameral congress considers and passes legislation for the entire country according to procedures established by a federal constitution. In 1984 the U.S. Congress passed the first major piece
of crime victim legislation, the Victims of Crime Act. The Act was
amended and improved in 1986 and 1988, and currently is funded
through 1994 at $150 million per year. These funds mainly support
state-level agencies and programs aiding victims of crime.

The United States is a confederation of autonomous states—50 at
the present time—each with its own governor and legislative body, its
own constitution, a great degree of independence in establishing its gov-
ernance, its own criminal and civil laws and taxing powers, and the
authority to determine the nature and purposes of its social institutions.
Over the years, all of the states have established and funded some
amount of crime victim assistance. For example, almost all states have
crime victim compensation boards to reimburse victims for financial
losses resulting from criminal acts; all provide some funding for general
victim services, aiding victims of sexual assault, helping victims of
domestic violence, and other services.

The states are divided into counties for voting, taxation, court and trial processes, and other functions. Counties are composed of various municipalities, villages, townships, and other jurisdictions; each of these has executives, governing bodies, and limited power to pass local laws and administrative rules affecting their residents. The great majority of these local jurisdictions have victim assistance programs. Because of the number and diversity of these programs, coordination of effort is difficult at best; it depends heavily on the cooperation and the agreement of interests of the groups involved. Personal leadership at each level of operation (national, state, and local) is critical in influencing the ultimate delivery of victim services.

Victim Assistance at the National Level

Since the mid-1960s the United States Congress has considered and rejected numerous bills to compensate victims of crime. Progress was not made at the national level until the Republican administrations of the 1980s embraced the victims' movement as a natural extension of their conservative philosophy opposing criminal offenders. Those administrations created the President's Task Force on Victims of Crime in 1982, and backed the 1982 Omnibus Victims of Crime Act and the 1984 Crime Victim Assistance Act (Elias, 1986:20). Despite its support however, the federal government has been consistent in its view that public safety and assistance to crime victims are ultimately state concerns. Therefore, none of the national legislation, then or since that time, has provided sufficient funding to fully address the problems of compensation or other forms of victim assistance.

The Victims of Crime Act of 1984 created the Office for Victims of Crime (OVC), which remains the most significant federal agency for victim assistance. As a result of the Act, fines and fees levied against persons convicted of federal crimes are spent to assist crime victims throughout the country. No centralized agencies exist in individual states to receive and distribute the funds from the OVC; rather, federal funds go directly to state agencies and programs that provide victim assistance according to a plan developed by the OVC. These funds in turn filter down to support victim assistance programs at the county level, including local municipal, town, and village programs.

Assistance at the State Level

As noted above, states rather than the federal government have been in the vanguard of the victims' movement since the 1960s. The first major state legislation for compensating crime victims was passed in California in 1965 and was followed rapidly by similar legislation in other states. Crime victim compensation boards (their titles vary among states) continue to be administered centrally at the state level. In addition to federal funds provided by the OVC since 1984, states have raised their own funds to support the compensation boards through taxes, penalty assessments, or other means. In some cases, states support victim assistance programs which are administered by county-level prosecutors' offices. Various county programs also receive support funds from state agencies such as departments of mental health and family and social services.

Assistance at the County (Local) Level

Because most crime control and prosecutorial responsibilities are lodged at the county level, the local police, local prosecutors and courts, and local victims' advocates collectively provide the most direct and most significant assistance to crime victims. Many of the programs at this level tend to be victim-specific; they deal with a single group such as battered wives, abused or sexually molested children, rape victims, or geriatric victims. Their staffs tend to be a mix of professionals and volunteers working in close cooperation with criminal justice practitioners and hospital emergency room personnel. Among the most effective are the many Victim/Witness Assistance Programs. These are administered by county prosecutors' offices, which provide crime victims with support, monetary assistance, and legal advice.

Crime Victim Leadership Organizations

Many national (and state) organizations lobby for victims' rights and influence legislation on behalf of crime victims. Most prominent are the National Organization for Victims Assistance (NOVA), The National Victims Center (NVC), Mothers Against Drunk Driving (MADD), The National Committee for the Prevention of Child Abuse (NCPCA), and the National Coalition Against Sexual Assault (NCASA). These groups act as victim assistance coordinators for a vast network of volunteer, practitioner, and professional victim assistance programs at the national, state, and local levels. Their activities include public education, training, fund raising, lobbying, and information management.

Although they have no direct authority over the many victims' programs in the country, these professionally managed agencies have succeeded in coordinating the activities of the diverse victims' groups throughout the United States. Through their leadership over the years they have been able to bring together an array of public and private victims' programs and tie them into the network of state and federally funded programs. In addition, they have lobbied successfully at the federal and state levels for a variety of legislation benefiting victims. Generally these are private, nonprofit organizations that are supported by their members and by public and private grants and donations.

A Time for Introspection

Developments in crime victim assistance in the United States over the past 30 years have been truly remarkable. In the face of such progress, it is difficult to speak of shortcomings. Yet as the movement continues to mature, existing policy and/or operations should be reviewed and new or tangential directions should be charted in certain major, closely related areas.

Developing a General Welfare Perspective

From its beginning, the victims' movement in the United States has been influenced by a retributive philosophy. In fact, it originated with groups that had a strong anti-offender bias (Karmen, 1984:20). It has been difficult to disengage from this legacy, which has caused tensions among otherwise supportive individuals. They view such a philosophy as lacking dimension and perhaps as counterproductive (Walker, 1989:167,170). At a workshop on violence and public health, Marvin Wolfgang advocated a more comprehensive commonweal perspective. He suggested that efforts to deal with deviant behavior (and its victims) should extend beyond the criminal justice system and the notion of deserved punishment:

> Tensions between justice and public tranquility and order were guiding concerns in the quest of the Violence Commission (1969) to understand and to prevent violence. In that analytical and philosophical context, violent disorder was dissected with the cutting instrument of criminal law and the system of criminal justice. Although various theories were used to reveal the causes of violence, the primary inquiry was from the viewpoint of violative and unlawful behavior.
>
> The Founding Fathers seemed prescient in their deliberations and constitutional framing. They inscribed another viewpoint and objective into this nation's first legal document; namely, the promotion of the general welfare .... The disorders of violence are as much challenge to the general health and welfare of our nation as they are to the system of justice and law (Wolfgang, 1985:9).

By adopting such a general welfare perspective, advocates for crime victims' would include among their concerns the "offender/victims"—that is, offenders who themselves are victims of discrimination, racism, poverty, and related conditions. Promoting programs to assist these high-risk individuals would be consistent with the overall goals of victim advocacy: *to prevent victimization* as well as to support victims of violence. A strong commitment to helping individuals in these offender/victim groups would contribute directly to a reduction in victimization. The major caution, then, is that in the fervor to achieve a universal bill of rights for victims, the movement must not forget that many offenders are victims in their own right. A movement ideology that sponsors gains for crime victims at the expense of constitutional and human rights eventually may lose support.

Victim Compensation Programs

Victims' advocates should be concerned about the fact that so few victims of crime actually are assisted by violent crime compensation boards. A major reason, it seems, is the symbolic nature of the political commitment to victims' assistance on the part of federal and state lawmakers, which results in seriously inadequate program funding. A 1991 national survey of VCCBs revealed:

> that a paucity of funds in almost all state programs accounts in part for limitations on the numbers and amounts of compensation awards. Many states have set the maximum award per victimization at unrealistically low levels, which obviate the original intent; those states which offer more generous benefits are in danger of overexpending their resources. North Carolina's VCCB is so hard pressed, for example, that it has been forced to disseminate funds on a first come, first served basis (McCormack, 1991:338).(3)

The survey showed wide variations among the states in claims filed, awards made, and awards-to-claims ratios.

This study and others (Chappel, 1988; Elias, 1986; Friedman et al., 1982; Gattuso-Holman, 1976, Karmen, 1984) have pointed out that in addition to lack of funds, lack of information about the programs is a major reason why victims do not file claims. Chappel suggests, "Perhaps the most significant (limitation) of these (VCCBS) is the lack of public awareness of the very existence of the programs, a situation that can be explained in many jurisdictions by poor mechanisms devised to bring the programs to the attention of eligible crime victims" (1988:380). According to *Compensating Victims of Crime*, the 1992 report of the Office of Justice Programs of the National Institute of Justice, only 10 program directors said that "victims in their state were adequately informed about the compensation program . . . if programs made more victims aware of their rights to compensation, they likely would diminish the average claim paid to those victims, unless there were major increases in funding." The report also stated that "almost half the program directors said that existing funds for program administration were inadequate"; even if "better outreach efforts increased the number of claims, many states would be unable to process the increased case load in an efficient and timely manner" (NIJ, 1992:13,14).

The remoteness of most VCCBs from their clients also seems to contribute significantly to the low level of claims. Most state VCCBs have only one central office. If outreach is to be successful, more decentralized, community-based locations must be established in urban neighborhoods, where victimization is most prevalent. Again, in reference to the 1992 NIJ report cited above, researchers pointed to the decentralized, highly effective VCCB of Denver, Colorado, "in which separate victim compensation boards were established in each of the state's judicial districts, administered by local district attorney's (prosecutor's) office". The report mentions a number of bureaucratic objections to such programs. Supporters of such decentralized programs, however, believe that the administrators "would be more sensitive to victims' interests and needs and because compensation decisions would be made by local officials [they] would insure better coordination with locally delivered victim service programs".

Victim/Witness Assistance Programs

Victim/Witness Assistance Programs (VWAPs) administered by prosecutors suffer from the same lack of legislative commitment as compensation boards (Roberts, 1990:107). Their problems are compounded by (1) the "functional" or system-facilitating nature of the programs—that is, the offer of assistance to victims who agree to cooperate in the prosecution of the offender—and (2) the fact that they provide virtually no outreach to crime victims whose crimes are not cleared by arrest. In regard to the first of these elements, Elias points out that:

> Within criminal justice, officials often consider victims as a threat or interference in their activities. And victim programs may be even more threatening, unless tailored to official objectives. Witness management schemes, for example, may promote official goals, but expensive victim assistance programs may drain scarce resources and thus be resisted. . . . This suggests that only victim advocacy carefully tailored to parallel official goals will be likely to be successful, even if such schemes do not serve victim interests very well or perhaps at all (1986:238).

As to the second element, the lack of services to victims of uncleared crimes, VWAP coordinators in New Jersey reported, "It would be unusual for [us] to be provided with information concerning crimes that were not currently being handled by the prosecutor's office." The data in that report revealed that in the 21 New Jersey counties, slightly more than 100 victimizations connected with uncleared crime came to the attention of VWAP coordinators each month (McCormack, 1992:8).

Police and Crime Victims

The policing establishment in the United States generally has not lived up to its potential for assisting crime victims. Of the approximately 15,000 state and local police departments in the country, only a handful have effective programs for post crime victim assistance. In an earlier version of this paper I cited a State of New Jersey survey of 'chiefs of police' conducted in 1988. In the lead question in the survey, the chiefs were asked whether, in addition to the normal crisis intervention response to reported crime, they had formal programs of victim assistance. Of the 51 responding agencies, 47 replied in the negative. The chiefs also were asked whether, in their opinion, coordinating immediate aftercare assistance to crime victims was an appropriate use of police resources. Forty-five said "no." The following statement was typical of the negative responses:

> There is no way that police agencies can take on any additional roles with respect to social services. We are already taxed with victims procedures, domestic violence programs, alcohol and drug dependency programs and there is no assistance from the state with respect to manpower or budget increases. They are living in a dream world—do more with less. These recent additional responsibilities defy all reason. Most chiefs of police feel that, in time, police work will have to be returning to general police work and will designate social agencies to deal with social problems. We are being dumped on because we work 365 days a year and around the clock. It is more economical to throw things in the direction of law enforcement.

On the basis of this survey and more than 40 years of research and experience with policing nationwide, it is clear to me that police view victims as an added burden on their already overtaxed resources rather than as an opportunity to enrich their jobs and perform a vital service to their communities. Victims' advocates should focus more attention on the police as a prime source of victim assistance. They are the first at the scene of a crisis, and with proper indoctrination and training can significantly affect the impact of victimization. One of the surest ways for the police to achieve the professional status they seek is through this type of community service. Perhaps the victims' movement should sponsor such recognition more aggressively in return for a more responsive role in victims' affairs on the part of the police.

Summary

The major areas of concern described above must be addressed if the victims' movement is to continue to grow and mature. To reach its full potential and to expand on its remarkable achievements since the 1960s, the movement must seek out issues that will augment its political base. By embracing a wider spectrum of national victim concerns—particularly those related to victims in lower socioeconomic groups—and by assuming a general welfare position rather than a retributive stance, victims' advocacy will attract a wider constituency. The Office for Victims of Crime points the way in its "Report to Congress: April 1990". It suggests that new challenges are arising, which were not addressed in the original or amended forms of The Victims of Crime Act. These include hate crimes resulting in murder, rape, assault, and vandalism against persons of a particular race, religion, or sexual orientation. The report also highlights the epidemic of drugs and violence and recommends that victims' advocates show concern for the impact of such crimes on residents of the affected neighborhoods. In addition, the report suggests that the emergence of new populations of drug-addicted babies and the lack of victim assistance programs in high-crime neighborhoods should be concerns of the victims' movement. These new initiatives are essential if the victims' movement in the United States is to realize its potential to serve society's victims fairly and effectively.

REFERENCES

Chappel, D. 1988. "The implementation of victims' rights in North America." In M.C. Bassiouni (Ed.) *Nouvelles estudes penales: International protection of victims.* Toulouse, France: Eres, pp. 377-384.

Cole, G.F. 1983. *The American system of criminal justice,* third edition. Monterey, CA: Brooks/Cole Publishing Company.

Department of Justice, Office of Justice Programs. 1992. *Compensating crime victims: A summary of policies and practices.* Washington, DC: U.S. Government Printing Office.

Department of Justice, Office for Victims of Crime. 1990. *Victims of crime act of 1984 as amended: A report to Congress by the Attorney General.* Washington, DC: U.S. Government Printing Office.

Elias, R. 1986. *The politics of victimization: Victims, victimology and human rights.* New York, NY: Oxford University Press.

Friedman, Kenneth, Helen Bischoff, Robert Davis, and Andresa Person. 1982. *Victims and helpers: Reactions to crime.* Washington, DC: National Institute of Justice.

Gattuso-Holman, Nancy A. 1976. "Criminal sentencing and victim compensation legislation: Where is the victim?" In Emilio C. Viano (Ed.) *Victims and society.* Washington, DC: Visage, pp. 363-367.

Hunt, Morton. 1970. "Up against the wall, male chauvinist pig." *In From Playboy: The sexual revolution.* Chicago, IL: Playboy Press, pp 93-103.

Karmen, Andrew. 1990. *Crime victims: An introduction to victimology,* 2nd edition. Monterey, CA: Brooks/Cole.

McCormack, Robert J. 1998. *Police chief's survey on crime victim assistance: State of New Jersey.* Trenton State College, unpublished.

_____. 1991. "Compensating victims of violent crime." *Justice Quarterly,* Volume 8, Number 3, September, Washington, DC, pp.329-346.

_____. 1992. "Outside the victims system: Crimes 'not cleared by arrest' or 'downgraded'." Paper presented at the Annual Meeting of the American Society of Criminology, New Orleans, Louisiana, November.

Miers, David. 1978. *Responses to victimization: A comparative study of compensation for criminal violence in Great Britain and Ontario.* Abingdon, Oxon: Professional Books Limited, p. 51.

Roberts, Albert R. 1990. *Helping crime victims: Research, policy and practice.* Newbury Park, CA: Sage Publications, Inc.

Schwendinger, Julia R., and Herman Schwendinger. 1983. *Rape and inequality.* Beverly Hills, CA: Sage Publications, Inc.

Siegel, Larry J., and Joseph J. Senna. 1991. *Juvenile delinquency: Theory, practice and law,* St. Paul, MN: West Publishing Company.

United States. 1982. *President's task force on victims of crime: Final report.* Washington DC: U.S. Government Printing Office.

Time Magazine. 1986. "Growing pains at 40," March 19.

Walker, Samuel. 1992. *The police in America: An introduction.* New York, NY: McGraw-Hill, Inc..

Wolfgang, Marvin E. 1985. "Interpersonal violence and public health care: New Directions, new challenges." In U.S. Department of Health and Human Services, *Surgeon General's workshop on violence and public health report.* Washington, DC: DHHS, pp.9-18.

Young, Marlene. 1987. "Who's looking out for victims." Interview by Robert McCormack for *Law Enforcement News,* New York, NY, November 24.

Chapter 12

Victims' Perceptions of Criminal Justice

Deborah P. Kelly, Ph.D.

This article considers the criminal justice system from the crime victim's perspective. Victims are the people behind crime statistics. They are the individuals who suffer the injuries inflicted by criminals and who reveal the existence of crime when they report it. Victims are the key to apprehending criminals and the justification for the state's subsequent prosecution, yet they are often the people we know least about.

Volumes have been written on the rights of defendants. The role of prosecutors has been studied and the decisions of judges are reported in casebook after casebook. Much has been written on discretion and attrition in the judicial process, yet we seldom consider how these decisions affect the injured party. We know comparatively little about how crime victims view the judicial process, though their cooperation is central to its operation.

Once a victim reports a crime to the police, the state—police, prosecutors, and judges—takes over. What actually happened to the victim frequently seems to matter only insofar as it guides law enforcement officials in determining how much attention to give the complaint and how to classify the offense. For the most part, victims' opinions are rarely solicited; personal costs incurred by the victim are considered irrelevant. Instead, what was once a private matter now becomes the business of strangers to be handled mainly as they see fit.

---

*B.A., University of Vermont, 1974; M. A., 1977, Ph.D., Johns Hopkins University, 1982. Assistant Professor, Department of Government, American University.

Source: Kelly, D.P. (1984). Victims' perceptions of criminal justice. *Pepperdine Law Review, 11,* 15-22. Reprinted by permission of *Pepperdine Law Review.*

The working assumption of the criminal justice system is that, despite this transfer of interest, victims will come forward and cooperate, because although the state brings the case, without the victim's cooperation, there may be no case. Such cooperation is not always forthcoming. A national study of prosecutorial decision-making concluded that witness problems were the primary reason why violent crimes were dismissed.[1] However, subsequent research found that prosecutors often misjudged the victim in trying to anticipate the victim's behavior and strength as a witness. Cannavale, in his study of witness cooperation, concluded that many prosecutors labeled as "uncooperative" witnesses who only lacked information about when to show up and what to do.[2]

These findings suggested that victims were not necessarily uncooperative; more often they were confused. Such confusion is understandable. Consider the judicial process from the victim's perspective: Victims are introduced to a system grounded on the legal fiction that victims are not the injured party. Victims soon learn they have no standing in court, no right to counsel, no control over the prosecution of their case, and no voice in its disposition. In an attempt to alleviate these problems, programs have been developed to educate witnesses as to their role in the criminal justice process, reduce their confusion, and thereby minimize the prosecutors' problems with witness noncooperation.[3] The theory was that if the state helped victims, victims would in turn help the police to apprehend and the prosecutors to convict offenders.

To the extent that victim/witness programs have been analyzed, they generally have been evaluated from an administrative perspective. For example, studies have considered whether new programs reduced unnecessary police appearances and waiting time, produced more cooperative witnesses, decreased case dismissals, and increased conviction rates.[4] This research perspective, while important in identifying what the courts need from victims, neglects an equally important inquiry; what do victims want from the justice system?

This paper will address that question and also explain why victims' needs should be considered. The comments in this paper are based on a study in which over 100 personal interviews were conducted with felony crime victims in metropolitan Washington, D.C.[5] In the course of these

---

1. Institute for Law and Social Research, Expanding the Perspective of Crime Data: Performance Implications for Policymakers (Washington, D.C. 1977); Brian Forst, Arrest Convictability as a Measure of Police Performance, paper presented at American Society of Criminology (November 1981).

2. F. CANNAVALE, WITNESS COOPERATION, INSTITUTE FOR LAW AND SOCIAL RESEARCH (1975).

3. See VICTIM RIGHTS AND SERVICES: A LEGISLATIVE DIRECTORY 1984 (Washington, D.C.: The National Organization for Victim Assistance 1984).

4. See, e.g., A. LITTLE, COMMISSION ON VICTIM WITNESS ASSISTANCE: FINAL EVALUATION REPORT (Washington, D.C. 1977).

5. For further explanation of methodology and findings see Kelly, Delivering Legal Services for Victims: An Evaluation and Prescription, 8 JUST. SYS. J. (Spring 1984 forthcoming).

interviews, respondents were asked about their contacts with and attitudes toward police, medical, and court personnel. Additionally, respondents were asked to evaluate special services such as victim compensation programs, crisis centers, and victim/witness units.

Victims' needs can be divided into two general categories: (1) relief from the administrative inconvenience of going to court, and (2) more participation in the judicial process. This article will initially review victims' administrative problems and then will address victims' requests for more systemic reforms to increase their status in the criminal justice process.

ADMINISTRATIVE INCONVENIENCE

Studies which have focused almost exclusively on administrative inconvenience have created the impression that victims are primarily troubled by the administrative run-around—especially the loss of time (delay, waiting, postponements) and monetary concerns (missed pay, transportation, babysitting).[6] Although these problems occur, such studies mask more fundamental problems victims experience with law enforcement. Indeed the purpose and design of such studies frequently predetermines their results. Their purpose is often to better manage witnesses and promote their cooperation. Their design is to ask victims specific questions such as: "Did you have trouble with transportation, parking, or finding the court building?" As victims are usually not asked more substantive questions about their role in the judicial process, it is logical that their responses are limited to issues of court-related inconvenience.

Programs which have been developed to compensate victims for crime costs and minimize their court-related inconvenience are available in varying degrees throughout the country.[7] In spite of these extensive services, however, many victim's concerns remain unanswered:

1. Services are frequently provided to those select witnesses the state needs to make its case. As most cases are dismissed or plea bargained, many victims never benefit from such programs because they are not needed to testify or provide further evidence. As one woman stated: "After I identified the guy at lineup I never heard from anyone again. They got what they needed and dumped me." Other victims were excluded when their complaints were dropped in plea negotiations.

---

6. UNITED STATES DEP'T OF COM., BUREAU OF THE CENSUS, THE MILWAUKEE CRIME FOLLOW-UP SURVEY, FINAL SURVEY REPORT (1976).

7. See VICTIMS RIGHTS AND SERVICES, *supra* note 3, for complete list for available services and legislative activity in this area.

2.   Services may be provided which are relatively unimportant to victims, while other more important needs are overlooked. For example, although many victims experience problems with transportation, babysitting, and parking, most do not judge these problems as serious.[8] Their wishes for greater participation are rarely addressed in these programs.

3.   Some victim/witness assistance programs exist in name only. Frequently they enable prosecutors to manage rather than *assist* victims. In one jurisdiction in the Washington, D.C. area, for example, the victim/witness unit primarily serves bench warrants and tracks down key witnesses who leave the court's jurisdiction.

Although it is clearly important that services have been developed to remedy these problems, other critical concerns remain overlooked. Existing services address administrative difficulties associated with the court and the crime but rarely affect the more fundamental issue of expanding the role of victims in the judicial process.

STRUCTURAL REFORM

Above all, victims want their personal interests recognized by the judicial system. They are surprised to learn how little their opinions matter and how rarely their interests are considered. They soon find that, as Gilbert Geis observed: "Their role is like an expectant father in the delivery room—necessary for things to have gotten underway in the past but at the moment rather superfluous and mildly bothersome."[9]

Victims' comments clearly indicate that they deeply resent being excluded from deliberations. To illustrate, when 100 rape victims were asked how they would improve police and court procedures, most wanted increased participation and status in the judicial system. Though victims are legally irrelevant to the state, their proposals reflect that the case is extremely relevant to them.

Victims' evaluations of the police were strongly related to how much information police provided on the case, how frequently victims were contacted, and how considerate police were of their feelings. In all cases the rule was, the more involved victims perceived themselves to be, the more satisfied they were with police services.

Victims want the police to provide information on the status of their assailant. They want to be called when the defendant is arrested and told whether he is in jail, released on bail, or roaming the neighborhood. Victims want this information—*regardless* of their utility to the case. Addi-

---

8. See Kelly, *supra* note 5, for analysis of victims' court-related problems.

9. Geis, *Victims of Crimes of Violence,* VIOLENCE AND CRIMINAL JUSTICE 63 (D. Chappell & J. Monahan, eds. 1975).

tionally, they want police officers to support, not second-guess, their behavior. Victims objected when, for example, police commented, "That's what you get for living in the city" or "You should have known better than to go out alone." Victims urged police to focus on the offender's behavior, not the victim's; to investigate the crime, not the victim's judgment in dating the offender, leaving a window open, or jogging at night.

Victims also want more recognition from the legal system. Specifically, they want to be informed of deliberations, included in case developments, and offered an opportunity to participate in determining what happens to their assailant.

Victims also want better legal representation of their interests. Statistical analysis revealed that victims judged prosecutors in part as a client views private counsel—the better the perceived representation, the more favorable the evaluation. This evaluation was not primarily based on the disposition of the case. Rather, the more frequently victims heard from the prosecutor and were consulted about the case, the more satisfied they were with prosecutors' services. However, many felt that they were excluded, their case was not well prepared, and no continuity in personnel was provided which required them to repeat their story to a series of new prosecutors.

Postponements were particularly difficult to tolerate. Studies show that witnesses' opinions of the court deteriorate as the number of postponements increases.[10] Sixty percent of the victims interviewed had their court date postponed at least once. Delay in court hinders the victim's recovery. As one woman stated: "Your life is on hold until it's over." Victims believed continuances were granted with little consideration for their feelings. Additionally, decisions on case dispositions and sentencing were usually made regardless of victims' interests. It is these imbalances that victims seek to correct.

Why Listen to Victims?

There are at least four major reasons to correct the present judicial imbalance and institutionalize victims' roles in the criminal process.

1. Victim/witness satisfaction with the judicial process is essential to its operation. The court systems are often held in low esteem by those who participate in it. Contrary to other institutions, the more contact witnesses have with the courts, the lower their evaluation.[11] These negative evaluations may have long-term effects. Once witnesses experience

---

10. M. Knudten, R. Knudten & A. Meade, *Will Anybody be Left to Testify? Disenchantment with the Criminal Justice System*, THE NEW AND THE OLD CRIMINOLOGY 207-22 (E. Flynn & J. Conrad, eds. 1978).

11. YANKEVICH, SKELLY & WRIGHT, THE PUBLIC IMAGE OF THE COURTS: HIGHLIGHTS OF A NATIONAL SURVEY OF THE GENERAL PUBLIC (Williamsburg, Va.: National Center for State Courts 1978).

delay, intimidation, or financial loss, they may be reluctant to participate in the court system again. As an editorial in the *San Francisco Examiner* noted: "It is unreasonable and self-defeating to expect that citizens, no matter how dedicated, will automatically keep subjecting themselves to personal loss and inconvenience in the name of justice."[12]

Negative assessments may be contagious. As the National Advisory Commission observed: Witness problems "contribute to an undercurrent of popular dissatisfaction that is undermining the public's respect for the American court system."[13] As with any consumer complaint, when one person has a bad experience—whether it is with a restaurant or a movie—the story spreads. Others avoid the same restaurant or skip the movie. The same holds true for the court system. The lack of enthusiasm displayed by most citizens upon receiving a notice for jury duty, and the creative reasons offered for being excused from service, are common examples of the citizenry's reluctance to participate in the court system.

Victims' satisfaction is particularly important. Studies have shown that an estimated 87 percent of reported crime comes to police attention through victims' reports.[14] Furthermore, research on the criminal investigation process shows that victims generally provide police with information critical to solving the case.[15] In short, the criminal justice system depends on victims; if they decide the inconvenience of participating is too great, more crimes will be committed with impunity.

2. Presently the criminal justice system only exacerbates the loss of control victims experience. Even if, for example, their transportation and parking is paid for, victims must still regain control over what once were their orderly lives. When victims are included and informed only at the state's whim, this loss of control is compounded. Information is an important first step toward re-establishing control, but it is not enough. It is critical that at some point in the judicial process victims be given an opportunity to speak up, whether at a pretrial conference, plea negotiation, or sentencing. Establishing the victims' right to participate would help reduce their sense of disorder and demonstrate a new found respect for their rights.

3. Attorneys frequently object to increased victim participation because they assume such involvement is synonymous with harsher penalties, retribution, obstruction, and delay. There is no evidence to support these assumptions; the evidence that exists suggests the contrary. In Florida, for example, pretrial settlement conferences which included

---

12. *Quoted in* F. CANNAVALE, WITNESS COOPERATION, *supra* note 2, at 16.

13. NATIONAL ADVISORY COMMISSION ON CRIMINAL JUSTICE STANDARDS AND GOALS, TASK FORCE REPORT ON COURTS 1-2 (1973).

14. Hawkins, *Who Called the Cops?: Decisions to Report Criminal Victimization*, 7 L. & SOC'Y REV. 427, 441 (1973) (citing Black, *Production of Crime Rates*, 35 AM. SOCIOLOGICAL REV. 733, 736 (1970)).

15. *See generally* P. GREENWOOD, J. CHAIKEN & J. PETERSILIA, THE CRIMINAL INVESTIGATION PROCESS (1977)

victims, police officers, prosecutors, defense attorneys, and judges in deliberations found that cases were disposed of more quickly. Victims did not demand that prosecutors "throw the book" at offenders, but rather, usually agreed with recommendations. Victims frequently turned down invitations to participate, but those police officers and victims who attended pretrial conferences felt more positive toward the courts as a result.[16] Similarly, a study of jurisdictions with victim-impact laws found that, with one exception (Ohio), sentences did not increase.[17] This may suggest that the victims' primary concern is how they are treated, not what punishment the defendant incurs.

4. Due process may be extended to victims without compromising defendants' rights. Currently, experimental programs exist that require the judicial process to recognize victims. Fourteen states have recently approved Victims' Bills of Rights, which vary in scope but generally formalize victims' rights to information, due process, participation, and notice. Such legislation will benefit both victims and potential victims. It is a public statement that the courts' concerns extend beyond administration, budget, and defendants' rights.

Victim-impact statements also provide opportunities for victim participation. Some fourteen states, as well as the federal courts, now have statutes which allow victims' viewpoints to be considered at sentencing. Additionally, the President's Task Force on Victims of Crime called for a constitutional amendment to guarantee "a victim's right to be present and heard at all critical stages of judicial proceedings."[18] Most recently the National Judicial College and the American Bar Association adopted guidelines to increase victims' participation in the judicial process.[19]

Today, many victims' concerns are receiving attention. However, to truly address victims' needs, the criminal justice system must not limit reforms to "courtesies and conveniences." The judicial system must respond to victims' major objection—the criminal justice system's indifference to their personal opinions and interests. Not only do we owe it to victims to provide opportunities, services, and procedures which correct this, but on an administrative level, we depend on victims to help in crime control. It is only fair that victims' rights be taken more seriously. Victims do not ask to conduct or sing solo; they merely ask that their voices be allowed to join the chorus.

---

16. Heinz & Kerstetter, *Pretrial Settlement Conference: Evaluation of a Reform in Plea Bargaining*, 13 L. & SOC'Y REV. 349 (1979).

17. New York State Crime Victims Board, A Quick Assessment and Evaluation of Victim Impact Statement Law (unpublished study, May 1983).

18. *See* THE PRESIDENT'S TASK FORCE ON VICTIMS OF CRIME: FINAL REPORT 114-15 (Washington, D.C., Dec. 1982).

19. *See* VICTIMS COMMITTEE, CRIMINAL JUSTICE SECTION, ABA GUIDELINES FOR FAIR TREATMENT OF VICTIMS AND WITNESSES IN THE CRIMINAL JUSTICE SYSTEM (Washington, D.C. 1983)

In sum, analysis both refutes the idea that the victims' sole concern is retribution and underscores that to do something *for* victims is not the same as doing something *to* defendants. Victims' status and satisfaction with the judicial process may be improved by instituting reforms which expand their involvement and recognize that crime involves more than the state and the defendant.

Chapter 13

Victim Impact Statements and Victim Satisfaction: An Unfulfilled Promise?

Robert C. Davis
Barbara E. Smith
Victim Services Agency
New York, New York 10007

ABSTRACT

Victim impact statements have been widely heralded as a means of promoting victim involvement in criminal court decisionmaking and of increasing victim satisfaction with the justice process. This article reports on the results of a field test that examined the effects of impact statements on victim perceptions of involvement and satisfaction with the justice system. Participants were randomly assigned to one of three groups: (1) victims were interviewed and victim impact statements were written and distributed to court officials, (2) victims were interviewed but no statements were written, and (3) victims were not interviewed. No effects of victim impact statements were found on any of a multitude of measures of victim perceptions. The article concludes that, while impact statements are a relatively low-cost and noncontroversial way to involve victims, they might do little to promote satisfaction with the justice system.

During the 1970s, many studies documented that large numbers of victims and witnesses were failing to cooperate with officials in the prosecution of criminal cases in large urban courts (e.g., Cannavale and Falcon, 1976; Davis, Russell, and Kunreuther, 1980). Researchers also dis-

Source: Davis, R.C., & Smith, B.E. (1994). Victim impact statements and victim satisfaction: An unfulfilled promise? *Journal of Criminal Justice, 22,* 1-12. Reprinted by permission of Elsevier Science.

covered that many victims and witnesses were dissatisfied with their experiences with the justice system (e.g., Davis, 1983; Smith, 1979; Kelly, 1984). Some criminal justice experts argued that the two problems were connected and that both stemmed from frustration of victims and witnesses over their virtual exclusion from the adjudication process. They suggested that allowing victims a greater degree of participation would reduce disaffection and give victims an incentive to cooperate with officials (e.g., Goldstein, 1982; Rosett and Cressey, 1976; DuBow and Becker, 1976).

Certainly, there was plenty of correlational evidence to suggest a link between victim participation and satisfaction with the courts. Several studies indicated the existence of a link between victim participation, particularly participation that might influence criminal justice proceedings, and victim satisfaction. Davis, Russell, and Kunreuther (1980) found that victims who were consulted about their wishes by judges or prosecutors were more satisfied with case outcomes than victims who were not consulted. A study by Smith (1981) indicated that victims' satisfaction increased when they *believed* they had influenced the criminal justice process (whether or not they had actually done so). Hagan (1982) demonstrated that victims' evaluations of sentencing decisions were more positive when they attended the sentencing. Hagan's study also suggested a link between victim involvement and acceptance of case disposition: victims who attended court were less likely to demand severe sentences. A study of rape victims by Kelly (1984) showed that a sense of participation is more critical to victims' satisfaction than how severely defendants are punished.

Others have stated that an increased role for victims in the justice process will help promote their psychological recovery from crime (Kilpatrick and Otto, 1987). Giving victims a role in prosecution, it is argued, could help lessen feelings of helplessness and loss of control induced by victimization and give victims a sense of increased equity (Zehr and Umbreit, 1982; Young, 1987).

Based on these ideas, pilot programs were started in several locations to give victims a greater voice in decisions made about their cases. In Dade County, Florida victims were given the opportunity to attend pretrial settlement conferences along with judges, attorneys, arresting officers, and defendants. At the conferences all parties participated in discussing the incident and in determining an appropriate disposition (Kerstetter and Heinz, 1979). This experiment was later replicated in three additional sites (Clark et al., 1984). At the same time the Vera Institute's Victim Involvement Project (VIP) stationed representatives in courtrooms to communicate victims' interests to officials in Brooklyn, New York Criminal Court. The advocates asked victims what outcomes they desired and made certain that this information was relayed to prosecutors (Davis, Kunreuther, and Connick, 1984).

Evaluations of these early experiments in victim participation were not particularly encouraging. The experiments did serve to convince skeptics that allowing victims to participate was not necessarily harmful to the interests of defendants: in all of the field tests scarcely any victims used their opportunities to speak in order to demand unreasonable punishment. However, the programs were expensive to run. Moreover, at the four sites where pretrial settlement conferences were held, most victims failed to attend the conferences, and evidence was mixed as to whether the conferences had any effects on satisfaction with case processing or case outcomes (Kerstetter and Heinz, 1979; Clark et al., 1984). Researchers studying VIP were unable to find a discernible effect on victims' satisfaction with case outcomes or on their perceptions of the court's responsiveness to their needs or desires (Davis, Kunreuther, and Connick, 1984). Davis et al. concluded that programmatic action alone was unlikely to bring about sufficient change to increase victim satisfaction. They argued that legislative action was needed mandating that victims be given the chance to express their opinions orally or in writing.

Victims' Rights Legislation and Victim Impact Statements

During the 1980s state governments and the federal government in the United States implemented a vast array of legislation guaranteeing victims' rights in the criminal justice process. In 1981 the federal government took the initiative by declaring a Victims' Rights Week to focus national attention on victim issues. Soon afterward, provisions were made for victims to be informed of proceedings in their cases and, in some instances, to be consulted about the course of prosecution. In 1982 the federal government established a Presidential Task Force on Victims of Crime. The Task Force recommended that victim impact statements—assessments of the physical, financial, and psychological effects of crime on individual victims—be taken and distributed to judges prior to sentencing. That recommendation was implemented at the federal level when the 1982 Omnibus Victim and Witness Protection Act became law, mandating that victim impact statements be provided at sentencing in federal cases.

By the mid-1980s victim impact statements had become a popular vehicle for increased victim participation. By 1982, twelve states had passed impact statement laws (Hudson, 1984). By 1984 the number of states with such laws was twenty-two (Davis, Fischer, and Paykin, 1985), and, by August 1987, forty-eight states had provisions authorizing some form of victim participation in conjunction with sentence imposition (McLeod, 1988:3). Victim involvement at sentencing has been endorsed by the American Bar Association and the National Judicial College (Kelly, 1990).

Victim impact statement legislation was intended to augment the role of victims in criminal justice proceedings. Victim impact statements offered victims the opportunity to relate the harm done to them by the crime and to express their concerns with the expectation that this information would be considered in sentencing decisions. This was expected to lead to court decisions that better reflected the harm done to victims and to greater victim satisfaction with the courts.

However, some researchers and victim advocates have warned of possible dangers of raising victims' expectations (by telling them that they might influence sentencing decisions) if those expectations are not realized. Indeed, some research has suggested that victims might be less satisfied when they expect to influence sentence decisions but do not than when they have no such expectation (Villmoare and Neto, 1987; Erez and Tontodonato, 1989). One clinical psychologist has maintained that

> Providing rights without remedies would result in the worst of consequences, such as feelings of helplessness, lack of control, and further victimization. . . . Ultimately, with the crime victims' best interests in mind, it is better to confer no rights at all than "rights" without remedies. (Kilpatrick and Otto, 1987)

Others have questioned the motivation behind the spate of victim rights legislation in the 1980s, which was generally introduced and supported by conservatives. Talbert (1988), Hellerstein (1989), and others have contended that attention to victim harm and concerns erodes the rights of defendants and jeopardizes the principles of equity and proportionality in sentencing. Some have expressed suspicion that conservative support for victim rights is motivated less by a concern for the interests of victims than by a desire to abridge the rights of the accused (Henderson, 1985).

Empirical Research on the Effects of Victim Impact Legislation on Victims

The concerns raised about victim rights legislation make it important to examine empirically whether the legislation actually benefits victims. Since the late 1980s, researchers have begun to produce empirical data to try to determine how the right to submit an impact statement affects victim satisfaction. Erez and Tontodonato (1989) examined 500 felony cases, some of which had victim impact statements taken and some of which did not, according to prosecutor files. These authors found greater satisfaction with sentences among victims who said they completed victim impact statements than among victims who did not complete them. However, the effect of completing a victim impact statement was quite small, accounting for only two percent of the variation in satisfaction with sentencing.

Moreover, serious methodological problems make the results diffi-cult to interpret. The survey of victims had a low response rate (25 per-cent), which raises concerns about representativeness. Further, in addressing the effect of impact statements on satisfaction, the study used a correlational approach: it compared satisfaction in cases in which impact statements were completed with satisfaction in cases in which they were not completed. The authors suggested in another article (Erez and Tontodonato, 1990) that whether victims were asked to complete statements was up to the discretion of prosecutors. Indeed, cases with and cases without impact statements reportedly differed in many ways. Factors such as the seriousness of the case and prosecutors' perceptions of victims appear to have influenced which cases did and which did not have statements prepared. The authors attempted to control for con-founding factors in their analysis, but there could have been factors they failed to control. Finally, their independent variable—whether or not an impact statement was prepared—was based on victims' reports, and the authors noted that 20 percent of the victims who claimed not to have filled out impact statements had in reality completed them (statements were contained in prosecutors' files).

Another study of the effect of impact statements on victim satisfac-tion was carried out in Brooklyn. This study was conducted as a quasi-experiment. Davis (1985) compared outcome measures for victims in a court part in which impact statements were taken with victims in a sim-ilar court part in which no statements were taken. (Cases were assigned to the two parts on alternate days, and checks verified that the two groups of cases were comparable in terms of charges and victim charac-teristics.) The study's findings with regard to victim satisfaction were not encouraging: there was no evidence that victims in the experimental court part felt a greater sense of participation or increased satisfaction relative to those in the control part.

The present study was an attempt to improve on the earlier New York study by using a true experimental design. In the current study, cases were randomly assigned to one of three treatments: (1) impact statements were taken and distributed to officials; (2) impact statement interviews were done, but no statement was prepared; and (3) no inter-view was conducted. Use of these three conditions permitted an assess-ment of the effects of impact statements on victim satisfaction and on sentences.[1]

In order to implement a design that randomly assigned cases to treat-ments, it was necessary to create a victim impact statement program in a court in which one did not exist previously. The reason was that administrators of an existing program would be unlikely to permit with-holding the privilege of completing an impact statement from victims who normally would be allowed to do so. Therefore, the present researchers set up a new program in Bronx County, New York Supreme

Court with the cooperation of the judiciary and the Bronx County District Attorney's Office.

One of the advantages of setting up a new impact statement program was that it was not necessary to rely on procedures that court officials had developed and implemented and that might not be seen as distinctive or special by victims. In the Brooklyn study, the present researchers had been concerned that officials did not make clear to victims the purpose of the impact statement interview. Erez and Tontodonato too wondered whether the victim impact interview had been meaningful to victims in their study:

> If the purpose of filling out a victim impact statement is to provide the psychological gratification of being heard, it should be conducted in a more ceremonial fashion so that it is distinctively remembered by the victims as the occasion during which they voiced their feelings, concerns, and wishes. (1989:14)

In the current research there was an opportunity to create a distinctive impact statement interview process. The researchers were able to hire, train, and supervise the staff, who were taught to conduct the interviews in an empathic fashion. It was possible to develop a protocol that emphasized the reasons why the questions were being asked and what would be done with the information that victims provided. In addition, to make the treatment even more potent, a telephone follow-up was conducted thirty days later to verify that the impact information collected from the victim at the grand jury remained accurate. In short, everything within reason was done to ensure that victims would understand the purpose of the impact statement procedure.

METHOD

The experiment was conducted in Bronx Supreme Court, Bronx, New York. Between July 1988 and April 1989, 293 victims of robbery, nonsexual felonious assault, and burglary went through the intake procedure. These crimes were selected based on two considerations. First, it was desirable to include victims of serious crimes, who would be likely to have experienced significant impact; it would not have benefitted the experiment to include, for example, victims of larcenies or petty assaults. Second, because large numbers of victims were needed, the decision was made not to focus on homicide or rape, crime categories in which the impact is great but the numbers of victims are relatively small. Because each of these two crimes is handled by a special unit of the Bronx District Attorney's Office (which provided the research subjects) and these units are located in different places, it would not have been feasible to include homicide or rape victims in the program *in addition to* victims of the other felonies.

Sixty-nine percent of the subjects were victims of robbery, 21 percent were victims of felonious assault or attempted homicide, and 10 percent were victims of burglary. Twenty percent of the victims knew their offenders prior to the crime. Only about half of the victims had completed high school, and 52 percent had household incomes of less than $15,000 per year. The median age of the sample was 25 years.

Treatments

Each victim was assigned to one of three treatments: (1) the victim was interviewed and a victim impact statement was written and distributed (104 victims); (2) the victim was interviewed but no statement was written (100 victims); (3) only the victim's name and address were recorded (89 victims).

Victims were interviewed—statement written. Victims for whom victim impact statements were written were told by a caseworker (hired by the research project specifically to prepare impact statements) that they would be interviewed and that a statement, based on the answers they gave to the questions in the interview, would be written and distributed to the judge, defense attorney, and prosecutor. It was explained to these victims that because impact statements would be prepared for them, court officials might have more information about how they were affected by the crimes. Victims also were told that judges would have this information during sentencing.

In addition, these victims were told that someone from Victim Services Agency would try to contact them by phone or letter about one month later in order to ask them what coming to court had been like and to update the information in their victim impact statements if necessary. They were also told that the researchers would contact them when their cases ended to ask them how they felt about the final dispositions.

The victim impact interview typically took five to ten minutes. Victims were asked about the impact of the crime in five areas of their lives: physical impact, property loss or damage that occurred as a direct result of the crime, any subsequent financial loss (such as hospital bills or pay lost due to time missed from work), psychological impact, and behavioral impact (any changes in routines or habits as a result of the crime—for example, if they had trouble sleeping or took different routes to work). Victims in the Impact Statement Group (like all the victims, regardless of treatment group) were given pamphlets from the Crime Victim's Assistance unit located in the Bronx Criminal Court, and they were told that they could go to the CVAU office if they needed information, referrals, or counseling.

A transcript of the impact interview was xeroxed immediately and turned over to the prosecutor assigned to the case. The caseworker then wrote a victim impact statement, based on the victim's responses to the interview questions, and distributed it to the prosecutor and to the defense attorney through the District Attorney's Supreme Court Bureau Chief. Copies of the statement were forwarded also to the appropriate judge for each case. One copy was sent through the mail as soon as a judge was assigned to the case; another copy was delivered to the chief clerk of the Supreme Court, who enclosed the statement with the file containing the presentence report and delivered it to the judge just prior to sentencing.

Victims were interviewed—no statement written. This treatment was included in order to evaluate whether the victim impact *interview* itself had a therapeutic effect for the victim. This treatment also produced a comparison group for determining whether the impact statement procedure resulted in sentences that better reflected the harm done to the victims.

The victims in this treatment group were administered the same interview as the victims for whom statements were written. The caseworker explained to them that Victim Services Agency was interested in learning more about the experiences of crime victims and that the present researchers would like some background information about the effects of the crimes on their lives. The interview questions were posed, but none of the descriptive responses was written down.

These victims also were told that someone from Victim Services Agency would try to reach them by phone or mail about one month later to ask them what coming to court was like and again when their cases ended to ask them how they felt about the case outcome. Each of these victims was given a CVAU pamphlet. The prosecutor received a copy of a form that reflected only the victim's and defendant's names, the charge, and the docket number.

Victims in the control group. The caseworker told these victims that Victim Services Agency was trying to learn more about the experiences of crime victims and that someone from Victim Services Agency would contact them by phone or by mail about one month later in order to ask them what coming to court was like and again when their cases ended in order to ask them how they felt about the case outcome. Like victims in the other two treatment groups, these victims were given CVAU pamphlets. Only the names and addresses of these victims were recorded. The prosecutor received a memo saying that these victims were controls in the study and that only their names and addresses were recorded.

Procedures

Intake. All victims were brought by the prosecutors assigned to their cases to the Victim Services Agency project office, usually after their testimony to the grand jury. Victims were assigned to treatments through the use of a log sheet that was prenumbered with victim identification numbers and a corresponding treatment group for each of the numbers. The treatments were preassigned based on a random numbers table.

The random assignment was not begun, however, until after the first 32 victims had been interviewed. These initial interview subjects, all of whom had impact statements taken for them, originally were intended to be a pretest group. However, it became necessary to include them in the experiment when intake proved to be far slower than anticipated. Analyses revealed no significant differences between these 32 victims and later subjects assigned to the impact statement groups (see below for details).

Follow-up. Telephone contact for first follow-up interviews was attempted approximately one month after case intake. Interviews were completed with 202 of the 293 victims in the sample. The first follow-up interview was very short; it took approximately two minutes. The victims were asked questions about their experiences going to court: Did they have a chance to express their concerns about their case to the prosecutor? Did they feel that the prosecutor understood how the crime affected them? Did they feel that they had been treated respectfully? Each of these questions had a 5-point scale for response options. In addition, the victims were asked their age, highest level of education, and approximate annual income. Those for whom victim impact statements were written were also asked questions to update the information in their statements. The impact statements subsequently were revised, and the judges received updated versions at the time of sentencing. Few of these updates included new information.

Victims were contacted by phone for a second follow-up interview when their cases were disposed. One hundred and fifty-seven of the victims were reached. (No second follow-up interviews were attempted for the fifty victims whose cases were still pending as of February 1990—at least 10 months after indictment). The second follow-up interview generally took five to ten minutes. After establishing that the victims knew the dispositions of their cases, the interviewer asked them questions concerning perceptions of involvement and treatment by court officials that were similar to those asked in the first follow-up (30 days after intake). They were also queried about their satisfaction with the outcome and the handling of their cases: Do you think that court officials were aware of how you were affected by the crime when they sentenced the defendant? Are you satisfied with the outcome of your case? Do you feel that you had a chance to participate in the sentencing? Do you think that victims should have a greater say in how the courts decide cases? Again, each question had a 5-point scale for response options.

Subgroup Differences

Tests were run to determine whether there were differences among the subgroups in the sample. A major aim was to verify first that there were no differences between the first 32 impact statement victims included in the sample before random assignment was begun and the 72 subsequent victims in that group. (The original intention was to use the first 32 victims for pretesting only. However, it became apparent that the slow rate of intake would necessitate incorporating these victims into the main study.) Fortunately, no differences were found between the cases of the first 32 victims and later cases in terms of the nature of the charge (chi-square = 1.90, df = 3, n.s.), the severity of the charge (t [98] = 0.09, n.s.), the victim-offender relationship (chi-square = 0.64, df = 1, n.s.), the offender's prior record (t [101] = 0.76, n.s.), the victim's age (t [75] = –1.26, n.s.), the victim's education (t [72] = 0.75, n.s.), or the victim's income (t [30] = –1.13, n.s.). Based on these results, and necessity, the first 32 victims were included in the Impact Statement Group.

Differences between victims who did and victims who did not complete follow-up interviews also were assessed. Comparisons were limited to those that could be made based on data in District Attorneys' files; the information on victim characteristics that was obtained from follow-up interviews was not used in these comparisons. Victims who never completed an interview were compared with victims who completed the first follow-up interview only and with victims who completed the second follow-up interview. No differences were found among the three subsamples in terms of the nature of the charge in the case (chi-square = 4.16, df = 6, n.s.), the offender's prior record (F = 1.12, df = 2,286, n.s.), or the victim-offender relationship (chi-square = 2.13, df = 2, n.s.). However, a difference emerged for charge severity (F = 3.21, df = 2,283, p = .04): persons who completed the second follow-up interview tended to be victims of somewhat less serious crimes than persons who completed neither follow-up interview or persons who completed the first follow-up interview only. A probable explanation for this difference is that those cases still open at the study's conclusion—for which no second follow-up interviews with the victims were attempted—are likely to have been more serious cases.

Finally—and most importantly—the three treatment groups were examined to ensure that they were comparable prior to the experimental manipulation. No differences were found among the three conditions in terms of the charge type (chi-square = 8.10, df = 6, n.s.), the charge severity (F = 0.78, df = 2,283, n.s.), the victim-offender relationship (chi-square = 0.26, df = 2, n.s.), the offender's prior record (F = 0.29, df = 2,286, n.s.), victim age (F = 0.13, df = 2,212, n.s.), victim education (F = 1.66, df = 2,209, n.s.), or victim income (F = 0.67, df = 2,103, n.s.).

RESULTS

First Interview

In the interviews conducted one month after victims testified before a grand jury, the respondents were asked a series of questions about their perceptions of involvement in the court process and their treatment by court officials. The distribution of responses to those questions is displayed in Figure 1, broken down by treatment groups.[2] Differences in perceptions among treatment groups were minimal, and none was significant ($F = 2.58$, $df = 2,196$, $.05 < p < .10$ for belief that coming to court was a waste of time; $F = 0.86$, $df = 2,195$, n.s. for ability to express concerns to DA staff; $F = 1.35$, $df = 2,194$, n.s. for belief that DA staff understood the impact of crime on the victim; $F = 0.24$, $df = 2,196$, n.s. for belief that prosecutors were interested in the effect of crime on the victim; and $F = 1.39$, $df = 2,195$, n.s. for belief that prosecutors treated the victim with respect). In fact, the minimal differences that emerged among the treatment groups ran contrary to expectation: on all measures, the Victim Impact Statement groups gave the least positive responses.

Second Interview

Surprisingly, in the interviews administered upon case disposition, only about half of the participants in the Victim Impact Statements condition (56 percent) and the interview only condition (48 percent) recalled being asked by someone in court how the crime had affected them. Those percentages were significantly higher than the figure (32 percent) for control group participants with a similar recollection (chi-square = 5.80, $df = 2$, $p = .05$). However, it is noteworthy that about half of the victims who received the experimental treatment did not remember it.

Figure 2 shows the distribution of responses regarding the effects of treatments on victims' perceptions of involvement in the court process following disposition. There were no differences among treatment groups that approached statistical significance on any of these measures ($F = 0.29$, $df = 2,152$. n.s. for belief that officials were concerned: $F = 0.08$, $df = 2,139$, n.s. for belief that officials were aware of the crime's impact; $F = 1.52$, $df = 2,137$, n.s. for belief that victims had a chance to participate; and $F = 0.02$, $df = 2,147$. n.s. for belief that coming to court was a waste of time).

Figure 1
Victim Perceptions of the Court Process One Month After Victim Impact Statements (VIS) Were Taken

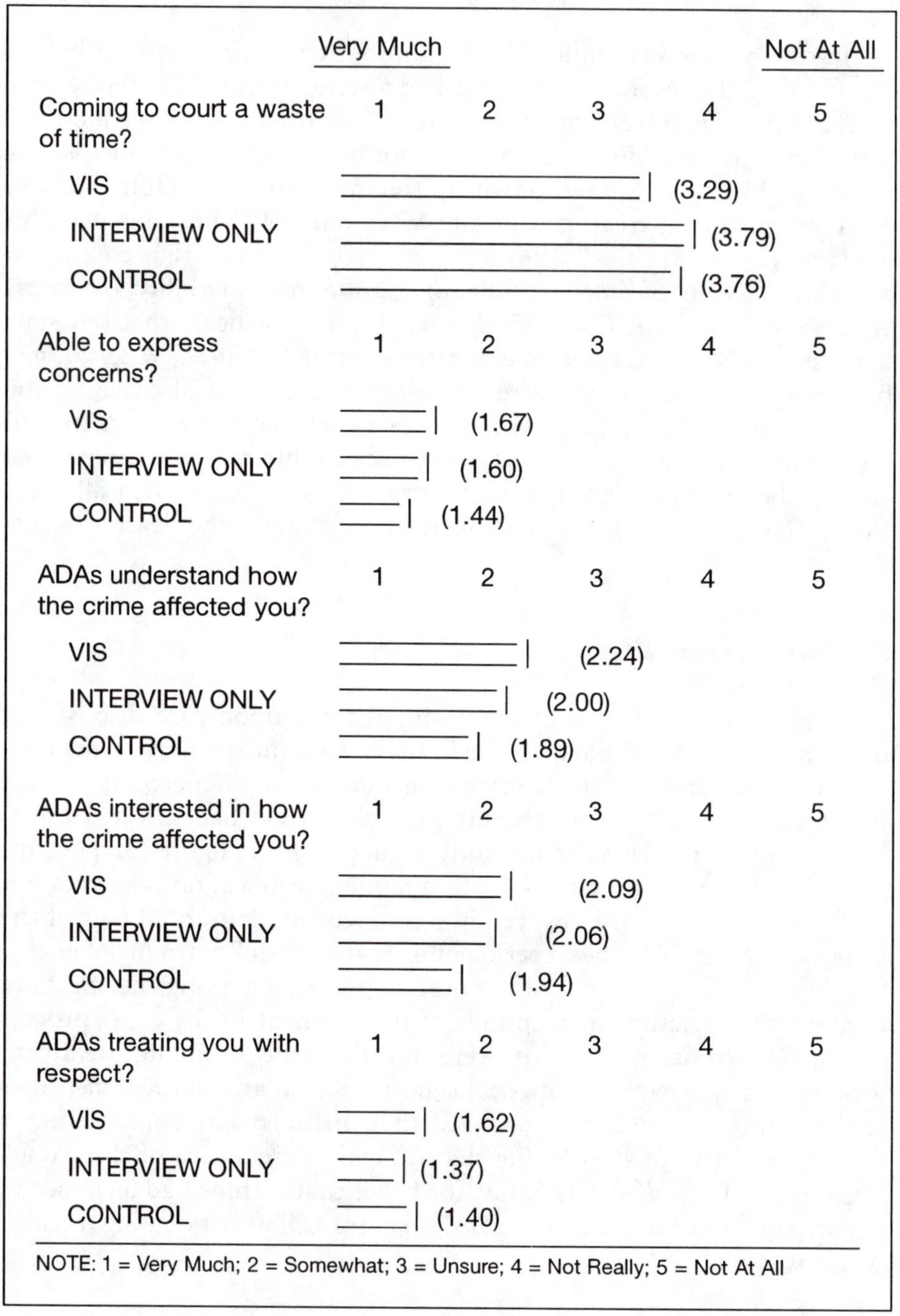

	Very Much				Not At All

Coming to court a waste of time?   1   2   3   4   5

- VIS — (3.29)
- INTERVIEW ONLY — (3.79)
- CONTROL — (3.76)

Able to express concerns?   1   2   3   4   5

- VIS — (1.67)
- INTERVIEW ONLY — (1.60)
- CONTROL — (1.44)

ADAs understand how the crime affected you?   1   2   3   4   5

- VIS — (2.24)
- INTERVIEW ONLY — (2.00)
- CONTROL — (1.89)

ADAs interested in how the crime affected you?   1   2   3   4   5

- VIS — (2.09)
- INTERVIEW ONLY — (2.06)
- CONTROL — (1.94)

ADAs treating you with respect?   1   2   3   4   5

- VIS — (1.62)
- INTERVIEW ONLY — (1.37)
- CONTROL — (1.40)

NOTE: 1 = Very Much; 2 = Somewhat; 3 = Unsure; 4 = Not Really; 5 = Not At All

Figure 2
Victim Perceptions of Involvement in the Court Process at the Time of Disposition

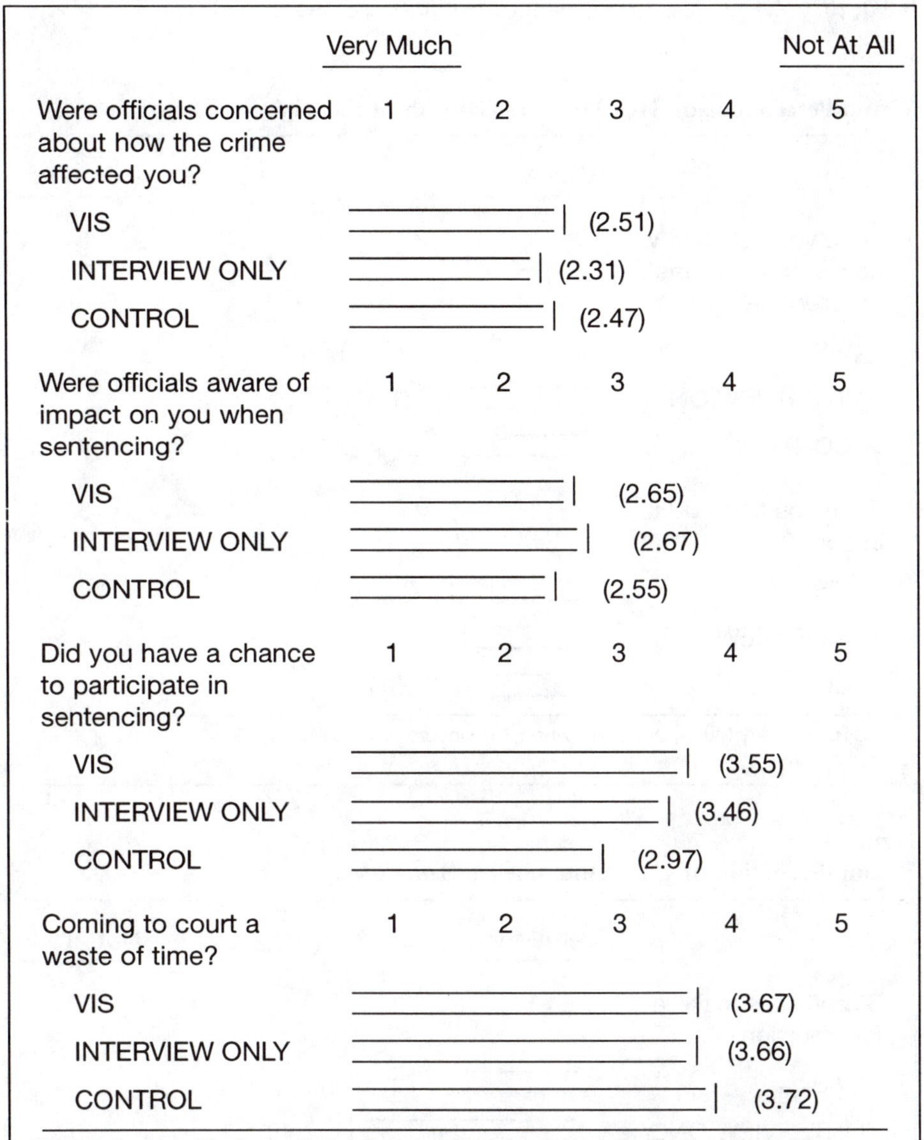

	Very Much				Not At All

Were officials concerned about how the crime affected you?

    1   2   3   4   5

  VIS — (2.51)
  INTERVIEW ONLY — (2.31)
  CONTROL — (2.47)

Were officials aware of impact on you when sentencing?

    1   2   3   4   5

  VIS — (2.65)
  INTERVIEW ONLY — (2.67)
  CONTROL — (2.55)

Did you have a chance to participate in sentencing?

    1   2   3   4   5

  VIS — (3.55)
  INTERVIEW ONLY — (3.46)
  CONTROL — (2.97)

Coming to court a waste of time?

    1   2   3   4   5

  VIS — (3.67)
  INTERVIEW ONLY — (3.66)
  CONTROL — (3.72)

NOTE: 1 = Very Much; 2 = Somewhat; 3 = Unsure; 4 = Not Really; 5 = Not At All

Figure 3 shows the distribution of responses to questions about victim perceptions of treatment in court. Again, there were no significant differences in these measures among the treatment groups ($F = 1.32$, $df = 2,140$, n.s. for satisfaction with handling; $F = 0.60$, $df = 2,152$, n.s. for perceptions of fair treatment). Finally, Figure 4 displays the distribution of responses regarding victim satisfaction with case outcomes. Differences among treatment groups were minor, and they failed to approach statistical significance ($F = 0.25$, $df = 2,141$, n.s. for belief that officials made a fair decision; $F = 0.10$, $df = 2,152$, n.s. for satisfaction with case outcomes).

Figure 3
Victim Perceptions of Treatment by Officials at the Time of Disposition

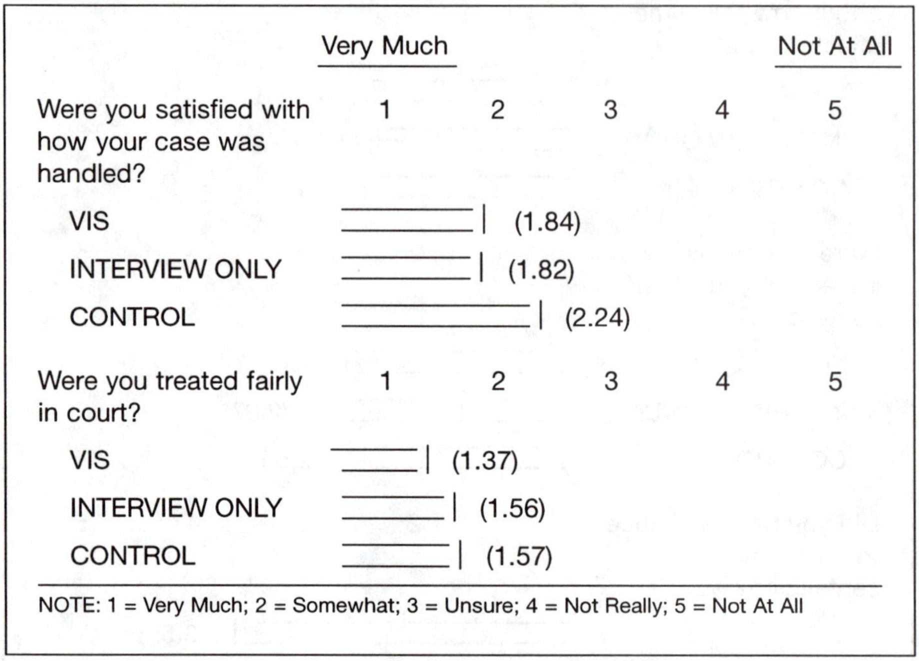

	Very Much				Not At All
	1	2	3	4	5
Were you satisfied with how your case was handled?					
VIS	========| (1.84)				
INTERVIEW ONLY	========| (1.82)				
CONTROL	===========| (2.24)				
Were you treated fairly in court?	1	2	3	4	5
VIS	=====| (1.37)				
INTERVIEW ONLY	======| (1.56)				
CONTROL	======| (1.57)				

NOTE: 1 = Very Much; 2 = Somewhat; 3 = Unsure; 4 = Not Really; 5 = Not At All

Figure 4
Victim Perception of Case Outcomes at Time of Disposition

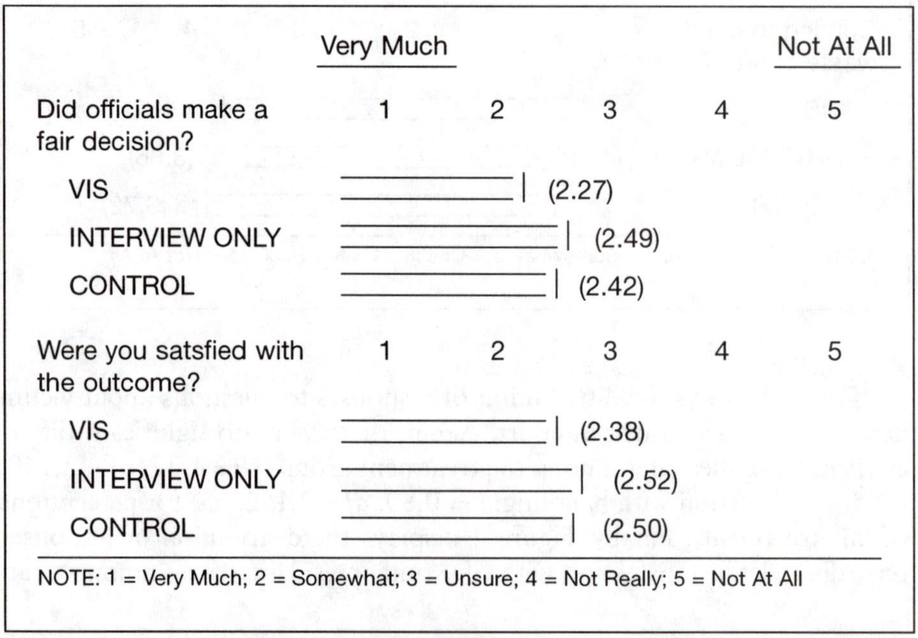

	Very Much				Not At All
	1	2	3	4	5
Did officials make a fair decision?					
VIS	===========| (2.27)				
INTERVIEW ONLY	=============| (2.49)				
CONTROL	=============| (2.42)				
Were you satsfied with the outcome?	1	2	3	4	5
VIS	============| (2.38)				
INTERVIEW ONLY	==============| (2.52)				
CONTROL	=============| (2.50)				

NOTE: 1 = Very Much; 2 = Somewhat; 3 = Unsure; 4 = Not Really; 5 = Not At All

CONCLUSIONS

The results do not support the idea that victim impact statements are an effective means to promote victim satisfaction with the justice system. There was no indication that impact statements led to greater feelings of involvement, greater satisfaction with the justice process, or greater satisfaction with dispositions. In this respect, the present results are consistent with our earlier quasi-experiment in Brooklyn (Davis, 1985), which also found no effects of impact statements on victim satisfaction. The present results also are basically consistent with those from the correlational study by Erez and Tontodonato (1989), which found that, at best, impact statements might account for a couple of percentage points of the variation in victim satisfaction with sentences.

The results of the two previous studies mentioned above could be dismissed as *implementation failure*. That is, it could be argued that the impact statement procedures—designed and carried out by court officials—might not have been sufficiently distinct from the rest of the court process or that the purpose of impact statements might not have been explained well to victims. However, that was not the case with the Bronx experiment reported here. The caseworkers in the present study strongly emphasized to victims why they were being interviewed and how the information would be used. Of course, a critic could argue that the Bronx impact statements procedure was not very potent either. Indeed, how powerful could it have been if only slightly over half of the victims who went through it remembered being asked by someone in court how the crime affected them?

The response to that criticism is that the treatment we designed and implemented in the present study was more distinct and meaningful to victims than most impact statement procedures currently in use in courts across the United States. True, it would be possible to design a procedure that is more elaborate. For example, the interview could be greatly lengthened; victims could be asked to come to court for the interview on a day when they were not participating in other events; and so forth. However, such a procedure would bear little or no resemblance to the way impact statements are produced in the real world of criminal courts. Even if such an impact statement treatment increased victim satisfaction, the results would be of academic interest only. If additional replications of the experiment reported here yield similar results, supporters of victim participation will have to question whether impact statements are, indeed, a "magic pill" to increase victim satisfaction with the justice system. If they are not, then what means are available to promote victim satisfaction?

Victim allocution—allowing victims to make oral statements to the court at sentencing—might offer a more effective way to promote victim satisfaction through participation. A study of the effects of a California allocution statute suggested that most victims who spoke expressed positive feelings about the experience of allocution (Villmoare and Neto, 1987). However, victims who spoke were no more satisfied with the justice process than were those who chose not to speak. Moreover, allocution is more controversial than impact statements since an in-person plea from a seriously debilitated victim could have far greater influence on a judge or jury than a written statement.

It might be time to ask whether part of the reason impact statements have failed to increase victim satisfaction could be that many victims do not seek increased participation in the justice process. It is true (as discussed above) that several studies have linked increased participation to victim satisfaction with the justice process. However, these studies used correlational methods; thus, their results are open to different interpretations. Other studies have suggested that only about half of all victims are interested generally in participating in the justice process (Davis, Tichane, and Grayson, 1979) or specifically in taking advantage of allocution rights (Villmoare and Neto, 1987).

Basic research is needed to ascertain the proportion of victims who want to participate more fully in the justice process and to determine who these victims are. It is necessary also to find out *how* victims want to participate. Is it enough to keep them informed? To allow them to be in court during sentencing? To prepare written impact statements? To permit them to allocute? What victims want might or might not be compatible with the aims of the justice system and the rights of the accused. However, until we understand what victims want, we cannot debate their proper role in the justice process intelligently.

ACKNOWLEDGEMENTS

This research was supported by grant # 88-IJ-CX-0004 from the National Institute of Justice.

NOTES

1. Sentencing results are reported elsewhere; see Davis and Smith (1991).

2. To estimate the size of experimental effect detectable with the sample size we employed, we conducted a power analysis for the dependent measure we considered most important (satisfaction with case outcome). Assuming a one-tailed test, a .05 confidence level, and a power of 90 percent, our experiment would be able to detect as significant a between-group difference of 1.03, out of a five-point scale. Results would be similar for other measures.

REFERENCES

Cannavale, F., and Falcon, W. (1976). *Witness cooperation.* Lexington, MA: D.C. Heath.

Clark, T.; Housner, J.; Hernon, J.; Wish, E.; and Zelinski, C. (1984). *Evaluation of the structured plea negotiation project.* Washington, D.C.: Institute for Law and Social Research.

Davis, R.C. (1985). *First year evaluation of the victim impact demonstration project.* New York: Victim Services Agency.

————— (1983). Victim/witness noncooperation: A second look at a persistent problem. *J Crim Just* 11:233-87.

————— Fischer, P., and Paykin A. (1985). Victim impact statements: The experience of state probation officers. *Journal of Probation and Parole* 16:18-20.

Davis, RC.; Kunreuther, F.; and Connick, E. (1984). Expanding the victim's role in the criminal court dispositional process: The results of an experiment. J *Crim Law* 2:491-505.

Davis, R.C.; Russell, V.; and Kunreuther, F. (1980). *The role of the complaining witness in an urban criminal court.* New York: Vera Institute of Justice.

Davis, R.C., and Smith, B.E. (1991). The effects of victim impact statements on sentencing decisions. Paper submitted for publication.

Davis, R.C.; Tichane, M.; and Grayson, D. (1979). *Mediation and arbitration as alternatives to prosecution in felony arrest cases.* New York: Vera Institute of Justice.

Dubow, F., and Becker, T. (1976). Patterns of victim advocacy. In *Criminal justice and the victim,* ed. W.F. McDonald. Beverly Hills: Sage Publications.

Erez, E., and Tontodonato, P. (1990). The effect of victim participation in sentencing on sentence outcome. *Criminology* 28:451-74.

————— (1989). Victim participation in sentencing and satisfaction with justice. Paper presented at the annual meeting of the Western Society of Criminology at Orange, California.

Goldstein, A.S. (1982). Defining the role of the victim in criminal prosecution. *Miss L J* 52:515-61.

Hagan, J. (1982). Victims before the law: A study of victim involvement in the criminal justice process. *J Crim Law* 73:317.

Hellerstein, D.R. (1989). The victim impact statement: Reform or reprisal? *Am Crim L Rev* 27:391-430.

Henderson, L.N. (1985). The wrongs of victim's rights. *Stanford L Rev* 37:937-1021.

Hudson, P. (1984). The crime victim and the criminal justice system: Time for a change. *Pepperdine L Rev* 11:23-62.

Kelly, D.P. (1990). Victim participation in the criminal justice system. In *Victims of crime: Problems, policies, and programs,* ed. A. Lurigio, W. Skogan, and R. Davis. Newbury Park, CA: Sage Publications.

————— (1984). Victims' perceptions of criminal justice. *Pepperdine L Rev* 11: 15-22.

Kerstetter, W.A., and Heinz, A.M. (1979). *Pretrial settlement conference: An evaluation.* Report of the University of Chicago Law School to the National Institute of Justice. Chicago: University of Chicago Law School.

Kilpatrick, D., and Otto, R. (1987). Constitutionally guaranteed participation in clinical proceedings for victims: Potential effects on psychological functioning. *The Wayne Review* 34:17.

McLeod, M. (1988). *The authorization and implementation of victim impact statements.* Washington D.C.: National Institute of Justice.

Presidential Task Force on Victims of Crime (1982). *Final report.* Washington, D.C.: U.S. Government Printing Office.

Rosett, A., and Cressey, D. (1976). *Justice by consent: Plea bargains in the American courthouse.* New York: J. B. Lippincott.

Smith, B.E. (1981). *Non-stranger violence: The criminal court's response.* Alexandria, VA: Institute for Social Analysis.

————— (1979). *The prosecutor's witness: An urban/suburban comparison.* Unpublished Ph.D. dissertation, State University of New York at Stony Brook.

Talbert, P. (1988). The relevance of victim impact statements to the criminal sentencing decision. *UCLA Law R* 36:199-232.

Villmoare, E., and Neto, V.V. (1987). *Victim appearance at sentencing hearings under the California victims' bill of rights.* Washington, D.C.: National Institute of Justice.

Young, M.A. (1987). A constitutional commandment for victims of crime: The victims' perspective. *Wayne L Rev* 4:51-68.

Zehr, H., and Umbreit, M. (1982). Victim-offender reconciliation: An incarceration substitute. *Fed Prob* 46:63-68.

Chapter 14

Restorative Justice:
Justice That Promotes Healing

Daniel Van Ness
Karen Heetderks Strong

While restorative justice advocates have constructed a variety of models, there appear to be three fundamental propositions upon which most agree a restorative system should be constructed. First, restorative justice advocates view crime as more than simply lawbreaking, an offense against governmental authority; crime is understood also to cause multiple injuries to victims, the community and even the offender.[1] Second, proponents argue that the criminal justice process should help repair those injuries.[2] Third, they protest the government's apparent monopoly over society's response to crime. Victims, offenders and their communities also must be involved at the earliest point and to the fullest extent possible. This suggests a cooperative effort, with government responsible for maintaining a basic framework of order, and the other parties responsible for restoring community peace and harmony. The work of government must be done in such a way that community building is enhanced, or at least not hampered.[3] Let us consider each of these premises in turn.

---

[1] *See, e.g.,* Howard Zehr, *Changing Lenses: A New Focus for Crime and Justice* (Scottsdale, PA: Herald Press, 1990), 181-186.

[2] *See, e.g.,* Martin Wright, *Justice for Victims and Offenders* (Philadelphia: Open University Press, 1991), 114-117 (proposing a system with the primary aim of restoring—or even improving—the victim's prior condition).

[3] The challenge to structure community-government cooperation is developed further in subsequent sections of this book.

Source: Van Ness, D., & Strong, K.H. (1997). Restorative justice: Justice that promotes healing. In D. Van Ness & K.H. Strong, *Restoring justice.* Cincinnati, OH: Anderson. Reprinted by permission of Anderson Publishing Co.

Proposition 1. Justice requires that we work to restore victims, offenders and communities who have been injured by crime.

Crime leaves injured victims, communities and offenders in its wake, each harmed in different ways and experiencing correspondingly different needs. To promote healing, then, society must respond appropriately, considering the needs and responsibilities of each party.

Victims are those who have been harmed by the offender; this harm may be experienced either directly or secondarily. *Primary* victims, those against whom the crime was committed, may sustain physical injury, monetary loss and emotional suffering. These may be only momentary in duration or may last a lifetime. Because of the varying circumstances of victims, similar injuries may produce substantially different effects. In at least two respects, however, all victims have common needs: the need to regain control over their own lives, and the need for vindication of their rights. Being victimized is by definition an experience of powerlessness—the victim was unable to prevent the crime from occurring. As a result, primary victims often need help regaining an appropriate sense of control over their lives. As Justice Kelly discovered, victimization is also the experience of being wronged by another, bringing with it the need for vindication, for an authoritative and decisive denunciation of the wrong and exoneration of the one who was wronged. In addition to primary victims, *secondary* victims are indirectly harmed by the actions of offenders. These secondary victims can include the family members or neighbors of victims and offenders, and their injuries and needs must also be considered in constructing a restorative response to crime.

In order to consider the injuries and needs of the "community," we need to be clear about the meaning of that term. It is used in many different ways. We sometimes use it to refer to a community in geographic terms—the neighborhood in which we live, for example—a "local community." With the coming of increased mobility and transience, however, some have suggested that a more useful definition is nongeographic, emphasizing instead a "community of interest."[4] Such communities are identified by the willingness of their members "to take actions on behalf of the community not only that they would not take on their own behalf,

---

4   John Braithwaite discusses the relevance of expanding concepts of community to crime prevention strategies:

> This possibility comes even more to life if we consider the views of theorists who suggest that in modern urban societies the networks of individuals become less spatially localized, the locus of inter-dependency shifts from neighborhood to communities of interest based on workplace, occupation, and leisure activities. These alternative communities of interest might become alternative foci for communitarian crime control initiatives. Thus crime prevention associations might be set up in workplaces as in Japan; professional associations can be asked by government to set up monitoring and disciplinary committees to deal with fraud and malpractice in the profession; football associations can be asked to step in where the police have failed to solve problems of crowd hooliganism. John Braithwaite, *Crime, Shame, and Reintegration* (New York: Cambridge University Press, 1989): 172-173.

but that are quite possibly detrimental to their own interests."[5] They are characterized, then by a fundamental sense of duty, reciprocity and belonging.[6] Finally, the word is sometimes used loosely in everyday conversation as a synonym for society as a whole.[7] Each of these communities—the local community, the community of interest and society as a whole—may be injured by crime in different ways and degrees, but all will be affected in common ways as well: the sense of safety and confidence of their members is threatened, order within the community is threatened and (depending on the kind of crime) the common values of the community are challenged and perhaps eroded. However, the injury to the first two appear to be more direct than does the general injury to society as a whole. Consequently, when we use the term "community" we will be referring to local communities and communities of interest.[8]

Finally, the injuries of offenders must also be addressed. These injuries can be thought of as either *contributing* to the crime or *resulting* from the crime. By contributing injuries we mean those that existed prior to the crime and that prompted in some way the criminal conduct of the offender. For example, it has sometimes been argued that some victims of child abuse become abusers themselves, and that some substance abusers commit crimes to support their addictions. While these contributing injuries, these prior conditions, do not excuse the criminal choices of offenders, any attempt to bring healing to the parties touched by crime must address them.[9] Resulting injuries are those caused by the crime itself

---

[5]   Frederick Schauer, "Community, Citizenship, and the Search for National Identity," *Mich. L. Rev.* 84 (1986): 1504.

[6]   See Ian R. Macneil, "Bureaucracy, Liberalism, and Community—American Style," *Nw. U. L. Rev.* 79 (1984-85): 900, 937.

[7]   Macneil distinguishes between what we call the community of interest and society:

        It is necessary to distinguish sharply community thus viewed from society as a whole, and particularly from any idea of Leviathan as embodying society. It is possible, of course, to lose one's self to—and gain community with—Leviathan; witness any popular war or mass movement, or indeed even the very modest loss of self in standing up during the abominably bad singing of the Star Spangled Banner at football games. But this kind of community, patriotism—particularly the sense of belonging—only rarely has any of the continuity, nonsporadic duration, completeness, and intensity of the smallest community, the family, or even of other small communities. And when it does, the world shakes. Moreover, in the modern state large scale community is necessarily a bureaucratic community, which has significant consequences both for the nature of community and for bureaucracy. (Ibid., 936-937.) (citations omitted)

[8]   One of the important implications of the distinction between "community" and "victim" is that the community may not necessarily speak for the interests of the victim (*see* Chapter Eight of this book). But the opposite is also true: the victim does not necessarily speak for the community either. Kai-D. Bussmann, "Morality, Symbolism, and Criminal Law: Chances and Limits of Mediation Programs," in Heinz Messmer and Hans-Uwe Otto, eds., *Restorative Justice on Trial* (Dordrecht, The Netherlands: Kluwer Academic Publishers, 1992), 320.

[9]   There are at least three occasions to address offenders' adverse circumstances. First, when those circumstances would prevent offenders from discharging their obligations (for example, they are unable to pay restitution because they are unemployed); second, when the circumstances directly contributed to the decision to commit the crime (for example, when the crime was committed to support a drug habit); and third, when the victim and offender have identified circumstances that they agree should be addressed, even though they did not contribute directly to the crime nor would they prevent completion of the sentence (for example, illiteracy).

or its aftermath. These may be physical (as when the offender is wounded during the crime or incarcerated as a result of it), emotional (as when the offender experiences shame[10]) or moral and spiritual (since the offender has chosen to injure another). Further, offenders will likely be injured by the criminal justice system's response, which further alienates them from the community, strains family relationships, may lead to long-term employment disadvantages or prevent them from making amends to their victims.[11] Again, we are not arguing that offenders be relieved of accountability by recognizing "injuries." We are simply asserting that the injuries should be acknowledged and addressed in the response to crime. Unfortunately, there are no terms in the English language that appropriately describe this process. Consequently, we have adopted the admittedly awkward word "habilitation" to express this goal.

Proposition 2. Victims, offenders and communities should have opportunities for active involvement in the restorative justice process as early and as fully as possible.

Virtually every facet of our criminal justice system works to reduce victims, offenders and communities to passive participants. Because the current approach considers government to be the party harmed by crime, government's virtual monopoly over the apprehension, prosecution and punishment of offenders seems logical and legitimate.[12] Because of the legal presumption of innocence bestowed on all defendants, as well as the panoply of due process rights that are afforded them, defendants have few incentives to assume responsibility for their actions, and many incentives to remain passive while the government marshals its cases and their lawyers attempt to dismantle them. Because victims are not parties of interest in criminal cases, and rather are simply "piece[s] of evidence to be used by the state to obtain a conviction,"[13] they have

---

[10] *See* Braithwaite, *supra* note 4 for an extended discussion of how shaming can be both positive and negative for offenders and the community.

[11] We do not suggest that the offender should not experience pain as a result of his or her treatment in the criminal justice system. Retribution is a part of society's response to an offender, although we will argue that the suffering caused to the offender should come as the offender is held accountable for helping repair the injuries caused by the criminal behavior (*see* Chapter Six). Our point here is that the justice system itself may create new wounds, and that these must be considered and addressed in building a restorative justice system.

[12] As we will see in Chapter Eight, this state monopoly has a relatively short history; as late as the mid-nineteenth century victims were the dominant party in the criminal justice system, responsible for initiating and prosecuting criminal cases.

[13] Juan Cardenas, "The Crime Victim in the Prosecutorial Process," *Harv. J.L. & Pub. Pol'y 9* (1986): 371.

very limited control over what occurs and no responsibility to initiate particular phases of the process.[14] Finally, the direct participation of members of the community is also very limited, consisting almost exclusively of service on grand or petit juries.[15]

Restorative justice, on the other hand, places a much higher value on direct involvement by the parties. For victims who have experienced powerlessness, the opportunity to participate restores an element of control.[16] For an offender who has harmed another, the voluntary assumption of responsibility is an important step in not only helping others who were hurt by the crime but also in building a prosocial value system.[17] Likewise, the efforts of community members to repair the injuries to victims and offenders serves to strengthen the community itself, and to reinforce community values of respect and compassion for others.[18]

Proposition 3. In promoting justice, government is responsible for preserving order and the community for establishing peace.

The term "order" is sometimes used as though it were a synonym for public safety; politicians speak, for example, of the need for "law and order" as a means of ending "crime in our streets." Safety, however, is a broader, more inclusive concept than order; to put it another way, both order and peace are required to secure public safety. As ancient Jewish law incorporated notions of "shalom," so today we must think of "peace" as a cooperative dynamic fostered from within a community. It requires a community's commitment to respect the rights of its members and to help resolve conflicts among them. It requires that those members respect community interests even when they conflict with their individual interests. It is in this context that communities and their members assume responsibility for addressing the underlying social, economic and

---

[14]   While some states have retained vestiges of private prosecution on their law books (as we will see in Chapter Eight), Cardenas is correct in concluding:

> In sum, the practice of allowing crime victims to hire private attorneys to participate in state prosecutions is a vestige of the English origins of American justice. English common law rested on the notion that the best way to bring a public wrong to satisfactory resolution was to vest in the family of the wronged individual the right to pursue its own concept of vengeance. Critics of private prosecution argued that a public prosecution system was necessary to regulate private revenge and to place a restraint upon the avenging party. Today, almost without exception, American jurisprudence has incorporated this view, holding that a private individual no longer has any right to prosecute another for a crime. (Cardenas, *supra* note 13, at 383.)

[15]   The community does play a significant indirect role in that the criminal justice system is supported by taxes. Further, their community members have worked outside the criminal justice system to address various dimensions of crime prevention and response. Examples of this latter involvement include participation in crime watch programs and offender or victim assistance programs.

[16]   *See* Chapter Eight.

[17]   *See* Chapter Six.

[18]   *See* Chapter Seven.

moral factors that contribute to conflict within the community. "Order," on the other hand, is imposed on the community. It sets external limits on behavior and enforces those limits to minimize overt conflict and to control potentially chaotic factors. Like peace, a just order is important in preserving safety, and government has both the power and mandate to establish such an order.

Both order and peace are appropriate means to achieving safety. However, as imposed order increases, personal freedom decreases; hence, peace will be sought in a society that values freedom. Security built primarily on governmentally imposed order is detrimental to a free society, as conditions in police states throughout the world demonstrate. On the other hand, when the community fails to foster peace, it may be necessary for the government to intervene and impose order. The American civil rights movement is an example of that kind of action. Desegregation of public schools was met with violent resistance on the community level, and National Guard troops had to enforce sufficient order for African-American children to enter the schools. The community, content with preserving the interests of the powerful by seeking to preserve the status quo, had failed in its role to seek peace for all members.

Of course, describing peace as the community's responsibility and order as government's is somewhat simplistic. Each plays a role in achieving peace and order, as we see when community members form "neighborhood watch" programs to prevent crime or when government programs address economic and social injustices that inhibit peace. We wish to emphasize a point that is often forgotten in the debate about crime and criminal justice: *safety comes as both government and community play their parts in upholding order and establishing peace.*

Restorative Justice: A Visual Model

A series of figures will illustrate some of the features of restorative justice theory. Figure [1] illustrates how contemporary criminal justice focuses exclusively on the offender and the government. The government seeks to establish order by enacting laws and punishing those who violate them. Because the government's power is so great, due process safeguards have been developed over the centuries to ensure fairness in how offenders are treated. One consequence is that the offender's posture is defensive (and often passive) during the proceedings, while the government plays the active role. Criminal courts are arenas of battle in which the government is pitted against offenders in a high-stakes contest to determine whether the law has been violated, and if so, what form of retribution should be imposed.

Figure [1]

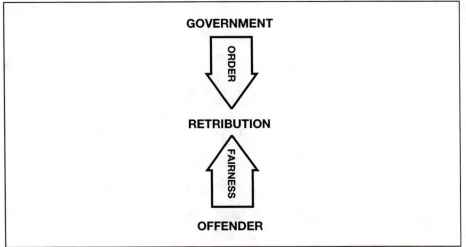

Figure [2] illustrates how restorative justice theory returns to the ancient view that there are actually four parties affected by crime: victim, offender, community and government. Restorative justice theory emphasizes that every crime involves specific victims and offenders, and that the goal of the criminal justice process should be to help them come to resolution (see Figure [3]). This response to crime is largely neglected by the criminal justice system and left to the civil courts to address. Resolution requires that the rights of victims be vindicated by exoneration from responsibility for the injuries they have sustained as well as by receiving reparation for those injuries.

Figure [2]

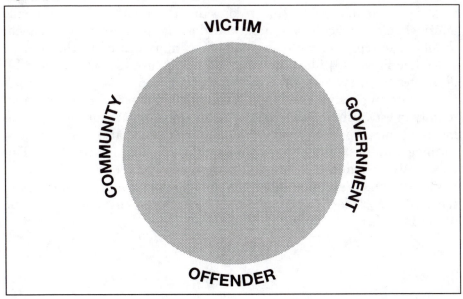

Figure [3]

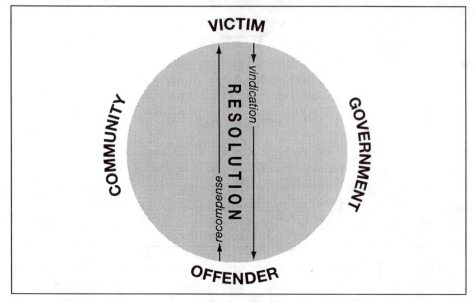

That is not all that is required. The offender must make recompense for there to be full resolution. Recompense and retribution are different. Retribution is defined as deserved punishment for evil done. The definition underscores an important aspect of a society's response to offenders, but it has two shortcomings. First, the active party, the punisher, is the government; the offender is merely a passive recipient of punishment. Second, punishment that does not help repair the injuries caused by crime simply creates new injuries; now both the victim and the offender are injured. "Recompense," on the other hand, is something given or done to make up for an injury. This underscores that the offender who caused the injury should be the active party, and that the purpose of punishment should be to repair as much as possible the injury caused by the crime.

While Figure [3] illustrates the micro response to crime, Figure [4] illustrates the macro response of crime prevention. It suggests the roles that restorative justice theory gives to the government and to the community in establishing safety. Safety is obtained in part through governmentally imposed order, but the community must also contribute by forming strong, stable, peaceful relationships among its members. This cooperative relationship between government and community is the basis for crime prevention. Combining Figures [3 and 4] reminds us of the need to consider both the micro and macro responses in conjunction with each other.

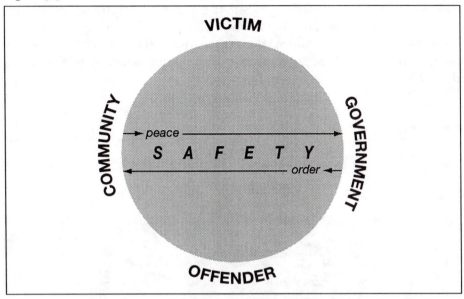

The victim's and the offender's need for resolution, and the government's and community's need for public safety, must be addressed in the same process (see Figure [5]). This dual thrust contrasts with the separation of civil and criminal law in most modern jurisdictions, a separation that can force either/or choices for victims and the government in

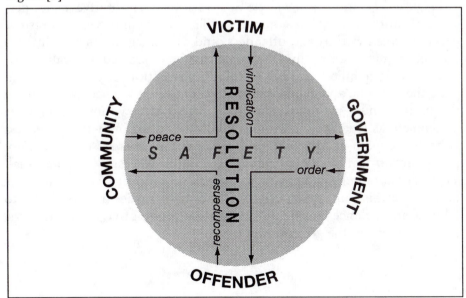

deciding whether and how to proceed against the offender. Figure [6] shows the restorative justice goals that govern the relationships of government with individual victims and offenders. The government helps reestablish order by ensuring that reparation takes place. It facilitates redress to victims through restitution and compensation while ensuring that offenders are treated with fairness.

Figure [6]

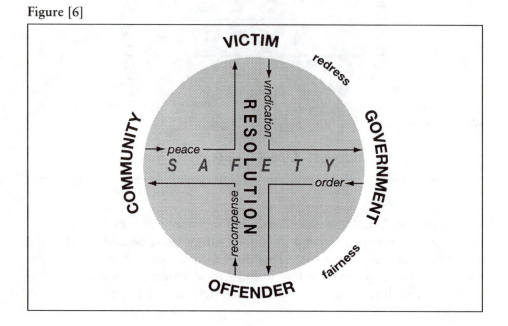

Figure [7] completes the circle by presenting a restorative justice perspective on the role of the community. The community seeks to restore peace between victims and offenders, and to reintegrate them fully into the community. For victims the goals can be expressed as healing; for offenders, as habilitation. The circular construction of the figures suggests the dynamic and dependent relationships that are necessary among the parties under restorative justice theory. Peace without order is as incomplete as recompense without vindication; healing without redress is as inadequate as rehabilitation without fairness. A society cannot select certain features of the model and omit others; all are essential. That very comprehensiveness is a fundamental aspect of the restorative pattern of thinking about crime. Restorative justice theory seeks to address and balance the rights and responsibilities of victims, offenders, communities and the government.

Figure [7]

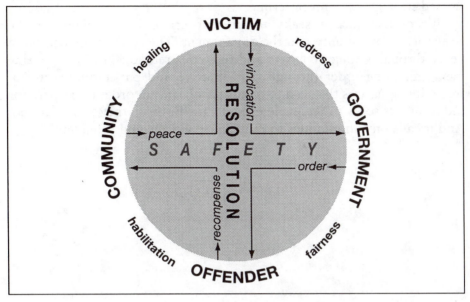

Conclusion

Restorative justice, then, focuses on repairing the harm caused by crime and reducing the likelihood of future harm. It does this by encouraging offenders to take responsibility for their actions and for the harm they have caused, by providing redress for victims and by promoting reintegration of both within the community. This is done through a cooperative effort by communities and the government.

Restorative justice is different from current criminal justice practice in a number of ways. It views criminal acts more comprehensively; rather than limiting crime to lawbreaking, it recognizes that offenders harm victims, communities and even themselves. It involves more parties; rather than including only the government and the offender in key roles, it includes victims and communities as well. It measures success differently; rather than measuring how much punishment has been inflicted, it measures how much harm has been repaired or prevented. And finally, rather than leaving the problem of crime to the government alone, it recognizes the importance of community involvement and initiative in responding to and reducing crime.

Restorative justice responds to specific crimes by emphasizing both recovery of the victim through redress, vindication and healing, and recompense by the offender through reparation, fair treatment and habilitation. It seeks processes through which parties are able to discover the truth about what happened and the harms that resulted, to identify the injustices involved and to agree on future actions to repair those harms.

It considers whether specific crimes are suggesting the need for new or revised strategies to prevent crime.

Restorative justice seeks to prevent crime by building on the strengths of community and the government. The community can build peace through strong, inclusive and righteous relationships; the government can bring order through fair, effective and parsimonious use of force. It emphasizes the need to repair past harms in order to prepare for the future. It seeks to reconcile offenders with those they have harmed. And it calls on communities to reintegrate victims and offenders.

About the Editor

Peggy M. Tobolowsky is currently Associate Professor and Associate Chair of Criminal Justice at the University of North Texas (UNT) in Denton, Texas. She also supervises ongoing research of the Criminal Justice Department's Center for Victim Studies, which fosters research, academic training, and continuing education concerning victims of crime and violence. Prior to joining the UNT faculty in 1989, Professor Tobolowsky's legal career included work as a litigator in private practice and as a federal prosecutor in the United States Attorney's Office for the District of Columbia. She received her Juris Doctor degree from George Washington University in 1977.

Tobolowsky's research interests include criminal law and procedure, crime victim issues, capital punishment, and pretrial release. Her articles on these subjects have appeared in journals such as the *American Journal of Criminal Law*, *Judicature*, the *New England Journal on Criminal and Civil Confinement*, and the *Journal of Contemporary Law*.

Index